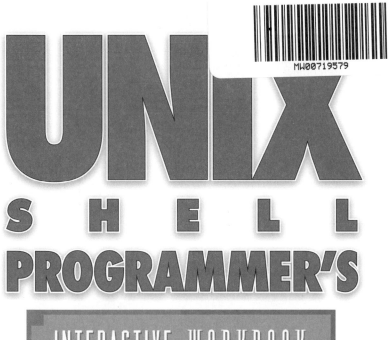

UNIX SHELL PROGRAMMER'S

INTERACTIVE WORKBOOK

CHRISTOPHER VICKERY

Prentice Hall PTR
Upper Saddle River, NJ 07458
http://www.phptr.com/phptrinteractive

ISBN 0-13-020064-6
90000
9 780130 200648

Editorial/production supervision: *Nick Radhuber*
Acquisitions editor: *Mark L. Taub*
Development editor: *Ralph Moore*
Marketing manager: *Dan Rush*
Manufacturing manager: *Alexis R. Heydt*
Editorial assistant: *Audri Anna Bazlen*
Cover design director: *Jerry Votta*
Cover designer: *Anthony Gemmellaro*
Art director: *Gail Cocker-Bogusz*
Series design: *Meryl Poweski*
Web site project manager: *Yvette Raven*

Prentice-Hall, Inc.
A Simon & Schuster Company
Upper Saddle River, NJ 07458

Prentice Hall books are widely used by corporations and government agencies for training, marketing, and resale.

The publisher offers discounts on this book when ordered in bulk quantities. For more information, contact: Corporate Sales Department, Phone: 800-382-3419; Fax: 201-236-7141; E-mail: corpsales@prenhall.com; or write: Prentice Hall PTR, Corp. Sales Dept., One Lake Street, Upper Saddle River, NJ 07458.

Printed in the United States of America
10 9 8 7 6 5 4 3 2 1

ISBN 0-13-020064-6

Prentice-Hall International (UK) Limited, *London*
Prentice-Hall of Australia Pty. Limited, *Sydney*
Prentice-Hall Canada Inc., *Toronto*
Prentice-Hall Hispanoamericana, S.A., *Mexico*
Prentice-Hall of India Private Limited, *New Delhi*
Prentice-Hall of Japan, Inc., *Tokyo*
Simon & Schuster Asia Pte. Ltd., *Singapore*
Editora Prentice-Hall do Brasil, Ltda., *Rio de Janeiro*

DEDICATION

To my mother, Doris W. Vickery.

"I suppose it's korny, but I'm glad I got bourne by you."

CONTENTS

FROM THE EDITOR

Prentice Hall's Interactive Workbooks are designed to get you up and running fast, with just the information you need, when you need it.

We are certain that you will find our unique approach to learning simple and straightforward. Every chapter of every Interactive Workbook begins with a list of clearly defined Learning Objectives. A series of labs make up the heart of each chapter. Each lab is designed to teach you specific skills in the form of exercises. You perform these exercises at your computer and answer pointed questions about what you observe. Your answers will lead to further discussion and exploration. Each lab then ends with multiple-choice Self-Review Questions, to reinforce what you've learned. Finally, we have included Test Your Thinking projects at the end of each chapter. These projects challenge you to synthesize all of the skills you've acquired in the chapter.

Our goal is to make learning engaging, and to make you a more productive learner.

And you are not alone. Each book is integrated with its own "Companion Website." The website is a place where you can find more detailed information about the concepts discussed in the Workbook, additional Self-Review Questions to further refine your understanding of the material, and perhaps most importantly, where you can find a community of other Interactive Workbook users working to acquire the same set of skills that you are.

All of the Companion Websites for our Interactive Workbooks can be found at `http://www.phptr.com/phptrinteractive`.

Mark L. Taub
Editor-in-Chief
Prentice Hall PTR Interactive

PREFACE

INTRODUCTION

Professional and casual programmers alike are finding that scripting languages, such as the *KornShell* programming language covered in this book, are valuable tools for developing powerful applications while writing a minimal amount of code.

The *KornShell* is both a scripting language and a command interpreter, which means that you can use the shell's programming features interactively, intermixed with commands you enter to run whatever processing programs you use in your work. UNIX calls its command interpreters *shells*, and there are a number of them available for UNIX systems besides the *KornShell*: the Bourne shell (*sh*), the Bourne-again shell (*bash*), the C shell (*csh*), and the TC shell (*tcsh*) among others. Microsoft Windows also provides rudimentary scripting features with its command interpreters for Windows 95/98 (*command.com*) and Windows NT/2000 (*cmd.exe*). The *KornShell* has the advantages of being a complete implementation of the POSIX shell standard and of being available for a wide range of platforms, including all major UNIX variants as well as for Microsoft Windows systems. The skills you develop as a *KornShell* programmer will carry over to a wide variety of programming platforms.

WHAT YOU'LL NEED

You will need a computer with the current version of the *KornShell* installed in order to use this book. The first chapter will make sure your system is set up correctly, including how to test whether you have the proper version of the shell and how to get a copy if you don't already have it. Your operating system may be any major version of UNIX, including Linux, or it might be Microsoft Windows, in which case you will also need a software package that enables UNIX programs to run under windows, specifically the U/WIN package which is actively being developed by David Korn (author of the *KornShell*) at AT&T Research. If you do work in a Windows environment, and if you have a choice about which one to use, you should use Windows NT/2000 because it supports more of the shell's features than either of the "9x" versions.

You will also need Internet access to use the book's Companion Web Site that is an integral part of this book.

HOW THIS BOOK IS ORGANIZED

Don't just read this book! It's an *interactive* workbook, and the way to use it is to interact with it and with your computer as you work your way through it. Each chapter has one or more Labs, and each Lab has one or more Exercises for you to do. The Exercises are written as a series of questions for you to answer, typically after running some commands on your computer. The answers to all the Exercise questions are given at the end of each Lab, along with an explanation of the concept being developed. Even if you are able to answer a question, you should always check the answer before going on to the next one because there is often explanatory material with the answer that you will need in order to answer the next question. Put a bookmark by the answers so you can get to them easily while working through the questions.

At the end of each Lab there is a set of Self-Review Questions that you can use to check if you are on the right track in mastering the material. The answers to these questions are given in Appendix A. There are additional practice questions for each chapter at the companion Web site for this book.

After the first chapter, which deals with setting up your computer, the remainder of the book introduces the *KornShell*'s programming constructs in what is intended to be a logical sequence of steps. This way of organizing the material was chosen for pedagogical reasons, but it has one characteristic you should be aware of: Some of the earlier material has you do things that you would do differently if you knew the material that comes later on. The goal has been to keep the focus on the part of the language you are learning rather than to introduce extraneous material in order to make each exercise a completely realistic task. The later chapters in the book will give you more realistic problems and solutions to work with.

Appendix B is an alphabetical reference guide to all of the *KornShell's* built-in commands, extracted from the definitive reference book on the *KornShell*, "The New *KornShell* Command and Programming Language" by Morris I. Bolsky and David G. Korn (Prentice-Hall, 1995). The book you are holding tries to cover as much of the *KornShell* as possible, but there are parts of the language that just don't fit into an introductory workbook. If you find that you want to learn more when you finish this book, the Bolsky and Korn book is the one to get. If you are interested in using the *KornShell* to develop programs with a Graphical User Interface on UNIX systems, you should also consider "Desktop *KornShell* Graphical Programming" by J. Stephen Pendergast, Jr. (Addison-Wesley, 1995).

Appendix C is a Glossary, with references back to the chapters. You might find this quicker than the index for tracking down key concepts.

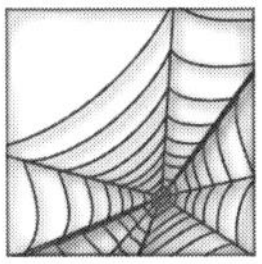

The companion Web site for this book is at:

`http://www.phptr.com/phptrinteractive/`

This Web site is closely integrated with the content of this workbook. Each chapter in the book ends with a set of "Test Your Thinking" exercises designed to give you practice with the material developed in that chapter, but the answers are not given in the book. Rather, you are encouraged to go to the Web site to compare your answers with those of others who are using the book. You will also find additional practice questions for each chapter there, along with hints and "coaching" comments for those questions. Finally, there is also an "Author's Corner" at the Web site where I've put some additional material that wouldn't fit in the book itself, where I will respond to questions about the book, and where I will post corrections to the book's content as needed.

I think of the Web site as a blend of traditional publishing with current trends in asynchronous learning, and I think that you will find it a lively source of help.

There is a CD-ROM packaged with this book called "UNIX: Using the Shell" published by CBT Systems Ltd. Although I was not involved in the development of this CD-ROM, it follows very much the same educational philosophy as this book. You can't just sit back and watch it go by, you have to think and answer questions as you go along. It doesn't provide the depth of coverage for the *KornShell* that the book does, but it does introduce you to some of the other UNIX shells, namely the Bourne and C shells. There were some technical errors in a pre-publication edition of the CD-ROM that I saw, so be sure to check the Author's Corner of this book's Web site for more information.

CONVENTIONS USED IN THIS BOOK

Variable names and statement types are *italicized*. Computer output is **boldface monospaced**. Interactive input and the names of commands are Courier. In Appendix B, the conventions are a little different, where boldface is used to indicate material that you must type as shown. Control codes are shown using normal text. For example, "Control-C" means to press the letter C while holding the "Ctrl" key on the keyboard, and "Newline" means the end-of-line code produced by pressing the "Enter" key on the keyboard.

NOTE : For lines of code in the book, when text that would appear as a single line on your computer screen doesn't fit a single line on the printed page, you will see a false line break, indicated by a backslash character (\ ), at the end of the first printed line.

ACKNOWLEDGEMENTS

This book began its life with the help of Jayne Demsky, my Prentice-Hall sales representative at Queens College, who put me in contact with the editorial people at Prentice-Hall PTR. Thank you, Jayne. The Prentice-Hall editors have been a great help, starting with Mark Taub, the series editor, and Jeff Gitlin, the series advisor. Mark and Jeff are the ones who came up with the structure of the interactive workbook series, and Ralph Moore has been the editor who made the format concrete and provided tremendous help in transforming my efforts into a real manuscript. Nick Radhuber in production gets a special vote of thanks for dealing with the time pressures imposed by my submission schedule with grace.

Kevin Wall was the technical reviewer for the book. Kevin has been invaluable in helping me get things right. His understanding of the *KornShell* is vast and deep, and the book has benefited greatly from his wisdom. I've learned a lot from Kevin, and hope I haven't distorted that knowledge too much in putting it in print.

I've used a computer running Windows NT while writing the book. One window holds the word processor, another one runs a *KornShell* login to the local computer, another two run *xterm* logins to *KornShell* logins on Solaris and DEC OSF/1 computers at Queens College. But the window that deserves special mention here is the one connected to the mail program that manages my subscriptions to the U/WIN users and U/WIN developers news groups. The people using these groups have been great sources of information about *KornShell* features and programming techniques. With David Korn as an active participant in these groups, they have provided a stimulating environment for working on the book.

You know how the author always ends the Acknowledgements by thanking his/her family for their patience and support during the difficult time of writing a book? Well, I can vouch that it's more than just lip service going on here. Many thanks to Nancy, Josh, and Alex for their support during the book's gestation period.

Christopher Vickery
Holliswood, NY
November 1998

ABOUT THE AUTHOR

Christopher Vickery is a professor of computer science at Queen's College of the City University of New York, where he teaches courses in software design and development. His home page on the Web is: *http://baggage.cs.qc.edu.*

CHAPTER 1

SETTING UP

Let's get started on the right foot.

CHAPTER OBJECTIVES

In this chapter, you will learn about:

Welcome to KornShell programming! The KornShell is a powerful computing environment that you can use both as a command interpreter and as a programming language. I know, a graphical user interface, with its bitmapped display, windows, icons, and mouse support, is great for much of the work you do with a computer. But the "old-fashioned" command line can't be beat as an efficient way to operate when you need to work in terms of a real computer instead of a desktop metaphor or when you have computing tasks that you want to automate.

In this book, you will do lots of exercises, and they all assume that you are using a computer that is configured so you can use the KornShell in a standard way. Even if you are already using the KornShell, you should go through this chapter carefully to make sure that your system is set up to operate in the standard way that we will assume throughout the remainder of the book. You can avoid a lot of aggravation later in the book if you make sure your system matches the one we will set up here.

LAB 1.1

LAB 1.1

RUNNING THE CURRENT KORNSHELL

LAB OBJECTIVES

After this lab, you will be able to:

- ✓ Set Up for LINUX and other UNIX Systems
- ✓ Set Up for MS Windows Systems

It's a fact of life that "the" KornShell has been under active development by David G. Korn of AT&T Research Laboratories for many years. The up side of this is that the shell continues to be available on more and more computing platforms. Today you can run the KornShell on virtually any UNIX system, including LINUX, Solaris, HP-UX, and many others, as well as on Microsoft Windows 9x and NT systems. You can write powerful programs using just a few lines of KornShell commands, and they will run the same way on all the systems that support the KornShell.

But there is a down side, too. It's that there are many "old" versions of the KornShell around that are missing features available in the current version. Also, because it is a big feature-rich software environment, there have been errors in some versions of the KornShell that are fixed in the most recent version.

The bottom line here is to verify that you have a current version of the KornShell up and running on your system or to get it up and running if you don't.

QUICK CHECK

If you have a system that you plan to use with this book and you think it's running the current version of the KornShell, log into it now, and press Control-V (press the "V" key while holding down the key labeled "Ctrl"). If you are running the current version of the KornShell, you should see a message that looks like the following:

```
Version M-12/28/93f
```

If you see a caret (^) when you press Control-V, you need to press the Escape key before Control-V to see the version message.

If you got that message or one like it that has a letter greater than **`f`** at the end, or one with a date later than `12/28/93` in it: *Congratulations, you are running a version of the KornShell that is compatible with this book and may skip the remainder of this Lab.* Go right on to Lab 1.2. However, if you got any other response when you pressed Ctrl-V, or if you don't have the KornShell running on your system, you will need to get it and install it on your system. If you are not an administrator for the system you are using, you will have to install a personal copy of the software, but if you *are* an administrator, you can install a copy for everyone who uses your system to share.

How you proceed now depends on whether you are running a UNIX system or Microsoft Windows. Depending on which applies to you, you should do Exercise 1.1.1 (UNIX) *or* 1.1.2 (Windows).

If for some reason you find yourself "stuck" with an earlier version of the KornShell, you may still be able to do most of the Exercises in this workbook. There are really just three major versions of the KornShell. The one we will use was released in 1993 and is known as *ksh93*. An earlier version was released in 1988 and is known as *ksh88*. There was also a version prior to 1988, as well as versions released by sources other than AT&T. For example, you can probably find "*pdksh*" on the Internet, and there is a version available commercially from Mortice Kern Systems (MKS), which at the time of this writing is being licensed by Microsoft for use with Windows 2000. Neither *pdksh* nor MKS *ksh* is compatible enough with *ksh93* to be able to recommend using them with this book. On the other hand, anything that works with *ksh88* will also work with *ksh93*. The Bolsky & Korn book cited in the Preface lists about seven pages of features that were added to *ksh88* to produce *ksh93*, but the vast majority of the features you will work with in this book will also work with *ksh88*. However, I have made no attempt in this book to cover those differences. If you have to work with *ksh88*, you should get a copy of the Bolsky & Korn book and look up anything from this book that doesn't seem to work right to see whether it is a version problem.

Some old versions of ksh *do not understand the Ctrl-V character. If you press Ctrl-V and don't see a version message, try the command* `what /bin/ksh` *(substitute the pathname your system uses if the KornShell is not in* `/bin/ksh`*), and you should see what version you have*

On Solaris, and possibly other systems that run the CDE (Common Desktop Environment), you will find an early version of ksh93 *as the command named* `dtksh`. *If you can't get the current version of ksh93,* `dtksh` *is better than ksh88 for doing the Exercises in this workbook.*

You can use `dtksh` *to build graphical user interfaces (GUIs) for your shell programs. Consult the Pendergast book (cited in the Preface) if you are interested in doing that sort of software development. That book is intended for experienced shell programmers who want to learn to program using the X Window System, or for experienced C/C++ programmers who already know how to program the X Window System. If you are using this workbook, you probably aren't in the category of "experienced shell programmers" (yet!), but you might be in the second category.*

LAB 1.1 EXERCISES

1.1.1 SET UP FOR LINUX AND OTHER UNIX SYSTEMS

The KornShell is an executable program named *ksh*. You can download an executable copy for most UNIX systems, including LINUX, using the following URL:

```
http://research.att.com/sw/tools/reuse
```

In the middle of this web page is a button marked *Binary* under a heading that says "Non-Commercial License Agreement and Available Software." Click the button, and you will go to a page that lists several software packages and gives you a menu of operating systems for each one. Select "*ast-base-97*" or "*ast-base-98*" (whichever lists your operating system), accept the license agreement, and proceed to download and install the software as instructed.

An alternative way to get the very latest release of the *KornShell* for AIX, HPUX, IRIX, Solaris, SunOS, or UnixWare is through Global Technologies Ltd., which you can contact using the following URL:

```
http://www.gtlinc.com
```

Once *ksh* is installed on your system, you have a choice of running it as your *default shell* or using some other shell as your default and running *ksh* as a command.

The way to make it your default shell is to use an interactive program named `chsh` (change shell) on some systems or `passwd` with a particular set of options on other systems. For example, I have a local account on a DEC OSF/1 system and use the `chsh` command to do this. I also have a networked account on a Solaris system, and the command I use is `passwd -r nisplus -e`. In either event, the command shows me the pathname of my current shell, and asks me for the pathname of the shell that I want to have as my new default. Once you change your default shell every time you log into your system, the KornShell will start running and will interpret the command lines that you type. If you are not sure about this, you might want to run the

KornShell as a separate command for a while until you are sure things are working smoothly.

Making a mistake in setting up your default shell can prevent you from logging into your system at all. In particular, if you have a network account (one that you can log into from any of the computers on a network), make sure the path to your default shell is valid, no matter which computer you use to log in.

If you want to run the KornShell as a command, just type the pathname to the `ksh` file in response to your default shell's prompt. If the directory containing `ksh` is in your `PATH` (we'll talk more about this later in this chapter), you can just type `ksh` as the name of a command.

Once you have installed `ksh` on your system, start it up either by logging in with it as your default shell or by running it as a command. Press Ctrl-V.

a) What happened? (answers to exercises are at the end of the Lab)

Because you are using a UNIX system, you should skip the next exercise, unless, of course, you also want to use the KornShell on a Windows system, too.

1.1.2 Set Up for MS Windows Systems

You can get the advantages of KornShell programming using MS Windows systems (Windows 95/98/NT/2000), but to do so you have to do something to make those systems work, more or less, like UNIX. There are several such packages available, but one, "U/WIN" (which stands for "UNIX for WINdows" but which is pronounced "You win") has the advantages of benefiting from David G. Korn's active involvement in its development and from the fact that it includes the latest version of the KornShell as part of the package.

You can download the current version of U/WIN from the following URL:

```
http://research.att.com/sw/tools/uwin
```

To quote that web page, "U/WIN binaries are available for educational, research, and evaluation purposes through this web site. Commercial licenses for U/WIN can be obtained from Global Technologies Ltd., Inc." You can also obtain the code on CD-ROM from Global Technologies if you prefer that route over doing the download. (The CD also contains a large number of UNIX utility programs compiled to run on a PC running U/WIN.) You can contact Global Technologies using the following URL:

```
http://www.gtlinc.com
```

You will have a pretty complete UNIX environment if you run U/WIN under Windows 2000 or NT. U/WIN is usable under Windows 95/98, but those systems cannot provide certain essential features needed to support several UNIX features. In particular, Windows 95/98 use the FAT file systems, which do not support many UNIX file system features. Similarly, those systems do not provide a rich enough multitasking environment to support some important UNIX process management features. Still, you can use most KornShell programming constructs, even under those systems, when running U/WIN.

Once you have downloaded and installed U/WIN, you will have a program group for U/WIN that includes an icon for running the KornShell in a window. If you are running Windows 2000 or NT, you will also be able to telnet into your system and use the KornShell that way.

Start a KornShell window using the icon in the U/WIN program group or telnet into your system and press Ctrl-V.

a) What happened?

____

____

LAB 1.1 ANSWERS

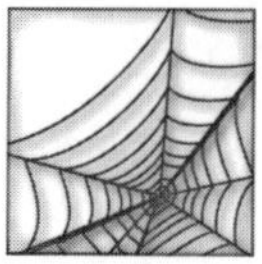

This section gives you some suggested answers to the questions in Lab 1.1, with discussion related to those answers. Your answers may vary, but the most important thing is whether or not your answer works. Use this discussion to analyze differences between your answers and those presented here.

If you have alternative answers to the questions in this exercise, you are encouraged to post your answers and to discuss them at the companion web site for this book, located at:

`http://www.phptr.com/phptrinteractive/`

1.1.1 ANSWERS

Once you have installed `ksh` on your system, start it up either by logging in with it as your default shell or by running it as a command. Press Ctrl-V.

a) What happened?

Answer: You should have seen a message such as `Version M-12/28/93f`

If the date is later than **`12/28/93`** or the letter at the end is greater than `f`, you're okay.

If you are running the shell using the `ksh` *command and get the wrong version, try typing the complete pathname to where the current version is installed. If that works, there is a problem with your* `PATH`*, which you will be able to fix later in this chapter. In this case, you can continue to work by typing the full pathname.*

If you think the shell is properly installed and you didn't get the correct version message, you are going to have to do some "sleuthing." Talking about the problem with someone who knows about your system can often lead to insight if you can't figure it out on your own.

1.1.2 ANSWERS

Start a KornShell window using the icon in the U/WIN program group or telnet into your system, and press Ctrl-V.

a) What happened?

Answer: You should have seen a message such as `Version M-12/28/93f`

If the date is later than `12/28/93` or the letter at the end is greater than `f`, you're okay.

If you have trouble getting U/WIN installed and running, there is an active mailing list for U/WIN users that you can join and ask for help. You can find out how to subscribe by selecting the "What's New" icon in the U/WIN program group. There is also a link to it from the U/WIN web site at AT&T.

LAB 1.1 SELF-REVIEW QUESTIONS

To test your progress, you should be able to answer the following question.

1) What does pressing Ctrl-V in response to a KornShell command prompt do?
   a) _____It displays the version of the KornShell that you are running.
   b) _____Something else.

Quiz answer appears in Appendix A, Section 1.1.

LAB 1.2

SETTING UP YOUR INTERACTIVE ENVIRONMENT

LAB OBJECTIVES

After this lab, you will be able to:

✓ Create Directories for Your Programs

LAB 1.2 SET UP YOUR PROFILE AND ENVIRONMENT FILE

This is a book about KornShell programming much more than it is about how to use the KornShell as your interactive shell for working with a UNIX or Windows system. However, there are several features of your interactive environment that have to be set up correctly in order for you to do the exercises throughout the book.

In this lab, you will set up the files and directories that have to be in place to use the KornShell effectively for program development

LAB 1.2 EXERCISES

1.2.1 CREATE DIRECTORIES FOR YOUR PROGRAMS

As you will see in the next lab, there are two types of KornShell programs, *scripts* and *functions*, and there are several ways to get those programs to run. In this exercise, you will create one directory for scripts and another one for functions.

Log into your account. This will make your *home directory* the same as your *current working directory.*

Run the following command:

```
pwd
```

a) What was displayed? (answers start on page 16)

____

____

Now list the part of the contents of your home directory using the following command:

```
ls -ld bin fun
```

b) What does the `-ld` part of this command do?

____

____

c) Were there any files or directories named `bin` or `fun` in your home directory?

If there were no files or directories named `bin` or `fun` in your home directory, create those directories now and verify them with the following commands:

```
mkdir bin fun
ls -ld bin fun
```

d) Are the directories in place now?

1.2.2 SET UP YOUR PROFILE AND ENVIRONMENT FILE

Setting things up properly to use the KornShell involves creating or modifying some files in your home directory. Before you do that, here is some background that will help you understand the rationale for what you are going to do with these files.

When you connect to your computer system, a program, usually named `login`, prompts you to enter your username and password, which it looks up in the system's user database (such as a file named `passwd` or in the Windows registry). That database also tells `login` the pathname of your home directory and the pathname of your shell program.

At this point, a *process* starts executing your shell (`ksh`). In general, you can use the terms *process* and *program* interchangeably, but there are real differences between the two. For example, on most systems, `login` and `ksh` are two *programs* (executable files) that are executed by the same *process*. *Processes* take a lot of time to create, so a general strategy is to try to minimize how many processes you create.

If you can do the same thing two different ways, one of which creates a new process and the other doesn't, choose the one that does not create a new process.

One important feature of a process is that each process has its own area of memory (called its *address space*), which includes a list of names and associated values, called its *environment*. The names in this list are called *environment variables*. (You will be learning a lot about variables throughout this book.)

A second important characteristic of processes is that one process can tell the operating system to create another process; the creating process is called the *parent* of the created process, called a *child*.

Finally, only one process can be executed by a hardware processor at a time. The operating system *schedules* all the processes on the system so that they all get to use the available processors in a fair and timely fashion.

Before your `login` process starts executing `ksh`, it makes the *current working directory* your home directory and puts three variables in the process's environment, named `LOGNAME` (value is the name you used for logging into the system), `HOME` (value is the pathname of your home directory), and `SHELL` (tells the pathname of your shell).

Log into your system and run the following commands:

```
print "My login name is $LOGNAME"
print "My home directory is $HOME"
print "My shell is $SHELL"
```

a) What printed?

____

____

On some systems, `login` initializes another environment variable named `PATH` to a default value, but on other systems, `PATH` is initialized in the step we are about to describe. Other variables, which won't concern us, that might be initialized by `login` include `MAIL` (tells the pathname of your incoming mailbox), and `TZ` (tells the name of the computer's "local time" time zone).

When the shell starts executing, it processes commands that it reads from a system-wide file named `profile`, normally in the directory named `/etc`. Then the shell processes commands from a file in your home directory named `.profile`, followed by the commands in your *environment file,* if it exists. Finally, the shell goes into *interactive mode* and prints a prompt string (by default, a dollar sign followed by a space), inviting you to type in commands. When you enter the `exit` command in response to this prompt, the shell process terminates and logs you out of the system. You can also terminate the shell process by pressing Ctrl-D in response to the shell's prompt for an interactive command.

The shell adds variables to its environment when it reads commands in the form `name=value`. For this exercise, we want to be sure the variables `PATH` and `FPATH` both have the proper values. As you can see from the previous paragraph, they can be set when the shell reads commands from `/etc/profile`, from `.profile` in your home directory, from your environment file, or by you when you respond to an interactive prompt. Unless they are set up for you by commands in `/etc/profile`, the best way to initialize `PATH` and `FPATH` is by editing your `.profile`.

If you put the characters tilde-slash (`~/` *) in front of a file name, it means the file is in your home directory, whether your current working directory is your home directory or has been changed by a* `cd` *command. You can accomplish the same thing by putting* `$HOME/` *in front of the file name. So your* `.profile` *is referred to as* `~/.profile`.

A dot at the beginning of a file's name makes it invisible to normal directory listings. This is done to keep from cluttering up your directory listings, especially in your home directory, with `~/.profile` *and numerous other housekeeping files that get put there. You can see these files by using the* `-a` *option of the* `ls` *command.*

I just checked and found about a dozen of these "hidden" files in the home directory of my U/WIN account and about 80 of them on my Solaris account.

To see whether you need to do anything to set up your `PATH` environment variable, run the following command:

```
typeset -x | grep "^PATH="
```

b) What (if anything) printed?

To see whether you need to do anything to set up your `FPATH` environment variable, run the following command:

```
typeset -x | grep "^FPATH="
```

c) What (if anything) printed?

When we mentioned your "environment file" before, we didn't say what its name was. That's because you get to pick the name yourself by assigning a value to the variable `ENV`.

The shell runs the commands in your environment file only when you start an interactive shell.

As you will see in the next exercise, you can run a copy of the shell in noninteractive mode, for example, to execute a shell script that you (or someone else) wrote. So that's where you put alias definitions and certain function definitions that wouldn't be used in scripts. Following this reasoning a bit further, it normally doesn't make sense to export `ENV` because the shell ignores it for noninteractive shells.

Run the following command to check whether you have an environment file:


```
print "My environment file is: $ENV"
```

d) What printed?

LAB 1.2 ANSWERS

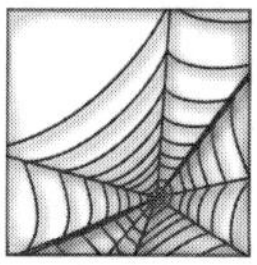

This section gives you some suggested answers to the questions in Lab 1.2, with discussion related to those answers. Your answers may vary, but the most important thing is whether or not your answer works. Use this discussion to analyze differences between your answers and those presented here.

If you have alternative answers to the questions in this exercise, you are encouraged to post your answers and to discuss them at the companion web site for this book, located at:

`http://www.phptr.com/phptrinteractive/`

1.2.1 ANSWERS

a) What was displayed?

Answer: It depends on the pathname to your home directory. For me, the interaction looked like the following:

```
$ pwd
/home/vickery
$
```

The shell's default prompt string is a dollar sign followed by a space, but as you will see in Lab 4.3.2, "Quote Variable References," you can easily change it to something more interesting. For now, we'll show the default prompt in our interactions.

Naturally, your home directory will have a different path than mine.

b) What does the `-ld` part of this command do?

Answer: It specifies a long listing using directory names.

By default, the `ls` command shows the contents of any directories you name on the command line, but the `d` option tells the command to list just the name of the directory instead. The `l` gives a long listing, which will let us verify whether we are looking at files or directories.

c) Were there any files or directories named `bin` or `fun` in your home directory?

Answer: Well, it depends! Here is what we want your interaction to look like:

```
$ ls -ld bin fun
drwxr-xr-x   2 vickery  users    1024 Oct  7 17:02 bin
drwx------   2 vickery  users     512 Jun 17 17:19 fun
$
```

We are interested in just the first four and last three characters on these two lines. The middle parts will be different for you, depending on several issues that aren't important to us here, such as your username and default permissions.

The first four characters, `drwx`, say that the names `bin` and `fun` are directories for which you have read, write and execute permissions. If the first letter is anything other than a *d*, it means that you have something other than a directory with the name `bin` (or `fun`), probably a regular file. If that is the case, you have a regular file with one of these names, and you should change its name using an `mv` command.

The two directories we are setting up here are going to hold two kinds of shell programs that you write, scripts (which go in `bin`*) and functions (which go in* `fun`*). Don't use a different name for* `bin` *unless you have a really good reason for doing so. It's the standard name to use for the directory that holds your own copies of executable programs, such as the* KornShell *scripts you will be writing.*

The name fun is not so standard, and it would be okay to pick another name if you want to. (Maybe "fun" seems too frivolous!) However, throughout this book we will refer to your ~/fun directory, meaning this directory. If you pick another name, you will have to mentally change all the references in the book from ~/fun to the directory name you are using.

d) Are the directories in place now?

Answer: Yes.

If your answer is anything other than "yes," repeat the material in this exercise, and redo the mkdir command until you get these directories properly created.

1.2.2 ANSWERS

a) What printed?

Answer: Your interaction should look like the following:

```
$ print "My login name is $LOGNAME"
My login name is vickery
$ print "My home directory is $HOME"
My home directory is /home/vickery
$ print "My shell is $SHELL"
My shell is /bin/ksh
$
```

Your results may differ, depending on your username, home directory location, and where the KornShell is stored on your system. In fact, it is possible that one or more of the messages will print nothing after the word *is*. If that happens, you can still continue with the material in this book, but you should take missing values as "red flags," indicating that your system is configured in some nonstandard way.

If the name of your shell is anything other than ksh *(or possibly* dtksh*), either you are running the* KornShell *as a separate program after logging in using a different shell by default, or there is a problem that you need to deal with before proceeding.*

b) What (if anything) printed?

Answer: Your answer depends on how your `PATH` environment variable is set up. Your interaction might look like the following:

```
$ typeset -x | grep "^PATH="
PATH=/usr/bin:/usr/local/bin:/home/vickery/bin
$
```


This command line consists of two parts. The first part (`typeset -x`) tells the shell to print a list showing the names and values of all the shell's *exported* variables, which could be quite long, and which should include `PATH`. The second part (`grep "^PATH="`) invokes the `grep` utility to search the output of the `typeset` command for the string `PATH=` at the beginning of a line (indicated by the ^ at the beginning of the string). You will learn more about this type of command in Chapter 4, "Simple Variables." For now, just type the command exactly as shown and observe the output.

If nothing printed when you typed the command, either `PATH` is not set up at all, which is highly unlikely, or it is not exported. You can see whether it is set by running the following command:

```
print $PATH
```

If *that* command prints nothing, you should check with the person who set up your system; there should be a `PATH=` command in `/etc/profile` so that each user will have an initial setting for this environment variable.

If a `print` command shows that `PATH` has a value, but the `typeset -x` command doesn't show it, it means you have to use your favorite text editor to add the following command to your `~/.profile`:

```
export PATH
```

You will need a good text editor for preparing many of the programs in this book, as well as to do housekeeping operations, such as putting commands in your configuration files.

There is one text editor that is available on all UNIX systems, `vi`. *Where we want to indicate "edit a file," we will show a* `vi` *command in this book. However, if you want to use* `vi` *you should strongly consider switching to* `vim` *("vi-improved"), which is widely available at no cost for most systems. Another widely used text editor is* `emacs`, *which is also widely available at no cost for most systems. If you don't already know* `emacs`, *you will find* `vim` *easier to learn.*

If you are using U/WIN, you can use any DOS or Windows text editor. These editors normally add an extra character to the end of each line of text (an ASCII carriage return) that UNIX editors do not use, but you can often turn this behavior off, or you can just not worry about it because the KornShell *will not have problems with the extra characters. If you choose to use a Windows editor, I recommend "The Programmer's File Editor," which is available at no cost from Alan Philips of Lancaster University Computer Center:*

`http:// www.lancs.ac.uk/people/cpaap/pfe/`

If you are using the X Window System, the best editor to use is `nedit` *by Mark Edel of Fermi National Labs. Binaries for most platforms, and source code you can use to build it yourself, are available from:*

`ftp://ftp.fnal.gov/pub/nedit`

Now, back to your PATH. When you run a command, it has a set of environment variables, just as the shell itself does; however, the shell's environment variables will not necessarily be part of the command's environment, unless you declare the variable to be exported. You will see in the next lab that there are ways to run commands so that they automatically share all the shell's environment variables, but for those cases where this does not happen automatically, you need to tell the shell to export the variable. You need to export PATH because it tells the shell what directories to look in to find executable files. If you write a shell program that runs other programs (which describes almost all shell programs), your shell program needs to have its `PATH` set correctly so that the shell can find these other programs.

`PATH` is a list of directories, separated by colons (:) that the shell will search to find executable files, including the shell scripts that you will be learning to write in this book. If it's not already there, you need to add `~/bin` to this list. (Remember, the tilde (~) is automatically taken by the shell to mean the pathname to your home directory.) If there was no `PATH=` command in your `~/.profile`, you could accomplish this by adding the following line to that file:

```
PATH="~/bin:$PATH"
```

More concisely, you can combine this with the `export` command:

```
export PATH="~/bin/:$PATH"
```

The shell looks through the directories in your `PATH` *in the left-to-right order that they appear in the variable's value string. The previous command tells the shell to* prepend *your* `bin` *directory to this list, which means that if you put a program in* `~/bin` *that has the same name as another command in the system, your program will run instead of the system's command. This is generally a good thing, but not always. Imagine if you unwittingly create a program with the same name as one of the ones that came with the system, then tried to run someone else's script that uses that program. If your* `bin` *directory was before the system's* `bin` *directory and* `PATH` *is exported, the script wouldn't work right. For this reason, many people* append *directories to the value established in* `/etc/profile`*, using a command in* `~/.profile`*, like the following:*

```
export PATH=$PATH:~/bin
```

You might also consider adding dot (.) to your `PATH`. That represents the current working directory, no matter what `cd` command(s) you might have executed to change to other directories. That can be convenient when you are developing programs in a directory that you set up for doing development work, but it can expose you to certain security risks if you are running your system as the superuser.

c) What (if anything) printed?

Answer: If `FPATH` *is set up correctly, you will see a colon-separated list of directories, including at least your* `~/fun` *directory.*

If the correct information was not displayed, using the same logic as in the discussion about `PATH`, you need to add a command such as the following to your `~/.profile`:

```
export FPATH=$FPATH:~/fun
```

If `/etc/profile` *does not have a command to assign a value to* `FPATH` *(on some systems it does, and on some systems it doesn't), you will end up with a colon (:) at the beginning of your* `FPATH` *value, which the shell will interpret as "the current directory followed by the remaining directories in the value string." That is, it's the same as having dot (.) at the beginning of your* `FPATH`*. The same thing holds for* `PATH`*. If you don't want this behavior, you will need to use one of the parameter expansions covered in Chapter 10, "Patterns, Expansions, and Substitutions," to deal with the problem.*

Run the following command to check whether you have an environment file:

```
print "My environment file is $ENV"
```

d) What printed?

Answer: If the variable `ENV` *is set, you should see the name of your environment file. If not, you will see only the first part of the message. Your interaction might look something like the following:*

```
$ print "My environment file is: $ENV"
My environment file is: /home/vickery/.kshrc
$
```

If nothing prints after the colon (:) in the message, it means that there is no `ENV=` in your `~/.profile`, so add the following command to that file (or one similar to it if you prefer to use a different file name):

```
export ENV=~/.kshrc
```

Normally, there is no need to export `ENV`, but it doesn't do any harm, and there are some situations where it actually is needed to get your interactive shell to process the commands in your environment file.

At this point, you don't know about functions, aliases, or the `set` command, which are the commands you would normally put in an environment file, so to get you started, we'll just show you an example without explaining the contents. As you learn more features of the shell, you can develop your own version of this file. Note that the following file contains sample personal preferences that you should modify to match your own way of working.


```
print This is .ksrhc

# Set up to use arrow keys for command line editing
EDITOR=vim        # Editor to invoke from inside more
VISUAL=emacs      # Command line editing style
emacs_keybind     # Make arrow keys work

# Set up to use less instead of more
PAGER=less
export LESS='-EaP?n?f%f .?m(File %i of %m) \
..?lt%lb/%L:?pt%pB\%:?bt%bB/%B:-...?e(end)?xNext\:
  %x..'

# Redefine the ls and rm commands for interactive use.
LSFLAGS=-F  # Put slashes after directory names, etc.
RMFLAGS=-i         # Always ask before deleting files

alias ls="command ls $LSFLAGS"
alias rm="command rm $RMFLAGS"

# Set some shell options
set -o nolog # Keep function defs out of history file
set -o noclobber  # Don't overwrite existing files

# Add some new command names -- aliases
alias ..="cd .."  # Go up one directory
alias m=$PAGER     # more (or less)
alias md=mkdir     # Like DOS
alias rd=rmdir     # Like DOS
alias q=exit       #


# Add some new command names -- functions
```

```
function l  {
  ls -l  "$@" | $PAGER
  }
function la {
  ls -la "$@" | $PAGER
  }
```

It's common practice on UNIX systems for programs to read commands from a file when they start up to set up a user's preferences for the program. Such files typically have names that begin with ~/. (to make them hidden files in the user's home directory), followed by the name of the program (ksh, in this case), followed by `rc` *(short for "read commands"). Knowing this can remove some of the mystery from looking at a list of the hidden files in your home directory.*

LAB 1.2 SELF-REVIEW QUESTIONS

To test your progress, you should be able to answer the following questions.

1) What is the *environment* of a process?

a) _____The computer that executes it.
b) _____The user who runs it.
c) _____The other programs in memory at the same time.
d) _____A list of variables with associated values.
e) _____Its network neighborhood.

2) What is an environment variable?

a) _____A name and its associated value that is part of a process's environment.
b) _____A peripheral device that works in different ways at different times.
c) _____A peripheral device that always works the same way.
d) _____A symbol that is exported to a process's external environment.
e) _____Anything that affects the weather.

3) What does it mean to *export* a variable?

a) _____To send the variable to another computer.
b) _____To send a copy of the variable to another computer.
c) _____To make its name and value available to a process' children.
d) _____To make its name and value available to a process' parents.
e) _____To put the variable on a ship bound for another country.

4) The KornShell always reads command from `~/.kshrc`, if that file exists.

a) _____True
b) _____False, because it never reads commands from that file.
c) _____False, because it reads commands from that file only if it contains an `ENV=` command.
d) _____False, because it reads commands from that file only if its name is the value of the variable named `ENV`.
e) _____False, because it always reads commands from a file named `~/envfile`, if it exists, instead.

5) Use the numbers 1–6 to indicate the sequence in which the following events occur (1 is first, 6 is last).

a) _____The shell executes the commands in the environment file.
b) _____Login reads the user's name and password.
c) _____The shell executes the commands in `~/.profile`.
d) _____The shell executes the commands in `/etc/profile`.
e) _____The login process executes the shell.
f) _____The shell prints a prompt and waits for the user to type a command.

Quiz answers appear in Appendix A, Section 1.2.

LAB 1.3

EDITING AND RUNNING SCRIPTS AND FUNCTIONS

LAB OBJECTIVES

After this lab, you will be able to:

- ✓ Define and Run a Script
- ✓ "Dot" a Script
- ✓ Define and Run a Function

There are two kinds of shell programs, *scripts* and *functions*. A script is a list of commands that you put into a file and that the shell processes by reading the file. The `/etc/profile`, `~/.profile` and your environment file are examples of scripts, albeit special ones, because the shell executes them automatically. The scripts we will be concerned with from here on are the ones that you write to create new commands. If you put a set of commands in a file and have everything set up properly, you can use the name of the script file as a new command name. Just type its name, and the shell will execute the commands inside it.

There are two ways to run a script. You can run it as a command that has its own, private environment, or you can run it so that it shares the environment of your interactive shell's process. You will learn about setting up and running scripts both ways in this lab.

Functions are normally smaller pieces of code that also provide new commands that you can use. The key difference between a script and a function is that once the shell reads the definition of a function, it keeps a copy of it in its own address space (memory), so that running the script again takes less time. Scripts, on the other hand, are read from their disk files every time they are run.

This lab will make sure you are set up to run scripts and functions properly.

LAB 1.3 EXERCISES

1.3.1 DEFINE AND RUN A SCRIPT

For a script file to work as a command, the file containing the script must be in one of the directories listed in your `PATH` (or you must type the complete pathname of the script file), and the file must be executable. At this point, `~/bin` is a directory that is listed in your `PATH`, so all you need to do to define and run a script is to create an executable file in that directory.

Run the following sequence of commands. (Expect to see two error messages.)

Be sure you don't already have a file named `s131` *in your* `bin` *directory.*

```
s131
> bin/s131
s131
chmod +x bin/s131
s131
```

a) What happened the three times you entered the `s131` command?

---

b) What was the purpose of the > command?

---

c) What was the purpose of the `chmod` command?

Now, let's work with a script that actually does something! Because we're trying to check your setup, put the following commands in `~/bin/s131` to cause it to show some information about your configuration:

```
# s131 Print the values of some variables.

print "This is $0"
print "My Process ID is $$"
print "FPATH is $FPATH"
print "VAR_131 is \"$VAR_131\""
```

Now use the following commands to give a value to the variable `VAR_131` and to run the new command. Do *not* export the variable `VAR_131`.

```
VAR_131=KornShell
s131
```

d) What printed?

---

e) What happens to the process ID if you run this command again?

1.3.2 "DOT" A SCRIPT

The second way to run a script is to "dot" it. That is, you type a dot (.), followed by a space and the name of the script (or function) that you want to run. When you run a script this way, it uses the shell's environment instead of having its own.

Run the following pair of commands to see the implications of dotting a script compared with running it as a command. You should not have changed `s131` or `VAR_131` since the previous exercise.

```
print $$
. s131
```

a) What is the process ID of your interactive shell?

b) What is the script's process ID when you dot it?

Now add the following commands to the end of `~/bin/s131`:

```
VAR_131=changed
print "Now VAR_131 is \"$VAR_131\""
```

Now you can see another of the shell's features. called *subshells*. You can run the command(s) in a subshell by putting parentheses around it (or them). To see this in action, run the following commands using your newly changed `s131` script:

```
s131
print $VAR_131
( . s131 )
print $VAR_131
. s131
print $VAR_131
```


c) Under what conditions can a script change the value of one of the shell's environment variables?

____

____

There is another way that you can run a script that you should know about, but that does not apply to you if you are running the KornShell as your interactive shell. It's called *she-bang* notation. Normally, the shell treats everything to the right of a sharp symbol (#) on a line as a comment and ignores it. However, if the first line of a file starts with a sharp symbol, followed by an exclamation mark (`#!`) (which is popularly pronounced "she-bang"), versions of UNIX will look for the name of a program on the remainder of the line to process the contents of the file.

d) On such systems, what could you put on the first line to cause the program to be executed as a KornShell script, even if the KornShell is not your interactive shell?

____

____

1.3.3 Define and Run a Function

You will learn a lot about writing functions in Chapters 2, "Command Syntax," and 5, "Parameters." In this exercise, we will show just the basics about how to define and run one of the two kinds of functions you can write for the Korn-Shell.

You can define a function from the command line. Try this by entering the following lines:

```
function f133 {
  print "This is function $0"
  }
```

Now run your function by typing its name, `f113`, as a command.

a) What printed?

____

____

Once a function becomes more complex than this, it pays to put the definition in a file. Enter the following function definition in the file `~/fun/f133`:

```
function f133 {
  print "This is function $0"
  print "My process ID is $$"
  print "Var_133 is \"$VAR_133\""
  VAR_133=changed
  print "VAR_133 is now $VAR_133"
  }
```

Now, to make a point, here is a trick question for you: Run the following sequence of commands:

```
VAR_133=KornShell
f133
```

b) What printed, and why?

____

____

To continue with the trick, run this command:

```
. f133
```

c) What printed, and why?

That's the end of the tricks. Now, run the following sequence of commands:


```
. ~/fun/f133
print $VAR_133
( f133 )
print $VAR_133
(. f133)
print $VAR_133
f133
print $VAR_133
VAR_133=KornShell
. f133
print $VAR_133
```

d) What makes the first command different from the dot command in the previous question?

If you have set your account up so that you can use the up and down arrow keys to move through your command history, you will find your function definition in the list of commands you have entered. You can turn this feature of the shell off by using the command:

```
set -o nolog
```

e) What are the four ways that you ran the function?

f) Under what conditions does a function run using the shell's process?

___

___

g) Under what conditions can a function change a shell's environment?

___

___

Finally, to see the role of `FPATH` in your setup, create the following function definition in a file named "`~/fun/notf133a`"

```
function f133a {
  print "This is $0"
  }
```

Now run the following sequence of commands:

```
f133a
cp ~/fun/notf133a ~/fun/f133a
f133a
rm fun/f133a
f133a
```

h) What happened when you ran the function each time?

___

___

___

___

___

___

Lab 1.3 Answers

This section gives you some suggested answers to the questions in Lab 1.3, with discussion related to those answers. Your answers may vary, but the most important thing is whether or not your answer works. Use this discussion to analyze differences between your answers and those presented here.

If you have alternative answers to the questions in this exercise, you are encouraged to post your answers and to discuss them at the companion web site for this book, located at:

`http://www.phtpr.com/phptrinteractive/`

1.3.1 Answers

a) What happened the three times you entered the `s131` command?

Answer: The first two times, you should have received an error message. The last time, nothing happened. Your interaction should have looked like the following:

```
$ s131
-ksh: s131: not found
$ > ~/bin/s131
$ s131
-ksh: s131: not found
$ chmod +x ~/bin/s131
$ s131
$
```

The error message begins with the name of the program that encountered the error—your interactive shell. The dash (-) in front of the shell's name was put there by `login` to tell the shell that it is a *login shell*, which is how it knows that it is supposed to process `/etc/profile`, `~/.profile`, and your environment file.

After the name of the shell is the name of the program the shell was trying to execute (`s131`) and the message, `not found`, which means that the shell was not able to find an executable file named `s131` in any of the directories listed in `PATH`.

b) What was the purpose of the > command?

Answer: It creates the file named `~/bin/s131`.

This is an example of output redirection, which will be covered in Chapter 2, "Command Syntax."

Creating the file in the proper directory isn't enough. The second `s131` command still produces the "not found" error message, even though the file is in a directory listed in `PATH`.

c) What was the purpose of the `chmod` command?

Answer: It turns on the execute permission bits for the file.

You should consult your system's documentation for the `chmod` command if you are not already familiar with it. Here's a simplified quick review: Every file or directory has nine permission bits associated with it–read, write, and execute permissions for the "user" (owner), the owner's group, and for "others"—everyone else who uses the system. By default, a file is created with read and write permissions for the owner and read permission for the owner's group and for everyone else. The `chmod` command used here turned on the execute permission bits for the owner, group, and others. If you wanted to make the file executable only by you, you could have used the following command instead of the one shown:

```
chmod u+x ~/bin/s131
```

If you want to make the default set of permissions for files you create *not* allow reading by anyone but yourself, put this command in your `~/.profile` or (if you want it to apply only to your interactive sessions) your environment file:

```
umask 77
```

Because `chmod` and `umask` are standard UNIX commands, you should consult your system's documentation for more information on their use. The *KornShell* provides its own version of `umask` that is a superset of the standard UNIX command; it is summarized in Appendix B, "Reference."

Now that the file exists in the proper directory and is executable, typing it as a command "works." There is no error message. However, nothing else happens because there are no commands in the script! The shell processes the commands in a script until there aren't any more. In this case, the shell finds "no more" commands as soon as it looks for the first one. This is not an error condition, it just isn't a very useful script, except for our purposes of studying what it means for a file to be in one of the directories listed in `PATH` and to be executable.

After entering the commands in `~/bin/s131` *and running the command again:*

d) What printed?

Answer: Your interaction should look something like the following:

```
$ s131
This is s131
My Process ID is 18728
FPATH is :/home/vickery/fun
VAR_131 is ""
$
```

Now the script runs and prints some interesting information. First, it prints its own name by using `$0` in the `print` command. You will learn about using special variables such as this one in Chapter 4, "Simple Variables."

The next line shows the script's *process ID*. The kernel assigns every process a unique ID number when it is created, and you can print a process's ID number using `$$` in a `print` command. Your process ID is undoubtedly different from the one I got when I ran the command. The next question will deal with this issue further.

The next two lines show the values of two variables, `FPATH` and `VAR_131`; however, the second one prints nothing inside the quotation marks. (We put literal quotation marks (`\"`) in this print statement to show that `VAR_131` does not have a value inside this script.) The issue is that `FPATH` is an exported variable (provided you set up your `~/.profile` correctly earlier) and you can print its value from inside the script, but `VAR_131` is *not* exported, and you cannot print its value from inside the script. We will look at this issue more in the next exercise, so remember what happened here!

e) What happens to the process ID if you run this command again?

Answer: It changes. Your interaction should look something like the following.

```
$ s131
```

```
This is s131
My Process ID is 25678
FPATH is :/home/vickery/fun
VAR_131 is ""
$
```

On some systems, the kernel "recycles" process IDs more quickly than on others, so you might see these numbers repeat on such systems. However, all systems guarantee that every process that exists at any moment in time will have a unique process ID, compared with all other processes that exist at that same moment.

1.3.2 ANSWERS

a) What is the process ID of your interactive shell?

Answer: It depends on what ID the kernel assigned your interactive shell's process when it started.

If you recall, the same process that executes `login` also executes `ksh` on most systems, so we have to use careful wording here to be precise. The real point of this question, however, comes in the answer to the next question.

b) What is the script's process ID when you dot it?

Answer: It is the same as the shell's. Your actual process ID will probably have a different number, but your interaction should look something like the following:

```
$ print $$
4006
$ . s131
This is s131
My Process ID is 4006
FPATH is :/home/vickery/fun
VAR_131 is "KornShell"
$
```

Now you can see the difference between dotting a script and running it as a command. When you dot it, it executes as part of the *same process as the shell*, as indicated by the common process ID number printed by the shell and by the script. An important implication of this feature of dotting a script is that *all* the shell's variables are available to a script when it is dotted—not just the ones that have been exported. This is demonstrated by the value displayed when the script prints `$VAR_131`.

c) Under what condition can a script change the value of one of the shell's environment variables?

Answer: If it is dotted and not run in a subshell. Your interaction should have looked like the following:


```
$ s131
This is s131
My Process ID is 6609
FPATH is :/home/vickery/fun
VAR_131 is ""
Now VAR_131 is "changed"
print $VAR_131
KornShell
$ ( . s131 )
This is s131
My Process ID is 4006
FPATH is :/home/vickery/fun
VAR_131 is "KornShell"
Now VAR_131 is "changed"
$ print $VAR_131
KornShell
$ . s131
This is s131
My Process ID is 4006
FPATH is :/home/vickery/fun
VAR_131 is "KornShell"
Now VAR_131 is "changed"
$ print $VAR_131
changed
$
```

The first time `s131` executes, it has its own process, and its environment includes only the variables exported by the shell. The value of `VAR_131` was assigned a value inside the script, but it had no effect on the value of the variable in the shell's environment.

When `s131` executes the second time, it is dotted, but the parentheses make it run in a subshell. Now it runs in the shell's process and has access to all the shell's variables, including those not exported, and it can change `VAR_131`, but the change *does not affect the shell's environment because commands in a subshell get a* copy *of the shell's environment*. They don't actually have access to the shell's environment directly.

Finally, when `s131` is dotted without running it in a subshell, it uses the shell's process, can access all the shell's variables, and *can modify the shell's environment.*

d) On such systems, what could you put on the first line to cause the program to be executed as a KornShell script, even if the KornShell is not your interactive shell?

Answer: The first line might look like the following (depending on where the shell is installed):

```
#! /bin/ksh
```

In this case, the operating system kernel will create a new process to run a noninteractive copy of the shell, which will read commands from the file, execute them, and terminate. If you are running the KornShell as your interactive shell and you invoke a script that starts this way on most systems, the shell recognizes the situation and runs the command as a subshell, instead of going through the overhead of having the kernel create another process.

On many systems, if the first line of a script file has a sharp (#) in the first column and nothing else on the line, the kernel will run a different shell, the C shell. Be sure you don't start your KornShell *scripts this way, or they won't run properly on such systems.*

1.3.3 ANSWERS

a) What printed?

Answer: Your interaction should look like the following:

```
$ function f133 {
> print "This is function $0"
  }
$ f133
This is function f133
$
```

You typed in the keyword *function* followed by the function *name* (`f133`), and an open brace ({), and when you pressed the Enter key at the end of the line, the shell issued its *continuation prompt (>)*, indicating that it expects you to type more information to complete the function definition that you have started. You typed a `print` command, and ended the function definition by typing a close brace (}) in response to the next continuation prompt. The shell prompted you to enter another command, and you typed the name of the function you just defined, and it executed.

b) What printed, and why?

Answer: Your interaction should have looked like the following:

```
$ vi ~/fun/f133
```

Here you should enter the lines indicated in the function definition file.

```
$ f133
This is function f133
$
```

This is the output of your previous definition of `f133`, not the new one you just entered into `~/fun/f133`.

If the shell has a definition for a function, creating or editing a file in `~/fun` *will not cause the shell to recognize the new definition automatically.*

c) What printed, and why?

Answer: The original function ran again.

Once a function has been defined, as you will shortly see, dotting it and running it as a command are equivalent. The point of the trick is that we still haven't seen how to get the *new* definition to take effect.

d) What makes the first command different from the dot command in the previous question?

Answer: This command gives an explicit pathname for the file to be dotted. The previous one just named the function.

There are several issues to sort out here, although the conclusions will turn out to be not too complicated. For scripts, the file must be in one of the directories in `PATH`, or you may specify the pathname of the file explicitly. In either case, script files must have their execute permission bit(s) set or the shell will issue a "not found" message.

However, for function definitions that you put inside a file, the file does not have to have its execute permission bit(s) set, and if you give the file's pathname explicitly (by starting it with a tilde, in this case), the shell will read the function definition from the file. When you typed the first command for this question, the shell read the new function definition and used it to replace the previous definition that you had entered from the command line but it did not run the function. The fact that we used the `~/fun` directory for this file and the fact that the file's name and the function's name are the same are irrelevant for now.

e) What are the four ways that you ran the function?

Answer: In a subshell, dotted in a subshell, as a command, and as a dotted command.

Putting the command in parentheses—whether dotting the command or not–causes it to run in a subshell, as the first two invocations of `f133` illustrate. The second two invocations ran the function without using a subshell.

f) Under what conditions does a function run using the shell's process?

Answer: All four ways use the shell's process. Your interaction should have looked like the following:

```
$. ~/fun/f133
$ print $VAR_133
VAR_133 is "KornShell"
$ ( f133 )
This is function f133
My process ID is 4006
Var_133 is "KornShell"
VAR_133 is now changed
$ print $VAR_133
KornShell
$ (. f133)
This is function f133
My process ID is 4006
Var_133 is "KornShell"
```

```
VAR_133 is now changed
$ print $VAR_133
KornShell
$ f133
This is function f133
My process ID is 4006
Var_133 is "KornShell"
VAR_133 is now changed
$ print $VAR_133
changed
$ VAR_133=KornShell
$ . f133
This is function f133
My process ID is 4006
Var_133 is "KornShell"
VAR_133 is now changed
$ print $VAR_133
changed
$
```

LAB 1.3

You can see that all four executions printed the same process ID, which (because I did not log out and back in again) is the same as the shell's process ID in the previous exercise.

g) Under what conditions can a function change a shell's environment?

Answer: When it is not run in a subshell.

The first two invocations of `f133` did not change the value of `VAR_133` that you printed from the command line, but the last two invocations—which were not run in subshells—did.

h) What happened when you ran the function each time?

Answer: There was an error the first time, but the function executed both the second and third times. Your interaction should have looked like the following:

```
$ vi ~/fun/notf133a
```

Here you should enter the lines indicated in the function definition file.

```
$ f133a
-ksh: f133a: not found
$ cp ~/fun/notf133a ~/fun/f133a
```

```
$ f133a
This is f133a
$ rm ~/fun/f133a
$ f133a
This is f133a
$
```


If you create a file with the same name as a function definition that it defines *and* you put that file in one of the directories listed in your `FPATH` variable, then run the function, the shell will locate the file and process all the commands in it (including any additional function definitions you might have put in it) and will then run the newly defined function. The shell doesn't read the file again unless you explicitly dot it, as shown by the fact that you can run the function again, even after removing the file containing the definition.

Any time you change the contents of a function definition file, you must dot it for the changes to take effect on the function definitions that the shell works with.

The behavior described in the previous paragraph is not well documented. For example, the Bolsky & Korn book cited in the Preface says the file has to be in a directory that is listed in both *the* `PATH` *and the* `FPATH` *variables. This is not true in current versions of the* KornShell.

You can put several related function definitions in one file, with the file name being the name of the first function that will be run, and they will all be defined when that first one runs.

LAB 1.3 SELF-REVIEW QUESTIONS

To test your progress, you should be able to answer the following questions.

1) A script always runs as a separate process from the shell.
   - **a)** _____True.
   - **b)** _____False. It always runs using the shell's process.
   - **c)** _____False. It runs as a separate process only if you dot it.
   - **d)** _____False. It runs as a separate process only if it is run in a subshell.
   - **e)** _____False. It runs as a separate process unless you dot it.

2) A function always runs as a separate process from the shell.
a) _____True.
b) _____False. It always runs using the shell's process.
c) _____False. It runs as a separate process only if you dot it.
d) _____False. It runs as a separate process only if it is run in a subshell.
e) _____False. It runs as a separate process unless you dot it.

3) How do you run a command (or commands) in a subshell?
a) _____Put them in a file and dot it.
b) _____Write them inside parentheses.
c) _____Write them inside curly braces.
d) _____Write them inside square brackets.
e) _____You can't do it.

4) What two conditions must be met for the shell to run a command as a script? (Pick the best answer.)
a) _____There must be a function with the name of the command, and it must be dotted.
b) _____There must be an executable file with the name of the script, and it must be in one of the directories in the `PATH` variable.
c) _____There must be proper definitions for `PATH` and `FPATH`.
d) _____The script must contain a comment (beginning with a sharp symbol [#]) and a `print` command in the script.
e) _____You can't do it.

5) Once a function has been defined, it starts faster than a script because the shell no longer has to read its commands from a file.
a) _____True
b) _____False

Quiz answers appear in Appendix A, Section 1.3.

CHAPTER 1

TEST YOUR THINKING

The projects in this section are meant to have you utilize all of the skills that you have acquired throughout this chapter. The answers to these projects can be found at the companion web site to this book, located at:

`http://www.phptr.com/phptrinteractive/`

Visit the web site periodically to share and discuss your answers.

Create another directory and add it to your `PATH`. Put two different scripts with the same name but different outputs in the two directories.

1) Which one gets executed when you run "the" command? Explain what is going on.

Create a script and a function definition file with the same names but different outputs.

2) Which one runs when you use the name as a command? Explain what is going on.

3) Discuss the advantages and disadvantages of writing functions, compared with scripts, based on what you have learned so far.

4) Discuss the advantages and disadvantages of running programs as subshells or not, based on what you have learned so far.

C H A P T E R 2

COMMAND SYNTAX

You may already be familiar with many of the elements of UNIX command lines. This chapter makes sure you understand how the KornShell *recognizes the significant parts of individual commands.*

Chapter Objectives

In this chapter, you will learn about:

In essence, the shell spends its life repeatedly doing just two things:

1. Obtaining a string of text, called a *command line.*
2. Executing the command line.

The shell can read command lines interactively from a user's keyboard, it can read them from a file (called a *shell script* or *shell program*), or it can receive one command line as a parameter when it starts executing. When the shell is in *interactive mode,* Step 1 includes writing some text, called a *prompt string,* on the user's screen before reading a command line. However, Step 2 is the same, regardless of how the command line was obtained.

Before executing anything, the shell breaks a command line into individual single commands, then it executes those commands. Often, there is just one command in a command line, but there are also several useful ways to put more than one command in a single command line. This chapter starts with individual commands, and the next chapter goes on to command lines with multiple commands in them.

LAB 2.1

COMMAND PARTS

LAB OBJECTIVES

After this lab, you will be able to:

- ✓ Identify Command Names
- ✓ Identify Parameters
- ✓ Document a Program's Syntax

In this lab, you will practice identifying the parts of single commands. As a shell programmer, you should tell people how to invoke the commands that you write, so this lab also includes some practice in using standard notation for doing that.

LAB 2.1 COMMAND SYNTAX

Every command has three parts, the *name, option parameters,* and *positional parameters.*

The option parameters are sometimes called *flags* or *switches*. Some option parameters, depending on the particular command involved, are followed by a name or value, known as the option's *argument*. You will also see the option parameters and positional parameters collectively referred to as *command arguments,* so you need to be careful when you see the word *argument* used.

There always has to be a command name, but the option parameters and/or positional parameters can be left out if they aren't needed. Like any programming language processor, the shell can't handle commands unless they follow certain *syntax rules*.

FOR EXAMPLE

In any command, the name has to be given first, followed by the option parameters, then the positional parameters, as follows:

```
ls -lF myfile mydir
```

Here, the command name is `ls`, there is one option parameter, `-l`, and there are two positional parameters, `myfile`, and `mydir`. Option parameters are identified by their *option letters*, which are `l` and `F` in this example, and positional parameters are identified by their left-to-right position in the command. In this example, `myfile` is the *first* positional parameter, and `mydir` is the *second* positional parameter.

If you don't follow the syntax rules when you write commands, the shell prints an error message. Unfortunately, following the syntax rules doesn't guarantee that the command does what you want it to do! It just means that the shell recognizes it as an executable command.

A command *name* can be pretty much anything that looks like a name: letters, underscores, and digits are usually used, with upper- and lowercase letters being distinct, provided your file system differentiates between upper- and lowercase file names. As you will see soon, there are different *types* of commands; the rules for valid names vary somewhat from one command type to another, but if you don't try to be tricky, there should be no surprises here. When you start making up your own command names, remember that there is a UNIX convention that command names are kept short to reduce typing overhead. For example, the command to list the files in a directory is `ls` instead of `list`.

You are probably are already familiar with many standard UNIX command names, such as `cp`, `rm`, `mv`, `cd`, *and* `mkdir`. *On the other hand, there are lots of command names you probably have not yet heard of. Because this book is about creating new commands (shell scripts and functions), not about using UNIX, we'll assume that you have either online or printed copies of the UNIX manual pages for looking up those UNIX commands that you aren't already familiar with.*

Most UNIX systems have the manual pages available on line. You use the `man` *command to find out how to use a command, including the* `man` *command itself. (Type* `man man` *to find out how to use the* `man` *command.)*

There are conventions for the *option parameters* part of a command, although you probably will come across commands that don't follow these conventions carefully. The conventions are as follows:

- Each option starts with a dash (-) or a plus (+) followed immediately by a letter.
- An option letter can be followed by an *argument* value (the name of a file, for example). If there is an argument, it should be separated from the option letter by a space.
- Multiple option letters can be combined after one dash or plus. For example, `-lF` in the previous example is shorthand for `-l -F`. No more than one option letter in a group may take an argument.

By the way, if you don't know all the options for the `ls` *command, try this:*

Riddle: *"What do* e, h, j, k, v, w, y, *and* z *have in common?"*

If an option is the kind of thing that is either present or absent, its presence is indicated using a dash (-), but if it is the kind of thing that can be turned on or off, the convention is to use a dash to turn it on ("in the usual way" is a favorite phrase here), and to use a plus (+) to turn it off.

This convention can be counterintuitive until you get used to "the usual way" of using a dash to indicate the presence of an option.

Option parameters are optional (*duh!*), which implies that the positional parameters could start any place after the command name. Normally, a program can tell that it has reached the end of the options by seeing something that doesn't start with a dash or a plus. However, there is a special code, two dashes (--), that you can use to mark the end of the options, in case you have a positional parameter that starts with a dash.

If you don't mind the extra typing, it's a good idea always to put a double dash after the options because it never does any harm, and it eliminates the chance that you will forget it when you really do need it.

Is it a dash, a hyphen, or a minus sign? There is only one key on the keyboard that you can use to type it, so it really doesn't matter what you call it. We use dash *because it's the shortest word. Similarly for* dot, period, *or (if you are British)* full stop. Dot *is easiest to say and to write, so that's what we'll use.*

LAB 2.1 EXERCISES

2.1.1 IDENTIFY COMMAND NAMES

What is the command name for each of the following commands?

a) `print -n file-1 file-3 file-2`

____

____

b) `ls -1`

c) `/bin/sort -r file-1`

d) `/usr/local/bin/ls`

2.1.2 IDENTIFY PARAMETERS

For each of the following commands, list all the option parameters, all the option arguments, and all the positional parameters:

a) `cat -n file-1 file-3 file-2`

b) `ls -acdfgil -- -file`

c) `sort -ro outfile -k 1.14 -`

d) `print These are not options.`

e) `set -x`

2.1.3 Document a Program's Syntax

When you write a program, you should tell people what it does and how to use it. On UNIX systems, the traditional way to do this is to write a *manual page* containing the documentation for your program, written in a standard format. As we pointed out earlier, people who want to know how to use the program look at the manual pages using the `man` command.

You are probably already familiar with man pages, because they are the standard way to document UNIX commands.

In this exercise, you will review the notation used in the "Synopsis" section of a man page, and you will practice writing your own.

You will see in Chapter 8, "Option Processing," that being able to write a standard synopsis for a command translates directly into writing commands that allow users to use options and parameters to control your command.

There is a trend moving away from traditional man pages toward web pages for user documentation. Also, programs with graphical user interfaces, unlike the command-line programs you will be writing, often include much (if not all) of their user documentation in the program itself

by means of a help menu. The material in this exercise can be used in all three types of user documentation.

In the synopsis for a command, square brackets (`[]`) are used to enclose items that may be omitted (such as options).

a) Write a synopsis for a command named `myscript` that allows, but does not require, option parameters called `-a` and `-b`.

If an option takes an argument, that option is listed separately, with a descriptive word showing the type of argument the command expects.

b) Add to your `myscript` synopsis an option `-f` that takes the name of a file as an argument.

If a parameter may be repeated, that is indicated by putting ellipses (`...`) after the item in the synopsis.

c) Change your `myscript` synopsis to indicate that instead of option `-f` followed by one file name argument, there may be *(i)* zero or more file name positional parameters, or *(ii)* one or more file name positional parameters.

Sometimes two options are mutually exclusive. That's indicated by putting a vertical bar (`|`) symbol between them in the synopsis.

Don't confuse the vertical bar in a command's synopsis with the vertical bar used to connect commands in a pipeline (Lab 3.1, "Command Sequences"). They are totally unrelated to each other.

d) Change your `myscript` synopsis to show that it is all right for the user to specify the `-a` option, the `-b` option, neither option, but not both options.

LAB 2.1 ANSWERS

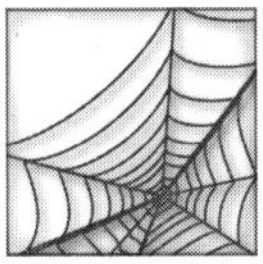

This section gives you some suggested answers to the questions in Lab 2.1, with discussion related to those answers. Your answers may vary, but the most important thing is whether or not your answer works. Use this discussion to analyze differences between your answers and those presented here.

If you have alternative answers to the questions in this exercise, you are encouraged to post your answers and discuss them at the companion web site for this book, located at:

http://www.phptr.com/phptrinteractive/

2.1.1 ANSWERS

What is the command name for each of the following commands?

a) `print -n file-1 file-3 file-2`

Answer: The command name is `print`.

b) `ls -1F`

Answer: The command name is `ls`.

c) `/bin/sort -r file-1`

Answer: The command name is `/bin/sort`.

d) `/usr/local/bin/ls`

Answer: The command name is `/usr/local/bin/ls`.

Command names can be simple names or pathnames of files.

2.1.2 ANSWERS

For each of the following commands, list all the options, all the option arguments, and all the positional parameters:

a) `cat -n file-1 file-3 file-2`

b) `ls -acdfgil -- -file`

c) `sort -ro outfile -k 1.14 -`

d) `print These are not options.`

e) `set -x`

Answer: The following table lists the answers:

Name	Options and Arguments	Parameters
a) `cat`	`-n`	`file-1`, `file-2`, and `file-3`
b) `ls`	`-acdfgil`	`-file`
c) `sort`	`-r`, `-o`, and `-k` `outfile` is the argument for `-1.14` is the argument for `-k`	`-`
d) `print`	None	`These`, `are`, `not`, and `options.`
e) `set`	`-x`	None

The `ls` command illustrates having a positional parameter that looks like an option because it starts with a dash, but the double dash before it indicates that it really is a positional parameter.

By the way, did you figure out the answer to that riddle?

Riddle Answer: *The letters* e, h, j, k, v, w, y, *and* z *are the only lower case letters that are* not *options for the* `ls` *command!*

Option letters are case-sensitive. The `ls` *command differentiates between the* (`f`) *and* (`F`) *option letters, for example.*

When a command processes its parameters in the standard way, the double dash is neither an option parameter nor a positional parameter; it's just a syntax marker.

The `sort` command illustrates combining options with option arguments. Note that the dash at the end of this command is a positional parameter. There has to be a letter after the dash to make it an option (or two dashes to make it mark the end of the option parameters).

A single dash is commonly used where the name of an input file would normally appear but where the user wants the input to come from the standard input device. (Standard input, output, and errors are introduced in Lab 2.3, "Redirecting Standard Input and Output.")

2.1.3 Answers

a) Write a synopsis for a command named `myscript` that allows, but does not require, option parameters called `-a` and `-b`.

Answer: The synopsis should be written as follows:

```
myscript [ -ab ]
```

You could also write this synopsis like this:

```
myscript [-a] [-b]
```

However, this format gets unwieldy if there are a lot of option letters (look at the man page for `ls`!), so the convention is to join them together, as shown in the first answer.

As a user, you generally have the choice between entering commands with one dash before all the option letters or using a separate dash for each letter. Some old commands require you to do it one way or the other. You will learn to write scripts and functions that give users the choice in Lab 5.2, "Processing Option Parameters."

b) Add to your `myscript` synopsis an option `-f` that takes the name of a file as an argument.

Answer: The addition should look like this:

```
myscript [-ab] [-f file]
```

The convention is to list each option that takes an argument separately, although a user would also be able to invoke this command with the option letters connected, as in the following example:

```
myscript -af a_file
```

c) Change your `myscript` synopsis to indicate that instead of option `-f` followed by one file name argument, there may be *(i)* zero or more file name positional parameters, or *(ii)* one or more file name positional parameters.

Answer: For zero or more file name parameters, you should have made the following change:

```
myscript [-ab] [file...]
```

The ellipses could go outside the brackets in this situation without changing the meaning.

For one or more file name parameters, you should have made the following change:

```
myscript [-ab] file...
```

d) Change your `myscript` synopsis to show that it is all right for the user to specify the `-a` option, the `-b` option, neither option, but not both options.

Answer: You should have made the following change:

```
myscript [-a | -b]
```

The square brackets (`[]`) show that it is all right to leave out both options, and the vertical bar (`|`) shows that if one is used, the other one cannot be used.

LAB 2.1 SELF-REVIEW QUESTIONS

To test your progress, you should be able to answer the following questions.

In this lab, you should have learned to identify the parts of a command, the name, option parameters, option arguments, and positional parameters. You also practiced writing a description of a command's syntax using standard man page conventions.

1) What are the parts of a command, in left-to-right order?
- **a)** _____name, voltmeters
- **b)** _____parameters, options, name
- **c)** _____name, arguments, parameters
- **d)** _____name, option parameters, positional parameters
- **e)** _____command, syntax, option arguments

2) If an option parameter must be followed by a string, that string is called which of the following?
- **a)** _____answer
- **b)** _____name
- **c)** _____argument
- **d)** _____file
- **e)** _____option string

3) Which of the following commands are not syntactically valid, given the following syntax synopsis? (There may be more than one answer.)

```
a_cmd [-abc] [-d fish] fowl...
```

a) _____a_cmd Hawk
b) _____b_cmd chicken
c) _____a_cmd -ab Pheasant
d) _____a_cmd -a -c -d gold
e) _____a_cmd -d sword Snipe
f) _____a_cmd -a -b -c -d cod pigeon

4) Which *syntax synopses* could describe this *command*:
gather rosebuds
a) _____gather [-abcdgoldfish] flowers
b) _____gather -a|b [flowers]
c) _____gather flower_1 flower_2
d) _____gather flowers...
e) _____gather [-f flowers]

Quiz answers appear in Appendix A, Section 2.1.

LAB 2.2

COMMAND TYPES

LAB OBJECTIVES

After this lab, you will be able to:

- ✓ List All Built-In Commands
- ✓ Use Two Built-In Tools: `print` and `whence`
- ✓ Execute External Commands
- ✓ Define Aliases
- ✓ Write and Run a Simple Function

A command can be *built-in, external,* a *function,* or an *alias*. This lab examines how the shell determines the type of a command, and how each type is executed. It also shows you how to use the `whence` command to find out whether a command is built-in, external, a function, or an alias.

LAB 2.2 BUILT-IN COMMANDS

Built-in commands are the ones, as their name implies, that are built into the shell itself. If a command name is one of these, the shell has a routine in its own memory that it calls on to do whatever the command calls for.

FOR EXAMPLE

There is a built-in command, `print`, that prints whatever parameters are given on the command line.

EXTERNAL COMMANDS

There are two kinds of external command files—those that contain binary machine code and those that contain shell scripts.

Binary machine code is generated by using a text editor to create a *source file* in a high-level language such as C, C++, or Java, then *compiling* the source file into an *object* file (or a *class* file, in the case of Java). The object file then has to be *linked* to *library files* to produce an executable file (or loaded into a Java Virtual Machine with other class files, in the case of Java). The resulting program executes very quickly, but there is a lot of overhead involved in getting from the code the programmer writes to the final product.

Shell scripts, on the other hand, are ready to run as soon as they have been typed using a text editor. When you have more shell programming tools under your belt, you will look at the relative efficiency of executing equivalent built-in, external-binary, and external-script programs to get a better feeling for what the trade-offs are between shell programming and compiled language programming.

One of the big advantages of shell programming is that you can edit, test, and correct your code in a very rapid cycle compared with conventional programming languages.

The code for external commands comes from files. The shell keeps a list of directories, where it looks for external commands. Alternatively, you can type the full pathname of the file as the command name.

■ FOR EXAMPLE:

The `ls` command is kept in the `/usr/bin` directory on most UNIX systems, and that is one of the directories the shell searches when you type a command name. You should be able to get the same results if you type `/usr/bin/ls` as if you type just `ls`, except for the number of key strokes.

ALIASES

An *alias* is simply a second name for a command. Aliases are normally used to save typing for interactive work, not for shell programming. In fact, if you define an alias from the command line, it won't be understood inside a shell script.

■ FOR EXAMPLE:

The syntax for defining an alias is very simple. For example,

```
alias p=print
```

makes p an alias for the print command.

Note that there must be no spaces before or after the = sign.

A *tracked alias* is an alias that the shell defines itself to improve its efficiency during an interactive session. The first time the shell does a search to locate the directory containing an external command, it saves the complete path name to the command so that it can find and run it faster in the future.

■ FOR EXAMPLE

The command `ls` is normally a tracked alias for `/usr/bin/ls`.

The name tracked alias *might seem to mean that something is an alias that the shell is keeping track of, but it doesn't. It means the shell is using its internal alias mechanism to keep track of a command file's location in the file system.*

FUNCTIONS

A *function* is a way to group a set of commands as if they were a single one, just like a shell script. The big difference between a function and a shell script is that a function works like a built-in command. Instead of reading a file to find out what commands to execute, the shell keeps track of the commands internally, which is much more efficient. You will be writing both functions and scripts as you progress through this workbook.

There are two ways to start the definition of a function. One uses the word *function,* followed by the name of the function. The other starts with the name of the function, followed by a pair of parentheses. After starting either way, you simply enclose the statements that make up the function between opening (`{`) and closing (`}`) braces. You will see the distinction between these two forms in Lab 6.1,"Typed Variables and Scope," where you will see that starting with *function* is better.

■ *FOR EXAMPLE*

Here is a function that creates command named `l` that pipes the output of an `ls` command to `more`:

```
function l {
  ls "$@" | more
  }
```

This example is very similar to an alias definition. The difference is that you can pass parameters to functions, but not to aliases. The "`$@`" on the `ls` command is an example of this; it represents whatever parameters the user types as arguments when entering an `l` command. You will practice passing parameters to functions in Chapter 4, "Variables and Parameters."

LAB 2.2 EXERCISES

2.2.1 LIST ALL BUILT-IN COMMANDS

Run the following command:

```
builtin
```

a) What are the results?

UNIX commands that write text to the screen can be "piped" to a system utility called `more`. This utility instructs UNIX to show the output of the command, one screen at a time. At the bottom of the screen, UNIX prompts you to hit the space bar to see the next screen, or to press the `q` key to quit.

Now, run the following command:

```
builtin | more
```

b) How are the results different?

Better yet, you should be able to use another command, `less` that does the same thing as `more`, but with additional options. If you are running `ksh` under U/WIN, `less` is `more`. That is, they are the same program. If you don't have a copy of `less`, you can get the source code from the Free Software Foundation. There is a link to it on the web site for this book at:

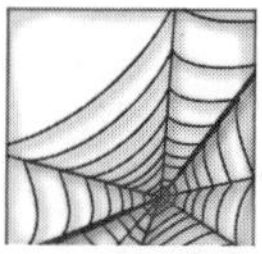

http://www.phptr.com/phptrinteractive/

Now, run the following command:

```
builtin | wc
```

c) What are the results? What do you think they mean?

d) How many built-in commands does the shell recognize on your system?

2.2.2 Use Two Built-In Tools: Print and Whence

The built-in commands you will use in this exercise are basic tools for exploring the capabilities of the shell.

You will use both of them throughout the book to find out more about how each part of the shell works and to help you write efficient shell programs.

The first tool is `print`, which prints whatever parameters appear on its command line. (You can ignore the option parameters for `print` for now.)

Use `print` to write your name on the console.

a) What command did you enter? What are the results?

You may be familiar with the UNIX command, `echo`*, which is pretty much the same as* `print`*. The problem is that there are different versions of* `echo` *for different versions of UNIX and for different shells, and some of them behave differently from one another. However, there is only one* `print` *for* `ksh`*, which can do anything that any of the various* `echo` *commands can do. So the best strategy is always to use* `print`*.*

Enter the following command:

```
whence -v builtin print whence
```

b) What are the results?

---

c) What happens if you don't use the `-v` option for these?

2.2.3 Execute External Commands

One of the directories that contains external commands is `/usr/bin`.

Use `ls /usr/bin` to see a list of some external commands.

a) What are the results?

You probably already know that the shell variable, `PATH`*, holds the list of directories where the shell automatically looks for external commands, but that topic is put off for now. We return to it in Chapter 4, "Simple Variables."*

Verify that you can run an external command by typing the full path name of the executable file using `/bin/ls`.

b) What are the results?

The shell provides built-in versions of several external-binary programs.

Verify that you can run `print` both ways. If that doesn't work, try `echo` instead.

c) What are the results? If it doesn't work, can you explain why?

2.2.4 Define Aliases

Run the following command:

```
alias p=print
```

a) What does this command do?

____

____

Verify that you can use the two versions of the command interchangeably to print your name.

b) What commands did you enter?

____

____

Create a script file named `mn` and containing a `p` command to print your name.

c) What two commands did you enter?

____

____

Using a text editor to create a script was covered in Chapter 1, "Setting Up."

Run your script and *verify that it doesn't work!*

d) What error message did you get?

____

____

e) Why doesn't the script work? Explain the error message.

____

____

f) How *can* you get `p` to work as an alias for `print` *inside your script?*

---

g) Why was the script called `mn`?

Use `whence -a ls` to see where the `ls` external command is in your file system.

h) What are the results?

2.2.5 Write and Run a Simple Function

Type the following function definition and run it:

```
function mdt {
  print It is now
  date
  }
```

a) What are the results?

Type the following function definition and run it:

```
mdt()
```

```
{
  print It is now
  date
}
```

These two examples, in addition to using the `function` *and* `()` *forms for defining functions, illustrate two different styles for placing braces around a function definition. You can use either style for placing braces or you can invent your own. The important thing is to pick a style, and to use it consistently. Consistent indenting and brace placement make your code easier to read and much easier to debug. The shell, however, is indifferent to the style you decide to use for placing braces.*

b) What are the results? Explain any differences.

Type `functions mdt` to see that the shell has kept a copy of the function definition internally, even though there is no file containing the definition.

c) Why was the function named `mdt`?

d) What type of command is `functions`? Why is it called `functions` instead of `function`?

e) What happens if you type `functions` without any parameters?

LAB 2.2 ANSWERS

This section gives you some suggested answers to the questions in Lab 2.2, with discussion related to those answers. Your answers may vary, but the most important thing is whether or not your answer works. Use this discussion to analyze differences between your answers and those presented here.

If you have alternative answers to the questions in this exercise, you are encouraged to post your answers and to discuss them at the companion web site for this book, located at:

`http://www.phptr.com/phptrinteractive/`

2.2.1 ANSWERS

Run the following command:

```
builtin
```

a) What are the results?

Answer: Your interaction should look something like this:

```
$ builtin
```

<Lots of lines of output, ending with... >

```
/bin/uname
unset
vmap
vpath
```

```
wait
/bin/wc
whence
$
```

We'll let the dollar sign ($) represent the shell's prompt for you to enter a command. How to customize this is a favorite topic of books on the shell. Although this book is primarily about shell programming instead of shell usage, you'll get some ideas about how to customize your shell prompt when we cover shell parameters in Chapter 4, "Simple Variables." For now, we'll just use the $ prompt you would see if you didn't do any customization.

This command lists all of the built-in commands on your system. There are about five dozen built-in commands in the 1993 version of the KornShell. You will get to learn about a large portion of them as you proceed through this workbook!

Now, run the following command:

```
builtin | more
```

b) How are the results different?

Answer: This command presents only a screenful of output at a time. Your interaction should look something like this:

```
$ builtin | more
.
:
[
alarm
alias
/bin/basename
< Enough lines to fill up the screen... >
--More--
```

Yes, those first three lines of punctuation marks really are command names! You saw the first one, the "dot command," in Chapter 1 when you tested your ksh setup. You can try running the colon ( ) command now (it's the null command and by itself, won't do anything), but I don't recommend trying the left-bracket ([) command because it won't work by itself. It's a command for making tests that is provided for backward compatibility with earlier versions of sh and the KornShell. You will learn how to make tests with the *KornShell* in Chapter 6, "Control Structures."

The last line is the prompt from more, telling you it is waiting for you to press Space to see the next screenful or q to quit.

Now, run the following command:

```
builtin | wc
```

c) What are the results? What do you think they mean?

Answer: You should see three numbers, the first two of which are the same, like this:

```
$ builtin | wc
61        61       397
$
```

They represent the number of lines and the number of words output by the builtin *command. They are the same because* builtin *outputs one word per line. The third number is the number of characters in the output of the* builtin *command.*

The wc (or word count) command counts the number of words, lines, and characters in a file and prints them out. So, for the output shown, there were 61 lines and 61 words (because there was one word on each line), and a total of 397 characters output by the builtin command, which includes the letters in the words as well as any spaces and end-of-line characters.

d) How many built-in commands does the shell recognize on your system?

Answer: Your answer may vary, but the output from the last question shows that there are 61 built-in commands that ksh *recognizes.*

The sample output was generated on a system running U/WIN on Windows NT. The same command run on a SparcStation running Solaris showed 62 commands. The difference is the newgrp command, which can't be implemented under Windows NT because that operating system doesn't implement the UNIX model of user's groups.

A powerful feature of the KornShell is that programmers can add their own built-in commands to the shell by constructing a shared library containing the code for the command. If you know how to program in C/C++, you can see how to do this in the Author's Corner at:

`http://www.phptr.com/phptrinteractive/`

2.2.2 ANSWERS

Use `print` to write your name on the console.

a) What command did you enter? What are the results?

Answer: You should have entered the following command:

```
print Your Name
```

Note that your own name should be used instead of Your Name.

The results should be as follows:

```
$ print Your Name
Your Name
$
```

Of course, if your name doesn't happen to be Your Name, your results might not be quite the same!

Enter the following command:

```
whence -v builtin print whence
```

b) What are the results?

Answer: The results should be as follows:

```
$ whence -v builtin print whence
builtin is a shell builtin
print is a shell builtin
```

```
whence is a shell builtin
$
```


The `whence` command lets you find out the type of any command name you give it. By default, `whence` doesn't say too much about the names of built-in commands, but you can use its `-v` option to make the output more "verbose."

c) What happens if you don't use the `-v` option for these?

Answer: The output would be as follows:

```
$  whence builtin print whence
builtin
print
whence
$
```

That's not very interesting output, which is why you did it first with the `-v` option.

2.2.3 Answers

Use `ls /usr/bin` to see a list of some external commands.

a) What are the results?

Answer: A long list of file names should appear.

The exact list depends on what system you are using. If you don't get a list, your system may use `/bin` instead of `/usr/bin`; try that instead.

Verify that you can run an external command by typing the full pathname of the executable file using `/bin/ls`.

a) What are the results?

Answer: A list of the files in the current directory should appear.

Verify that you can run `print` both ways. If that doesn't work, try `echo` instead.

b) What are the results? If it doesn't work, can you explain why?

Answer: Suppose you tried to print your name. Then your output should be similar to the following:

```
$ print your name
your name
$ /bin/print your name
your name
```

If you used `echo` *instead of* `print`*, your results should be similar to the following:*

```
$ echo your name
your name
$ /bin/echo your name
your name
$
```

You might have to adjust the pathname for the external command, depending on your system's set-up. In addition, your system might or might not have an external version of `print` and/or `echo`.

If you have trouble getting this exercise to work, you can look at your list of built-in commands and try both the built-in and external versions of any commands that have slashes in their names. Both versions should show the same results, even if it is just an error message.

2.2.4 ANSWERS

Run the following command:

```
alias p=print
```

a) What does this command do?

Answer: This command sets up the alias `p` *for the command* `print`.

Verify that you can use the two versions of the command interchangeably to print your name.

b) What commands did you enter?

Answer: The commands you entered and the respective results should be similar to the following:

```
$ print Your Name
Your Name
$ p Your Name
Your Name
$
```


Create a script file `mn` containing a `p` command to print your name.

c) What two commands did you enter?

Answer: You should have given one command to start your editor and a `chmod` *command to make your file executable. Your interaction with the editor should look something like the following:*

```
$ vi mn
```

< *Put the line* `p Your Name` *in the file.* >

```
$ chmod +x mn
```

The first command starts your editor, which might be `vi` as shown here, or another editor of your choice. After editing the file, you should give it execute permission with the `chmod +x` command, as covered in Chapter 1, "Setting Up."

Run your script and *verify that it doesn't work!*

d) What error message did you get?

Answer: Your interaction should look something like the following:

```
$ mn
mn: line 1: p: not found
$
```

Instead of printing your name, the shell prints an error message when you try to run the command.

If your error message says `mn: not found` *instead of* `mn: line 1: p: not found`*, it means the shell couldn't find the* `mn` *command instead of the* `p` *command as expected. This problem could be because (1) you didn't use the* `chmod +x` *command to make the script executable, (2) you used a different name for the command when you built it, (3) your current directory isn't one of the places the shell looks to for commands, or (4) there is an invalid "she-bang" (* `#!` *) in the first line of your script. In the case of (3), you can use* `./mn` *to run the command, and in the case of (4), you should refer to Chapter 1, "Setting Up," to see how to use she-bang, if you need it at all.*

e) Why doesn't the script work? Explain the error message.

Answer: The format of the message is `<command name>: <line number>: <command name>: <message>`*. So the shell reports that the first line of the command file* `mn` *contains the command* `p` *but the shell cannot find a command by that name to execute.*

In other words, the alias command for `p` that you typed in before does not apply to command lines inside the script.

f) How *can* you get `p` to work as an alias for `print` *inside your script?*

Answer: *You would have to put the* `alias p=print` *command inside the script file.*

Aliases are used to save typing during interactive sessions. Inside scripts, you should use the names of actual commands instead.

g) Why was the script called `mn`?

Answer: It's a UNIX-style command name, short for "my name."

Use `whence -a ls` to see where the `ls` external command is in your file system.

h) What are the results?

Answer: Your results should be similar to the following:

```
$ whence -a ls
ls is a tracked alias for /bin/ls
$
```

If you use `whence` to examine any external command, the shell will report that it is a tracked alias.

The pathname for your `ls` command may be different, but it should appear as a pathname, which the shell is keeping track of for you.

As you saw in Question f, the only way to get the shell to recognize an alias inside a script is to define it there. The "tracked alias" mechanism cannot be used to make an alias known inside a script. The shell's tracked alias mechanism does work inside scripts, it just doesn't have anything to do with the aliases you define with the `alias` command.

2.2.5 ANSWERS

Type the following function definition and run it:

```
function mdt {
  print It is now
  date
  }
```

a) What are the results?

Answer: After you type in the function definition, the results should look like the following:

```
$ mdt
It is now
WWW MMM DD HH:MM:SS ZON YYYY
$
```

The actual date and time will be displayed in the format indicated, where WWW is the weekday, MMM is the month, DD is the day of the month, HH:MM:SS are the current time (24-hour clock), ZON is the local time zone, and YYYY is the year.

The output of the `date` command is always exactly 28 characters (plus a line terminator) in the format indicated. This fixed structure makes it relatively easy to pull out specific parts in a program. For example, the hours and minutes part is always in character positions 11-15 if you count the leftmost character as position zero.

Type the following function definition and run it:

```
mdt()
{
  print It is now
  date
}
```

b) What are the results? Explain any differences.

Answer: The results should be exactly the same as for the previous question. There is a difference between the two types of function definitions, but it has to do with the scope of variables, which is a topic in Chapter 6, "Advanced Variable Usage." Until you start using variables in functions, there is no difference between the two forms.

If you are a C, C++, or Java programmer, you might be tempted to use the function definition style that uses parentheses, but don't. Using the `function` *keyword style lets you have local variables, and the parentheses form does not.*

Type `functions mdt` to see that the shell has kept a copy of the function definition internally even though there is no file containing the definition.

c) Why was the function named `mdt`?

Answer: It prints a message, the date, and the time.

Who says UNIX commands have cryptic names?

Using cryptic command names like this is fine if you are the only one who is going to have to remember what the names mean, and it can make interactive sessions more productive for you. However, if you are writing programs that you will keep around for a long time or that other people besides yourself will use, use more descriptive command names.

d) What type of command is `functions`? Why is it called `functions` instead of `function`?

Answer: It's a built-in command. If it were called `function`*, it would conflict with the keyword used to define a function.*

It may seem strange to use the plural form of the word to find out about just one function, but (*i*) it's also used to list all function definitions (see next question), and (*ii*) it would be *really* strange to define one function using the plural form as the keyword!

The reason for bringing this entire point up is to help you start thinking about the rules the shell follows as it processes command lines. That kind of thinking will help you develop a realistic model of how the shell works, which, in turn, will help you write programs that make the most effective use of the shell's facilities.

e) What happens if you type `functions` without any parameters?

Answer: You get a list of all of the function definitions the shell knows about.

If you are using the default settings for the shell, you will see both the names and definitions of all the functions, but if you have entered the command `set -o nolog`, any function definitions you have given since then are not displayed, just the function names.

Note that there is just one definition for `mdt`. The second one replaced the first one, even though you entered it using a different format. There are two ways to enter functions, but there is only one set of function definitions possible per function name.

LAB 2.2 SELF-REVIEW QUESTIONS

To test your progress, you should be able to answer the following questions.

1) A command can be both a built-in command and an external command, and produce the same results.
   a) _____True
   b) _____False

2) Which of the following is the purpose of the `whence` command?
   a) _____To print the location of a file you give it
   b) _____To find out the type of a command you give it
   c) _____To find out the type of a file you give it
   d) _____To print whatever parameters appear on its command line

3) When invoked, a function acts just like a script.
   a) _____True
   b) _____False

4) What would print if you enter the following command?
   `Functions *`
   a) _____Nothing.
   b) _____The names of all files named `functions`, no matter which type.
   c) _____An error message, because there is no command named `Functions`.
   d) _____The names, and possibly the definitions, of all functions defined in your shell.
   e) _____A prompt for you to enter the remainder of a function definition.

5) Which of the following items is a difference between functions and aliases?
   a) _____There are no differences. They are the same thing.
   b) _____Aliases can have parameters, but functions cannot.
   c) _____Functions can have parameters, but aliases cannot.
   d) _____Function definitions have to be typed in manually, but aliases can be read from a file.
   e) _____Alias definitions have to be typed in manually, but function definitions can be read from a file.

Quiz answers appear in Appendix A, Section 2.2.

LAB 2.3

REDIRECTING STANDARD INPUT AND OUTPUT

LAB OBJECTIVES

After this lab, you will be able to:

- ✓ Redirect `stdin` and `stdout` (< and >)
- ✓ Control Clobbering! (>> and >|)
- ✓ Redirect `stderr` (2>)
- ✓ Link *file descriptors* for Redirection (`n>&`)
- ✓ Use a *here document* for `stdin` (<<)

Every command that the KornShell runs has three *standard I/O devices* that it can use as it executes:

stdin	The standard input device, normally the user's keyboard.
stdout	The standard output device, normally the window in which `ksh` is running.
stderr	The standard error device, also normally the window in which `ksh` is running. Used for error messages.

Each of these devices is associated with a small integer, called a *file descriptor,* or *fd,* which are 0, 1, and 2 for *stdin, stdout,* and *stderr*, respectively. You will see how to do I/O using other fds than these three in Chapter 11, "I/O Trap Processing." In this lab, you will learn the syntax for getting the shell to connect the standard devices to files instead of the keyboard and screen.

There are six basic symbols you can use to tell the shell to redirect I/O for a command. They can appear anywhere within the command, but by convention, they appear at the right end.

`< filename`	Connect *stdin* to `filename` instead of to the user's keyboard.
`> filename`	Connect *stdout* to *filename* instead of to the console window. The file will be overwritten if it already exists.
`>| filename`	Same as >, but works even if the shell's `noclobber` option is set.
`>> filename`	Connect *stdout* to `filename`, but instead of overwriting the file, append text to whatever is already there.
`>& n`	Link two file descriptors so that they refer to the same file.
`<< symbol`	Used for *here documents*.

LAB 2.3 EXERCISES

2.3.1 REDIRECT `stdin` AND `stdout` (< AND >)

The UNIX `cat` command, without any options or parameters, copies *stdin* to *stdout*. Thus, it provides a convenient tool for practicing I/O redirection.

Use `cat` without any options or parameters, and observe that it writes out whatever you type in. Use Control-C (`^C`) or Control-D (`^D`) to stop.

Control-C cancels (kills) a program, and Control-D indicates the end of input from a terminal. The `cat` *command is programmed to stop when it comes to the end of its input (*`^D`*). Canceling a program is generally considered a heavy-handed way to get it to stop.*

You can use the `stty` *command to change what characters you type to perform these operations.*

a) What did you observe?

b) What two devices are *stdin* and *stdout* connected to?

Redirect *stdout* so that `cat` copies what you type to a file named `out`. Do this twice, once with the redirection symbol and file name *before* the command name, and again with them *after* the command name.

c) What did you observe?

Possible Problem! *If you redirect* stdout *to a file that already exists, you may get an error message. Use the command* `set -o noclobber` *to overcome this problem. You'll learn why this works in the next exercise.*

d) Does it matter whether you put the output redirection before or after the command name?

Now that you have a file with something in it, redirect *stdin* so that `cat` displays the contents of `out` in your console window.

Verify that input redirection can be placed either before or after the command name and still work.

e) What did you observe?

f) Write a `cat` command that uses both input and output redirection so that `cat` copies the file `out` to `out1`.

g) Do you have to specify input redirection before output redirection, or doesn't the order matter?

h) Use `cat out1 > out2 > out3` to find out what happens if you specify input or output redirection twice in the same command.

2.3.2 Control Clobbering! (>> and >|)

Now, about that "possible problem" mentioned in the previous exercise. The UNIX philosophy has traditionally been that if you tell the system to do something, you really mean it, and you don't want to be bothered with messages asking you if you really do mean it.

This approach is particularly appealing when you are writing scripts that need to run without stopping every step of the way to ask the user whether or not to do what the script says.

On the other hand, this behavior can have pretty grim consequences—there is no way to "undelete" files on UNIX systems, the way you can with some other systems. So the shell lets you have it both ways.

There is a shell option, `noclobber`, that you can turn on or off to cause the shell to prevent overwriting existing files or not, as you wish.

There are lots of shell options having to do with many, many features of the shell. They are all listed in Appendix B, "Built-In Command Summary," so you can refer to them. The exercises will tell you when you need to use one of them.

Run the following commands:

```
set -o noclobber
touch out out1
cat out > out1
```

a) What does the error message mean?

____

____

Now run these commands:

```
set -o noclobber
touch out out1
cp out out1
```

b) Why is there no error message this time?

c) What does `set -o noclobber` do?

Use `set +o noclobber` to turn the `noclobber` option off and try to redirect the output of `cat` to an existing file again.

d) What does `set +o noclobber` do?

Repeat the previous two operations, but use `set -C` and `set +C` instead of `set -o noclobber` and `set +o noclobber`.

e) Is there any difference between `set -o noclobber` and `set -C` or between `set +o noclobber` and `set +C`?

The `>>` and `>|` redirection symbols also handle the `noclobber` issue.

If you use `>>`, the output file will be created if it doesn't exist, but if it does already exist, the new output gets written to the end of the file.

If you use `>|`, the output is always written to the output file, even if it already exists.

You can think of `>|` *as a "*`noclobber override`*." It clobbers* `noclobber` *for just the command that uses it.*

Turn on the `noclobber` option and use `cat` with `>>` to make two copies of `out` in `out1`.

f) What commands did you type?

g) How can you verify that `out1` contains two copies of `out`?

With the `noclobber` option still set, use `>|` to overwrite `out1` with a single copy of `out`, and verify that `out1` has been overwritten.

h) What command did you use?

i) How did you verify that the file was overwritten?

2.3.3 Redirect `stderr` (2>)

You can also redirect *stderr* using the `>`, `>>`, and `>|` symbols by putting the *fd* for *stderr*, (`2`) just before the redirection symbol. There must be no spaces between the *fd* and the redirection symbol.

Use stdout for the "normal" output of a command and stderr for error messages. If the person using your script redirects stdout to a file, error messages will still show up on the console. If the user doesn't want to see the error messages or wants them to go to a file, he or she can redirect stderr.

Try to use `cat` to copy a nonexistent file to *stdout*. (Use whatever file name you wish for the name of the nonexistent file.)

a) What error message did you see?

Now use (`2>>`) to modify the previous `cat` command so the error message is appended to a file named `error.log`. Run `cat` this way twice and verify that `error.log` contains both error messages.

b) What commands did you use?

c) Did you see both error messages in `error.log`?

d) If 2> means to redirect *stderr*, what do 0< and 1> mean?

____

____

e) Write a `cat` command that copies file `out` to file `out1` using *fd* numbers for *stdin* and *stdout*.

____

____

f) Remembering that `>out1 >out2` means to redirect *stdout* to `out2`, as you saw earlier, what do you think `1>out3 2>out3` means?

____

____

You can redirect any fd, *not just stdin, stdout, and stderr, using this notation. You'll see how to do I/O with other* fds *in Chapter 11, "I/O and Trap Processing."*

2.3.4 Link File Descriptors for Redirection (n > &)

If a program writes output to two different *fds* (for example *stdout* and *stderr*), you can get the shell to make both *fds* go to the same file by redirecting one *fd* to the file, and then linking the second *fd* to the first one using the *link fd* redirection symbol, (n>&). In this symbol, the n is a number telling what *fd* you want to link.

FOR EXAMPLE

```
cat >out 2>&1
```

The `>out` part says that *stdout* will go to file `out`. The `2>&1` part says that *fd* 2 (*stderr*) will go to the same place as *fd* 1 (*stdout*).

Watch the spacing on this. There must be no spaces between the fd *number, the (>), and the ampersand.*

a) Why must there be no space between the `2` and the (>)?

____

____

b) Why must there be no space between the (>) and the ampersand?

____

____

Spaces after the ampersand are optional.

c) Why can there be a space between the ampersand and the `1`?

____

____

Remember that I/O redirection symbols are processed by the shell in left-to-right order.

d) What is the difference between the following two commands:

```
cat out1 out2 >out3 2>& 1
cat out1 out2 2>& 1> out3
```

____

____

2.3.5 Use a Here Document for `stdin` (<<)

When you start writing scripts and functions, you will find that sometimes you want a command's *stdin* to consist of some text that you will supply.

You could type the text into a file and redirect the command's *stdin* to come from the file, but that can get messy because the user needs both your script or function and the text file to use the program.

The shell provides a mechanism for dealing with this problem by letting you put the text right inside the script using a mechanism called a *here document.*

Here documents *have another big advantage over external files: The shell will process references to variables in* here documents, *but not for data coming from an external file. You'll see how to work with variables in Chapter 4, "Simple Variables," and the importance of this point should become clear then.*

For now, you can use the shell's interactive mode to see how a *here document* works.

■ FOR EXAMPLE

The following interaction sends two lines of text to a `cat` command's *stdin* using a *here document*:

```
cat <<!
This is the first line of a here document!
This is the last line of a here document.
!
```

The syntax is to type << followed immediately by any symbol you want to use as a *marker* (which was a single exclamation point in this example).

Then, starting on the next line, the shell reads lines until it comes to one that contains *only* the marker symbol you used (there must be no spaces before it) and passes the lines before the marker line as the *stdin* data for the command.

a) What effect did the exclamation mark after the word *document* have?

b) Modify the example so that it uses a dot as the symbol marking the end of the *here document.*

c) Can you use the word *the* as the symbol?

You can combine other types of redirection with *here documents.*

Type a `cat` command with a *here document* for *stdin*, and redirect *stdout* to a file.

d) What does the command do?

LAB 2.3 ANSWERS

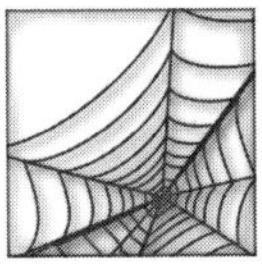

This section gives you some suggested answers to the questions in Lab 2.3, with discussion related to those answers. Your answers may vary, but the most important thing is whether or not your answer works. Use this discussion to analyze differences between your answers and those presented here.

If you have alternative answers to the questions in this exercise, you are encouraged to post your answers and to discuss them at the companion web site for this book, located at:

```
http://www.phptr.com/phptrinteractive/
```


2.3.1 Answers

Use `cat` without any options or parameters, and observe that it writes out whatever you type in. Use Control-C (`^C`) or Control-D (`^D`) to stop.

a) What did you observe?

Answer: Your interaction should look something like the following, depending on what you typed:

```
$ cat
hello
hello
good-bye
good-bye
```

< Press Control-C or Control-D to exit >

```
$
```

Note that each line is printed right after you type it. This tells you that `cat` does not need to read the entire input "file" before it starts generating the output.

b) To what two devices are `stdin` and `stdout` connected to?

Answer: `stdin` *is connected to your keyboard, and* `stdout` *is connected to your terminal window.*

A great deal of flexibility comes from the fact that programs such as `cat` can work equally well with disk files or I/O devices such as keyboards, screens, and printers.

The UNIX design is based on the idea that "everything looks like a file." That means that programs can work with things as diverse as files, I/O devices, network connections, and memory using the same basic I/O operations. The best programs take advantage of this philosophy and do not make unnecessary assumptions about what type of device they read from or write to.

Redirect *stdout* so that `cat` copies what you type to a file named `out`. Do this twice, once with the redirection symbol and file name *before* the command name, and again with them *after* the command name.

c) What did you observe?

Answer: Your interaction should look something like the following:

```
$ > out cat
hello
good-bye
^D
$ more out
hello
good-bye
$ cat > out
hello again
good-bye again
^D
$ more out
hello again
good-bye again
$
```

The (`^D`) in this interaction represents the place where you pressed `Control-D`. Of course, your interaction will look different, depending on what you typed.

This answer uses `more` to look at the contents of the file named `out`, but a better command to use is `less`, which has a lot of options for customizing its behavior.

The Author's Corner at the Web page for this book (`http://www.phptr.com/phptrinteractive/`) tells you where to get `less` if you don't already have it and how to customize it for your own use.

d) Does it matter whether you put the output redirection before or after the command name?

Answer: "Everyone" puts redirection symbols at the end of commands, not at the beginning. However, as this exercise shows, they can go either place.

There are actually some cases where putting redirection before the command name makes a difference and can be useful. Until you know what those cases are, stay with the standard way of doing things and always put them at the ends of your commands.

Verify that input redirection can be placed either before or after the command name and still work.

e) What did you observe?

Answer: Depending on what data you typed, your interactions should look something like the following:

```
$ < out cat
hello again
good-bye again
$ cat < out
hello again
good-bye again
$
```

As with output redirection, input redirection, works regardless of whether it is placed before or after the command name. This is not unique just to the `cat` command; it's a general principle.

f) Write a `cat` command that uses both input and output redirection so that `cat` copies the file `out` to `out1`.

Answer: Your answer should look something like the following:

```
$ cat < out > out1
$ more out1
hello again
good-bye again
$
```

g) Do you have to specify input redirection before output redirection, or doesn't the order matter?

Answer: They can be specified in either order, as the following interaction illustrates:

```
$ cat > out1 out <
$ more out1
hello again
good-bye again
$
```


The "natural" way to specify both is to put input redirection before output redirection. Because it's always a good idea write code so that someone looking at it later will have the least number of surprises, it makes sense to write redirection "the natural way," even though it makes no difference to the shell.

h) Use `cat out1 > out2 > out3` to find out what happens if you specify input or output redirection twice in the same command.

Answer: Depending on how many bytes are in your file `out1`*, your interaction should look something like the following:*

```
$ rm -f out2 out3
$ cat out1 > out2 > out3
$ ls -l out1 out2 out3
-rw-r--r--   1 Administrator None      12 Jul 16 20:02 out1
-rw-r--r--   1 Administrator None       0 Jul 16 20:02 out2
-rw-r--r--   1 Administrator None      12 Jul 16 20:02 out3
$
```

The `rm` command removes files `out2` and `out3` to make the results of the test unambiguous. The `-f` option forces the command to skip any queries or messages—in this case to suppress any messages in case the files don't exist.

Look at the *size* column of the output from the `ls` command (just before the date). It shows that both `out2` and `out3` were created, but that `out2` has zero bytes, whereas `out3` is the same size as `out1`.

You could use the `diff` *command to verify that* `out1` *and* `out3` *have identical contents. The command* `diff out1 out3` *will produce no output if there are no differences between the files. Consult your UNIX documentation if you are not familiar with how to use the* `diff` *command. If you want a challenge, run the command,* `diff3 out1 out2 out3`*, and interpret the results.*

In summary, both `out2` and `out3` were created, but only `out3` got the data that was output by the `cat` command.

The shell sets up I/O redirection for a command before it executes the command itself. Redirection can be specified anywhere within the command line, but it is processed by the shell in left to right sequence. Every time the shell comes to an output redirection, it creates the specified output file, but actual output is written only to the rightmost output file specified in the command.

EXERCISE 2.3.1 SUMMARY

A command, including any shell script that you write, reads "normal" input from *fd* 0, writes "normal" output to *fd* 1, and writes "error" output to *fd* 2. Because I/O redirection is handled by the shell before it runs the command, programs normally do not know whether the three *fds* are connected to the user's keyboard and monitor or to files, and should not make any assumptions that would conflict with this model. As you will see in the next Lab, the standard I/O *fds* can also be connected to the standard I/O *fds* of other commands in command *pipelines*, a powerful programming construct.

You can make a test in your script to tell whether an fd is connected to a file or a terminal. You will see how to do that in Chapter 7, "Basic Tests."

2.3.2 Answers

Run the following commands:

```
set -o noclobber
touch out out1
cat out > out1
```

a) What does the error message mean?

Answer: You should get something like the following:

```
$ set -o noclobber
$ touch out out1
$ cat out > out1
-ksh: out1: file already exists [File exists]
$
```

The `touch` command will create empty files named `out` and `out1` if they do not already exist. (If either does already exist, `touch` silently sets its last modification time to "now," but that has nothing to do with this exercise.)

The error message says that the program `ksh` found that the file named `out1` already exists. Why didn't the message come from `cat` instead of `ksh`? Because it is the *shell* that sets up the I/O redirection and finds the problem. The `cat` command never got to run.

Now run these commands:

```
set -o noclobber
touch out out1
cp out out1
```

b) Why is there no error message this time?

Answer: There was no error message (file `out` really did get copied over file `out1`) even though the `noclobber` option is set because `noclobber` is a shell option, and it affects only things the shell does, such as output redirection.

The `cp` command has no way of knowing what options are set in the shell; `cp` and `ksh` are totally separate programs.

c) What does `set -o noclobber` do?

Answer: It prevents you from using redirection to overwrite an existing file.

The `noclobber` option can help keep you from making mistakes, but having it set doesn't protect you, except for things the shell knows about, like output redirection.

Use `set +o noclobber` to turn the `noclobber` option off, and try to redirect the output of `cat` to an existing file again.

d) What does `set +o noclobber` do?

Answer: It turns the `noclobber` option off. You should see something like the following:

```
$ set +o noclobber
$ touch out out1
$ cat out > out1
$
```

No problem! Use of the plus sign turns the option off (which is the shell's default behavior), and the shell lets you redirect output to an existing file without complaint. The new file overwrites whatever was in the old one.

e) Is there any difference between `set -o noclobber` and `set -C`, or between `set +o noclobber` and `set +C`?

Answer: As the following sequence shows, there is no difference:

```
$ set -C
$ touch out out1
$ cat out > out1
-ksh: out1: file already exists [File exists]
$ set +C
$ touch out out1
$ cat out > out1
$
```

It really doesn't matter to the shell which form of the `set` command you use; they are identical. There are some shell options that can be set only using the `-o option` form because there is no short form available. See Appendix B, "Command Summary," for a complete list of both forms.

Use the `set -o noclobber` *form in scripts and functions because it makes your programs much easier to read. The* `set -C` *form can save you a few keystrokes when entering commands interactively, but you have to learn what option letter goes with what option name.*

Turn on the `noclobber` option, and use `cat` with `>>` to make two copies of `out` in `out1`.

f) What commands did you type?

Answer: You could have used the following sequence of commands:

```
$ rm -f out1
$ touch out1
$ set -C
$ cat out out >> out1
```

The first two commands make sure `out1` exists but is empty.

Even with `noclobber` set, `>>` redirection lets you add material to the end of an existing file.

Note that the `cat` command has file `out` appearing as a parameter twice. If you specify multiple parameters, `cat` reads from each of them, one after the other, so this `cat` command makes two copies of `out` in `out1`.

g) How can you verify that `out1` contains two copies of `out`?

Answer: Because the file is so small, you could just print it out, like the following:

```
$ more out1
hello again
good-bye again
hello again
good-bye again
$
```

You could also use `ls -l` to see what the file sizes are, but that wouldn't tell you whether they actually contain the same information or not.

You can use the `sdiff` command to do a side-by-side comparison of two files. You would need to use the `-w 80` option to make the output fit in to an 80-character-width window. If the files are long, you would probably pipe the output to `less` or `more`.

With the `noclobber` option still set, use >/ to overwrite `out1` with a single copy of `out` and verify that `out1` has been overwritten.

h) What commands did you use?

Answer: The following sequence of commands would do what was asked:

```
$ rm -f out1
$ touch out1
$ set -o noclobber
$ cat out >| out1
$ sdiff -w80 out out1
hello again                                     hello again
good-bye again                                  good-bye again
$
```

You could have used the `diff` command to make sure the files were the same, but `sdiff` lets you look at the contents.

Some other shells use `>!` the way the KornShell uses `>|`. That is, it uses an exclamation mark instead of a vertical bar for overriding the `noclobber` option. Don't get the two symbols confused. The KornShell doesn't use exclamation marks for anything having to do with redirection.

i) How did you verify that the file was overwritten?

Answer: The `rm` and `touch` commands guaranteed that `out1` exists but has zero bytes in it.

Logically, the solution given doesn't prove that `out1` was appended to rather than overwritten. You could `cat` another file over it if you aren't sure whether it was overwritten or appended to.

2.3.3 ANSWERS

Try to use `cat` to copy a nonexistent file to *stdout*. (Use whatever file name you wish for the name of the nonexistent file.)

a) What error message did you see.

Answer: Here is an interaction that uses `out1` *as the nonexistent file:*

```
$ rm -f out1
$ cat out1
-ksh: cat: out1: cannot open [No such file or directory]
$
```

The `rm` command guarantees the file doesn't exist, and `cat` then reports that it cannot open the file, as expected.

Now use (`2>>`) to modify the previous `cat` command so the error message is appended to a file named `error.log`.
Run `cat` this way twice and verify that `error.log` contains both error messages.

b) What commands did you use?

Answer: Your interaction should look like the following:

```
$ rm -f out1 error.log
$ cat out1 2>>error.log
$ cat out1 2>>error.log
$ more error.log
-ksh: cat: out1: cannot open [No such file or directory]
-ksh: cat: out1: cannot open [No such file or directory]
$
```

In this case, we removed both `out1` and `error.log` at the beginning to make sure the results are unambiguous.

c) Did you see both error messages in `error.log`?

Answer: As expected, `error.log` *did end up with two copies of the error message in it.*

d) If `2>` means to redirect `stderr`, what do `0<` and `1>` mean?

Answer: Redirect stdin *and* stdout*, respectively.*

The three standard file descriptor numbers are 0 for *stdin*, 1 for *stdout*, and 2 for *stderr*.

e) Write a `cat` command that copies file `out` to file `out1` using *fd* numbers for *stdin* and *stdout*.

Answer: The following interaction shows the `cat` *command and verifies that it worked.*

```
$ cat  0<out  1>|out1
$ more out1
  hello again
  good-bye again
$
```


Note the use of `1>|` for output redirection. If you know the file doesn't exist or you know that the shell's `noclobber` option isn't set, you could have used just `1>`.

f) Remembering that `> out1 > out2` means to redirect `stdout` to `out2`, as you saw earlier, what do you think `1>out3 2>out3` means?

Answer: It means that both stdin *and* stderr *are redirected to the same file,* `out3`*, but it doesn't work, as the following interaction shows:*

```
$ rm -f out3
$ set -o noclobber
$  cat out 1>out3 2>out3
-ksh: out3: file already exists [File exists]
$
```

The problem is that the shell sees two separate output redirections. When it sees `1>out3`, it creates file `out3` with zero bytes. Then, when it sees `2>out3`, the file `out3` already exists and the redirection fails because the `noclobber` option is set and `>|` wasn't used. The `cat` command was never run because the problem was detected by the shell.

If `noclobber` had not been set, the shell would have run the `cat` command, but there is another subtle issue here that you won't see using `cat`, which is that a program that writes to both *stdout* and *stderr* might produce a different sequence of output lines using this form of redirection rather than *linked fds*, which is covered in the next exercise. The issue is based on the fact that the operating system buffers output written to *stdout* but not to *stderr*.

You could try to deal with this problem by using `1>>out3  2>>out3` or `1>|out3  2>|out3`, but those won't work either. This entire, complex topic can be summarized in the following Tip:

Don't try to use separate redirections to send information from two fds to one file

.

2.3.4 ANSWERS

a) Why must there be no space between the 2 and the >?

Answer: Consider this command:

```
cat out 2 >out2
```

This would copy the files named `out` and `2` (because `2` is a valid file name) to `out2`.

If you find files with names like `1` or `2` in a directory, it probably means someone made typing errors when they were trying to redirect fds. But you never know, they might be real files, so double-check before deleting them!

b) Why must there be no space between the > and the ampersand?

Answer: Consider this command:

```
cat out 2> & out2
```

To understand this, you have to "think like the shell." When it sees the `2>` token, it knows the next thing must be the name of the file you want *stderr* redirected to, but the next thing it sees is the ampersand, which is its "background job" indicator, which you will cover in the next lab. That doesn't make any sense, and it issues an error message saying the ampersand was "unexpected." The `cat` command never gets run.

The shell uses spaces to tell it how to divide the parts of a command line into syntactic elements. If you want to link fds, the fd number, the >, and the ampersand must all be a single syntactic element with no spaces within it.

c) Why can there be a space between the ampersand and the `1`?

Answer: There is no ambiguity. Once the shell sees `2>&`, it knows that the next thing has to be an fd number, and it doesn't matter whether there is a space before it or not.

Pay attention to where spaces are required, where they are optional, and where they are prohibited in command lines. These are all common sources of syntax errors.

d) What is the difference between the following two commands:

```
cat out1 out2 >out3 2>& 1
cat out1 out2 2>& 1> out3
```

Answer: The first command redirects stdout *(fd 1) to* `out3`*, and then redirects* stderr *to the same place as* fd `1` *(i.e., to* `out3` *also). The second one redirects* stderr *to the same place as fd 1, which is still connected to your screen, then it redirects* stdout *to the file* `out3`*. The net effect of the second command is the same as the following command:*

```
cat out1 out2 > out3
```

Remember the left-to-right order that the shell uses to process redirection symbols. The *fd* association is done in left-to-right order, just like all other redirection operations.

2.3.5 Answers

a) What effect did the exclamation mark after the word *document* have?

Answer: It had no effect; it is part of the content of the here document.

The marker symbol can appear inside the *here document,* but when it is the only thing on a line, it marks the end of the *here document.*

b) Modify the example so it uses a dot as the symbol marking the end of the *here document.*

Answer: Your interaction should look something like the following:

```
$ cat <<.
> This here document is two lines long.
> Here is a dot:. It is not the dot that ends this doc.
> .
This here document is two lines long.
Here is a dot: . It is not the dot that ends this doc.
$
```


Again, you put the marker symbol inside the *here document,* but when it appears alone on a line, it marks the end of the document.

The > symbols on the second, third, and fourth lines are the prompt the shell shows when it is waiting for you to type parts of a command line that extend to multiple lines on the screen.

As this answer shows, you can use a dot without problems, but there are other punctuation marks you cannot use. For example, you couldn't use a > symbol because that would look like output redirection to the shell, and you will get a syntax error message.

c) Can you use the word *the* as the marker symbol?

Answer: Yes you can, as the following interaction shows:

```
$ cat << the
> the time is now
> So, words work fine as terminators too.
> the
the time is now
So, words work fine as terminators too.
$
```

Note that the first line starts with the marker symbol, but has more characters on the same line, so it doesn't terminate the here document.

You can use just about anything you like as the termination symbol for here documents, unless it looks like some other syntax element to the shell, such as a redirection symbol. For clarity, it's best to use something that won't be confusing to the person reading your script.

Common symbols used to end here documents *include the word* `END` *(using capital letters makes it stand out) or some exclamation marks (* `!!!` *). It's a good idea to pick one symbol and use it for all the* here documents *you write. The consistency will help you and the people who read your code to spot your use of* here documents *more easily.*

Three plus signs (+++) might seem like a good termination symbol for here documents *because it's easy to spot, but that's the code that tells many modems to go into their "command mode!"*

Type a `cat` command with a *here document* for *stdin*, and redirect *stdout* to a file.

d) What does the command do?

Answer: It copies the here document *to the file. Your interaction should look something like the following:*

```
$ rm -f out
$ cat << !!! > out
> This is here.
> That is there.
> Never the twain shall meet.
> !!!
$ more out
This is here.
That is there.
Never the twain shall meet.
$
```

This example shows the syntax for using both << and other redirection for a single command, but it's not the kind of thing you would normally do in interactive mode. *Here documents* are used almost exclusively inside scripts and functions.

LAB 2.3 SELF-REVIEW QUESTIONS

To test your progress, you should be able to answer the following questions.

1) What does *fd* stand for?
   a) _____file directory
   b) _____file descriptor
   c) _____format directive
   d) _____free distribution
   e) _____future domain

2) Aside from potential differences in readability, it does not matter in what order you put input redirection, output redirection, and the command name in the command.
   a) _____True
   b) _____False

3) What happens if you specify output redirection more than once for the same command?
   a) _____None of the redirections have any effect except the first one.
   b) _____None of the redirections have any effect except the last one.
   c) _____All the files are created, but only the first is written to.
   d) _____All the files are created, but only the last is written to.
   e) _____The shell prints a syntax error message.

4) Which of the following does everything having to do with I/O redirection:
   a) _____The command being executed.
   b) _____The shell.
   c) _____The operating system.
   d) _____The network. (*Hint: not this answer!*)

5) Which of the following commands redirect *stdout*? (There may be more than one answer.)
   a) _____`cat a_file b_file 2> error.log`
   b) _____`cat > a_file b_file`
   c) _____`print hello 3> there`
   d) _____`print hello 1> there`
   e) _____`print hello > there`

6) Which `cat` command writes both *stdout* and *stderr* to a file named `out`?

a) _____`cat a b > out 2>& 1`
b) _____`cat a b > out 2> &1`
c) _____`cat a b 2>&1 > out`
d) _____`cat a b 2> &1 out`
e) _____`cat a b 2 >& 1 out`

7) Which of the following is *not* a valid marker symbol for a *here document?*

a) _____`!!!`
b) _____`+END+`
c) _____`>out`
d) _____`END`
e) _____`+++`

8) Which of the following commands might fail if `noclobber` is set?

a) _____`print hello |cat`
b) _____`print hello > out`
c) _____`print hello >| out`
d) _____`cat < out`
e) _____`print Not this one!`

Quiz answers appear in Appendix A, Section 2.4.

CHAPTER 2

TEST YOUR THINKING

The projects in this section are meant to have you utilize all of the skills that you have acquired throughout this chapter. The answers to these projects can be found at the companion web site to this book, located at:

`http://www.phptr.com/phptrinteractive/`

Visit the web site periodically to share and to discuss your answers.

1) Write a syntax synopsis for the `sort` command. There are several versions of `sort` available on different UNIX systems. Write your synopsis for the one that has the following options and parameters:

Options `b, c, d, f, i, m, M, n, r`, and `u` do not take arguments.

The following options take the arguments indicated:

`k`	`keydef`
`o`	`output`
`t`	`char`
`T`	`directory`
`z`	`recsz`

The option `y` takes an *optional* argument called `kmem`.

Any number of file names, possibly none, are positional parameters.

2) Write five examples of valid `sort` command lines following the synopsis you wrote for questions 1.

3) Explain the similarities and differences between the `noclobber` option, `>>`, and `>1`.

4) How would you write a print command that writes its normal output to a file named `normal`, and any error messages to a file named `errors`?

CHAPTER 3

COMPOUND COMMANDSYNTAX

If one command is good, two must be better!

CHAPTER OBJECTIVES

In this chapter, you will learn about:

So far, you have been generally entering just one command per command line, but even working in that framework, it has been impossible not to put multiple commands in one line on occasion. When a command generates too much output on the screen, you have to pipe the output to `more` or `less`. Most people who have used UNIX much are familiar with this use of pipelines already.

In this chapter, you will look systematically at the various ways that the shell supports multiple commands in single command lines. We will look at these features mostly using the interactive features of the shell, but you will also find them extremely valuable as you write shell programs, too.

LAB 3.1

COMMAND SEQUENCES

LAB OBJECTIVES

In this lab, you will learn about:

- ✓ Sequential Execution (;)
- ✓ Run Multiple Commands Concurrently Using &
- ✓ Pipelines (|)
- ✓ Conditional Commands (&& and ||)
- ✓ Co-Processes (|&)

So far, you have looked at individual commands, but much of the power of UNIX shells comes from the ways you can combine multiple commands in a single command line. The KornShell supports a particularly rich set of features for combining commands, so even if you are already comfortable with pipelines, you will find things in this lab that will probably be new to you.

LAB 3.1 EXERCISES

3.1.1 SEQUENTIAL EXECUTION (;)

The simplest way to combine commands is just to type one after the other, separated by semicolons.

Type in this command line and observe what happens:

```
print hello; sleep 2; print hello again
```

a) What is the rule the shell follows for executing commands that are separated by semicolons?

b) What effect would a semicolon at the end of the command line have?

c) Is it necessary to have a space after the semicolons?

Run the following sequence of commands as one command line, using semicolons to separate the individual commands: *(i)* remove the file named `out`, *(ii)* print a message so the output goes into `out`, and then *(iii)* use `cat` to print the contents of `out`.

d) What does the shell do first, break the command line into commands, or process redirection symbols?

____

____

For this exercise, there is no difference between typing all three commands as part of one command line and typing three separate command lines. Each command begins executing when the one to its left finishes. You will see that this feature can be useful later on, but for now, the semicolon is just a piece of syntax that lets you string multiple commands together on one command line.

3.1.2 Parallel Execution (&)

Note that this exercise is affected by two shell options. Run the following command before you start this exercise to be sure these options are set "correctly," at least for now:

```
set -o monitor +o notify
```

The ampersand is used to separate commands that you want the shell to run in parallel. If the last (or only) command on a line is followed by an ampersand, the shell will prompt you for another command line without waiting for the previous command to finish.

FOR EXAMPLE

Try this command line:

```
print hello & sleep 2 & print hello again &
```

Wait at least 2 seconds after you type this command, and press Enter again. The numbers in square brackets are *job numbers*.

a) How many jobs were there, and what were their numbers?

b) Run the command line again. Did you get the same job numbers?

The other numbers are *process ids.*

c) Did you get the same set of process ids the two times you ran the command?

When the shell runs an external command, it normally does so by telling the operating system's kernel to create a process *to run the command. The shell itself runs as a process, and built-in commands are run as part of the shell's process. Using processes judiciously can affect the efficiency of your scripts greatly.*

The term job refers to the processes that you can control using the shell. For example, putting an ampersand at the end of a command creates a background job, a process that runs in parallel with the shell itself.

a) How many background jobs did you create by entering the preceding command line?

b) How do you know when a background job finishes executing?

The plus or dash next to some of thev "Done" messages tells you the "current" background job (+) and the "next" one (–). These can sometimes be useful for interactive work with jobs.

Change the command line so that the `sleep` command's parameter is 10 instead of 2. After you press Enter at the end of the command line, wait about 5 seconds and press Enter again, then wait another 5 seconds or more, and press Enter a third time.

c) Explain the sequence of "Done" messages that you see.

The shell's *monitor* option can be used to control whether "one" messages are printed or not. Use `set +m` or `set +o monitor` to turn it off.

Give the command, `set +m`, and try the last command again.

d) What difference does it make?

The shell's `notify` option can be used to control *when* "Done" messages are printed, if they are being printed.

Run the following command to turn *monitor* and *notify* both on:

```
set -o monitor -o notify
```

Now run the following command line, but do not type anything for at least 5 seconds after you enter it:

```
print hello& sleep 5& print again&
```

e) Explain what the `notify` option does.

The shell has several commands for managing background jobs (`fg, bg, jobs`) that can make your interactive sessions more productive. See Appendix B, "Built-In Commands Summary," for material on these commands.

3.1.3 PIPELINES (|)

When UNIX was first introduced, its shell's *pipeline* facility was seen as one of its most innovative features, a feature that shaped the use of the operating system in profound ways.

Many utility programs, called *filters*, were written that read data (almost always text) from *stdin*, manipulated the data, and wrote results to *stdout*. Each filter was designed to do just one thing, and users would connect sequences of filters together, called *pipelines*, to create customized tools to meet their needs.

You've already created some simple pipelines in this chapter, such as the one that counted the number of built-in commands and the one that kept the list of built-in commands from scrolling off the screen.

In this exercise, you'll practice using some "classic" UNIX filters in a pipeline.

Type the names of the days of the week into a file named `days`, one day per line.

a) Run a `cat` command that copies the `days` file to *stdout* twice.

Pipe the output of this `cat` command to the command `tr a-z A-Z`.

b) What does this `tr` command do to the output of the `cat` command?

Pipe the output of the previous `tr` command to another one: `tr -d DAY`.

c) What does this `tr` command do?

Pipe the output of the second `tr` to `sort`, and pipe the output of `sort` to `uniq`.

d) What do these two commands do?

Pipe the previous output to `cut -c1-2`.

e) What does `cut` do?

Pipe the output of `uniq` to `tee out` instead of to the `cut` command. After running the command, look at the file `out`.

f) What does `tee` do?

All of the commands in this pipeline are well-known UNIX filters. If you are not already familiar with them, it would be worth your while to look them up and to set up some similar pipelines to practice using the various options they support. You are encouraged to share your favorite pipeline with others at the companion web site for this book, located at:

`http://www.phptr.com/phptrinteractive/`

3.1.4 CONDITIONAL COMMANDS && AND ||

In this exercise, you will learn two operators that are designed specifically for use in scripts, even though you will use the shell's interactive mode to look at them.

EXIT CODES

To understand how these operators work, you need to know that each command you run leaves behind an *exit code* that you can test to determine whether the command completed "normally" or "not normally." (The command itself decides what its exit code will be; you'll see how to do this for your own functions and scripts in Chapter 7, "Basic Tests.") For now, you can think of these exit codes as logic values, where normal completion is indicated by a value of "true" and not-normal completion is indicated by a value of "false."

The shell has a pair of built-in commands named `true` and `false` that do nothing but set their exit codes and terminate. In this lab, we will use these two commands to substitute for "real commands" that set their exit codes based on what happens when they run.

You will see when you write your own functions and scripts that you use numbers for exit codes: Zero means "true" and any other number means "false."

The standard value for false is 1. Don't use another value unless you have a particular reason for doing so.

Next, you need to think about the logical operators `and` and `or` because the `&&` operator works like `and` and the `||` operator works like `or` for exit codes. If you combine two logic values using `and`, the result is true if the first value *and* the second value are both true, and false otherwise. If you combine two logic values using `or`, the result is true if the first value *or* the second value is true (or both).

The secret to understanding `&&` is that if you use it to connect two commands, the shell will run just enough commands to figure out what the result of the `&&` operator will be, and nothing more. Furthermore, the shell guarantees that it will execute the commands in left-to-right sequence until it knows the result of the `&&` operator.

a) Run the following two command lines and explain the output:

```
true && print hello
false && print hello
```

____

____

b) What happens if you have multiple `&&` operators in one command line? For example, what is the output of this command:

```
true && true && false && print hello
```

____

____

The shell makes the same guarantees about || as it does for `&&`: It always processes commands in left-to-right order and stops as soon as it can determine the value of the || operation.

c) Run the following two command lines and explain the output:

```
true || print hello
false || print hello
```

____

____

You can use `&&` to guarantee that a command runs only if another one completed successfully.

You can use || to print an error message if another command fails to complete successfully.

3.1.5 Co-Processes (|&)

The shell's co-process facility is an advanced topic that is usually used only in shell scripts. Still, it makes sense to see the syntax now because it's based on the principles of I/O redirection.

Use co-processes when you want to generate input for a program programmatically but need more flexibility than you get with here documents.

The idea of a co-process is an extension of a pipeline. You start a command as a co-process, and then you can write information to its *stdin* (and read information from its *stdout*) from your script.

You start a co-process by putting the co-process symbol (`|&`) at the end of a command. You can then write to the co-process using the `-p` option of the `print` command. How to read from a co-process will have to wait until Chapter 11, "I/O and Trap Processing."

Type the following commands to see a co-process at work:

```
rm -f out
cat >out |&
print -p hello
cat out
```

a) What is the purpose of the `rm` command?

____

____

b) Which command runs as a co-process?

____

____

c) What happens to the file `out` if you now run this command?
`print -p hello again`

____

____

The co-process runs as a background job.

Use the built-in command `jobs` to verify that you have a background job running.

d) Explain the output of the `jobs` command.

____

____

Use the `kill %cat` command to get rid of your co-process.

e) What happened when you ran the `kill` command?

____

____

f) What happens if you run another `print -p` command now?

____

____

Using the `kill` command to get rid of a background job is a crude way to terminate it. In Chapter 11, "I/O and Trap Processing," you will get to see the normal way to tell a co-process to terminate, by closing its stdin.

LAB 3.1 ANSWERS

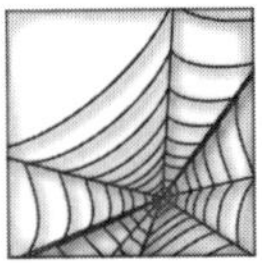

This section gives you some suggested answers to the questions in Lab 3.1, with discussion related to those answers. Your answers may vary, but the most important thing is whether or not your answer works. Use this discussion to analyze differences between your answers and those presented here.

If you have alternative answers to the questions in this exercise, you are encouraged to post your answers and discuss them at the companion web site for this book, located at:

`http://www.phptr.com/phptrinteractive/`

3.1.1 ANSWERS

Type in this command line and observe what happens:

```
print hello; sleep 2; print hello again
```

a) What is the rule the shell follows for executing commands that are separated by semicolons?

Answer: Your interaction with the shell should look something like the following:

```
$ print hello; sleep 2; print hello again
hello
```

There should be a 2-second delay at this point.

```
hello again
$
```

The `sleep` command does nothing for the number of seconds specified in its parameter. It's useful here to show that the second `print` command doesn't start until the previous command (`sleep`) completes. You will see how to make two commands run at the same time in the next exercise.

b) What effect would a semicolon at the end of the command line have?

Answer: It would have no effect, but you couldn't put it at the beginning of the command line, as the following interaction shows:

```
$ ;print hello
-ksh: syntax error: `;' unexpected
```

In some programming languages (such as Pascal) the semicolon is a command *separator;* in others, such as C, it is used as a command *terminator.* The KornShell lets you use it either way; you just can't put it at the *start* of a command line.

c) Is it necessary to have a space after the semicolons?

Answer: No, but putting a space after each semicolon makes the command line easier to read.

Paying attention to what an interactive command looks like is not very important, but making your programs easy to read is crucial. It will save someone (maybe you!) a lot of trouble when the code has to be changed later on.

Run the following sequence of commands as one command line, using semicolons to separate the individual commands: *(i)* remove the file named `out`, *(ii)* print a message so the output goes into `out`, then *(iv)* use `cat` with *stdin* redirected to come from `out` to print the contents of `out`.

d) What does the shell do first—break the command line into commands or process redirection symbols?

Answer: Your command line should look something like the following:

```
$ rm out; print hello > out; cat <out
hello
$
```

It must be that the shell breaks the command line into separate commands before it processes redirection because the redirections have to be associated with two different commands.

In fact, the shell has to redirect the `print` command before it processes the indirection for the `cat` command. Otherwise, the input redirection would have failed with a "No such file or directory" error message.

Understanding the sequence in which the shell processes command lines can be hard to master, but it pays off in helping you to understand how to use the shell most effectively and for understanding what happens when things go wrong!

3.1.2 Answers

Try this command line:

```
print hello & sleep 2 & print hello again &
```

Wait at least 2 seconds after you type this command and press Enter again. The numbers in square brackets are *job numbers*.

a) How many jobs were there, and what were their numbers?

Answer: Your interaction should look something like the following:

```
$ print hello & sleep 2 & print hello again &
[1]     257
[2]     269
[3]     261
$ hello
hello again
```

The cursor should have been on a blank line here when you pressed Enter *the second time.*

```
[3] + Done print hello & sleep 2 & print hello again &
[2] - Done print hello & sleep 2 & print hello again &
[1] Done print hello & sleep 2 & print hello again &
$
```

There are three jobs, one for each command. Their numbers are 1, 2, and 3, unless you have some other jobs already running.

As each job is started, it is given the first unused number greater than zero as its job number.

b) Run the command line again. Did you get the same job numbers?

Answer: Yes, you should get the same job numbers. For example, your second interaction should look something like the following:

```
$ print hello & sleep 2 & print hello again &
[1]       60
[2]       257
[3]       190
$ hello
hello again
```

The cursor should have been on a blank line here when you pressed Enter *the second time.*

```
[3] + Done print hello & sleep 2 & print hello again &
[2] - Done print hello & sleep 2 & print hello again &
[1] Done print hello & sleep 2 & print hello again &
$
```

The only difference should be the numbers printed on the second, third, and fourth lines.

c) Did you get the same set of process ids the two times you ran the command?

Answer: You probably got different process numbers, as shown in the previous output, but the situation is a bit more complex than for job numbers. Notice, for example, that my second set of process ids included 257, which was also one of the ones in the first set.

Every process running on the system has a unique process id, but job numbers are unique only within a single invocation of the shell. Thus, if you log into the system twice you could have two jobs numbered 1, but they would always have different process ids.

d) How many background jobs did you create by entering the command line above?

Answer: Three.

If you failed to put the `&` at the end of the command line, you would get very similar results, but the third command would not be run as a background command, and you would see only two job numbers in square brackets. In that case, your answer would have been *two*.

e) How do you know when a background job finishes executing?

Answer: The shell prints the job number in square brackets and the word Done.

The printing of these Done messages and the timing of their printing are controlled by the shell's `monitor` and `notify` options. Be sure you have entered the `set -o monitor +o notify` command correctly, as shown at the beginning of this Exercise.

Change the command line so that the `sleep` command's parameter is 10 instead of 2. After you type Enter at the end of the command line, wait about 5 seconds and press Enter again, then wait another 5 seconds or more, and press Enter a third time.

f) Explain the sequence of "Done" messages that you see.

Answer: Your interaction should look something like the following:

```
$ set -o monitor +o notify
$ print hello & sleep 10 & print hello again &
[1]     263
[2]     249
[3]     212
$ hello
hello again
```

<This is where you should wait 5 seconds and press Enter.*>*

```
[3] + Done print hello & sleep 10 & print hello again &
[1] Done print hello & sleep 10 & print hello again &
$ <This is where you should wait an additional five seconds, and press
  Enter again.>
[2] + Done print hello & sleep 10 & print hello again &
$
```

Don't panic! It's very hard to follow all this as it is happening. However, once you understand `monitor` *and* `notify`, *it should make sense, at least as you read through the discussion that follows.*

Answer: Jobs 1 and 3 (the two `print` *commands) completed within the first 5 seconds, but job 2 (the* `sleep` *command) did not complete until after 10 seconds.*

Here's a blow-by-blow description of the output:

1. After you typed the `print/sleep/print` command line, the three jobs started, and you see the three lines of output with job numbers and process ids.
2. The shell then issued the next prompt (**$**).
3. The "hello" message was printed. It appears on the same line as the prompt because you didn't get a chance to type anything between the moment that the prompt was printed and the moment that the print command executed.
4. The "hello again" message printed. It appears on the next line in the "usual" way.
5. The shell waits for you to type in a command line. There is no prompt on that line because the two messages were printed after the shell issued the prompt.
6. After a few seconds, knowing that the two print commands have completed, you press `<Enter>`, which causes the shell to issue another prompt, but before it does...
7. The shell "releases" the Done messages for jobs 3 and 1, *then* prints another prompt for you.
8. You wait long enough for job 2 to complete and press `<Enter>` again, which causes the shell to issue another prompt, but before it does...
9. The shell "releases" the Done message for job 2, then it issues the last prompt.

10. You wait long enough for job 2 to complete and press Enter again, which causes the shell to issue another prompt, but before it does...
11. The shell "releases" the Done message for job 2, then it issues the last prompt.

Give the command `set +o monitor` and try the last command again.

g) What difference does it make?

Answer: Your interaction should look something like the following:

```
$ set +o monitor
$ print hello & sleep 5 & print hello again &
[1]     254
hello
[2]     232
[3]     212
$ hello again
```

<*You should wait at this point for at least 5 seconds, then press* Enter.>

```
$
```

The Done messages don't print now. (*Whew!*) In the output shown, the "hello again" message printed on the same line as the shell's prompt, and you don't get another prompt until you press Enter again. You could have typed another command line instead of just pressing Enter, but that would have made the output still more confusing.

Turning off the monitor option to get rid of the Done messages can make your interactive sessions less cluttered. The shell does not print job or Done messages if you use `&` *commands in scripts (unless you dot them, as described in Chapter 1, "Setting Up"), so how you set monitor will have no effect on those programs.*

A difference between scripts and functions is that commands in functions generate job and Done messages if the monitor option is on, but commands in scripts never do.

Now run the following command line, but do not type anything for at least 5 seconds after you enter it:

```
print hello& sleep 5& print again&
```

h) Explain what the notify option does.

Answer: Your interaction should look something like the following:

```
$ set -mb
$ print hello & sleep 5 & print hello again &
[1]      270
hello
[2]      266
[3]      255
[1] Done print hello & sleep 5 & print hello again &
$ hello again

[3] + Done print hello & sleep 5 & print hello again &
```

<There should be a 5 second delay here, but you didn't type anything.>

```
[2] + Done print hello & sleep 5 & print hello again &
```

<At this point, you must press Enter *to get the next prompt.>*

```
$
```

The difference is that the last Done message came out even though you did not "release" it by pressing Enter to get another shell prompt.

Turning on the notify option (`-b`) is useful if you have long-running jobs and you want to find out when they complete, even if you don't happen to be actively interacting with the shell at the time. However, turning it off can make your interactive sessions easier to deal with if you tend to run a lot of short-lived jobs.

3.1.3 Answers

Type the names of the days of the week into a file named `days`, one day per line.

a) Run a `cat` command that copies the `days` file to `stdout` twice.

Answer: Your command line and the resulting output should look like the following:

```
$ cat days days
Sunday
Monday
Tuesday
Wednesday
Thursday
Friday
Saturday
Sunday
Monday
Tuesday
Wednesday
Thursday
Friday
Saturday
$
```

The `cat` command processes its parameters in left-to-right order, without regard for the possibility that it might be told to output the same file more than once.

Note the way the days' names are capitalized. The next part of the exercise will be affected by how you did it.

Pipe the output of this `cat` command to the command, `tr a-z A-Z`.

b) What does this `tr` command do to the output of the `cat` command?

Answer: Your interaction should look like the following:

```
$ cat days days | tr a-z A-Z
SUNDAY
MONDAY
TUESDAY
WEDNESDAY
```

```
THURSDAY
FRIDAY
SATURDAY
SUNDAY
MONDAY
TUESDAY
WEDNESDAY
THURSDAY
FRIDAY
SATURDAY
$
```

The `tr` command is a filter that translates the characters it reads from `stdin`. In this case, it translates all lowercase letters to uppercase letters. The two parameters passed to it are `a-z`, which tells it to translate all lowercase letters, and `A-Z`, which tells it to translate them into their corresponding upper-case letters.

You often use `tr` if you are looking for a word and don't care whether it is given in upper- or lowercase. If you translate everything to uppercase (or everything to lowercase), you have to test each word only once instead of two or more times.

There are slightly different versions of `tr` available. If it doesn't work right for you, you'll have to check your system's documentation to see exactly how to code the parameters. The forms used in this exercise should work with all versions, but if you have trouble, the first thing to try would be to put square brackets (`[]`) around the `a-z` and the `A-Z`, like this: `tr [a-z] [A-Z]`.

Pipe the output of the previous `tr` command to another one: `tr -d DAY`.

c) What does this `tr` command do?

Answer: Your command line and output should look like the following:

```
$ cat days days | tr a-z A-Z |tr -d DAY
SUN
MON
TUES
WENES
THURS
```

```
FRI
STUR
SUN
MON
TUES
WENES
THURS
FRI
STUR
$
```

The `-d` option causes `tr` to delete all occurrences of the letters listed. Note that both the `D`s in `WEDNESDAY` and both the `A`s in `SATURDAY` were deleted. If we wanted to translate days of the week into abbreviations, like Saturday `->` `SAT`, we would have had to use a different approach, one of which is suggested in the Self-Review Questions for this lab. Or, instead of using UNIX commands, we could use the KornShell's pattern substitution features, described in Chapter 10, "Patterns, Expansions and Substitutions."

Remember that `tr` *works on* characters, *so* `-d DAY` *means to delete the characters D, A, and Y, not the* word *"DAY." Using* `-d ADY` *would have been the same as using* `-d DAY`.

Pipe the output of the second `tr` to `sort`, and pipe the output of `sort` to `uniq`.

d) What do these two commands do?

Answer: Now your command line and the output should look like the following:

```
$ cat days days | tr a-z A-Z |tr -d DAY | sort | uniq
FRI
MON
STUR
SUN
THURS
TUES
WENES
$
```

The `sort` command has a number of options you can specify that make it very versatile, yet even in its simplest form with no options it is very useful. In this case, it sorted the days of the week alphabetically, giving a list that started `FRI`, `FRI`, `MON`, `MON`,... Unlike `tr`, which operates on characters, `sort` operates on *lines* of text.

The `uniq` command also works on lines of input: it writes out each line only if it is different from the one before it. That is, it removes duplicate input lines.

Try running the `uniq` command alone. It will read lines from your keyboard, and you can type in various words, repeating some several times, if you want to get a good idea of how `uniq` works.

Pipe the previous output to `cut -c1-2`.

e) What does `cut` do?

Answer: Your command line and output should look like the following:

```
$ cat days days | tr a-z A-Z |tr -d DAY | sort | uniq | cut -c1-2
    FR
    MO
    ST
    SU
    TH
    TU
    WE
    $
```

The `cut` command cuts out parts of lines, and the `-c` option says to cut out certain columns. In this example, everything except columns 1 and 2 is cut from each line, and what is left is written to *stdout*.

If a command line gets too long to fit on one line of the screen, just keep typing, and the shell will recognize the full command line, even if you can't see it all on the screen. Also, you can press Enter *in the middle of a command line, and the shell will automatically prompt you to continue typing, provided that it can tell that there "must be" more to the command. For example, if you press* Enter *after a pipe character, the shell knows that another command must follow. Finally, you can type a backslash character (\), immediately followed by* Enter *and the shell will prompt for additional input, even if what you have typed so far appears to be a complete command line.*

Pipe the output of `uniq` to `tee out` instead of to the `cut` command. After running the command, look at the file `out`.

f) What does `tee` do?

Answer: Your command lines and output should look like the following:

```
$ cat days days | tr a-z A-Z |tr -d DAY | sort | uniq | tee out
FR
MO
ST
SU
TH
TU
WE
$ cat out
FR
MO
ST
SU
TH
TU
WE
$
```

The documentation for `tee` calls it a *pipe fitting,* which is pretty accurate! It splits its *stdin* so it goes to both to its *stdout* and to any file(s) named as parameter(s), like directing water coming into a pipe so that it goes to two (or more) spigots.

3.1.4 ANSWERS

a) Run the following two command lines and explain the output:

```
true && print hello
false && print hello
```

Answer: Your interaction should look like the following:

```
$ true && print hello
hello
$ false && print hello
$
```

In the first command line, the `print` command is executed, because after the `true` command completes "normally," the shell has to run the second command to see whether it is evaluating `true && true` (result would be *true*) or `true && false` (result would be *false*).

In the second command line, the `print` command is not executed. After the `false` command completes the shell knows that executing the second command won't affect the result of the && operator: `false && false` would give `false` as its result, but so would `false && true`. So executing the `print` command can't affect the result of `&&`, and it doesn't get run.

b) What happens if you have multiple `&&` operators in one command line? For example, what is the output of this command:

```
true && true && false && print hello
```

Answer: The print command does not run.

The result is *true* only if *all* the commands have true exit codes. So the example given does not print anything. Only `true && true && true && print hello` would have printed anything.

c) Run the following two command lines and explain the output:

```
true || print hello
false || print hello
```

Answer: Your interaction should look like the following:

```
$ true || print hello
$ false || print hello
hello
$
```

The first command line does not produce any output because once `true` sets its exit code, there is no need to execute the `print` command; the shell already knows that the result of evaluating || will be true. If the `print` command returns `false`, the expression will be `true || false` (result is *true*), but if `print` returns a value of `true` (which is what it always does return), the expression will be `true || true` (result is also *true*). So there is no need to run the `print` command, and the shell doesn't run it. The second command line requires both commands to be executed. When the shell finds that the first exit code is *false*, it has to execute the second command to see if the result of evaluating || will be *true* (if the exit code from `print` is *true*) or *false* (if the exit code from `print` is *false*.)

3.1.5 ANSWERS

Type the following commands to see a co-process at work:

```
rm -f out
cat >out |&
print -p hello
cat out
```

a) What is the purpose of the `rm` command?

Answer: Your interaction should look like the following:

```
$ rm -f out
$ cat >out |&
$ print -p hello
$ cat out
hello
$
```

That's not very exciting to look at, but it does demonstrate how a co-process works.

The `rm` command is used to make sure the file `out` doesn't exist, to make sure the first `cat` command doesn't fail, in case the `noclobber` option is set.

b) Which command runs as a co-process?

Answer: The first `cat` command, because it ends with the co-process symbol (`|&`).

The co-process symbol has both the pipe (|) and background (&) symbols in it, and that's very descriptive. The command runs in the background, and you can write to its *stdin* or read from its *stdout*, the way you can use pipelines to get information into and out of filters.

Putting the co-process symbol before the output redirection symbol in the command line won't work. The `cat` *command starts running as a co-process before the shell sets up the redirection.*

c) What happens to the file `out` if you now run this command?
`print -p hello again`

Answer: Your interaction should look like the following:

```
$ print -p hello again
$ cat out
hello
hello again
$
```

The `cat` co-process is still running and still connected to file `out`, so writing another line to it with `print -p` makes file `out` get bigger, which the `cat` command in this interaction demonstrates.

Use the built-in command `jobs` to verify that you have a background job running.

d) Explain the output of the `jobs` command.

Answer: Your interaction should look like the following:

```
$ jobs
[1] +  Running                    cat > out |&
$
```

You can see the job number (`[1]`), the plus indicator showing that this is the "current" job, a note that says the job is running, and the command line that the job is running. For more information about the shell's job control features, you can look at Appendix B, "Built-In Command Summary."

Use the `kill %cat` command to get rid of your co-process.

e) What happened when you ran the `kill` command?

Answer: Your interaction should look like the following:

```
$ kill %cat
[1] + Terminated                    cat > out |&
$
```

The "Terminated" message is just like the "Done" messages you have already seen in Lab 2.3. If you don't see the "Terminated" message, it's because you have the shell's monitor option turned off. That is, the monitor option controls both "Done" and "Terminated" messages.

This form of the `kill` command, using `%`, followed by the name of the command that is running in the background is like using ^C to terminate a regular command that has it *stdin* connected to your keyboard. (You can use the job number instead of the command name with `kill`, if you prefer.)

f) What happens if you run another `print -p` command now?

Answer: Your interaction should look something like the following:

```
$ print -p Hello, hello, . ... Are you there?
-ksh: print: no query process [Bad file descriptor]
$
```

You can get the idea that you can't use `print -p` if you don't have a co-process running, but there is more information here to think about. First, the error message comes from ksh—its built-in command `print` in particular. After that, the `no query process` pretty clearly means there's no co-process. (There's no good reason for the difference in terminology.) Finally, the `Bad file descriptor` part of the message confirms what we mentioned before: the co-process runs like part of a pipeline with its *stdin* redirected from the keyboard to the output of `print -p`.

LAB 3.1 SELF-REVIEW QUESTIONS

To test your progress, you should be able to answer the following questions.

1) If you separate two commands with a `;`, the shell does not start the second one until the first one completes, even if the first one takes a long time to run.
   a) _____True
   b) _____False

2) Which of these command lines might *not* print `hello`?
   a) _____`print hello | cat`
   b) _____`print hello >| out; cat out`
   c) _____`print hello >| out & cat out`
   d) _____`print hello;`
   e) _____`print hello&`

3) What does this pipeline do? (Assume that `days` means is the days of the week file used in this lab.)
   `cat days | tr a-z A-Z | cut -c 1-3`
   a) _____Nothing
   b) _____It creates a new file named `DAY`
   c) _____The `cut` command prints an error message
   d) _____It prints `MON, TUE, WED,` etc.

4) What does this command line do? (Assume that there really is a command named `fribble`.)
   `fribble || print Fribble failure!`
   a) _____It always prints `Fribble failure!`
   b) _____It never prints `Fribble failure!`
   c) _____It prints `Fribble failure!` if the `fribble` command does not exit normally.
   d) _____It prints `Fribble failure!` if the `fribble` command does exit normally.
   e) _____The shell prints `Invalid ||`

5) Assuming that all the individual commands exist, what does this command line do?

```
feeble && fiend && foe && fumble && \
print fee-fie-fo-fum!
```

a) _____It prints `Feeble fiends are foes of fumbles.`
b) _____It prints `fee-fie-fo-fum` if *all four* of the other commands exit normally.
c) _____It prints `fee-fie-fo-fum` if *any one or more* of the other commands exits normally.
d) _____It never prints `fee-fie-fo-fum` regardless of how the other commands exit.
e) _____It prints `I smell the blood of an Englishman!`

6) What command can be used to write to *stdin* of a program running as a co-process?
a) _____`print -p`
b) _____`write -coprocess`
c) _____`writecoprocess`
d) _____`print -coprocess`
e) _____`print |&`

Quiz answers appear in Appendix A, Section 3.1.

LAB 3.2

LAB 3.2

COMMAND GROUPS

LAB OBJECTIVES

After this lab, you will be able to:

- ✓ Group commands { } and ( )
- ✓ Use Groups to Control I/O Redirection
- ✓ Use Groups to Control && and | |

In this lab, you will learn how to use braces and parentheses to group commands within a command line to control I/O redirection and the order in which && and | | are evaluated by the shell. Braces and parentheses also have purposes other than these two; for example, you have already used braces to enclose the statements in a function definition.

LAB 3.2 EXERCISES

3.2.1 GROUP COMMANDS { } AND ( )

There are lots of reasons for using braces and parentheses to group commands, but this lab will look at just two: *(i)* you can redirect I/O for all the commands in a group as a unit, and *(ii)* you can override the left-to-right order that the shell uses to process && and | |.

Although braces and parentheses are pretty much equivalent, as far as the things you will do in this lab, they are significantly different in the way the shell interprets them.

■ FOR EXAMPLE

If you run these two commands, you will get different results:

```
print hello}
print hello)
```

The first command prints the brace character (`}`), and the second one gives a syntax error. To deal with these differences, which aren't important for this lab, use the following rules for both braces and parentheses grouping. It will make both of them work the same way for the purposes of this lab:

RULES FOR THIS LAB ONLY

1)Put a space between each parenthesis or brace and the commands that precede or follow it.

2)Put a semicolon after the last command in each group of commands that appears inside a pair of braces or parentheses.

You can always *follow these rules if you want to, but they aren't always necessary in situations outside this lab.*

a) Write a single command to print "hello" from inside *braces*, using the rules just given.

____

____

b) Write a single command to print "hello" from inside *parentheses*, using the same rules.

c) Put two print statements that run one after the other inside a pair of *braces*.

d) Put the same two print statements inside a pair of *parentheses*.

3.2.2 Use Groups to Control I/O Redirection

The *stdout* from all the commands in a group can be redirected by putting the redirection operator just outside the parentheses or braces used for grouping.

Group two `print` statement inside braces using semicolons, and redirect the standard output for the group to a file named `out`.

a) Look at the file and verify that the output from both commands is in `out`.

Try the same thing with parentheses instead of braces.

b) Was there any difference?

Inside braces, pipe the output of `cat` to `tr a-z A-z`, and redirect *stdin* for the entire pipeline to come from your days of the week file. Do the same thing with parentheses.

c) Did the `days` file go to the `cat` command or to the `tr` command?

Run this command line:

```
{print hello; cat;} < days
```

d) How do you interpret the output you see?

e) Which of the following two command lines do you think would run more efficiently?

```
{print hello; print again} > out
print hello > out; print again >> out
```

3.2.3 USE GROUPS TO CONTROL && AND ||

If you put commands connected by `&&` or `||` inside parentheses or braces, they get evaluated before any `&&` or `||` operators outside the parentheses /

braces. Thus, you can use grouping to override the default pattern of executing commands in left-to-right order.

Use the fact that the `print` command always returns an exit code of *true* as you do this exercise.

a) What will print if you run the following command line:

```
print one && print two || print three && print four
```

b) Now use parentheses so that the same sequence of commands and operators prints just:

```
one
two
```

This little Exercise was a bit contrived. However, you will see that using grouping to control the sequence in which things are done is quite common when you learn about expressions in Chapter 6, "Advanced Variable Usage."

LAB 3.2 ANSWERS

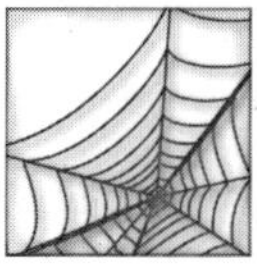

This section gives you some suggested answers to the questions in Lab 3.2, with discussion related to those answers. Your answers may vary, but the most important thing is whether or not your answer works. Use this discussion to analyze differences between your answers and those presented here.

If you have alternative answers to the questions in this exercise, you are encouraged to post your answers and to discuss them at the companion web site for this book, located at:

`http://www.phptr.com/phptrinteractive/`

3.2.1 ANSWERS

a) Write a single command to print "hello" from inside *braces*, using the rules just given.

Answer: Your interaction should look like the following:

```
$ { print hello; }
hello
$
```


If you don't put the space between the {and the `print`, you will get an error message. The space before the semicolon`;` is optional. Note that the semicolon is a command separator and does not print because the shell removes it before running the `print` command.

You don't know how to print a message with a semicolon in it yet. You can use quotes (Lab 4.3) if you need to do that.

b) Write a single command to print hello from inside *parentheses*, using the same rules.

Answer: Your interaction should look like the following:

```
$ ( print hello ; )
hello
$
```

This command line would work without spaces after the `(`or before the`)`, but they don't do any harm and they do make the parentheses and braces work the same way, for now.

The spaces after the opening parenthesis and before the closing parenthesis are important if you try to nest one set of parentheses inside another set. You will see this in Chapter 6, "Advanced Variable Usage."

c) Put two print statements that run one after the other inside a pair of braces.

Answer: Your interaction should look like the following:

```
$ {print hello; print again;}
hello
again
$
```

You need the first semicolon (`;`) to separate the two `print` statements. If you forget the second one the shell will pass the closing brace as a parameter to `print`. Having done that, the shell will see that it does not have a closing brace to match the opening one and will prompt you (with a >) to complete the command line. This is not an "interesting" syntax rule—just stick in that semicolon for now.

d) Put the same two print statements inside a pair of *parentheses*.

Answer: Your interaction should look like the following:

```
$(print hello; print again;)
hello
again
$
```

This exercise has demonstrated that you can do the same things, as far as grouping is concerned, with either parentheses or braces.

3.2.2 ANSWERS

Group two `print` statement inside braces, using semicolons, and redirect the standard output for the group to a file named `out`.

a) Look at the file and verify that the output from both commands is in `out`.

Answer: Your interaction should look like the following:

```
$ rm -f out
$ { print hello ; print again ; } > out ; cat out
hello
again
$
```

The `rm` command is there to make sure that the file really is created by the command lines shown and not left over from some other exercise.

Both `print` commands have their output redirected to the same file, using just one output redirection.

Try the same thing with parentheses instead of braces.

b) Was there any difference?

Answer: Your interaction should look like the following:

```
$ rm -f out
$ ( print hello ; print again ; ) > out ; cat out
```

```
hello
again
$
```


The `cat` command at the end of the second command line in this and the previous question could have been given on separate command lines, but doing it this way illustrates that the redirection applies to the grouped commands, not to the entire command line.

Inside braces, pipe the output of `cat` to `tr a-z A-z` and redirect `stdin` for the entire pipeline to come from your days of the week file. Do the same thing with parentheses.

c) Did the `days` file go to the `cat` command or to the `tr` command?

Answer: Your interaction should look like the following:

```
$ { cat | tr a-z A-Z } < days
SUNDAY
MONDAY
TUESDAY
WEDNESDAY
THURSDAY
FRIDAY
SATURDAY
$ ( cat | tr a-z A-Z ) < days
SUNDAY
MONDAY
TUESDAY
WEDNESDAY
THURSDAY
FRIDAY
SATURDAY
$
```

Because `tr` gets its input from the output of `cat`, using the pipeline connector (|), it must be that `days` went to the first command in the pipeline, the `cat` command.

Run this command line:

```
{print hello; cat;} < days
```

d) How do you interpret the output you see?

Answer: Your interaction should look like the following:

```
$ { print hello; cat;} < days
```

```
hello
Sunday
Monday
Tuesday
Wednesday
Thursday
Friday
Saturday
$
```

Because `print` doesn't read from *stdin,* the redirection goes to the first command inside the command group that *does* read from *stdin,* the `cat` command. So the `print` command prints "hello" and then the `cat` command runs and copies the `days` file to *stdout.*

e) Which of the following two command lines do you think would run more efficiently?

```
{print hello; print again} > out
print hello > out; print again >> out
```

Answer: Both command lines accomplish exactly the same thing, but it is more efficient to redirect the entire group, as in the first command line, than it is to do separate redirections within the group.

Setting up redirection involves interacting with the I/O system each time it is done, so doing it once is faster than doing it twice. On the other hand, command grouping is done internally by the shell, and doesn't take as much time as an interaction with the I/O system.

You will find that there will often be more than one way to do something, but that picking the more efficient way will affect the speed of your programs dramatically. You can't see the difference in this case unless you're using a really slow computer, but there will be plenty of cases where you can easily see the effects of how efficiently you do something because you can easily set up loops that make individual commands run many, many times, which will magnify seemingly small speed differences

3.2.3 ANSWERS

a) What will print if you run the following command line?

```
print one && print two || print three && print four
```

Answer: Your interaction should look like the following:

```
$ print one && print two || print three && print four
one
two
four
$
```

Notice that "three" did not get printed!

Because `print` always give an exit code of *true*, the command line is equivalent to `true && true || true && true` as far as deciding what to execute is concerned. Going from left to right, `true && true || X` is *true*, no matter what *X* is, so the `print three` command is skipped. Still going from left to right, the shell has a result of true after the first three commands and has to execute the fourth one to decide whether the entire sequence is true or not.

b) Now use parentheses so that the same sequence of commands and operators prints just:

```
one
two
```

Answer: There are several ways to do this. The author believes that the easiest way is to force the shell to process the last two commands as a group. Using this technique, your interaction would look like the following:

```
$ print one && print two || (print three && print four;)
one
two
$
```

By making the third and fourth commands a group, the command line reduces to `true && true || (X)`, which means that the shell does not need to evaluate *X*, and neither the third nor the fourth `print` command is executed.

You will seldom need to deal with this sort of complexity in "normal" shell programming, but if you do, you can follow the same advice C/C++ and Java programmers get: Use parentheses to make clear what you want to do.

Unfortunately, extra parentheses in shell programs can affect efficiency because commands inside parentheses are run in a subshell, although the KornShell minimizes this problem, compared with other shells.

LAB 3.2 SELF-REVIEW QUESTIONS

To test your progress, you should be able to answer the following questions.

1) Braces and parentheses are always equivalent, as far as the shell is concerned.

a) _____True
b) _____False

2) What happens if you type the following command line?

`{print hello}`

a) _____The shell prints an error message.
b) _____The shell prompts you to enter another command.
c) _____"`hello}`" is printed.
d) _____"`hello`" is written to the file `out`.
e) _____The file `out` is replaces by the file `hello`.

3) It is more efficient to apply a single redirection to a command group than it is to apply redirection to each command inside the group.

a) _____True
b) _____False

4) If you redirect *stdin* to a command group, it always goes to the first command in the group.

a) _____True
b) _____False

5) What does this command print?

`(print x || print y) && print z`

a) _____x
b) _____x and y
c) _____x and z
d) _____x and y and z
e) _____z

6) What does this command print?

```
print x || (print y && print z)
```

a) _____x
b) _____x and y
c) _____x and z
d) _____x and y and z
e) _____z

Quiz answers appear in Appendix A, Section 3.2.

CHAPTER 3

TEST YOUR THINKING

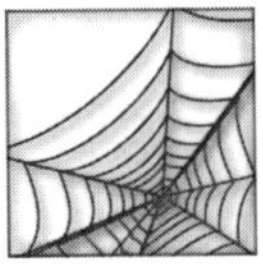

The projects in this section are meant to have you utilize all of the skills that you have acquired throughout this chapter. The answers to these projects can be found at the companion web site to this book, located at:

`http://www.phptr.com/phptrinteractive/`

Visit the web site periodically to share and discuss your answers.

1) Write a function named `overwrite` that copies `file_a` over `file_b`, even if `file_b` exists.

a) Make the function work, no matter how the shell's options are set and without changing the settings of any shell options.

b) Now rewrite the function so that it *does* change the setting of a shell option to do the same thing.

c) How can you see if your answer to Question 1b affects the `noclobber` setting after you run your function?

d) You might have written your function starting either `function overwrite {` or `overwrite() {`. Whichever way you wrote it, now rewrite it using the other form, and answer Question 1c again. (The results should be different.)

e) Discuss the advantages and disadvantages of using `>|` instead of `set +o noclobber` inside the two types of functions.

2) Write a command Line that reads a file named `Months` that contains the names of the months, one per line, and writes a new file named `mons` that contains the three-letter abbreviation for each month. The abbreviations in `mons` must be all lowercase, regardless of how the names are capitalized in `Months`.

CHAPTER 4

SIMPLE VARIABLES

Bread is the stuff of life.
Variety is the spice of life.
Variables are the stuff of programs.

CHAPTER OBJECTIVES

In this chapter, you will learn about:

Variables are at the heart of the shell's power and flexibility. You can use them to control the shell's behavior, the shell uses them for its own "housekeeping," and they are key elements of virtually all shell programs. In this chapter, you will learn how to manage some of the shell's variables, as well as ones that you use in your own programs.

LAB 4.1

TERMINOLOGY

LAB OBJECTIVES

After this lab, you will be able to:

✓ Use Proper Terminology for Variables

Before diving into the topics related to using variables, you need to know the terms that are used to refer to variables in different contexts. Unfortunately, some terms are used in ambiguous ways, and you will also need to know some of the common cases in order to reduce the chances for confusion.

There is a Glossary of Terms in Appendix C. You will use that as the basis for the exercises in this lab, so you might want to stick a bookmark there now to make it easy to find during the lab.

There are really only a few terms you need to master in this lab, so it will be a short one. However, it's important to get them under control right away to avoid headaches later on.

Variables are *names* for *values*. The name of a variable never changes, but its value may very well change as your program runs. The very term *variable* reflects this ability to change, or vary, the value associated with a name. The shell allows you to *assign* a value to a variable, and later on you can *reference* the variable name and the shell will *substitute* the value for the name. A new variable can be created just by assigning a value to a new variable name, which is called *initializing* the variable. If you try to reference a variable that hasn't been initialized yet (a reference to an *uninitialized* variable), you will get "nothing" as the value, which may or may not be an error, depending on the circumstances.

Substituting the value of a variable for its name is also called *evaluating* the variable. There are also times when the shell evaluates a variable without doing substitution, so evaluation is a more general term than substitution.

There are three ways variables are used:

1. You may create and use variables to help your programs perform their intended tasks.
2. You may assign values to variables that the shell consults in the process of doing its own work.
3. The shell assigns values to variables that you can reference to help your programs do their work.

FOR EXAMPLE

You will see examples of the first way to use variables throughout this book.

The `PATH` variable is an example of the second usage for variables. The value you assign to it is a list of directories that contain executable files, and the shell consults this list to find the external commands you run.

You already have seen "half" of an example of the third way variables are used: When you run a command or function, you know that you can specify option parameters and positional parameters for the command on the command line. The "other half" of this usage is that the shell *passes* those parameters as the values of a set of *parameter variables* that the program can evaluate to determine the particulars about what the user wants to do. The term *arguments* is sometimes used to refer both to parameters on the command line and to the corresponding parameter variables inside a script or function.

This lab will give you some practice defining these terms yourself. By the end of the chapter, you should have a working knowledge of all the concepts given here (and more!).

LAB 4.1 EXERCISES

4.1.1 USE PROPER TERMINOLOGY FOR VARIABLES

This exercise provides some practice using the proper terms for talking about variables. You don't need to know anything about actually using variables to do this practice.

Consult the Glossary in Appendix C, then write your own definitions of each of the following terms:

a) variable

____

____

b) name

____

____

c) value

____

____

d) reference

____

____

e) evaluate

f) substitute

g) assign

h) initialize

i) parameter variable

j) pass (a parameter)

LAB 4.1 ANSWERS

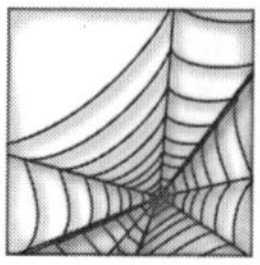

This section gives you some suggested answers to the questions in Lab 4.1, with discussion related to those answers. Your answers may vary, but the most important thing is whether or not your answer works. Use this discussion to analyze differences between your answers and those presented here.

If you have alternative answers to the questions in this exercise, you are encouraged to post your answers and to discuss them at the companion web site for this book, located at:

`http://www.phptr.com/phptrinteractive/`

4.1.1 ANSWERS

Consult the Glossary in Appendix C, then write your own definitions of each of the following terms:

a) variable

Answer: A variable is a `{name, value}` *pair.*

b) name

Answer: A variable name is a token used to identify a variable.

The rules for making variable names allow you to use any combination of letters (upper- and lowercase letters are different from each other), digits, and underscore characters (_). The first character of a variable name must not be a digit. In Lab 6.2, "Arrays and Compound Variables," you will see that you can also use *compound variables* that have variable names with dots in them.

You will also see some variables that have various punctuation marks in their names and some that start with, and contain nothing but, digits. These are variables that the shell creates itself, and they have names that "break the rules" in part so that you won't accidentally create variable names that conflict with them. The variables that you create have to follow the letters-digits-underscores rule. You will learn about many of the shell's variables with special names in this chapter.

c) value

Answer: The value part of a variable is the information associated with a name.

Values are usually text strings, but the KornShell allows you to have *typed variables* that are optimized for such things as doing arithmetic using variable values as numeric operands.

d) reference

Answer: A reference means to use a variable's name in such a way that the shell substitutes its associated value.

A reference to a variable starts with a dollar sign (`$`), which is followed immediately by either the name of the variable or the name of the variable enclosed in curly braces (`{}`). The curly braces are usually, but not always, optional.

FOR EXAMPLE

You can print the value of `PATH` using either of the following commands:

```
print $PATH
print ${PATH}
```

Most people use the first form, without the braces, whenever possible because it is easier to type, and you will see later that there are certain places where the shell even lets you omit the dollar sign.

e) evaluate

Answer: The shell evaluates a variable by substituting its value when you give it a reference to the variable.

FOR EXAMPLE

If you type the command, `print $PATH`, it prints the *value* of the `PATH` variable, which in this case is a list of directories separated by colons (`:`)

because the shell substitutes the value of `PATH` for this reference to the `PATH` variable before running the `print` command.

f) substitute

Answer: The process the shell applies when it changes a reference to a variable into the corresponding value.

g) assign

Answer: A value is associated with a variable by assigning the value to it.

You can assign a value to a variable by typing the name, an equal sign (=), and the value you want to assign as a command. There must be no spaces between the name and the equal sign or between the equal sign and the value. Enclose the value in quotes if it contains any spaces.

FOR EXAMPLE

You can assign the value `/usr/bin:/usr/me/bin` to `PATH` with the following command:

```
PATH=/usr/bin:/usr/me/bin
```

h) initialize

Answer: The first time a value is assigned to a variable, the variable is initialized. *Before that, the variable is* uninitialiazed.

It's generally all right to reference an uninitialized variable. As you will see later in this chapter, the value of an uninitialized variable is just nothing.

i) parameter variable

Answer: Inside a script or function definition, a program can determine what the command line parameters were by referencing a special set of variables called parameter variables.

Parameter variables are examples of shell variables with "illegal" names: their names are numbers (1, 2, 3,...) identifying which position they occupy on the command line (first, second, third,...).

j) pass (a parameter)

Answer: The process by which the shell transforms a command line parameter into a parameter variable is called passing a parameter *to the script or function.*

You will also see the term *argument* used to refer to both command line parameters and parameter variables, in addition to its use you saw in Lab 2.1 to denote the value that follows some option parameters.

At this point, you might find some of these answers more abstract than you like. The remainder of this chapter should make them much more concrete for you.

LAB 4.1 SELF-REVIEW QUESTIONS

To test your progress, you should be able to answer the following questions.

1) One way to create a variable is to assign a value to a name that hasn't yet been used as a variable.

a) _____True
b) _____False

2) What is meant by the term *argument*?

a) _____It refers to the name you have substituted for a variable's value.
b) _____It refers to a parameter variable inside a script or function.
c) _____It can refer both to parameters on the command line and to the corresponding parameter variables inside a script or function.
d) _____It refers to a referenced variable that has not been initialized.
e) _____It refers to an initialized variable that has not been referenced.

3) The first character of a variable name must be a dollar sign but cannot be any other punctuation mark because of a potential conflict with the shell's built-in variables.

a) _____True
b) _____False

4) Which of the following is a valid assignment command?

a) _____`This one is valid`

b) _____`valid = this one`

c) _____`this one = valid`

d) _____`this_one = valid`

e) _____`this_one="a valid one"`

Quiz answers appear in Appendix A, Section 4.1.

LAB 4.2

EVALUATING AND ASSIGNING VALUES

LAB OBJECTIVES

After this lab, you will be able to:

- ✓ Evaluate Simple Variables
- ✓ Assign Values to Variables Using =
- ✓ Use `unset` to Uninitialize a Variable

Variables have many uses, but the primary one used in shell programming is *substitution*. If a command line contains a reference to a variable, the shell substitutes its value before executing the command. Variable substitution is one of the most versatile features of the shell; you will see new uses for it over and over as you develop your shell programming skills.

LAB 4.2

LAB 4.2 EXERCISES

4.2.1 EVALUATE SIMPLE VARIABLES

The easiest way to see the effects of evaluating a variable is to put a *reference* to it in a `print` statement. You have already done this in Chapter 1, "Setting Up," when you checked your `PATH` and `FPATH` variables. Because we want to see the effects of assigning new values to variables in this lab, those two variables are not good ones to study; changing them could adversely effect your setup. Instead, this lab will use a variable whose value you see every time you enter a command.

Everyone gets tired of the default prompt string, `$`, sooner or later, and the shell provides a variable to let you customize it to almost any extent you might wish. Each time the shell displays a prompt for you to enter a command, it does so by evaluating and printing the variable named *PS1*.

SETTING UP FOR THIS LAB

If you have already customized your prompt string, run the following command so your interactions will start out looking like the ones in these exercises:

```
PS1="$ "
```

Don't skip these exercises even though you already know how to customize your prompt string. The exercises deal with principles of using variables, and they use the prompt string only as an example that makes it easy to see the effects of your work.

Now run the following command:

```
print $PS1
```

a) Explain the output.

____

____

If you reference a variable that has not yet been assigned a value, the shell uses an empty string as the value. You probably have not assigned a value to a variable named *PS1X*, but if by any chance you have, just pick another variable name to use in place of *PS1X* in the following items.

b) Put a reference to a variable named *PS1X*, followed by a reference to *PS1* in a `print` command and compare the output with the previous `print` command.

Most of the time, referencing an uninitialized variable is harmless, but sometimes it happens because of an error in your program. In such cases, you can get the shell to tell you (with an error message) whenever it evaluates any uninitialized variable. The command `set -o nounset` *turns on this feature, and* `set +o nounset` *turns it off.*

You have a choice of whether to put braces around the variable's name in a reference most of the time, but one situation where you *must* use braces is when the shell can't tell where a variable name ends. Is `$PS1X` a reference to *PS1* followed by an X, or is it a reference to an uninitialized variable named *PS1X*?

Write a command that prints the *value* of *PS1* with a character X on each side of it. There must be no spaces between the Xs and the value of *PS1*.

Remember, `print X$PS1X` *would print an X followed by the value of PS1X, which is an uninitialized variable. You will have to use braces.*

c) What command did you write?

Now print the value of *PS1*, a dash, and the value of *PS1X* between Xs. Do not print any spaces, and don't use any unnecessary braces.

d) What command did you use?

The shell manages a number of interesting variables that you can evaluate.

e) Print the values of the following variables and tell what you think each one is: *PS2, RANDOM, SECONDS, PWD, HISTCMD*.

4.2.2 ASSIGN VALUES TO VARIABLES USING =

One way you can assign a value to a variable is to write a command in the form `name=value`, where *name* is the name of the variable and `value` is the value you want to assign to it. There must be no spaces or tabs on either side of the equal sign.

Assign the value `hello` to the variable *PS1*.

a) What happened to your prompt string?

Assign the value `Kalamazoo` to the variable *city*, then use a reference to `city` to print `Kalamazoo, MI`. Do not use a variable reference to print `MI`.

b) What two command lines did you use?

You can put multiple assignment commands in a command line. Unlike sequences of other commands, you do not need to separate them by semicolons.

When you put multiple assignment commands in a command line, separating them with semicolons or not determines whether the assignments have an effect beyond the current command line or not.

Assign the value `Syracuse` to the variable *city* and the value *NY* to the variable *state* in one command line, then use references to these variables to print `Syracuse, NY.`

c) What command line did you enter?

You can change the value of a variable by doing another assignment to it.

Assign `Minot` and `ND` to *city* and *state*, then print the new values.

d) What *single command line* would accomplish this?

The value of a variable can include references to other variables.

Use the following command to create a new variable named *CityState* and initialize it to the values of *city* and *state*, joined together.

```
CityState=${city}${state}
```

Note that there are no spaces between the two variable references on the right side of the equal sign.

e) What result do you get if you print a reference to *CityState*?

Once you assign a value to a variable, it does not change until you assign another value to it, even if its value was assigned using references to other variables.

Now use the following command to change the value of *city* to `Bismarck`.

```
city=Bismarck
```

f) What happens if you now print the values of *city* and *CityState*?

4.2.3 Use *unset* to Uninitialize a Variable

The first time you assign a value to a variable, the variable comes into existence.

Other programming languages require you to *declare* that a name represents a variable before you can use it (the shell supports this feature too; see Lab 6.1, "Typed Variables and Scope") but, in general, you can get the shell to create a new variable any time you want to, just by picking a name and assigning a value to it.

Sometimes you will want to get rid of a variable, usually as a way to check that your script or function is doing what you expect it to do, rather than as a normal programming technique.

Remember, if you reference a variable that doesn't exist yet, the shell substitutes an empty string for the value.

The way to get rid of a variable is to use the shell's built-in *unset* command.

Print references to the variables *city*, *state*, and *zip*, each surrounded by equal signs. The variables *city* and *state* should still be initialized from the previous exercise, but *zip* should not be initialized at this point.

> **a)** What happens when you print the value of *zip* compared with the other two?

Note: *Once it comes to a non-assignment command name (such as* `print`*), the shell normally does not expect to find any more assignment commands unless the shell's* `keyword` *option has been turned on. If you get strange behavior using equal signs in this exercise, use the command* `set +o keyword` *to turn this option off and try the command again.*

Now use an `unset` command to make *city* and *state* uninitialized, and print the three variables, surrounded by equal signs, again.

> **b)** What is the purpose of printing the equal signs in this and the previous command?

To investigate `unset` further, you need to look at the list of variables that the shell maintains internally. The built-in command `set` prints a list of them all, one per line. The list is probably quite long. You can see exactly how long by running the following command line:

```
set | wc -l
```

c) What does this command line do?

You can see an individual variable's entry in the shell's list of variables by piping the output of `set` to a `grep` command.

FOR EXAMPLE

The following command line will print the line for the variable *RANDOM* that you looked at earlier:

```
set | grep ^RANDOM=
```

The UNIX `grep` *command is used to find strings in files (or* stdin*). If you aren't already familiar with this command, you can get an idea of how to use it by working through this and other exercises in this book. But* `grep` *is one of the most commonly used UNIX commands in shell programs, so you should study your UNIX reference material to become familiar with its rich set of features. Or better yet, pick up the UNIX Awk, Sed, and Grep Interactive Workbook by Peter Patsis (Prentice Hall, 1999). It's one of the "tools of the trade" that you will use a lot.*

Unfortunately, there are several different versions of the `grep` *command that have different rules for constructing the regular expressions (or patterns) the command searches for. Each has its own special uses. To avoid confusion in this book, we'll use only those* `grep` *commands that should work with all versions, even if they are not as fast or elegant as using a different version.*

Run the previous command, and observe the output.

d) What prevents `grep` from printing out variables that contain *RANDOM=* as part of their value?

e) What prevents `grep` from printing out a variable named *RANDOMIZE*?

Assign the value OH to the variable *state*, and verify that *state* is initialized, but that *city* and *zip* are not.

f) What command line(s) did you use?

You can use multiple -e *options to get* `grep` *to search for multiple strings. Each* -e *is followed by one of the strings you want to find.*

There is essentially no difference between a variable that is uninitialized and one that is initialized to an empty string, but you *can* see a difference if you try:

Uninitialize a variable named *y* (just to be sure your answers agree with mine), and print a reference to it immediately preceded by the letter *X* and immediately followed by the letter *Z*.

g) What command line did you use, and what was the output?

Now assign the value 123 to *y*, and print a reference to *y* surrounded by the characters *X* and *Z* again.

h) What command line did you use, and what was the output?

Now assign an empty value to *y* by pressing Enter right after the equal sign. Again, print a reference to it surrounded by X and Z, and use `set | grep ^y=` to see if the shell considers the variable to be initialized.

i) What did your output look like?

Now unset *y*, print a reference to *y* surrounded by the characters X and Z, and use `set | grep ^y=` to see if the shell still considers *y* to be initialized.

j) What did you observe?

LAB 4.2 ANSWERS

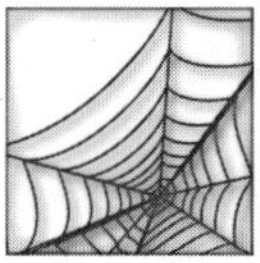

This section gives you some suggested answers to the questions in Lab 4.2, with discussion related to those answers. Your answers may vary, but the most important thing is whether or not your answer works. Use this discussion to analyze differences between your answers and those presented here.

If you have alternative answers to the questions in this exercise, you are encouraged to post your answers and to discuss them at the companion web site for this book, located at:

`http://www.phptr.com/phptrinteractive/`

4.2.1 ANSWERS

Run the following command:

```
print $PS1
```

a) Explain the output.

Answer: Your interaction should look like the following:

```
$ print $PS1
$
$
```

The second line is the output of the print command, which looks just like the shell's prompt on the third line because the "real" prompt is generated by evaluating *PS1* the same way is it was evaluated in the print statement.

b) Put a reference to a variable named *PS1X* followed by a reference to `PS1` in a `print` command and compare the output with the previous print command.

Answer: Your interaction should look like the following:

```
$ print $PS1X $PS1
$
$
```

The output looks just like the previous item's because the shell effectively ignores references to uninitialized variables, such as *PS1X*.

Write a command that prints the *value* of *PS1* with a character X on each side of it. There must be no spaces between the Xs and the value of *PS1*.

c) What command did you write?

Answer: Your command and its output should look like the following:

```
$ print X${PS1}X
X$ X
$
```

Four characters were printed: an X, a dollar sign, a space, and another X.

Don't confuse the dollar sign in the print *command with the dollar sign that gets printed. The former introduces a variable reference, and the latter happens to be part of the value of* PS1. *They are two totally different uses of the same character and have nothing to do with each other.*

Even though the shell "knows" there is a variable named *PS1* and that there is no variable named *PS1X,* it always takes the longest possible string of characters as the name. That is, it would have treated `$PS1X` as a reference to the variable name *PS1X.*

So the braces were needed because `print X$PS1X` would have printed X followed by the value of *PS1X,* which is an uninitialized variable. That is, it would have printed just a single X.

Why is there a space between the dollar sign and the final X in the output? Because the standard default prompt string is a dollar sign followed by a space. The command given in the "Setting Up for this Lab" showed how to use quotes to include the space in the value part of the variable, and this topic will be dealt with further in the next Lab.

Put a space at the end of prompt strings. It makes the cursor easier to see and makes it clearer where the prompt ends and the user's reply begins on the screen.

Now print the value of *PS1*, a dash, and the value of *PS1X* between Xs. Do not print any spaces and don't use any unnecessary braces.

d) What command did you use?

Answer: Your print *command and the resulting output should look like the following:*

```
$ print $PS1-X${PS1X}X
$ -XX
$
```

The output of the print command is five characters: a dollar sign, a space, a dash, and two Xs.

You could have put braces around *PS1* before the dash without changing the result, but they are not needed because a dash can't be used in a variable name. So the variable name unambiguously ends with the `1` before the dash. The braces are needed in the second variable reference so the shell can tell whether you are referencing the variable named *PS1XX* or the variable named *PS1X* followed by an X.

The two Xs are next to each other because *PS1X* is an uninitialized variable, When the shell evaluates an uninitialized string variable, it substitutes literally nothing for it. (It substitutes the value zero for numeric variables, but you won't use them until Lab 6.1, "Typed Variables and Scope.")

e) Print the values of the following variables, and tell what you think each one is: *PATH, PS2, RANDOM, SECONDS, PWD, HISTCMD.*

Answer: Your interaction would include the following `print` *commands, but your output would differ from that shown, for the reasons given below:*

```
$ print $PATH
/usr/bin:/usr/local/bin:/home/vickery/bin:.
$ print $PS2
>
$ print $RANDOM
11930
$ print $SECONDS
17669.347
$ print $PWD
/home/vickery
$ print $HISTCMD
539
$
```

PATH is a list of directories the shell will search for an external command when a command name is not in the shell's lists of built-in commands and functions. The directories are separated from each other by colons (:). This is the same output that was shown in Chapter 1, "Setting Up."

PS2 is the prompt string the shell uses when a command line is continued on an additional line on the screen. The default value is a right angle-bracket (>) followed by a space.

You can customize PS2 *just as you can customize* PS1. *Later on, you will see two more prompt strings that you might want to customize:* PS3, *used with the* `select` *built-in command (Chapter 9, "The Case and Select Statements"), and* PS4, *used with the* `trace` *option for debugging scripts (Chapter 11, "I/O and Trap Processing").*

The values of the other variables will depend on a number of conditions. *RANDOM* evaluates to a random number, and will be different each time it is evaluated. *SECONDS* is the number of seconds the current shell process has been running, and its value will change as real time elapses. (Printing it twice in one `print` command gives you an idea of how long it takes the shell to evaluate a variable.) *PWD* is the pathname of your present working directory (which probably has *your* login name in it instead of mine), and *HISTCMD* is a number that counts the number of commands you have entered.

You can re-execute a command if you know its HISTCMD *number by using the shell's built-in* `r` *command. Type* `r n`*, where* `n` *is the value of* HISTCMD *when the command was run. You can also use the* `r` *command to re-execute a command by typing any part of the command itself instead of its* HISTCMD *number.*

Assign the value `hello` to the variable *PS1*.

a) What happened to your prompt string?

Answer: Your command and the next command line should look like the following:

```
$ PS1=hello
hello
```

Notice that the cursor is right after the `o` of your new prompt string. The shell uses spaces to decide where parts of a command start and end, so even if you put a space at the end of the first line, it won't be part of the value assigned to *PS1*. Assign the default value ("`$ `") to *PS1* before continuing.

You can make up your own variables and assign values to them. Assign the value Kalamazoo to the variable *city*, then use a reference to `city` to print `Kalamazoo, MI`. Do not use a variable reference to print `MI`.

b) What two command lines did you use?

Answer: You should have entered the following two commands and printed the results as follows:

```
$ city=Kalamazoo
$ print ${city}, MI
Kalamazoo, MI
$
```

The first command assigns the value `Kalamazoo`, a string of characters, to the variable named *city*.

The second command prints a reference to the variable *city*, followed by a comma, a space, and the letters **MI**. The braces aren't really necessary in the second line because the comma unambiguously marks the end of the variable name, but using braces makes seeing the end of the variable name easier.

Using braces around all variable names is a bother when you are working interactively, but doing so in scripts is a good idea because it makes the code a bit easier to read. It's not so much of a bother to type the braces in a script because you type the command just once, then run it any number of times.

Assign the value *Syracuse* to the variable *city* and the value `NY` to the variable *state* in one command line, then use references to these variables to print `Syracuse, NY.`

c) What command line did you enter?

Answer: You should have used the following two commands:

```
$ city=Syracuse state=NY
$ print ${city}, ${state}
Syracuse, NY
$
```

The first line makes two variable assignments in one command line. You could have put a semicolon between them, but it's not necessary. The second line prints the values of the two variables, along with a comma and a space between them.

Notice that the commas in this and the previous item are there just so they will be printed. They aren't part of the variables in any way.

Assign `Minot` and `ND` to *city* and *state*, then print the new values.

d) What single command line would accomplish this?

Answer: There are two ways you could try do this, illustrating a subtle point about how the shell processes assignment commands:

```
$ city=Minot state=ND print ${city}, ${state}
$ Syracuse, NY
$ city=Minot state=ND ; print ${city}, ${state}
Minot, ND
$
```


The first command line didn't work! The variables still have their old values. However, putting a semicolon between the assignments and the `print` command *did* work.

It appears that the first command line did not actually change the values of *city* and *state*, but that is not really true.

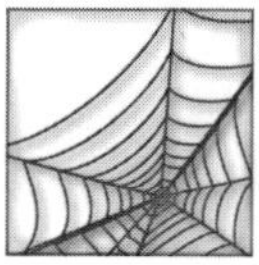

The full significance of the semicolon is covered in the Web pages for this Lab at:

`http://www.phptr.com/phptrinteractive/`

e) What result do you get if you print a reference to *CityState*?

Answer: Your interaction should look like the following:

```
$ CityState=${city}${state}
$ print $CityState
MinotND
$
```

If you tried to print a reference to `$City$State` *or* `$city$state`*, you are missing the point that* CityState *is the name of a single new variable.*

There are several things to notice about this interaction:

- First, the variable name uses capital letters to make it easier to read the separate "words" that make up the name. Instead, we might have used an underscore between the parts to make the variable name more meaningful: *city_state*, *CITY_STATE*, and *City_State* are all different variable names that might have been used. Note that these would all be the names of different variables because upper-

and lowercase letter differences are significant in shell names.

- Second, The curly braces weren't really needed in the assignment command. Because you can't put a dollar sign in a variable name, it would have been unambiguous to the shell where the *city* variable name ended, and the name *state* clearly ends at the end of the line.
- Finally, you could have combined the command lines, provided you put a semicolon before the `print` command.

Now, consider exactly why the two variable references were run together as they were in the first line. Look at the following interaction:

```
$ CityState=$city, $state
ksh: ND: not found [No such file or directory]
$
```

The space after the comma marks the end of the value part of the assignment, so the shell tries to use `$state` (which evaluates to `ND`) as the name of a command to execute. If you want to put spaces in the value of a variable, you can, but you have to use quotation marks, which is covered in the next Exercise.

Now change the value of *city* to `Bismarck`.

f) What happens if you print the values of *city* and *CityState*?

Answer: Your interaction should look like the following:

```
$ city=Bismarck
$ print $city $CityState
Bismarck MinotND
$
```

The interaction shows that the value of *city* changed, but that the value of *CityState* did not change.

You have to think about the shell's sequence of processing steps when doing shell operations.

The assignment to *CityState* involved referencing the variables *city* and `state`. First the shell evaluated the references to *city* and *state*, then it made the assignment to *CityState* using the results of those evaluations. Changing the value of *city* later on has no "backwards in time" effect on the original assignment to *CityState*. The only way to change the value of *CityState* again is to execute another assignment command with *CityState* on the left side of the equal sign.

There is a feature of the KornShell that will let you use one variable name to refer to the value of another variable (see the `typeset-n` *command in Appendix B) but the principle developed in this exercise is the general case and by far the most common.*

4.2.3 ANSWERS

Print references to the variables *city*, *state*, and *zip*, each surrounded by equal signs. The variables *city* and *state* should still be initialized from the previous exercise, but *zip* should not be initialized at this point.

a) What happens when you print the value of *zip* compared with the other two?

Answer: Your interaction should look like the following:

```
[$]: print =${city}= =${state}= =${zip}=
=Minot= =ND= ==
[$]
```

Note that there is nothing between the last two equal signs in the output. That is what an "empty string" looks like—nothing. (*zip* is nothing!) If you do see something between the last two equal signs, it means that *zip* has already been initialized on your system, in which case you can just continue with the exercise; you'll see more uninitialized variables shortly.

Now use an `unset` command to make *city* and *state* uninitialized and print the three variables, surrounded by equal signs, again.

b) What is the purpose of printing the equal signs in this and the previous command?

```
unset city state
print =${city}= =${state}= =${zip}=
== == ==
```


Now you've definitely seen nothing! By printing the equal signs, you can see exactly where the shell put the values of the variables, even though all three of the values are empty strings.

```
set | wc -l
```

c) What does this command line do?

Answer: Your interaction should look something like the following:

```
set | wc -l
     80
```

Because the `set` command lists the variables one per line, using the `-l` (line count) option on the wc command tells you how many variables are set. The number `80` is typical, but the value you got is undoubtedly different. That's a long list to look at, so the next step is to look at just the lines we are actually interested in.

There is nothing wrong with running a `set` *command with all the output going to the screen (possibly through* more*), it's just that there are a lot of variables there that would be really distracting to try to explain right now.*

Run the previous command and observe the output.

d) What prevents `grep` from printing out variables that contain *RANDOM* as part of their value?

Answer: Your interaction should look like the following:

```
set | grep ^RANDOM=
RANDOM=12345
```

Of course, your random number is probably different from the one I got.

The answer to the question might involve looking up quite a bit of information about `grep`. The argument to `grep`, `^RANDOM"` in this case, is called a *pattern* or *regular expression*. You can use a string of characters as the pattern, and `grep` will find the lines that contain them, such as the `RANDOM=` part of the pattern used in this example. The caret (`^`) at the beginning of the pattern is a special code that tells `grep` that we are interested only in lines that have `RANDOM=` at the *beginning* of the line. This way, a line would not print if, for example, the characters `RANDOM=` appeared to the right of an equal sign in the output of the `set` command.

e) What prevents `grep` from printing out a variable named `RANDOMIZE`?

Answer: The equal sign at the end of `RANDOM=` *prevents spurious matches like this one.*

As you can see, using `grep` to get exactly what you want, neither more nor less, can be a tricky piece of business. The skills you develop in working with `grep` will carry over to the rich set of pattern-matching features provided by the KornShell itself, which you will see in Chapter 10, "Patterns Expansions and Substitutions."

Assign the value `OH` to the variable, and verify that *state* is initialized but that *city* and *zip* are not.

f) What command line(s) did you use?

Answer: You could use the following interaction to answer this question:

```
$ state=OH
$ set | grep ^city=
$ set | grep ^state=
state=OH
$ set | grep ^zip=
```

There is no output from the commands that look for *city* and *zip*, which indicates that they don't exist as far as the shell is concerned. But `state` is an initialized variable, as the output from the third command line shows.

If you assigned values to city and zip after unsetting them in Question b, your results will be different from those shown here.

You could have combined all those commands into a single command line:

```
state=OH; set|grep -e ^city= -e ^state= -e ^zip=
```

This technique is somewhat more efficient than running separate commands for each variable because `set` *and* `grep` *are each called just once instead of three times. The* `-e` *option for grep is the "trick" that lets you search for several different patterns at the same time.*

Uninitialize a variable named *y* (just to be sure your answers agree with mine) and print a reference to it, immediately preceded by the letter X and immediately followed by the letter Z.

g) What command line did you use, and what was the output?

Answer: Your interaction should have looked something like the following:

```
unset y ; print X${y}Z
XZ
```

At this point, the "nothing" between the X and the Z should look familiar to you. The braces were needed around the variable name so the shell wouldn't try to print the value of a variable named *yZ*.

Now assign the value `123` to *y* and print a reference to *y*, surrounded by the characters *X* and *Z* again.

h) What command line did you use, and what was the output?

Answer: Your interaction should look like the following:

```
y=123 ; print X${y}Z
X123Z
```

This step is just verifying that things are progressing as expected. You already did this sort of thing earlier.

Now assign an empty value to *y* by pressing Enter right after the equal sign. Again, print a reference to it surrounded by X and Z, and use `set | grep ^y=` to see if the shell considers the variable to be initialized.

i) What did your output look like?

Answer: Your interaction should look like the following:

```
y=
print X${y}Z
XZ
set | grep ^y=
y=''
```

The print command shows that the value of *y* doesn't put any characters between the X and the Z, but the `set` command shows that *y* is indeed a variable with a value, but the value is the empty string. The two quotation marks are the shell's way of indicating that the value is a string containing nothing: There is nothing between the quotes.

Now unset *y*, print a reference to `y` surrounded by the characters X and Z, and use `set | grep ^y=` to see if the shell still considers *y* to be initialized.

j) What did you observe?

Answer: Your interaction should look like the following:

```
unset y
print X${y}Z
XZ
set | grep ^y=
```

This question shows that an uninitialized variable and a variable initialized to an empty string act in a similar way. (One exception is the shell's `nounset` option mentioned earlier.) However you can use the `set` command to see if a variable has actually been assigned a value.

Knowing whether a variable has been initialized to an empty string or has never been initialized at all can often be a powerful hint when debugging scripts and functions.

LAB 4.2 SELF-REVIEW QUESTIONS

To test your progress, you should be able to answer the following questions. At this point, you should be able to assign values to variables and make references to them, whether they are variables you created yourself or ones the shell maintains automatically.

1) Is `George_Washington` a valid variable name?
   a) _____Yes.
   b) _____No, because it has an underscore in it.
   c) _____No, because it is too long.
   d) _____No, because it has no digits in it.
   e) _____No, because it was already used by the first president.

2) Is `George Washington` a valid variable name?
   a) _____Yes.
   b) _____No, because it has a space in it.
   c) _____No, because it is too long.
   d) _____No, because it has no digits in it.
   e) _____No, because it is the name of a man, not a variable.

3) Is `George$Washington` a valid variable name?
   a) _____Yes.
   b) _____No, because it has a dollar sign in it.
   c) _____No, because it is too long.
   d) _____No, because it has no digits in it.
   e) _____No, because the dollar sign is not followed by a 1.

4) Is `1234_Skybar` a valid variable name?
   a) _____Yes.
   b) _____No, because it has an underscore in it.
   c) _____No, because it has too many digits in it.
   d) _____No, because it starts with a digit.
   e) _____No, because it is not George Washington.

5) Which command assigns the value `George Washington` to the variable `president`?
   a) _____`George Washington was a president.`
   b) _____`"George Washington" = president`
   c) _____`president=George Washington`
   d) _____`president="George Washington"`
   e) _____`The first president was George Washington.`

6) Which of the following command lines will definitely print "hello"?

a) _____`print $hello`

b) _____`h=hello print $h`

c) _____`h=hello ; print $h`

d) _____`hello=h print $hello`

e) _____`hello=h ; print $h`

Quiz answers appear in Appendix A, Section 4.2

LAB 4.3

QUOTING VARIABLES

LAB OBJECTIVES

After this lab, you will be able to:

- ✓ Quote the Value Part of an Assignment
- ✓ Quote Variable References
- ✓ Quote Single Characters

You saw an example of quoting in the previous lab as the way to include a space in a variable's value. We'll look at that use of quotes more carefully in this lab, see the difference between double and single quotes, and learn how to quote references to variables to affect how the shell evaluates them.

The goal in this lab is to learn how quotes affect variable values and variable references.

Lab 4.3 Exercises

4.3.1 Quote the Value Part of an Assignment

The shell uses spaces and tabs to tell where to separate the parts of a command. If you want to put spaces inside a part of a command, such as the value part of a variable assignment, enclose it in quotation marks.

The shell understands three different kinds of quotation marks, single ('), double ("), and back (`). This exercise deals with double and single quotes, the ones that are normally on the same key of the keyboard. Backquotes were used for command substitution *in the Bourne Shell and are recognized by the KornShell for compatibility, but as you will see in Lab 10.2.1, "Command Substitution," the KornShell provides a better way to do command substitution than using backquotes.*

The first item repeats what you may already have done in the previous lab:

a) Write a command that assigns the default value, a dollar sign followed by a space, to *PS1*.

Use double quotes in this exercise. You'll see how to use single quotes in the next exercise.

Put a right angle bracket (>) between the dollar sign and the space in your prompt string.

b) What does this tell you about quotes?

____

____

You have seen a lot of symbols that can be used to separate the parts of a command, such as the vertical bar for pipelines, the double ampersand for logical *and*, and so forth. They can all have their special meanings removed by putting them inside quotes, except for one symbol, the dollar sign.

Create a variable named *separators* that has as many command separator symbols as you can think of for its value, and print it.

c) What commands did you use?

____

____

4.3.2 QUOTE VARIABLE REFERENCES

In the previous exercise, you saw that double quotes remove the special meaning from the symbols that the shell uses to separate commands and for I/O redirection, but I didn't have you try quoting a dollar sign because that character is handled differently.

Use the following command to put the number of seconds you have been logged on inside square brackets, followed by a colon and a space, at the beginning of your prompt string.

```
PS1="[$SECONDS]: "
```

a) Now run a `sleep 2` command. What happened to the prompt string?

____

____

If you put a dollar sign inside *single* quotes, it loses its special meaning. That is, the shell treats it like any other character.

Use single quotes to assign the value `$SECONDS` to the variable *y* and print a reference to *y*.

b) What is the value of the variable *y*?

You can't get the shell to evaluate *SECONDS* by using the variable *y*. However, the variable *PS1* is special. If you put a reference to a variable in the value of *PS1*, the shell *will* evaluate the variable reference each time it displays a new prompt string.

c) How can you modify the assignment to *PS1* given above so that the "current value" of *SECONDS* is part of the prompt string?

This is a useful feature for customizing your interactive sessions, as the next two questions will demonstrate. However, it is not important for shell programs, where the shell does not issue prompts. Rather, the important concept here is to see the difference between single and double quotes with regard to how the shell handles dollar signs.

Recall that *PWD* is a shell variable that holds the pathname of your current working directory. Modify your *PS1* so it always shows the current directory.

d) Does your prompt change if you change directories?

The last question in this exercise sets your prompt string to include the value of *HISTCMD*, the variable that holds the current command number. This may seem like a rather obscure piece of information to look at each time you enter a command, but it will be the standard prompt used for the remainder of this workbook because it makes it easy to refer to individual commands in the discussion.

Many people like to put `$HISTCMD` *in their prompt string so they will know what command number to use with the shell's* `r` *built-in command. The* `r` *command reruns a previously entered command, using either the command number (what you see if you put the value of* HISTCMD *in your prompt string) or a piece of the previous command line, such as the initial few letters. See Appendix B, "Summary of Built-In Commands," for a summary of the* `r` *command and the* `history` *command that is often used in conjunction with it during interactive sessions.*

Instead of the current directory, put the command line number inside the square brackets of your command prompt.

e) What happens if you press Enter at the beginning of a line, compared with entering a command?

____

____

4.3.3 Quote Single Characters

There is another type of quoting you can use that works the same way as single quotes but applies to single characters. The backslash (\) character tells the shell that the next character is to be treated literally as that character, not as a character that might otherwise have significance to the shell as it analyzes the command line.

This type of quoting is sometimes called a *literal escape* or an *escape quote*.

The backslash as a quoting character has nothing to do with the ASCII `<Esc>` *code, even though the word escape is used for both, so don't confuse the two.*

■ FOR EXAMPLE

You could use the following command to set *PS1* the same way you set it in the previous exercise:

```
PS1=[\$HISTCMD]:\
```

a) What is the purpose of the second backslash in this command?

b) What happens if you type this command without typing a space after the second backslash?

Single quotes, double quotes, and backslashes all interact with each other in fairly predictable ways, as the following example illustrates.

■ *FOR EXAMPLE*

Run the following command:

```
y=hello; print "$y" '$y' \$y "\$y" '\$y' \\$y \" \'
```

c) Explain the results.

4.3.4 ANSWERS

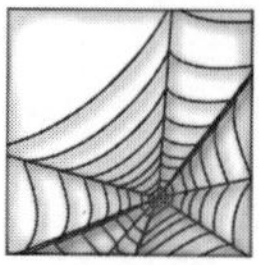

This section gives you some suggested answers to the questions in Lab 4.3, with discussion related to those answers. Your answers may vary, but the most important thing is whether or not your answer works. Use this discussion to analyze differences between your answers and those presented here.

If you have alternative answers to the questions in this exercise, you are encouraged to post your answers and to discuss them at the companion web site for this book, located at:

```
http://www.phptr.com/phptrinteractive/
```

4.3.1 ANSWERS

The first item repeats what you may already have done in the previous lab:

a) Write a command that assigns the default value, a dollar sign followed by a space, to *PS1*.

Answer: Your interaction should look like the following:

```
$ PS1="$ "
$
```

If your prompt wasn't the default string before, it should be at this point.

If you had typed the command without the quotes, the space after the dollar sign would have been dropped from the value of *PS1* because the shell discards all spaces and tab characters that are not inside quotes before it executes a command.

One of the first things the shell does when it processes a command line is to split it into syntactic units that it calls tokens (sometimes called words) using spaces, tabs, and other special characters to find the token boundaries. The last thing the shell does before it executes a command is to remove any quotation marks that aren't escaped with backslashes. The command being executed does not have any way to tell whether or not the user put quotes around the command line parameters.

This "token splitting" part of command line processing also explains why there can't be any spaces around the equal sign in an assignment command: The entire assignment command must be a single token when the command line is split.

Put a right angle bracket (>) between the dollar sign and the space in your prompt string.

b) What does this tell you about quotes?

Answer: Your interaction should look like the following:

```
$ PS1="$> "
$>
```


Normally, > would indicate output redirection, but putting it inside quotes removes this special significance.

Create a variable named *separators* that has as many command separator symbols as you can think of for its value, and print it.

c) What commands did you use?

Answer: Your interaction should look something like the following:

```
$ separators="; | & && || |& << < > >>" ; print $separators
; | & && || |& << < > >>
$
```

Putting these symbols inside quotes removes their special meaning.

4.3.2 ANSWERS

Use the following command to put the number of seconds you have been logged on inside square brackets, followed by a colon and a space, at the beginning of your prompt string.

```
PS1="[$SECONDS]: "
```

a) Now run a `sleep 2` command. What happened to the prompt string?

Answer: Your interaction should look something like the following:

```
$ PS1="[$SECONDS]: "
[804.376]: sleep 2
<Be patient for two seconds.>
[804.376]:
```

If you didn't happen to have been logged on for exactly 804.376 seconds when you ran the first command, you would have a different number inside the square brackets.

If there is no fraction displayed in your prompt, it means you are using a very old version of the shell. You need to get a more current version, as described in Chapter 1, "Setting Up."

The first prompt after you changed *PS1* shows the number of seconds and milliseconds since you logged on, which shows that you that you can put variable references inside double quotes and they still "work," in the sense that the shell substitutes the value for the reference.

However, the prompt string didn't change the next time the shell printed a prompt, even though the amount of time since you logged in has definitely increased. What happened? The shell evaluated `$SECONDS` when you typed in the first command, the one that assigned the value to `PS1`, and that became the permanent value of `PS1`. As you saw earlier, putting a variable reference on the right side of an equal sign causes the *current value* of the variable to be used in the assignment; the variable on the left side is not connected to the variable on the right side in any way. So 2 seconds later, *PS1* is still whatever it was at the time you assigned the value of *SECONDS* to it.

Use single quotes to assign the value `$SECONDS` to the variable *y* and print a reference to *y*.

b) What is the value of the variable *y*?

Answer: Your interaction should look something like the following:

```
[804.376]: y='$SECONDS' ; print $y
$SECONDS
[804.376]
```

By using *single* quotes, the value assigned to *y* includes the character dollar sign, followed by the letters *S-E-C-O-N-D-S*. It doesn't matter what the value of the variable *SECONDS* was because the shell didn't treat the dollar sign as the start of a variable reference, and didn't evaluate the `SECONDS` variable.

c) How can you modify the assignment to *PS1* given above so that the "current value" of *SECONDS* is part of the prompt string?

Answer: The solution is to use single quotes instead of double quotes, as the following interaction illustrates:

```
[804.376] PS1='[$SECONDS]: '
```

```
[844.628]
<Wait a few seconds, and press Enter again.>
[848.102]
```

Now the shell displays the updated number of seconds since you logged in every time it prints a prompt. Note that once a prompt is on the screen it doesn't change. The only change is when the shell writes another prompt.

Recall that *PWD* is a shell variable that holds the pathname of your current working directory. Modify your *PS1* so it always shows the current directory.

d) Does your prompt change if you change directories?

Answer: Your interaction should look something like the following:

```
[1001.339] PS1='[$PWD]: '
[/home/vickery]: cd bin
[/home/vickery/bin]: cd
[/home/vickery]:
```

Of course, your current directory probably has a different name from the one shown.

Because the value of *PS1* contains the string, `$PWD`, and because the shell does variable expansion of *PS1* every time it writes a prompt string, the prompt always displays the current working directory, regardless of its value at the time the initial assignment to *PS1* was made.

Instead of the current directory, put the command line number inside the square brackets of your command prompt.

e) What happens if you press Enter at the beginning of a line, compared with entering a command?

Answer: Your interactions should look something like the following:

```
[820.722]: PS1='[$HISTCMD}: '
[301]:
[301]: date
Fri Dec 31 23:59:59 EDT 1999
[302]: r 301
date
Tue Jan  1 00:00:01 EDT 1900
[303]:
```

The first line uses single quotes to "protect" the dollar sign so that it will become part of the value of *PS1*. From then on, each new command gets a new prompt.

On the first line numbered 301, the user just pressed Enter and the value of *HISTCMD* did not change. However, entering a command, as on the second line numbered 301, does change *HISTCMD*, and the prompt string was updated.

The command on line 302 illustrates the use of the shell's retry (`r`) command using a command number as the parameter, in this case, re-executing the `date` command. Note that the shell prints the recalled command line before re-executing it.

The shell will also show the command number in your prompt if the value of PS1 *contains an exclamation point (*`!`*), just the same as if it contained a reference to* HISTCMD*. This is for compatibility with older versions of the shell, which did not support the* HISTCMD *variable. Note that* HISTCMD *always means the current command number, no matter where you reference it, but the exclamation point works only when it is part of your* PS1.

4.3.3 Answers

```
PS1=[\$HISTCMD]:\
```

a) What is the purpose of the second backslash in this command?

Answer: The second backslash quotes the space following the colon.

If you ran this command without typing the space after the second backslash, you ran into another feature of backslash quoting, as the next question reveals.

b) What happens if you type this command without typing a space after the second backslash?

Answer: If you run the command without the trailing space, your interaction should look like the following:

```
[303]: PS1=[\$HISTCMD]:\
>
```

```
[304]:
```

What you have stumbled onto here is the special feature of the backslash when it is the very last character on the line. In this case, the backslash quotes the end-of-line character itself. The shell removes the end-of-line character from the command line and prompts you to continue typing the command.

In this example, you would have to type another backslash and space on the command-continuation line to get the new value of *PS1* to end with a space.

You can use backslash at the end of a line to let you type long lines without having some of your input scroll to the left and become invisible.

Run the following command:

```
y=hello; print "$y" '$y' \$y "\$y" '\$y' \\$y \" \'
```

c) Explain the results.

Answer: Your interaction should look like the following:

```
[304]: y=hello ; print "$y" '$y' \$y "\$y" '\$y' \\$y \" \'
hello $y $y $y \$y \hello " '
[305]:
```

The first output (`hello`) is the value of *y*, which shows that variable substitution takes place inside double quotes, as you already know.

The second and third outputs (`$y $y`) show that single quotes and the backslash both hide the special meaning of the dollar sign, and it is printed just like any other character.

The fourth output (`$y` again) shows that the backslash hides the special meaning of the dollar sign, even inside double quotes.

The fifth output (`\$y`) shows that single quotes remove the special meaning of both backslash and dollar sign.

The sixth output (\hello) shows that you can use the backslash to quote itself which, in this example, leaves the dollar sign unquoted, so the shell does variable substitution.

The last two outputs (" and ') show that the backslash can be used to quote double and single quotes.

LAB 4.3 SELF-REVIEW QUESTIONS

To test your progress, you should be able to answer the following questions.

1) Which of these commands would assign the value *George Washington* to the variable `president`?
   - **a)** _____`president = George Washington`
   - **b)** _____`president="George Washington"`
   - **c)** _____`president='George Washington'`
   - **d)** _____`president=George\ Washington`
   - **e)** _____All except choice a).

2) What does the following command do?

```
PS1='[$HISTCMD] $PWD> '
```

   - **a)** _____Nothing, because you can't put two variable references in the value part of an assignment.
   - **b)** _____It redirects the output of the prompt string to a file named `'`.
   - **c)** _____It makes the next prompt into `[]  >` because variable expansion is suppressed by the quotes.
   - **d)** _____It shows both the current command number and the current working directory in the prompt string.
   - **e)** _____It shows the same command number and directory name in all prompt strings, regardless of how many commands are entered and regardless of any `cd` commands.

3) What might the following command print?

```
print There have been \'$SECONDS\' seconds since I\'ve
  logged in.
```

a) _____An error message because there is an odd number of single quotes.
b) _____A prompt to continue the line because the second quoted string is not terminated.
c) _____An error message because you can't combine single quotes and backslashes.
d) _____A new prompt string containing an error message.
e) _____`There have been '123.456' seconds since I've logged in.`

Quiz answers appear in Appendix A, Section 4.3.

CHAPTER 4

TEST YOUR THINKING

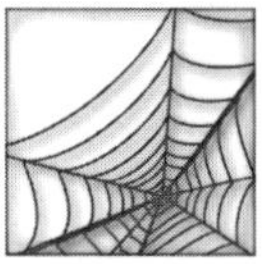

The projects in this section are meant to have you utilize all of the skills that you have acquired throughout this chapter. The answers to these projects can be found at the companion web site to this book, located at:

`http://www.phptr.com/phptrinteractive/`

Visit the web site periodically to share and discuss your answers.

1) Modify the function named `l` given as an example in Lab 2.2, "Command Types," so that it uses the value of a variable named `LSFLAGS` to control what options are used for the `ls` command. Try running the `l` function with different values assigned to `LSFLAGS` to verify that it works as expected.

2) Write an alias for the `rm` command that appends the current value of a variable named `RMFLAGS` to all `rm` commands the user enters interactively. Verify that it works properly. Be careful! Don't test this in a directory containing files you wouldn't want to delete accidentally.

C H A P T E R 5

PARAMETERS

The values of the parameters that you pass to a command control what the command does.

Chapter Objectives

In this chapter, you will learn about:

You have already seen that a command consists of a *command name* followed by some number of *parameters* (possibly none). The parameters are subdivided into *option parameters* and *positional parameters,* with the option parameters (also called *option letters* or just *options*) normally appearing to the left of the positional parameters. It doesn't matter whether the command is a shell built-in, a script, a function, or a command written in a language like C, C++, or Java—the shell passes all of the parameters you type on the command line to the command as a list of values.

In this chapter you will see how you can write code that uses the list of parameter values that the shell passes to a script or function. First you will learn about the special variables that you can use inside a script or function to find out how many values there are in the parameter list and what their values are. Then you will learn how to use a special command inside a script or function to process option parameters in the "standard way."

LAB 5.1

PARAMETERS

LAB OBJECTIVES

After this lab, you will be able to:

- ✓ Verify Your Set-Up
- ✓ Pass Parameters to a Function or Script
- ✓ Use Special Parameter Variables (`#` `@` `*`)
- ✓ Use `set` to Assign Positional Parameters
- ✓ Use `shift` to Access Positional Parameters

You have already seen parameters from a user's point of view. They are the tokens, such as file names, that you type after the options part of a command string. In this lab, you will see how functions and scripts find out what parameters are passed to them using a special set of variables provided by the shell.

SETTING UP FOR THIS LAB

You will be writing several scripts in this lab, so you should go over the material in Lab 1.3, "Editing and Running Scripts and Functions," if you haven't already done so, before you proceed. The first exercise checks to be sure you are set up correctly.

PASSING PARAMETERS

Once the shell has broken a command line into tokens and divided it into individual commands, it ends up with a sequence of tokens for each command, beginning with the command name and followed by a sequence of parameters. The parameters, by convention, begin with an optional sequence of option parameters, followed by another optional sequence of positional parameters, as you saw in Chapter 2, "Command Syntax." In this lab, the command name is the name of a function or script that you are writing, and you will learn to find out what parameter values were typed on the command line. Dealing with the options will be covered in Lab 5.2, "Processing Option Parameters." For now, you will work with commands and functions that don't use any options.

Options are passed to a script or function the same way that parameters are, so the term positional parameter *is used to refer to the parameters after the options. In this lab, there are no options, so the terms* `parameter` *and* `positional parameter` *will always refer to the same thing. In general, an option is a parameter associated with an option letter, and a position parameter is a nonoption parameter that is identified by its ordinal position on the command line (first, second, third, and so forth).*

When a shell program runs, the command line parameters are assigned to a set of variables named 1, 2, 3,... in left-to-right order, that you can reference from within the function or script. In this lab, you will practice looking at the values of those variables using `print` commands. Once you can do that, you will know how to use them for whatever purposes your programs require.

LAB 5.1 EXERCISES

5.1.1 VERIFY YOUR SET-UP

You need directories that the shell will look in for your scripts and function definitions. In Chapter 1, "Setting Up," you should have created directories name `bin` and `fun` under your home directory for this purpose, if they were not already there. You can use directories with other names if you want to, but all the exercises will assume those two names, so you'll have to make mental translations to your own directory names if they are not the same.

The shell uses two variables to tell it what directories to search when it looks for commands and functions, *PATH* and *FPATH*. You should also have set up these variables in Chapter 1.

> **a)** Print the values of *PATH* and *FPATH*. Is `~/bin` in your *PATH*, and is `~/fun` in your *FPATH*?
>
> ____
>
> ____

To write a script, you put a text file in `~/bin` and make it executable using `chmod +x <file name>`.

If you type a tilde (~) at the beginning of a pathname, the shell automatically substitutes the pathname of your home directory for it, which can save you a bit of typing. This "tilde notation" will be used throughout the labs and exercises to come.

Write a script named `s511` and put a command that prints "`This is script s511.`" to *stdout* in it.

> **b)** Make `s511` executable, use `cat`, `more`, or `less` (your choice) to show its contents, and run it. What is your output?
>
> ____
>
> ____
>
> ____
>
> ____

c) Run `s511`. What is your output?

To write a function, you put the definition in a text file in `~/fun`. If the function has the same name as an external command, you need to tell the shell that the function exists using the `autoload` built-in command. (Actually, `autoload` is an alias for `typeset -fu`, which you can type instead if you prefer. It's `typeset` that's really the built-in command.)

With the KornShell, you often have the choice of learning a new command name that's easier to type and has a more descriptive name, such as `autoload`, *or using a single command, such as* `typeset`, *that requires you to memorize and type special options to make it work. The choice is yours.*

The name of the function has to be the same as the name of the file, and the file has to be in your `~/fun` directory (or some other directory listed in your `FPATH`).

Write a function named `f511` and put a command that prints "`This is function f511.`" in it. Put a command that prints "`This is file fun/f511`" *after* the function definition in the same file.

Run the following command:

```
whence -a f511
```

d) What does the shell know about the function?

e) Run the function, run the `whence -a f511` command again, then run the function again. Explain the results.

You can delete `~/bin/s511` and `~/fun/f511` now if you want to clean things up.

5.1.2 Pass Parameters to a Function or Script

When you run a script or function, the parameters you type on the command line are passed to the program as the values of the *positional parameter variables*, named *1*, *2*, *3*, etc.

Create a script named `s512`. Put a `print` statement in it that prints references to the variables named *1* through *10*.

Note: *Normal variable names can't start with a digit, but the positional parameter variables inside a function or script are the exception to this rule. When you reference these variables, you need to put braces around the name if it is more than one digit, but you can skip the braces for the variables named 1-9.*

a) Print the script, then run it with your name as parameters and explain the results.

---

b) Now run the script again, but with each of the letters of the alphabet as parameters. Explain these results.

Create a function named `f512` with the same `print` statement in it as `s512` has. Run it twice, once with your name and once with the letters of the alphabet as parameters.

c) Is there any difference between running the function and running the script?

5.1.3 USE SPECIAL PARAMETER VARIABLES (# @ *)

The title of this exercise might look like curse words in a comic book, but it's really a list of three special variables the shell sets when a function or script is called. The *number* of parameter variables is given by the value of the number sign variable (#), and *all* the parameter variables are the value of the at (@) and asterisk (*) variables. The difference between @ and * has to do with quoting, as you will see.

Create a script named `s513` that prints each of these variables, and run it using the following commands.

```
s513 hello 123
s513 There are four words.
```

a) What did you observe?

Pass your name as a single parameter to `s513` with five spaces between your first and last names. Verify that it was received as a single value. *Hint:* Use quotes.

b) What command did you use? Were the spaces preserved?

Run a command *from the command line* that prints your name. Put five spaces between your first and last names, and don't use any quotes.

c) Explain how this item relates to the previous one.

Now run a `print` command from the command line that prints your name. Put five spaces between your first and last names, and *do* put double quotes around your name.

d) Explain how this item relates to Question *b*.

Now modify `s513` so that each of the variable references is enclosed in quotes. Run `s513` with your name, including the extra spaces, inside quotes.

e) Explain what you observed.

5.1.4 USE `set` TO ASSIGN POSITIONAL PARAMETERS

What is the difference between `$@` and `$*`? As mentioned before, it has to do with quoting, but you haven't learned enough tools to see the difference ... yet. This exercise will introduce you to the *KornShell's* mechanism for managing the positional parameters that you can access from the command line, and with that in place you will be able to see the difference between `$@` and `$*`.

The built-in command `set`, followed by a list of values, replaces the values that were passed to a command or function with the ones given in the set command. The shell also assigns new values to the special symbols, `$#`, `$@`, and `$*` when you use this form of the `set` command.

Thought Question: *You have already seen that a* `set` *command without any options or parameters will print the names of all variables and their values, and you have also already seen that* `set` *can be used to set shell options, such as* `noclobber`. *Think about how the shell figures out what it is supposed to do when it reads a* `set` *command that you type in. See the* Test Your Thinking *section of this chapter, item 1.*

Run this command from the command line to print the values of the three special variables #, @, and *:

```
print $#: $@: $*
```

a) Is the variable `#` defined? How many parameters were passed to `ksh` when it started running?

You can use the `set` command in an interactive session to give yourself a set of positional parameters to work with, just as if you were inside a script or function. We'll use this feature here to save the trouble of creating more script or function definition files.

Use a `set` command to set the positional parameters to the message, `My name is "Your     Name."` Use quotes so your first and last name, separated by five spaces, will be one parameter value.

Print the values of the special variables #, @, and *. (Use separate `print` commands.)

b) What are the values of the three parameter variables now?

Now run `s513` using `$@` as a parameter, and again using `$*`. Do *not* put any quotes in your command line.

c) How many positional parameter variables are passed in both cases, and what are their values?

Finally, to see the difference between @ and *, repeat the last two commands, but put `$@` and `$*` inside double quotes. Note the number of parameters passed and how the spaces between your first and last names are handled.

d) What is the difference between these two special variables?

5.1.5 USE `shift` TO ACCESS POSITIONAL PARAMETERS

The shell's built-in `shift` command is usually used inside loops, which you won't cover until Chapter 8, "Loops." Nonetheless, you can easily learn what it does now, and you will be ready to use it in loops later. In addition, this exercise will give you some good practice working with variables.

In its simplest form, the `shift` command moves parameter variables "down" in the set of positional parameter variables. That is, what was in variable 2 becomes variable *1*, what was in variable *3* becomes variable 2, and so on.

The `shift` command is usually used in scripts or functions when one part of the program "uses up" some of the parameter variables but another part of the program doesn't have a good way of knowing which variable is "next." In this case, the first part of the program shifts away the parameter variables it has dealt with, leaving the rest of the program to start with the "next" parameter in variable 1.

Use `set` to give the values *red, white,* and *blue* to positional parameters *1* through *3*. Print `$#` and `$@`, run the `shift` command, and print `$#` and `$@` again. Repeat the shift and print commands three more times.

a) What happens to the variable *1* each time you run `shift`?

Note that the `set` command in this exercise totally replaces the values of all the special variables and positional parameter variables. Whatever was left in them from the previous exercise is completely gone.

You can shift away more than one parameter variable at a time by specifying a number as a parameter to the `shift` command.

Set the positional parameters to the seven colors of the rainbow in the order *red, orange, yellow, green, blue, indigo,* and *violet.* Use a single `shift` command to get rid of *red, orange,* and *yellow,* then print what's left.

b) What commands did you use, and what was the result?

You should now have four colors left in your parameter variables. Try to shift away five variables.

c) What happens if you try to shift away more parameter variables than there are?

LAB 5.1 ANSWERS

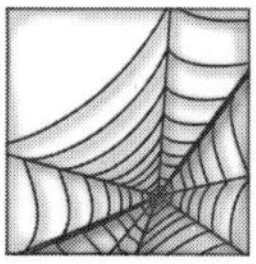

This section gives you some suggested answers to the questions in Lab 5.1, with discussion related to those answers. Your answers may vary, but the most important thing is whether or not your answer works. Use this discussion to analyze differences between your answers and those presented here.

If you have alternative answers to the questions in this exercise, you are encouraged to post your answers and to discuss them at the companion web site for this book, located at:

```
http://www.phptr.com/phptrinteractive/
```

5.1.1 ANSWERS

a) Print the values of *PATH* and *FPATH*. Are your `~/bin` and `~/fun` directories in them?

Answer: Depending on the path of your home directory, your interaction should look something like the following:

```
[5001]: print $PATH
... :/home/vickery/bin: ...
[5002]: print $FPATH
... :/home/vickery/fun: ...
[5003]:
```

Both *PATH* and *FPATH* are lists of directories separated by colons, and each should have the path to your `bin` and `fun` directories somewhere in them.

b) Make `s511` executable, use `cat`, `more`, or `less` (your choice) to show its contents, and run it. What is your output?

```
[5003]: vi ~/bin/s511
<Edit the file>
[5004]: chmod +x ~/bin/s511
[5005]: cat ~/bin/s511
print This is script s511
[5006]:
```

The file contains just one line of code, the `print` statement.

You could put the pathname of the program to run the script (`ksh`), in the first line of your scripts using "she-bang" notation (see the Glossary), but as long as you run your scripts from an interactive KornShell session, there is no need to do this for KornShell scripts because the shell will run the script just fine without it. In fact, it takes longer to run scripts using she-bang because a whole new copy of `ksh` has to be loaded into memory for execution.

c) Run `s511`. What is your output?

Answer: Your output should look like the following:

```
[5006]: s511
This is script s511
[5007]:
```

If the script doesn't run as expected, check that your PATH contains the directory where you put the script, and that the script has execute permission.

Write a function named `f511` and put a command that prints "`This is function f511.`" in it. Put a command that prints "`This is file fun/f511`" *after* the function definition in the same file.

Run the following command:

```
whence -a f511
```

d) What does the shell know about the function?

Answer: The shell reports that it is an undefined function. Your interaction should look something like the following:

```
[5007]: vi ~/fun/f511
<Edit the file>
[5008]: cat ~/fun/f511
function f511 {
  print This is function f511
  }
print This is file fun/f511
[5009]: whence -a f511
f511 is an undefined function
[5010]:
```

The shell does not use *FPATH* to find functions the way it uses `PATH` to find scripts. The shell can find a file named `f511` in one of the directories in your *FPATH* (`~/fun`), and it can verify that the file contains a function with the name `f511`, but until you execute the function the first time, the shell does not "dot" the file, so the function is not yet defined.

e) Run the function, run the `whence -a f511` command again, then run the function again. Explain the results.

Answer: Your interaction should look like the following:

```
 [5010]: f511
This is file fun/f511
This is function f511
[5011]: whence -a f511
f511 is a function
[5012]: f511
This is function f511
[5013]:
```

The first time you run an undefined function, the shell looks for a file with the same name in each of your *FPATH* directories and "dots" the file (runs the file as a script in the context of the interactive shell). The file does not have to be executable for this. Your script, `~/fun/f511`, contains both a function definition and a `print` statement, so the function becomes defined and the first line you see after line 5010 prints. Then the shell runs the newly defined function, leading to the second output line after line 5010. The `whence` command on line 5011 shows that the function is now defined, and line 5012 shows that the shell runs the function without dotting the definition file again.

You could delete `~/fun/f511` now and still use the `f511` function because the shell stores a copy of the function definition in its own memory and does not need the file any more. However, the shell does not remember function definitions across sessions, so if you log out and back in again, you would have to redefine the function. Chapter 1, "Setting Up," covered setting up your environment so that commands, such as ones that define functions you always want to use, get run automatically every time you log in.

5.1.2 ANSWERS

Create a script named `s512`. Put a `print` statement in it that prints references to the variables named *1-10*.

a) Print the script, then run it with your name as parameters, and explain the results.

Answer: Your interaction should look something like the following:

```
[5013]: cat ~/bin/s512
print $1 $2 $3 $4 $5 $6 $7 $8 $9 ${10}
[5014]: s512 Your Name
Your Name
[5015]:
```

Only the variables named *1* and *2* have been assigned values, so all the others produce empty strings.

Double-Check: *If the output is something like "Your Name Your0," it means you forgot to put braces around the reference to variable 10, and the shell interpreted it as a reference to variable 1, followed by the character 0. It's a lot easier not to type in the braces, but when they are needed, there is no way around it.*

b) Now run the script again, but with each of the letters of the alphabet as parameters. Explain these results.

Answer: Your interaction should look like the following:

```
[5015]: s512 a b c d e f g h i j k l m n o p q r s t \
u v w x y z
a b c d e f g h i j
[5016]:
```

Only the first 10 parameters are printed because that's as many as were referenced in the `print` command. The other letters were passed and are available, but there are no references to them in this script.

Create a function named `f512` with the same `print` statement in it as `s512` has. Run it twice, once with your name and once with the letters of the alphabet as parameters.

c) Is there any difference between running the function and running the script?

Answer: Your interactions should look like the following:

```
[5016]: f512 Your Name
Your Name
[5018]: f512 a b c d e f g h i j k l m n o p q r s t \
u v w x y z
a b c d e f g h i j
[5017]:
```

There's no difference between the script and the function, as far as positional parameters are concerned. One major difference between scripts and functions is that the shell processes functions more efficiently than scripts. The other major difference is that functions are run in the same context as the shell, whereas scripts run as separate processes. That is, running a function is like dotting a script.

5.1.3 ANSWERS

Create a script named `s513` that prints each of these variables, and run it using the following commands:

```
s513 hello 123
s513 There are four words.
```

a) What did you observe?

Answer: Your interactions should something like the following:

```
[5017]: cat ~/bin/s513
print '$# is ' $#
print '$@ is ' $@
print '$* is ' $*
[5018]: s513 hello 123
$# is 2
$@ is hello 123
$* is hello 123
[5019]: s513 There are four words.
$# is  4
$@ is  There are four words.
$* is  There are four words.
[5021]:
```

Line 5017 shows the contents of the script file. Note the single quotes around the first part of each `print` command. If they weren't there, the shell would evaluate the references to `#`, `@`, and `*` instead of passing the characters `$#`, and so forth, to `print` for printing.

The two command lines show that `$#` is set to 2 when there are two parameters (*hello* and *123*), and to 4 when there are four parameters (*There, are, four,* and *words.*). For both command lines, the values of `$@` and `$*` are the same—all the parameters on the command line.

Pass your name as a single parameter to `s513` with five spaces between your first and last names. Verify that it was received as a single value. *Hint:* Use quotes.

b) What command did you use? Were the spaces preserved?

Answer: The command line and output should look like the following:

```
[5021]: s513 "Your     Name"
```

```
$# is 1
$@ is Your Name
$* is Your Name
[5022]:
```

First, note that the value of # is 1. By putting "`Your     Name`" in quotes, it was passed as a single parameter to the script.

However, there is only *one* space between your first and last names in the output. What's happening here is that references to `@` and `*` expand to your name with the five spaces in between, but there are no quotes in this expansion, so the `print` statement is receiving your first and last names as two separate parameters. The extra blanks are squeezed out (by the shell) before the `print` commands get to run.

Run a `print` command *from the command line* that prints your name. Put five spaces between your first and last names, and don't use any quotes.

c) Explain how this item relates to the previous one.

Answer: Your interaction should look like the following:

```
[5022]: print Your     Name
Your Name
[5023]:
```

This print statement is equivalent to the print statement executed inside `s513` in the previous statement. The spaces between your first and last names are not passed to the `print` command, which prints each of the arguments it receives, separated by a single space.

Now run a `print` command from the command line that prints your name. Put five spaces between your first and last names, and *do* put double quotes around your name.

d) Explain how this item relates to Question *b*.

Answer: Your interaction should look like the following:

```
[5023]: print "Your     Name"
Your     Name
[5024]:
```

The quotes have to appear in the `print` command in order to preserve the spacing in the output. For this exercise, that means we have to modify the script to provide the quotes.

Now modify `s513` so that each of the variable references is enclosed in quotes. Run `s513` with your name, including the extra spaces, inside quotes.

e) What did you observe?

Answer: Your interaction should look like the following:

```
[5024]: vi ~/bin/s513
<Edit the script>
[5025]: cat ~/bin/s513
print '$# is ' "$#"
print '$@ is ' "$@"
print '$* is ' "$*"
[5026]: s513 "Your      Name"
$# is 1
$@ is Your      Name
$* is Your      Name
[5027]: s513 'Your      Name'
$# is 1
$@ is Your      Name
$* is Your      Name
[5028]:
```

Line 5025 shows the revised script. Note the use of double quotes around the variable references; if you had used single quotes, the variables would not have been expanded.

The second `print` command in the script, after variable substitution, would look like this:

```
print '$@ is ' "Your      Name"
```

That is, the shell will pass two parameters to the `print` command (after removing the quotation marks from them). The first parameter consists of the six characters `-$-@- -i-s- -` and the second one consists of the 13 characters `-Y-o-u-r- - - - - -N-a-m-e-`.

For this script, it doesn't matter whether you use single or double quotes on the command line, but it does matter inside the script.

Use single quotes where you want to prevent the shell from evaluating what look like variable references, use either single or double quotes where you want the shell to preserve spaces inside a parameter, and use double quotes where you want the shell to do variable substitution.

5.1.4 ANSWERS

Run this command from the command line to print the values of the three special variables #, @, and *:

```
print $#: $@: $*
```

a) Is the variable # defined? How many parameters were passed to `ksh` when it started running?

Answer: Yes, # is defined, and its value is 0. Your interaction should look like the following:

```
[5028]: print $#: $@: $*
0: :
[5029]:
```

Note the colon (:) immediately after the 0 in the output. That's what tells us the zero is the value of `$#` rather than one of the other parameters, which are both empty strings. (Note the position of the colons in the print command line.)

Use a `set` command to set the positional parameters to the message, `My name is "Your     Name."` Use quotes so your first and last name, separated by five spaces, will be one parameter value.
Print the values of the special variables #, @, and *. (Use separate `print` commands.)

b) What are the values of the three variables now?

Answer: # is 4, and the four arguments are "`My`*", "*`name`*", "*`is`*", and "*`Your Name`*". Your interaction should look like the following:*

```
[5029]: set -- My name is "Your     Name."
[5030]: print $#
4
[5031]: print "$@"
My name is Your     Name.
[5032]: print "$*"
```

```
My name is Your     Name.
[5033]:
```

This question confirms that the `set` command can be used to give values to positional parameter variables that you can reference using #, @, and *.

You should know how the output would have been different if you did not put quotes around $@ and $ in the `print` command. If not, you need to review the previous exercise.*

Putting a double dash after the `set` command name is a good habit to get into so you won't get tripped up when the first parameter looks like an option paramter.

Now run `s513` using `$@` as a parameter and again using `$*`. Do *not* put any quotes in your command line.

c) How many positional parameter variables are passed in both cases, and what are their values?

Answer: Both `$@` and `$*` are passed as five arguments, the words My, name, is, Your, *and* Name. *Your interaction should look like the following:*

```
[5033]: s513 $@
$# is 5
$@ is  My name is Your Name
$* is  My name is Your Name
[5034]: s513 $*
$# is 5
$@ is  My name is Your Name
$* is  My name is Your Name
[5035]:
```

The value of variable 4 for the command line has been split into two values when passed to the script. Note also that the five spaces between *Your* and *Name* have been reduced to one.

Finally, to see the difference between @ and *, repeat the last two commands, but put `$@` and `$*` inside double quotes. Note the number of parameters passed and how the spaces between your first and last names are handled.

d) What is the difference between these two special variables?

Answer: The difference is that a reference to `$@` *inside double quotes is passed as separated arguments, but a reference to* `$*` *inside double quotes is passed as a single argument.*

Your interaction should look like the following:

```
[5035]: s513 "$@"
$# is 4
$@ is  My name is Your      Name
$* is  My name is Your      Name
[5036]: s513 "$*"
$# is 1
$@ is  My name is Your      Name
$* is  My name is Your      Name
[5037]:
```

Now `"$@"` is passed as *four* variables, but `"$*"` is passed as *one* variable. The spaces inside parameter *4* are preserved in both cases.

Summary: *If you want to pass positional parameters to a script with embedded spaces preserved, put double quotes around the references to @ and *. If you want to preserve embedded spaces and pass the positional parameters as separate values, use "$@", but if you want to pass a* single *parameter containing* all *the positional parameters, use "$*". You will find this distinction most useful when you are using loops, which will be covered in Chapter 8, "Loops."*

5.1.5 ANSWERS

Use `set` to give the values *red, white,* and *blue* to positional parameter variables *1* through *3*. Print `$#` and `$@`, run the `shift` command, and print `$#` and `$@` again. Repeat the `shift` and `print` commands three more times.

a) What happens to variable `1` each time you run *shift*?

Answer: Variable `1`*, containing the left-most parameter, is discarded and replaced by the value of the next parameter to the right each time.*

Your interaction should look like the following:

```
[5037]: set red white blue
[5038]: print $#: $@
```

```
3: red white blue
[5039]: shift
[5040]: print $#: $@
2: white blue
[5041]: shift
[5042]: print $#: $@
1: blue
[5043]: shift
[5044]: print $#: $@
0
[5045]:
```

Command number 5037 assigns the values *red, white,* and *blue* to positional parameter variables *1, 2,* and *3.* Then the `print` command on line 5038 confirms that there are three variables with the values specified. The first `shift` command on line 5039 removes *red,* leaving two parameters, *white* and *blue,* as the `print` command on line 5040 confirms. At this point, the value of variable `1` is *white,* and the value *red* has been lost.

Set the positional parameters to the seven colors of the rainbow in the order *red, orange, yellow, green, blue, indigo,* and *violet.* Use a single `shift` command to get rid of *red, orange,* and *yellow,* and then print what's left.

b) What commands did you use, and what was the result?

Answer: The four colors green, blue, indigo, *and* violet *should remain after running the following commands.*

```
[5045]: set red orange yellow green blue indigo violet
[5046]: shift 3
[5047]: print $@
green blue indigo violet
[5048]:
```

The `set` command replaces all parameter variables with the seven values shown and sets the special variable # to 7. Shifting away three variables (line 5046) leaves the four shown by the `print` command.

c) What happens if you try to shift away more variables than there are?

Answer: The shell reports a "bad number" error, as the following interaction illustrates:

```
[5048]: shift 5
ksh: shift: 5: bad number
[5049]: shift 4
```

```
[5050]: print $#: $@
0:
[5051]:
```

You can shift all the parameter variables away, but not more than there are. Line 5049 shows that you can shift four variables away, and line 5050 shows that the variable # is now 0, and that the variable @ is now empty.

LAB 5.1 SELF-REVIEW QUESTIONS

To test your progress, you should be able to answer the following questions. At this point, you should be able to pass parameters to functions or scripts and to access those parameters from within a function or script.

1) What would be the value of the variable # inside `myfunc` when the following command line is run:

```
myfunc 12345
```

a) _____The empty string.
b) _____0
c) _____1
d) _____2
e) _____5

2) Assume `myfunc` is defined in a file named `~/fun/myfunc`. What happens the first time you run a `myfunc` command?
a) _____The shell prints a "not found" error message.
b) _____The shell executes `~/bin/myfunc`.
c) _____The shell executes `~/fun/myfunc`.
d) _____The shell executes `~/fun/myfunc` then executes the newly defined function.
e) _____The shell executes `~/bin/myfunc` then executes `~/fun/myfunc`.

3) Again assuming `myfunc` is defined in a file named `~/fun/myfunc`, what happens the second time you run a `myfunc` command?

a) _____Nothing, because the shell knows it has already executed this file.

b) _____Nothing, because the shell knows it has already executed this function.

c) _____Nothing, because the shell knows it has already executed `~/bin/myfunc`.

d) _____The shell executes `~/fun/myfunc` then executes the newly defined function.

e) _____The shell executes the already-defined function, `myfunc`.

4) After running `myfunc` the first time, you can modify or delete `~/fun/myfunc` and the shell will continue to use the definition it found the first time you ran it.

a) _____True

b) _____False

5) What is the difference between using `"$@"` and `"$*"` as a parameter to a command?

a) _____There is no difference because they are both in quotes.

b) _____The positional parameters will be passed as separate values using `"$@"`, but will be passed as a single value using `"$*"`.

c) _____The positional parameters will be passed as separate values using `"$*"`, but will be passed as a single value using `"$@"`.

d) _____`"$@"` reverses the order of the parameters, but `"$*"` does not.

e) _____`"$*"` reverses the order of the parameters, but `"$@"` does not.

6) What is the difference between using `$@` and `$*` as a parameter to a command?

a) _____There is no difference because neither is in quotes.

b) _____The positional parameters will be passed as separate values using `$@`, but will be passed as a single value using `$*`.

c) _____The positional parameters will be passed as separate values using `$*`, but will be passed as a single value using `$@`.

d) _____`$@` reverses the order of the parameters, but `$*` does not.

e) _____`$*` reverses the order of the parameters, but `$@` does not.

7) What will the following sequence of commands print?

```
set All good boys deserve fudge.
shift $#
print $#
```

a) _____Nothing
b) _____0
c) _____5
d) _____6
e) _____A "bad number" error message.

Quiz answers appear in Appendix A, Section 5.1.

LAB 5.2

PROCESSING OPTION PARAMETERS

LAB OBJECTIVES

After this lab, you will be able to:

- ✓ Use the `getopts` Command
- ✓ Use the *OPTIND* Variable
- ✓ Use the *OPTARG* Variable
- ✓ Customize `getopts` Error Messages

The shell provides a number of variables that you can use along with the built-in `getopts` command to find out what option parameters and arguments were passed to a script or function. Option processing is usually done using one of the control structures covered in Chapter 8, "Loops," so this lab's goal is to introduce you just to the `getopts` command and associated variables. You will learn the standard ways to do option processing after you have learned about the shell's control structures.

BACKGROUND FOR THIS LAB

The shell does not differentiate between option parameters and positional parameters in a command line. It simply passes everything between the command name and the end of the command (except I/O redirection) to the command, and it is up to the command to decide what to do with each of the parameters. Because the first parameters passed to most commands are options, programmers have to write virtually the same code to process the options for every different command or script that they work on. This is not only wasted duplication of effort, it leads to different commands having different rules for the proper syntax of the options: Can you put several option letters after one dash, or do you have to use a separate dash for each one? Does there have to be a space between an option letter and an argument that follows it? When the POSIX standard for shell programs and utilities was developed, it included a specification for the proper syntax for option parameters. To encourage programmers to adopt the standard, the `getopts` command was developed for use in shell scripts, and a corresponding function named `getopt()` was developed for C/C++ programmers. The `getopts` command doesn't do all the work of processing options, but it makes it easy to process them in the standard way.

Just to make things interesting, many UNIX systems provide a `getopt` *command (no 's' at the end) that does something similar to the* `getopts` *command. The* `getopt` *command is obsolete, but the* `getopt()` *function for C/C++ is not!*

Most UNIX systems have an external command named `getopts`, probably in the `/bin` directory. For efficiency, the KornShell also provides a built-in version that works the same way as the external one.

LAB 5.2 EXERCISES

5.2.1 USE THE `getopts` COMMAND

The `getopts` command takes (at least) two parameters, a list of option letters, and the name of a variable. When it runs, it puts the next option that it finds in the parameter variables into the variable named in the command.

FOR EXAMPLE

The following interaction illustrates using `getopts` from the command line:

```
[5051]: set -- -vu -do hello
[5052]: getopts douv optletter
[5053]: print $optletter
v
[5054]: getopts douv optletter
[5055]: print $optletter
u
[5056]: getopts douv optletter
[5057]: print $optletter
d
[5058]: getopts douv optletter
[5059]: print $optletter
o
[5060]:
```

You usually use `getopts` inside a script or function, but we will use the example as a model for experimenting with the `getopts` command by running it interactively.

a) What is the purpose of the double dash (`--`) on line 5051?

---

b) What would be output if you printed a reference to the special variables # and @ between lines 5051 and 5052?

---

c) Write a `set` command that would be equivalent to line 5051 but would use just two parameters instead of three.

---

d) Write another `set` command that would be equivalent to line 5051 but would use five parameters.

---

e) What would happen to *optletter* if the *getopts* command were run again?

5.2.2 USE THE *OPTIND* VARIABLE

The `getopts` command keeps track of which option parameter it is processing by means of a variable named *OPTIND* ("option index"). Each time `getopts` finishes with the option letters in a parameter, it adds one to the value of *OPTIND*, which means that when you finish processing a command or function's options, *OPTIND* will be the index of the first positional parameter on the command line.

a) What are the values of *OPTIND* and `@` after completing the previous exercise?

You can assign a value to *OPTIND*, and the next time you run `getopts`, it will start looking for option letters in the parameter number that you assigned to *OPTIND*. Almost always, you assign the value *1* to *OPTIND* because you want to process the options over again from the beginning. But you can use any number you want, depending on the nature of the program you are writing.

b) Set *OPTIND* to *1* and show that this lets you process the options over again from the beginning.

A script or function normally goes through two phases. In the first phase it uses `getopts` to process the option parameters. In the second phase, it processes the positional parameters. Because the second phase doesn't know how many option parameters there were, it is convenient to do a `shift` that puts the first positional parameter into parameter variable number *1*.

FOR EXAMPLE

After processing the option parameters in the example, we would like to shift `hello`, which is in parameter *3*, into positional parameter *1*.

Hint: You can do arithmetic in the parameter you pass to `shift`.

c) Write a `shift` command that uses *OPTIND* to put `hello` in parameter *1*, and verify that it works.

5.2.3 USE THE OPTARG VARIABLE

If an option requires an argument, put a colon (:) after its letter in the list you give to `getopts`, and `getopts` will automatically put the corresponding argument in the variable *OPTARG*. This variable is defined only after you run `getopts` *and* the option letter is one that had an argument.

Run the following commands:

```
set -- -c -b b_arg -a hello
OPTIND=1
```

a) What is the reason for assigning the value 1 to *OPTIND?*

Now run the following pair of commands three times

```
getopts ab:c optletter
print $OPTIND: $optletter $OPTARG
```

b) What is printed each time?

5.2.4 CUSTOMIZE getopts ERROR MESSAGES

A particularly valuable feature of `getopts` is that it automatically generates meaningful error messages if the user types in an invalid command line.

FOR EXAMPLE

If the user types an option letter that is not among those specified in the `getopts` command, it automatically prints an error message telling what option letter was unrecognized:

```
$ set -- -p
$ OPTIND=1
$ getopts abcdefghijklmnoqrstuvwxyz optletter
ksh: -p: unknown option
```

This `getopts` command accepts any lowercase option letter except `p`, which just happens to be the one specified in the `set` command. The error message tells the user exactly what option caused the problem.

```
set -- -a -b
OPTIND=1
getopts ab: optletter
```

a) What error message is displayed?

____

____

Write a script named `s524` that contains just the command `getopts ab: optletter`, and run it with command line of `s524 -a -b`.

b) What is the difference between the error message that prints now, compared with the previous one?

____

____

You can customize the error message by providing a string that describes argument values for the user. For example, if the user is supposed to provide a "bucket name" as the argument to the `-b` option you could code the `getopts` command as:

```
getopts ab:[bucket_name] optletter
```

Replace the `getopts` command in your `s524` script with the one above, and run it again without giving an argument after the `-b` option.

c) What error message did you get now?

____

____

LAB 5.2 ANSWERS

This section gives you some suggested answers to the questions in Lab 5.2, with discussion related to those answers. Your answers may vary, but the most important thing is whether or not your answer works. Use this discussion to analyze differences between your answers and those presented here.

If you have alternative answers to the questions in this exercise, you are encouraged to post your answers and to discuss them at the companion web site for this book, located at:

`http://www.phptr.com/phptrinteractive/`

5.2.1 ANSWERS

a) What is the purpose of the double dash (--) on line 5051?

Answer: It marks the end of the options to the set command, and the beginning of the parameters for it.

If the double dash were missing, `set` would interpret `-vu` and `-do` as its own options, and you would get an error message because `-d` is not a valid option for `set`.

b) What would be output if you printed a reference to the special variables # and @ between lines 5051 and 5052?

Answer: You would see the number 3 and the values of the three parameters, like the following interaction:

```
[5051a] print $#: $@
3: -vu -do hello
[5052]:
```

There are four options, but the user chose to write them as two parameters. The third parameter doesn't start with a dash, so it does not contain any options.

c) Write a `set` command that would be equivalent to line 5051 but would use just two parameters.

Answer: You could use `-vudo`*, as shown in the following command line. The remainder of the interaction would be identical to what was given in the example:*

```
[5051]: set -- -vudo hello
```

d) Write another `set` command that would be equivalent to line 5051 but would use five parameters.

Answer: You would use `-v -u -d -o`*, as shown in the following command line. Again, the remainder of the interaction would be identical to what was given in the example:*

```
[5051]: set -- -v -u -d -o hello
```

e) What would happen to `optletter` if the `getopts` command were run again?

Answer: It would be set to a question mark (?), as the following interaction shows:

```
[5060]: getopts -douv optletter
[5061]: print $optletter
?
[5062]:
```

In this example, when `getopts` sees `hello` with no dash at the beginning, it knows there are no more options and will set *optletter* to the question mark, no matter how many more times it is called.

The important thing to see here is that successive calls to `getopts` *return successive options in optletter. Even though you run exactly the same command line, the command behaves differently. The implication is that the command has a way of keeping track of which of the options it has already processed. Can you figure out how this is done? (Hints: (1) it can't be done inside the shell, because the external* `getopts` *command works the same way as the built-in command, and (2) this is a chapter on* variables.*) You will see the answer in the next exercise.*

5.2.2 Answers

a) What are the values of *OPTIND* and @ after completing the previous exercise?

Answer: OPTIND *is 3, and* @ has the three values, -vu, -do, and hello, *as shown by the following interaction:*

```
[5062]: print $OPTIND: $@
3: -vu -do hello
[5063]:
```

Note that the value of *OPTIND* (3) is the index of the first positional parameter, hello.

b) Set *OPTIND* to *1* and show that this lets you process the options over again from the beginning.

Answer:Your interaction should look like the following:

```
[5063]: OPTIND=1
[5064]: getopts douv optletter
[5065]: print $optletter
v
[5066]: getopts douv optletter]
[5067]: print $optletter
u
[5068]: getopts douv optletter
[5069]: print $optletter
d
[5070]: getopts douv optletter
[5071]: print $optletter
o
[5072]: print $OPTIND: $@
3: -vu -do hello
[5073]:
```

If you had set *OPTIND* to 2, you could have started with the -d option instead of -v.

c) Write a `shift` command that uses *OPTIND* to put `hello` in parameter *1*, and verify that it works.

Answer: You have to subtract one from the value of OPTIND, as the following interaction shows:

```
[5073]: shift OPTIND-1
[5074]: print $1
hello
[5075]:
```


The nice thing about line 5073 is that the same statement would put the first positional parameter into the variable *1,* regardless of how many options the user gave on the command line of the script (or in the `set --` command in our example) and regardless of how many options were put after each dash.

5.2.3 ANSWERS

a) What is the reason for assigning the value 1 to *OPTIND?*

Answer: The previous exercise may have left OPTIND at a value other than 1.

The `set` command has no effect on *OPTIND*; it just sets the values of all the parameter variables.

Now run the following pair of commands three times:

```
getopts ab:c optletter
print $OPTIND: $optletter $OPTARG
```

b) What is printed each time?

Answer: Your interaction should look like the following:

```
[5075]: set -- -a -b b_arg -c hello
[5076]: OPTIND=1
[5077]: getopts ab:c optletter
[5078]: print $OPTIND: $optletter $OPTARG
2: a
[5079]: getopts ab:c optletter
[5080]: print $OPTIND: $optletter $OPTARG
4: b b_arg
[5081]: getopts ab:c optletter
[5082]: print $OPTIND: $optletter $OPTARG
```

```
5: c
[5083]: getopts ab:c optletter
[5084]: print $OPTIND: $optletter $OPTARG
5: ?
[5085]:
```


Here you can see that *OPTIND* is stepping along through the parameters, skipping number *3,* because that was the position of the argument for the -b option. Also, note that line 5080 is the only one that prints a non-empty value for *OPTARG*. Whenever an option is followed by an argument, *OPTARG* is set to the value of the argument, but when an option does not have an argument, `getopts` unsets the value of *OPTARG*, so it prints as an empty string in those cases.

5.2.4 ANSWERS

Run the following commands:

```
set -- -a -b
OPTIND=1
getopts ab: optletter
```

a) What error message is displayed?

Answer: The shell says that an argument was expected following the `-b` *option, as the following interaction shows:*

```
[5085]: set -- -a -b
[5086]: OPTIND=1
[5087]: getopts ab: optletter
[5088]: getopts ab: optletter
ksh: -b: argument expected
[5089]:
```

Line 5087 doesn't cause a problem because `-a` doesn't take an argument, so it is recognized and accepted by `getopts`. However, when line 5088 is run, `getopts` finds the `-b` option with no argument after it and generates the error message shown. If you don't know what the `ksh:` at the beginning of the error message is, the next question will explain it.

Write a script named `s524` that contains just the command `getopts ab: optletter`, and run it with command line of `s524 -a -b`.

b) What is the difference between the error message that prints now, compared with the previous one?

Answer: It begins with `s524` *instead of* `ksh:`*, as the following interaction shows:*

```
[5089]: cat bin/s524
getopts ab: optletter
[5090]: s524 -b
s524: -b: argument expected
[5091]:
```

The error messages that `getopts` prints start with the name of the command that caused the error, followed by the option letter that was in error, and finally by an explanation of the problem.

(1) You can print your own command's name by referencing the special variable 0. Unlike variables 1 and beyond, you can't change the value of 0, but you can reference it. (2) If $0 shows the full pathname of the command and you want just the name of the command itself, check out Lab 10.3 to see how to get rid of the part you don't want.

```
getopts ab:[bucket_name] optletter
```

Replace the `getopts` command in your `s524` script with the one above, and run it again without giving an argument after the `-b` option.

c) What error message did you get now?

Answer: Your interaction should look like the following:

```
[5091]: cat bin/s524
getopts ab:[bucket_name] optletter
[5092]: s524 -b
s524: -b: bucket_name argument expected
[5093]:
```

The string inside the brackets is printed between `-b:` and `argument expected`. You can format this string to say anything you like. If you want spaces or other special characters inside the string, you have to put the string (or the entire options parameter of the `getopts` command) inside quotes.

Be sure there are no spaces between the colon (:) and the square bracket ([ ). A space would mark the end of the first parameter to `getargs`*, and it would treat the bracket as an invalid name for the variable that is supposed to receive the value of the option.*

If you decide to provide an error message for an option that takes an argument, make sure it will make sense when printed before "argument expected."

LAB 5.2 SELF-REVIEW QUESTIONS

To test your progress, you should be able to answer the following questions.

1) What is the first parameter of a `getopts` command?

a) _____The name of a variable containing valid options.
b) _____A list of valid option letters.
c) _____The name of a variable that will receive an option letter as its value.
d) _____The number of valid option letters.
e) _____The name of the person to contact if there is a problem.

2) What is the second parameter of a `getopts` command?

a) _____The name of a variable containing valid options.
b) _____A list of valid option letters.
c) _____The name of a variable that will receive an option letter as its value.
d) _____The number of valid option letters.
e) _____The name of the person to contact if there is a problem.

3) How do you indicate option letters that must be followed by an argument?

a) _____Put a colon after the option letter in the first parameter of the `getopts` command.
b) _____Put the name of the argument inside square brackets in the first parameter of the `getopts` command.

c) _____Put a colon after the option letter in the second parameter of the `getopts` command.
d) _____Put the name of the argument inside square brackets in the second parameter of the `getopts` command.
e) _____Assign the value `3` to `OPTARG`.

4) How do you indicate an option letter that is *optionally* followed by an argument?
a) _____You can't do that using `getopts`.
b) _____Put the word *optional* in the third parameter of the `getopts` command.
c) _____Put the word *optional* in the second parameter of `getopts` command.
d) _____Put the word *optional* inside square brackets after the colon in the first parameter of the `getopts` command.
e) _____Put two colons, an ampersand, and three asterisks after the option letter in the first parameter of the `getopts` command.

5) What command causes `getopts` to start processing option parameters from the beginning?
a) _____There is no command that will do that.
b) _____Just run `getopts` again after it reaches the end of the option parameters.
c) _____`OPTARG=1`
d) _____`OPTINDEX=1`
e) _____`OPTIND=1`

Quiz answers appear in Appendix A, Section 5.2.

CHAPTER 5

TEST YOUR THINKING

The projects in this section are meant to have you utilize all of the skills that you have acquired throughout this chapter. The answers to these projects can be found at the companion web site to this book, located at:

`http://www.phptr.com/phptrinteractive/`

Visit the web site periodically to share and discuss your answers.

Consider the following three invocations of the shell's built-in `set` command:

```
set
set -o noclobber
set alpha beta gamma
```

1) First tell what these three commands do. Then assume that built-in commands work the same way as scripts and functions do, and tell what variables the `set` command would need to use to process each command properly.

2) Write a script or function that prints the first five parameters (either option parameters or positional parameters), one per line, with the parameter number at the beginning of the line.

As you will see in Chapter 7, "Basic Tests," the following command line inside a script will cause the script to terminate if the value of the variable `optletter` is a question mark:

```
[[ optletter == "?" ]] && return
```

3) Use a series of these command lines in a script that prints as many as the first five option letters passed to the function, one per line.

In Lab 10.3 you will see how to write code that behaves differently, based on whether a variable has been initialized to an empty string or has never been initialized at all. You will also see how to have the shell print an error message if a variable has not been initialized or if its value is the empty string.

4) Give an example of how this knowledge could help you to debug a script.

CHAPTER 6

ADVANCED VARIABLE USAGE

Integers, floats, locals, and arrays. Master these and you're on your way to great shell programs!

Chapter Objectives

In this chapter, you will learn about:

Now that you have seen how to use shell variables to hold values, you are ready for some advanced features the KornShell provides for working with variables efficiently and effectively. Until now, we have looked only at *string* values, but you can improve the efficiency of your programs and write more powerful scripts if you let the shell know which of your variables hold *numbers*, and you can further improve matters by differentiating between numbers that have fractions *(floats)* and numbers that don't have fractions *(integers)*.

In this chapter you will also learn how to work with groups of variables efficiently. The KornShell provides two types of arrays *(indexed* and *associative)* that let you create a list of values that you can access using either a number or a name. You will also learn how to group variables in a hierarchy rather than in list form in this chapter.

LAB 6.1

TYPED VARIABLES AND SCOPE

LAB OBJECTIVES

After this lab, you will be able to:

- ✓ Declare Variables and Assign Values
- ✓ Write Arithmetic Expressions
- ✓ Use Arithmetic Expansion
- ✓ Control the Scope of Variables

Before you start writing "real" scripts, it's a good idea to see some of the principles of using variables effectively. This lab will introduce two of them, *types* and *scoping*.

LAB 6.1 EXERCISES

6.1.1 DECLARE NUMERIC VARIABLES AND ASSIGN VALUES

The KornShell provides four different primitive types of variables for you to use. The most commonly used type has values that are *strings*, and they don't need to be "declared" in any way. Just assign a value to a variable, and the shell creates a string variable to receive the value.

FOR EXAMPLE

If you type the following command, or put it in a script or function, the shell will create a variable named `a_variable`, and will give it the value `123.456`.

```
a_variable=123.456
```

Even though the characters to the right of the equal sign are a number, `a_variable` is still a string variable. There is going to be a bit of confusion here, because you can treat the value as a number and do arithmetic with it, but the *type* of the variable is *string*. You will see the significance of this fact as this Lab progresses.

The shell provides two commands to declare that variables are going to hold numeric values instead of strings, and the commands have the same names as the two numeric data types that the shell can work with, `integer` and `float`. Integers can be positive, zero, or negative numbers, but they may not have fractions. Floats have fractions and can represent a larger range of values than do integers, but arithmetic operations using them are slower.

You will see the fourth type of variable, called a *name reference*, at the end of this exercise. First, though, we'll start with the numeric types, the integers and floats.

Once you declare a variable to hold numeric value, the shell will always make sure it contains a value of the proper type, even if you attempt to assign a different type of value to it.

Run the following commands:

```
integer i j k
float   x y z
i=3.5 j=4.9 k=99.999
x=3.5 y=4.9 z=99.999
print i=$i j=$j k=$k x=$x y=$y z=$z
```

a) What happens if you assign a value with a fraction to an integer?

____

____

Now run the following commands:

```
i=hello x="hello, world!"
print $i $x
```

b) What happens if you try to assign a string to a numeric variable?

____

____

Now run the following commands:

```
j=y z=k
print j=$j k=$k y=$y z=$z
```

c) What happens if you try to assign the value of an integer variable to a float variable, and vice versa?

____

____

Now run the following commands:

```
m=3.7 n=Howdy! i=$m j=$n x=$m y=$n
print m=$m n=$n i=$i j=$j x=$x y=$y
```

d) What happens if you assign the value of a string variable, such as *m* or *n*, to integer or float variables?

____

____

The `integer` and `float` commands are actually predefined aliases for special forms of the `typeset` built-in command. The full `typeset` commands allow you to control how variables' values are formatted, as well as what types of values they hold.

Run the following commands:

```
typeset -i i j k
typeset -F x y z
i=3.5 j=4.9 k=99.999
x=3.5 y=4.9 z=99.999
print i=$i j=$j k=$k x=$x y=$y z=$z
```

e) How do these results compare with the results in Question a?

____

____

You can specify a radix (numeric base) for displaying integers using `typeset`. The base must be specified as a (decimal) integer from base 2 to base 64. The default base (if not specified) is 10.

Run the following commands:

```
typeset -i2 i=20
typeset -i16 j=20
print i=$i j=$j
```

f) What number bases were used to display the values of `i` and `j`?

____

____

Now run the following two commands:

```
typeset -i i j
print i=$i j=$j
```

g) Does `typeset` affect the value of an integer, or just how it is displayed?

Now run the following commands:

```
typeset -F3 x=1.23456
print x=$x
typeset -F2 x
print x=$x
typeset -F9 x
print x=$x
```

h) What does the digit after the `F` do to the value, and how it is displayed?

There is one more point to make here. Run the following commands:

```
typeset -i x
typeset -F x
print x=$x
```

i) What effect does changing a variable from type `float` to type `integer` and back have on its value?

The fourth type of variable is called a *name reference*. You won't see any examples that really need name references in this book, but there is no reason that you can't learn how they work now. The idea of a name reference is that you can use it to set up two different names for the same variable.

You declare a variable to be a name reference with `typeset -n`.

Run the following commands:

```
typeset +n alpha beta gamma delta
typeset -n gamma=delta
alpha=bye
beta=bye
gamma=hello
delta=aloha
print   alpha=$alpha   beta=$beta   gamma=$gamma
  delta=$delta
```

j) What does the first `typeset` command accomplish?

____

____

k) What is printed?

____

____

6.1.2 WRITE ARITHMETIC EXPRESSIONS

You may not be too surprised to learn that the reason for having arithmetic variables is so that you can do arithmetic with their values. The rationale for doing arithmetic in scripts or functions will become more evident after you learn how to get the values for variables from files or by interacting with the user, which you will see in later chapters. For now, you can find how to perform arithmetic calculations while remaining in the rather contrived realm of using interactive commands to assign values and print results.

The KornShell provides two ways to write arithmetic expressions. One is to use a special built-in command, `let`, and the other is to enclose the expression you want to compute in double parentheses.

Watch the spacing when you write the double parentheses; there must be no space between the two opening parentheses or between the two closing parentheses.

Watch the quoting when you write the expressions using `let`*; the shell may attempt to expand some characters such as '*' (for multiplication) if you don't quote them.*

Run the following commands:

```
integer i=3 j=5 k=7
let i=i+j
(( j = j + k ))
print i=$i j=$j
```

a) In the `let` command, do the `i` and `j` on the right side of the equal sign represent characters, or are they references to variables?

____

____

b) In the double parentheses command, do the `j` and `k` on the right side of the equal sign represent characters, or are they references to variables?

____

____

c) In both the `let` and the double parentheses commands, what arithmetic operation is being performed?

____

____

d) What do you observe about the use of spaces inside the double parentheses command?

____

____

The KornShell provides a rich set of arithmetic operators derived primarily from the C language. The following questions will introduce you to a sampling of some of them.

Run the following commands:

```
i=3 j=5
(( k = i++ )) ; print i=$i k=$k
(( k = ++j )) ; print j=$j k=$k
```

e) What does the double plus do, and what difference does it make whether it comes before or after the name of a variable?

____

____

Run the following commands:

```
i=3 j=5 k=7
(( i = i * j + k )) ; print i=$i
i=3 j=5 k=7
(( i = i * (j + k) )) ; print i=$i
```

f) What is the asterisk used for in arithmetic expressions?

____

____

g) What are parentheses used for in arithmetic expressions?

____

____

Run the following commands:

```
i=3 j=5
(( i += j ))  ; print i=$i
(( i %= j ))  ; print i=$i
(( i <<= 5 )) ; print i=$i
```

h) What is += equivalent to?

____

____

i) What does the `%` operator compute?

____

____

j) What does the `<<` operator compute?

____

____

String variables can be used to hold arithmetic expressions.

Run the following commands:

```
unset m
i=3 j=5 k=7
m="i*j%k"
(( k = m )) ; print "m=$m k=$k"
```

k) What is the difference between referencing the variable *m* inside the double parentheses and outside them in the `print` command?

____

____

You also can use references to a set of mathematical functions in your arithmetic expressions:

- `abs` Absolute value
- `acos` Arc cosine
- `asin` Arc sine
- `atan` Arc tangent
- `cos` Cosine
- `cosh` Hyperbolic cosine
- `exp` Exponential (base *e*)
- `int` Integer part of a float value
- `log` Logarithm (base *e*)
- `sin` Sine
- `sinh` Hyperbolic sine
- `sqrt` Square root
- `tan` Tangent
- `tanh` Hyperbolic tangent

Run the following commands:

```
float x y z
(( x = sqrt(2) ))
(( y = log(100000)/log(10) ))
(( z = cos(3.14159) ))
print x=$x y=$y z=$z
```

l) What did you observe?

____

____

6.1.3 USE ARITHMETIC EXPANSION

You have already seen how the shell substitutes the value of a variable for a reference to it when you use the dollar sign (`$`) in front of the variable's name. You will see more powerful ways that the shell can do substitutions in Chapter 10, "Patterns, Expansions, and Substitutions," but this is a good place for you to see one of these mechanisms, called *arithmetic expansion*.

You can reference the *value* of an arithmetic expression by putting a dollar sign in front of the opening double parentheses.

Run the following command:

```
print -- $(( sqrt(2) ))
```

There must be no spaces between the dollar sign and the first open parenthesis, or you will get a syntax error message from the shell.

a) What printed?

You can use arithmetic expansion anywhere you would use a variable reference.

Run the following commands:

```
readonly float two_pi=$(( 2 * 3.141592654 ))
float theta=180
print -- $(( cos(theta / 360 * two_pi) ))
```

b) What printed?

c) What did the first command do?

---

d) What happens if you try to run the following command?

```
two_pi=3.141592654
```

You can do assignments inside an arithmetic expansion. If there is more than one, the value of the last one is the value of the expansion.

Run the following commands:

```
float x y=5 z=7

print --$((x = sqrt (y * z), y = x/2 = y * 4 )) $x $y $z
```

e) What two values are the same, and why?

---

f) If the two values are the same, why did they print differently?

6.1.4 Control the Scope of Variables

The *scope* of a variable refers to where the variable's name and associated value can be used. If you assign a value to a variable using an interactive command, you can reference the same variable inside a script, and you will get the value you assigned to it interactively. Likewise, if you change the value of the variable inside a script, then reference the variable from the command line, you will see that the value of the variable was changed inside the script.

On the other hand, you can use `typeset` to create variables inside a function that are different from variables with the same name that exist outside the function. You say that the *scope* of such variables is *local to the function* in which they are defined, or just that they are *local variables* for short. Variables that are not local are called *global variables*.

Local variables are especially good to use in big programs, where it gets difficult to keep track of what all the global variables are being used for. They are also a way to make sure that the variables you use in your functions do not accidentally clash with variables of the same name that a user might be using for some other purpose.

The variables OPTIND *and* OPTARG *(Lab 5.2) are good examples of variables that should be made local to your functions.*

Prepare the following script, and put it in the file `~/fun/f614`:

```
# f614 -- Examine the scopes of some variables

#  Global variables

x=3
integer y=5

#  A function with a local variable.
function f614_ksh {

x=abc
y=2.71828
integer z=7

  print Inside f614_ksh: x=$x y=$y z=$z

  }
```

```
#  A function with all global variables.
f614_posix() {

x=def
y=1.41421
integer z=7

  print Inside f614_posix: x=$x y=$y z=$z

  }
```

Now run the following sequence of commands:

```
unset x y z
float z=3.14159
. ~/fun/f614
print x=$x y=$y z=$z
f614_ksh
print x=$x y=$y z=$z
f614_posix
print x=$x y=$y z=$z
```

a) What does the `unset` command accomplish?

____

____

b) What does the `dot` command accomplish?

____

____

c) What is the effect of running `f614_ksh` on the value of *x*?

____

____

d) What is the effect of running `f614_ksh` on the value of *y*?

---

e) What is the effect of running `f614_ksh` on the value of *z*?

---

f) What is the difference between running `f614_ksh` and `f614_posix`?

The notions of "global" and "local" variables are relative terms that apply to variables defined or given values inside *functions*. However, inside *scripts*, variables are local by default.

Enter the same set of commands that you just ran from the command line into a script file named `~/bin/s614`, then run the following commands:

```
unset x y z
float z=99.99
s614
print x=$x y=$y z=$z
```

g) What are the values of `x`, `y`, and `z` after running the script?

You can *export* a copy of variables so that scripts can use their values, but this is not the same as making a variable global.

Create the following script in a file named `~/bin/export_test`:

```
# export_test -- Demonstrate the effects of exporting
  a variable

print -- Before assignment, the value of x is $x.
x=good-bye
print -- After assignment, the value of x is $x.
```

Now run the following commands:

```
unset x
export_test
print $x
x=hello
export_test
print $x
export x
export_test
print $x
```

h) What does exporting a variable do?

____

____

Functions and dot commands use *the same environment* as the shell from which they are invoked.

Run the following two commands:

```
unset x y z
. s614
print x=$x y=$y z=$z
```

i) How does dotting the script affect the values of the three variables?

____

____

LAB 6.1 ANSWERS

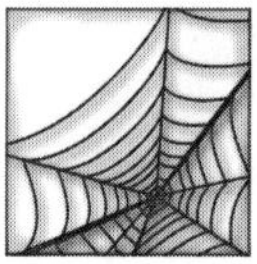

This section gives you some suggested answers to the questions in Lab 6.1, with discussion related to those answers. Your answers may vary, but the most important thing is whether or not your answer works. Use this discussion to analyze differences between your answers and those presented here.

If you have alternative answers to the questions in this exercise, you are encouraged to post your answers and to discuss them at the companion web site for this book, located at:

`http://www.phptr.com/phtprinteractive/`

6.1.1 ANSWERS

a) What happens if you assign a value with a fraction to an integer?

Answer: Your interaction should look like the following:

```
[6000]: integer i j k
[6001]: float   x y z
[6002]: i=3.5 j=4.9 k=99.999
[6003]: x=3.5 y=4.9 z=99.999
[6004]: print i=$i j=$j k=$k x=$x y=$y z=$z
i=3 j=4 k=99 x=3.5 y=4.9 z=99.999
[6005]:
```

The float variables, *x, y,* and *z* all retain their fractional parts, but no matter how large the fractional part of an integer variable, the shell silently drops the fractional part. The fraction is not rounded up, it is simply truncated. Also, because the range of a float variable is much larger than an integer variable, there is a possibility that integer overflow will occur, leaving the integer variable with an incorrect value.

The shell does not indicate when overflow occurs; it just leaves you with the wrong answer, so you need to be careful about this possibility when you write your code.

```
i=hello x="hello, world!"
print i=$i x=$x
```

b) What happens if you try to assign a string to a numeric variable?

Answer: Your interaction should look like the following:

```
[6005]: i=hello x="hello, world!"
ksh: hello, world!: arithmetic syntax error
[6006]: print i=$i x=$x
i=0 x=0
[6007]:
```

First, you see that you can assign the string "hello" to `i` (you could have assigned it to `x` too), but that you can't assign the string "hello, world!" to `x` (nor could you have assigned it to `i`), because the shell reports an "arithmetic syntax error." Question d will deal with the error message further.

For now, the important point is that whether the variable is an integer or a float, assigning a nonnumeric string makes the shell substitute the numeric value zero.

```
j=y z=k
print j=$j k=$k y=$y z=$z
```

c) What happens if you try to assign the value of an integer variable to a float variable, and vice versa?

Answer: Your interaction should look like the following:

```
[6007]: j=y z=k
[6008]: print j=$j k=$k y=$y z=$z
j=4 k=99 y=4.9 z=99
[6009]:
```

If you assign a float variable to an integer, the fraction part is truncated, and there is the possibility of arithmetic overflow. If you assign an integer variable to a float, the integer part is all there is to assign, so the fraction part of the result is zero; the integer value is preserved accurately.

```
m=3.7 n=Howdy! i=$m j=$n x=$m y=$n
print m=$m n=$n i=$i j=$j x=$x y=$y
```

d) What happens if you assign the value of a string variable, such as *m* or *n*, to integer or float variables?

Answer: Your interaction should look like the following:

```
[6009]: m=3.7 n=Howdy! i=$m j=$n x=$m y=$n
ksh: Howdy!: arithmetic syntax error
[6010]: print m=$m n=$n i=$i j=$j x=$x y=$y
m=3.7 n=Howdy! i=3 j=0 x=3.7 y=0
[6011]:
```

If, like *n*, the variable has a value that doesn't look like a number or a valid *arithmetic expression,* the shell assigns the value zero to the numeric variable and generates an error. (Arithmetic expressions are covered in the next exercise.) However if, like *m*, the variable has a value that looks like a number (or arithmetic expression), the shell assigns the value of that number to the numeric variable. If the string looks like a number with a fractional part and the variable receiving the value is an integer, the fraction part is lost.

Avoid mixing string and numeric variables in your assignments.

The shell is very flexible about letting you intermix string and numeric variables, which makes shell programming much easier to do than conventional programming languages like C, C++, and Java, in which every variable must have a declared data type, and the rules for what can be assigned to what are very rigid. The tradeoff is that it's relatively easy to make mistakes in shell programs if you forget what variables hold what types of values.

```
typeset -i i j k
typeset -F x y z
i=3.5 j=4.9 k=99.999
x=3.5 y=4.9 z=99.999
print i=$i j=$j k=$k x=$x y=$y z=$z
```

e) How do these results compare with the results in Question a?

Answer: Your interaction should look like the following:

```
[6011]: typeset -i i j k
[6012]: typeset -F x y z
```

```
[6013]: i=3.5 j=4.9 k=99.999
[6014]: x=3.5 y=4.9 z=99.999
[6015]: print i=$i j=$j k=$k x=$x y=$y z=$z
i=3    j=4    k=99    x=3.5000000000    y=4.9000000000
  z=99.9990000000
[6016]:
```

Except for the number of decimal places displayed for the floats, the values are the same. You'll see how to get finer control over the decimal places shortly.

```
typeset -i2 i=20
typeset -i16 j=20
print i=$i j=$j
```

f) What number bases were used to display the values of `i` and `j`?

Answer: Your interaction should look like the following:

```
[6016]: typeset -i2 i=20
[6017]: typeset -i16 j=20
[6018]: print i=$i j=$j
i=2#10100 j=16#14
[6019]:
```

The number after the `-i` is the radix that you want the shell to use when displaying the value of the integer. Decimal 20 in binary is 10100_2 (1*16 + 0*8 + 1*4 + 0*2 + 0*1), which the shell displays as `2#10100`. The hexadecimal representation of 20 is 14_{16} (1*16 + 4*1), which the shell displays as `16#14`. You can use numbers between 2 and 64 for the radix.

You can use the `radix#value` *notation on the right side of assignment statements if that is more natural for your particular program. The radix does not have to match the value (if there was any) given in the* `typeset -i` *command.*

```
typeset -i i j
print i=$i j=$j
```

g) Does `typeset` affect the value of an integer, or just how it is displayed?

Answer: Your interaction should look like the following:

```
[6019]: typeset -i i j
```

```
[6020]: print i=$i j=$j
i=20 j=20
[6021]:
```

The values of the two variables are both 20_{10}, regardless of the radix specified in the `typeset` command. In the code here, the `typeset` command takes away the radix specification for the two variables without changing their values. When you then print the variables, the shell uses the default radix, 10.

```
typeset -F3 x=1.23456
print x=$x
typeset -F2 x
print x=$x
typeset -F9 x
print x=$x
```

h) What does the digit after the `F` do to the value, and how it is displayed?

Answer: Your interaction should look like the following:

```
[6021]: typeset -F3 x=1.23456
[6022]: print x=$x
x=1.235
[6023]: typeset -F2 x
[6024]: print x=$x
x=1.23
[6025]: typeset -F9 x
[6026]: print x=$x
x=1.234560000
[6027]:
```

The digit after the `F` determines how many decimal places the shell will use when it prints the value of the variable. The number of places does not affect the value of the variable, only how it is displayed. Thus, for example, line 6022 shows that the shell rounds the displayed variable according to the normal rounding rules of arithmetic. Then line 6026 shows that the value of the variable was not changed, even after apparently truncating it on line 6023.

The "digit" after the `-F` can be any number you want, but the computer's accuracy is limited, so that too many digits will result in a lot of trailing zeros. Still, this is a valuable feature if you want to print columns of numbers that line up with one another.

```
typeset -i x
typeset -F x
print x=$x
```

i) What effect does changing a variable from type `float` to type `integer` and back have on its value (assuming that no overflow occurs)?

Answer: Your interaction should look like the following:

```
[6027]: typeset -i x
[6028]: typeset -F x
[6029]: print x=$x
x=1.0000000000
[6030]:
```

The fraction part got lost. There are ten zeros after the decimal point because that's the default number of places if you use `typeset -F` without giving a number.

The `float` command is actually an alias for `typeset -E`, which prints the value using scientific notation. Values larger than 9,999,999,999 or smaller than 0.00001 will print with the letter `e` (for "exponent"), followed by the exponent value. For example, 0.00001 prints as `1e-05`, which means "one times ten to the minus fifth power."

The `typeset` command has several options that give you control over how values will be printed. There is a complete list of them in Appendix B, "Built-In Command Reference."

```
typeset +n alpha beta gamma delta
typeset -n gamma=delta
alpha=hi
beta=bye
gamma=hello
delta=good-bye
print    alpha=$alpha    beta=$beta    gamma=$gamma    \
delta=$delta
```

j) What does the first `typeset` command accomplish?

Answer: It makes sure that there are no name references among the variables `alpha`, `beta`, `delta`, *and* `gamma`.

It's not likely that you have any name references, but if you start entering some of these commands and try to change something, you can get some difficult-to-understand errors. The `+n` turns "off" any name references you might already have set up, in much the same way that `set +o` can be used to turn off a shell option.

k) What printed?

Answer: Your interaction should look like the following:

```
[6030]: typeset +n alpha beta gamma delta
[6031]: typeset -n gamma=delta
[6032]: alpha=bye
[6033]: beta=bye
[6034]: gamma=hello
[6035]: delta=aloha
[6036]: print alpha=$alpha beta=$beta gamma=$gamma \
delta=$delta
alpha=bye beta=bye gamma=aloha delta=aloha
[6037]:
```

In this code, you assigned the value *aloha* to `delta` after assigning the value *hello* to `gamma`, so *aloha* is what shows up as the values for both `gamma` and `delta`. By using a name reference, you get to have two names for the same variable. You don't have two different variables with the same value, you have one variable with two names. Figure 6.1 should help make this concept clearer.

In Figure 6.1 the names of the variables are in the boxes on the left, and their values are in the boxes on the right. The names *alpha* and *beta* represent separate variables, each with its own value, but *gamma* and *delta* are two names that can be used to reference a single, shared value. You can't change the value of *gamma* without changing the value of *delta,* and vice versa.

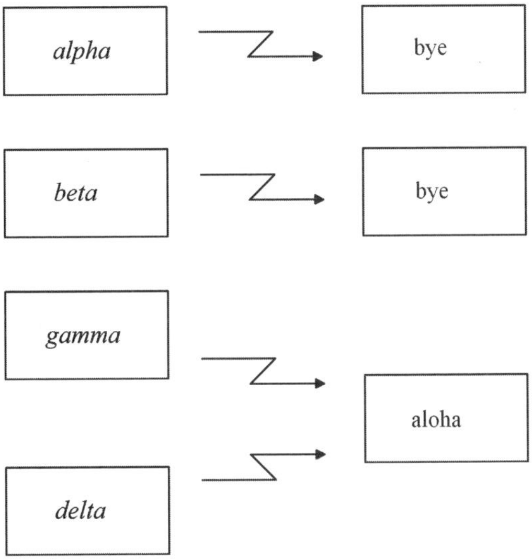

Figure 6.1

6.1.2 ANSWERS

```
integer i=3 j=5 k=7
let i=i+j
(( j = j + k ))
print i=$i j=$j
```

a) In the `let` command, do the `i` and `j` on the right side of the equal sign represent characters, or are they references to variables?

Answer: They are references to variables.

You are allowed to put in the dollar signs on the right of the equal sign if you want to, but you don't need to.

However, if you put a dollar sign in front of the variable name to the left of the equal sign, you will get an error message from the shell telling you "`assignment requires lvalue`*" because the shell will try to use the value of i as the name of the variable to receive the value of the assignment. An "*`lvalue`*" is something that makes sense to put on the left side of an equal sign, so it has to be the name of a variable.*

b) In the double parentheses command, do the `j` and `k` on the right side of the equal sign represent characters, or are they references to variables?

Answer: They are references to variables.

The shell doesn't require dollar signs in variable references in `let` and double parentheses commands because there is no ambiguity if you leave them out. Consider the following interaction:

```
meat=food
((potatoes=food))
print meat=$meat potatoes=$potatoes
meat=food potatoes=0
```

Even though neither *meat* nor *potatoes* is declared to be a numeric variable, the second assignment gives the value `zero` to *potatoes* because it is done in the context of an arithmetic expression. The first command interprets `food` as a value to be assigned to `meat` in the usual way, but you can't use the letters f-o-o-d as a number, so the shell interprets `food` as the name of a variable. Assuming that you haven't assigned any value to the variable named *food,* the shell quietly uses the value `zero`.

c) In both the `let` and the double parentheses commands, what arithmetic operation is being performed?

Answer: In both cases, the values of two variables are being added together.

If you have never written a computer program before, the statements may look like illogical equations; it would not make sense to say that something is equivalent to itself plus something else (unless, perhaps that something else is "nothing"). However, if you recognize the equal sign as the symbol for *assignment,* it should be clear that the two commands replace the current value of the variable on the left side of the equal sign with a new value that is computed using the arithmetic expression on the right side of the equal sign. Because of the timing (first compute the value on the right side, *then* assign it to the variable on the left side) it's perfectly legitimate to reference the original value of the variable to do the computation.

d) What do you observe about the use of spaces inside the double parentheses command?

Answer: It's all right to put spaces around the various parts of an arithmetic expression inside double parentheses.

The rule about no spaces in an assignment applies to `let` commands but not inside double parentheses. Because spaces make code easier to read, it's a good idea to use double parentheses instead of the `let` command. You can also use spaces in the expression part of a `let` command by putting the expression to the right of the equal sign in quotes, but by the time you type the word *let* and the quotes, you might as well type the double parentheses.

You can make multiple arithmetic assignments in one `let` *command line, just as you can do for nonarithmetic assignments. If you want to do the same thing inside double parentheses, separate the assignments with commas (,). The following three command lines are equivalent:*

```
let i=i+j  j=j+k
(( i = i + j )) (( j = j + k ))
(( i = i + j, j = j + k ))
```

Run the following commands:

```
i=3 j=5
(( k = i++ )) ; print i=$i k=$k
(( k = ++j )) ; print j=$j k=$k
```

e) What does the double plus do, and what difference does it make whether it comes before or after the name of a variable?

Answer: Your interaction should look like the following:

```
[6037]: i=3 j=5
[6038]: (( k = i++ )) ; print i=$i k=$k
i=4 k=3
[6039]: (( k = ++j )) ; print j=$j k=$k
```

```
j=6 k=6
[6040]:
```

The double-plus operator increments (adds 1 to) the value of a variable. Putting it to the left of the variable name does the incrementing *before* using the value of the variable to compute the value of the expression, whereas putting it to the right of the variable name does the incrementing *after* using the value of the variable. Thus, line 6038 assigns the value 3 to *k*, then adds one to the variable *i*, as the `print` command verifies. However, line 6039 first adds 1 to *j*, then uses that value (6) for the assignment.

```
i=3 j=5 k=7
(( i = i + j * k )) ; print i=$i
i=3 j=5 k=7
(( i = (i + j) * k )) ; print i=$i
```

f) What is the asterisk used for in arithmetic expressions?

Answer: Multiplication.

The first `print` command prints 38 (3+5*7). Note that multiplication is done before addition, using the rules of *precedence*. (Multiplication, division, and modulus are done before addition and subtraction.)

g) What are parentheses used for in arithmetic expressions?

Answer: To override the precedence rules and, occasionally, to make the expression more readable to humans.

The shell computes the value inside the parentheses, then uses that value to compute the rest of the expression. In this code, the value `56` prints, which is 3+5, or 8, multiplied by 7.

```
i=3 j=5
(( i += j ))  ; print i=$i
(( i %= j ))  ; print i=$i
(( i <<= 5 )) ; print i=$i
```

h) What is += equivalent to?

Answer: Your interaction should look like the following:

```
[6040]: i=3 j=5
[6041]: (( i += j ))  ; print i=$i
i=8
[6042]: (( i %= j ))  ; print i=$i
i=3
[6043]: (( i <<= 5 )) ; print i=$i
i=96
[6044]:
```

The expression `i += j` is equivalent to `i = i + j`. You can use this sort of typing shortcut for all the arithmetic operators whenever the right-hand side of an assignment can be written with the variable on the left-hand side as the first operand.

i) What does the `%` operator compute?

Answer: The remainder when you divide the first operand by the second.

In line 6042, the right-hand side is equivalent to 8%5 (because the value of *i* was changed in line 6041), so the result is *3* because 8 divided by 5 has a quotient of 1 (which is discarded) and a remainder of 3.

This "remainder operator" is usually called the modulus operator, *or* modulo, *and is normally shortened to* mod.

j) What does the << operator compute?

Answer: It shifts the bits in the variable to the left the number of positions specified.

This is one of several "bit manipulation" operators. Others include >> (shift right), & (bit-wise *and*), | (bit-wise *or*), ^ (bit-wise *exclusive or*), and ~ (bit-wise negation, also known as *one's complement*). You usually use these operators when you read data from some sort of device that uses a non-standard data encoding scheme and you need to convert it into values that you can work with in your programs.

The value printed after line 6043, `96`, is equal to the value of *i* times 2^5. Each position you shift the bits in an integer to the left doubles its value, so shifting 5 positions doubles the value 5 times, which is the same as 2^5 (32).

The bit-manipulation operators work only on variables of type *integer*.

```
unset m
i=3 j=5 k=7
m=i*j%k
(( k = m )) ; print m=$m k=$k
```

k) What is the difference between referencing the variable *m* inside the double parentheses and outside them in the `print` command?

Answer: Your interaction should look like the following:

```
[6044]: unset m
[6045]: i=3 j=5 k=7
[6046]: m=i*j%k
[6047]: (( k = m )) ; print m=$m k=$k
m=i*j%k k=1
[6048]:
```

Because *m* is a string variable, line 6046 assigns a 5-character string value to it. However, inside the double parentheses on line 6047, the shell interprets that value as an arithmetic expression, and assigns the value `3*5 modulo 7` to *k*. Because the multiplication and modulus operators have the same precedence, the shell evaluates them in left-to-right order, so the value is *15* `modulo 5`, or `1`. Outside the arithmetic expression, the `print` command shows that a reference to *m* is the string `i*j%k`, but `k` has the arithmetic value of `1`.

If you have declared a variable to be an integer or a float, then you don't need a double parentheses command to assign the value of an expression to it. If a numeric variable is on the left of an equal sign, the shell will treat variable names on the right side as references to the variables, even without dollar signs in front of them, and it will evaluate any values that look like expressions as well.

Thus, in this case, line 6046 could have been written `k=m ; print m=$m k=$k`*, with the same result.*

Avoid using this tip! It makes your code hard to understand unless you are doing a long sequence of calculations where (i) it is clear that you are doing arithmetic computations rather than string manipulations and (ii) the double parentheses would create a lot of clutter, which can make code difficult to read, too.

```
float x=3 y=5 z=7
(( x = sqrt(2) ))
(( y = log(100000)/log(10) ))
(( z = cos(3.14159) ))
print x=$x y=$y z=$z
```

l) What did you observe?

Answer: Your interaction should look like the following:

```
[6048]: float x y z
[6049]: (( x = sqrt(2) ))
[6050]: (( y = log(100000)/log(10) ))
[6051]: (( z = cos(3.14159) ))
[6052]: print x=$x y=$y z=$z
x=1.414213562 y=5 z=-1
[6053]:
```

First, you can see that x gets the square root of 2 and gets displayed with ten digits of precision. Next, the fact that *y* gets the value *5* indicates that the shell computes logarithms using base *e* (natural logs, or *ln*). Computing ln(100,000)÷ln(10) is the same as computing $\log_{10}(100,000)$. Finally, the value printed for cos(π) is *-1*, which indicates that the shell requires you to give the angle for the trigonometric functions in radians, not degrees. (The cosine of π radians is negative one, but the cosine of π degrees would have been +0.998.)

6.1.3 ANSWERS

Run the following command:

```
print -- $(( sqrt(2) ))
```

a) What printed?

Answer: Your interaction should look like the following:

```
[6053]: print -- $(( sqrt(2) ))
1.41421356237
[6054]:
```

It's always a good idea to put double dashes before the arguments of a `print` command, especially when the first value is an arithmetic expansion. If the result of the expansion is negative, the initial minus sign will erroneously indicate an option parameter if you don't put in the double dashes. Of course, the `sqrt()` function won't generate a negative result, but it's a good idea to put in the double dashes all the time.

The value printed is the square root of 2, with 12 digits of precision.

```
readonly float two_pi=$(( 2 * 3.141592654 ))
float theta=180
print -- $(( cos(theta / 360 * two_pi) ))
```

b) What printed?

Answer: Your interaction should look like the following:

```
[6054]: readonly float two_pi=$(( 2 * 3.141592654 ))
[6055]: float theta=180
[6056]: print -- $(( cos(theta / 360 * two_pi) ))
-1
[6057]:
```

The value printed, `-1`, is the cosine of 180°.

c) What did the first command do?

Answer: The first command declares two_pi to be a variable of type float, with a value of 2π.

You have already seen that you can use a reference to a variable on the right-hand side of a variable assignment command. The code in this example extends that concept to include references to the value of an arithmetic expression.

d) What happens if you try to run the following command?

```
two_pi=3.141592654
```

Answer: The shell prints an error message saying that two_pi is read only.

The `readonly` command declares that a variable cannot be unset and that its value cannot be changed from the command line, scripts, or functions. It's actually an alias for `typeset -r`. Because `float` is also an alias for a `typeset` command, line 6054 is equivalent to:

```
typeset -Fr two_pi=$(( 2 * 3.141592654 ))
```

If you declare a variable to be read only, it becomes a "constant," and you eliminate the chance that you might accidentally change its value.

Read-only variables are not absolutely constant. If you declare a variable that the shell changes, such as *SECONDS*, to be read-only, you can't change it any more, but the shell itself still can.

```
float x y=5 z=7
print -- $(( x = sqrt(y * z), y = x/2, z = y * 4 )) $x $y $z
```

e) What two values are the same, and why?

Answer: Your interaction should look like the following:

```
[6057]: float x y=5 z=7
[6058]: print -- $(( x = sqrt(y * z), y = x/2, z = y* \
4 )) $x $y $z
11.8321595662 5.916079783 2.958039892 11.83215957
[6059]:
```

The first and fourth numbers have the same value. The first one is the value of the last (rightmost) assignment in the arithmetic expansion, and the fourth one is the value of *z*, which is the variable that received the result of that same assignment.

f) If the two values are the same, why did they print differently?

Answer: They are the same value, but they are printed with different numbers of digits because z is declared as a float, but the expression does not have an associated precision.

FOR EXAMPLE

You can control the number of digits used to print the value of a variable by using the `typeset` command, but you don't have any way to control the precision used to print the results of arithmetic expansions when you use the `print` command. Instead of `print`, you can use the `printf` command, which is covered in Lab 11.1. Here is a `printf` command that shows the result of an arithmetic expansion, printed with three digits to the right of the decimal point:

```
printf "%.3f\n" $(( sqrt(2) ))
1.414
```

6.1.4 ANSWERS

Prepare the following script, and put it in the file `~/fun/f614`:
Now run the following sequence of commands:

```
unset x y z
float z=3.14159
. ~/fun/f614
print x=$x y=$y z=$z
f614_ksh
print x=$x y=$y z=$z
f614_posix
print x=$x y=$y z=$z
```

a) What does the `unset` command accomplish?

Answer: It makes sure that the three variables do not have types set for them from earlier commands you may have run.

In particular, it is important that *x* and *y* must not have types or values, because that would make it difficult to evaluate the effects of running this particular script.

b) What does the dot command accomplish?

Answer: It runs the script in the context of the current shell, as described in Chapter 1, "Setting Up."

When you dot this script, the assignment commands to the variables `x` and `y` are executed, and the shell memorizes the function definitions, but it does not execute the functions.

c) What is the effect of running `f614_ksh` on the value of `x`?

Answer: Your interaction should look like the following:

```
[6059]: unset x y z
[6060]: float z=3.14159
[6061]: . ~/fun/f614
[6062]: print x=$x y=$y z=$z
x=3 y=5 z=3.14159
[6063]: f614_ksh
Inside f614_ksh: x=abc y=2 z=7
[6064]: print x=$x y=$y z=$z
x=abc y=2 z=3.14159
[6065]: f614_posix
Inside f614_posix: x=def y=1 z=7
[6066]: print x=$x y=$y z=$z
x=def y=1 z=7
[6067]:
```

The variable *x* is never explicitly declared in any way, so it came into existence when the file was dotted (line 6061). Its value, printed by line 6062, appears to be numeric, but it's actually a string variable. Running `f614_ksh` gives it the value `abc`, which prints from inside the function (line 6063) and remains set at that value when control returns to the command line, where it is printed again at line 6064.

d) What is the effect of running `f614_ksh` on the value of *y*?

Answer: Its value is changed from 5 *to* 2.

The variable *y* was declared to be an integer variable with a value of `5` when the file was dotted on line 6061, as shown by the output from line 6062. When `f614_ksh` was executed on line 6063, *y* was assigned the value `2.71828`, which was truncated to *2* because the variable is an integer. The output from line 6064 shows that the variable *y* still has the value *2* when control returns to the command line.

e) What is the effect of running `f614_ksh` on the value of z?

Answer: Nothing, `z` *still has the value* 3.14159.

This is a trick question! There are *two* variables named *z*. There is the one defined as a float on line 6060, which has the value `3.14159` and which is not changed by executing `f614_ksh`. The fact that it is not changed by executing the function is shown by line 6064, which prints the value `3.14159` for *z*. The second variable named *z* is the one that was declared with the `typeset` command inside the function, and which has its value (7) printed as part of the execution of the function on line 6066.

If you use `typeset` (or one of its aliases, such as `integer` or `float`) inside a function definition and if you use the function keyword to define the function, the variable has "local scope." It exists only inside the function.

Local variables are recreated every time you run the function that contains their declaration. There is no direct way to preserve the value of a local variable from one execution of a function to another.

f) What is the difference between running `f614_ksh` and `f614_posix`?

Answer: When you run `f614_posix`, there is only one variable named z, and its value is changed by running the function.

The function definition style that uses parentheses instead of the `function` keyword does not support the notion of local variables, but it matches the semantics of the POSIX standard for shells.

Use local variables if it is logically possible whenever you write functions. This practice is especially critical for functions that might be run from the command line, where there is no way to know what variable names the user might already be using.

Enter the same set of commands that you just ran from the command line into a script file named `~/bin/s614`, then run the following commands:

```
unset x y z
float z=99.99
s614
print x=$x y=$y z=$z
```

g) What are the values of x, y, and z after running the script?

Answer: Your interaction should look like the following:

```
[6067]: unset x y z
[6068]: float z=99.99
[6069]: s614
x=3 y=5 z=3.14159
```

```
Inside f614_ksh: x=abc y=2 z=7
x=abc y=2 z=3.14159
Inside f614_posix: x=def y=1 z=7
x=def y=1 z=7
[6070]: print x=$x y=$y z=$z
x= y= z=99.99
[6071]:
```

The output from running the script shows that the functions worked the same way as when they were run from the command line, but the values of *x*, *y*, and *z* were not affected by running the script. The script works with its own set of variables, which is independent of the ones you work with when running commands interactively.

Create the following script in a file named ~/bin/export_test:
Now run the following commands:

```
unset x
x=hello
export_test
print $x
export x
export_test
print $x
```

h) What does exporting a variable do?

Answer: Your interaction should look like the following:

```
[6071]: unset x
[6072]: x=hello
[6073]: export_test
Before assignment, the value of x is .
After assignment, the value of x is good-bye.
[6074]: print $x
hello
[6075]: export x
[6076]: export_test
Before assignment, the value of x is hello.
After assignment, the value of x is good-bye.
[6077]: print $x
hello
[6078]:
```

On line 6073, `export_test` does not "see" the value of the variable *x* and prints nothing for its value in the "Before assignment" message. The script successfully assigns a value to *x*, as the second line of output following line 6073 shows, but that value is not assigned to the variable *x* defined at the command-line level, and line 6074 prints the value assigned to *x* before `export_test` was run. When `export_test` is run again after declaring that *x* is an exported variable, the script does have a variable named *x* with the value `hello` when it starts running, and it again is able to change the value of that variable successfully. However, the variable *x* inside the script is a *copy* of the variable defined from the command line, and changing its value inside the script does not affect the value of the command line variable, as shown by the output from line 6077.

A variable that is passed to a script using `export` *is called an* environment variable. *A program's environment is a list of variables and their values that are defined when the program starts running. When you run* `set` *(with no options or parameters) from the command line, the shell prints its own environment, which includes environment variables.*

```
unset x y z
. s614
print x=$x y=$y z=$z
```

i) How does dotting the script affect the values of the three variables?

Answer: Your interaction should look like the following:

```
[6078]: unset x y z
[6079]: . s614
x=3 y=5 z=3.14159
Inside f614_ksh: x=abc y=2 z=7
x=abc y=2 z=3.14159
Inside f614_posix: x=def y=1 z=7
x=def y=1 z=7
[6080]: print x=$x y=$y z=$z
x=def y=1 z=7
[6081]:
```

When you look at the variables from the command line (line 6080), they have the same values as the last time they were printed by the script (*def, 1,* and *7*) because they *are the same variables*. There are no copies being made; they are simply the same variables inside the script and outside it.

Dotting a script and running a function work the same way because they both run in the same environments and use the same variables.

LAB 6.1 SELF-REVIEW QUESTIONS

To test your progress, you should be able to answer the following questions.

1) If a variable is not declared as an integer, a float, or a name reference, it is which of the following?

a) _____an integer
b) _____a float
c) _____a name reference
d) _____a string
e) _____an error, because you have to declare the type of all variables.

2) What is the difference between the following two commands:

```
integer    perimeter
typeset -i perimeter
```

a) _____The first one makes *perimeter* an integer, but the second one makes it an index.
b) _____Both are wrong because *perimeter* is not a valid variable name.
c) _____They are the same in the sense that both declare *perimeter* to be a number with no fraction part.
d) _____The first one can be used only inside function definitions, but the second one can be used anywhere.
e) _____They are the same in the sense that both compute the distance around a geometric shape.

3) What will be the value of *y* after the following commands are executed?

```
float   x=5.678
integer y=$x
```

a) _____5.678
b) _____5
c) _____6
d) _____5678
e) _____There will be an error because you can't use a float as the value of an integer.

4) What will be the value of `y` after running the following commands? (Be careful.)

```
unset hello y
hello=1.234
float y=hello
```

a) _____*0* because *hello* is a string variable.
b) _____*1.234* because the value of *hello* looks like a valid floating-point number.
c) _____*hello* because *y* is a string variable.
d) _____*1234* because *y* is an integer variable.
e) _____There is an error because there is no dollar sign before `hello`.

5) What is the difference between ((…)) and $((…))?
a) _____There is no difference; the dollar sign is optional.
b) _____The first one is invalid because there has to be a dollar sign.
c) _____The second one is invalid because there must not be a dollar sign.
d) _____The first one is always valid, no matter what the ellipses represent but the second one is valid only if the ellipses represent a valid arithmetic expression.
e) _____The first one is a command that computes the expression represented by the ellipses, but the second one is a reference to the value of the expression represented by the ellipses.

6) What would the following code print?

```
integer i j k
i=123 j=246 k=369
(( i = i + j / k )) ; print $i
```

a) _____An error message, because you can't have spaces inside an arithmetic expression.
b) _____1
c) _____123

d) _____123.6666667
e) _____124

7) What is the difference between using the keyword to define a function and using the `POSIX` form with parentheses?

a) _____There is no difference.
b) _____You can have local variables if you use the `POSIX` form, but not if you use the `function` keyword.
c) _____You can have global variables if you use the `POSIX` form, but not if you use the `function` keyword.
d) _____You can have local variables if you use the `function` keyword, but not if you use the `POSIX` form.
e) _____You can have global variables if you use the `function` keyword, but not if you use the `POSIX` form.

8) What do dotting a script and running a function have in common?

a) _____Nothing.
b) _____They mean the same thing.
c) _____The variables in the environment from which they are run are copied into the environment of these commands.
d) _____The variables in the environment from which they are run are the same as the variables in the environment of these commands.
e) _____All scripts are functions, but not all functions are scripts.

9) What does the `export` command do?

a) _____It prints an error message every time it is run.
b) _____It doesn't do anything.
c) _____It makes variables global.
d) _____It makes variables local.
e) _____It tells the shell to copy a variable to the environment of a command.

Quiz answers appear in Appendix A, Section 6.1.

LAB 6.2

ARRAYS AND COMPOUND VARIABLES

LAB OBJECTIVES

After this lab, you will be able to:

- ✓ Use Indexed Arrays
- ✓ Declare and Use Associative Arrays
- ✓ Use Compound Variables and Discipline Functions

In this lab, you will learn to work with arrays and compound variables. There are two types of arrays, called *indexed arrays* and *associative arrays*. Both of them use a single variable name to hold a list of values, and you use another value, called a *subscript*, to tell which element of the array you want to use. An indexed array uses integer numbers between 0 and 4095 as subscripts. In Chapter 8, "Loops," you will see how to use loops to access the different elements of an indexed array in a systematic order. An associative array uses strings as subscripts. Associative arrays are also known as *property lists* or *hashtables*, and are used for many purposes in computer programming.

Finally, this lab also introduces you to a powerful feature provided by the KornShell, called *compound variables*. You will see that these variables allow you to create sets of related variables, and to write special functions, called *discipline functions*, that exploit some of the special features of compound variables.

LAB 6.2 EXERCISES

6.2.1 USE INDEXED ARRAYS

Any variable can be used as an indexed array simply by using a subscript to tell which element of the array you want to modify or use. Put the subscript inside square brackets.

Enter the following commands:

```
days[0]=Sunday days[1]=Monday days[2]=Tuesday
days[3]=Wednesday
days[4]=Thursday days[5]=Friday days[6]=Saturday
```

a) What is the name of the array variable?

____

____

b) How could you print the value of array element 5?

____

____

c) What happens if you try to print the value of *days[7]*?

____

____

d) What happens if you try to print the value of *days[4096]*?

---

e) What happens if you try to use -1 as a subscript?

---

f) What happens if you use 3.7 as a subscript?

---

g) What happens if you print a reference to `days` without using any subscript?

---

h) What happens if you use the string, `hello`, as a subscript?

Assign the value *5* to a variable named *TGIF*.

i) How can you use the value of *TGIF* to print the value of the sixth element of *days*?

Print the value of *days* using `@` as the subscript.

j) What did the shell print?

Enter the following command:

```
print ${#days[@]}
```

k) What number was printed, and how does it relate to the array, `days`?

Enter the following commands:

```
weekend[0]=6 weekend[1]=0
print There are ${#weekend[@]} \
days in the weekend.
print They are ${days[ weekend[0] ]} and \
${days[ weekend [1]]}.
```

l) Explain the output of the first `print` command.

---

m) Explain the output of the second `print` command

Assign the value `Birthday` to `days[31]` and assign the empty string to *days[99]*.

n) What happens if you print ${days[@]}and ${#days[@]} now?

6.2.2 Declare and Use Associative Arrays

An *associative array* is an array that uses strings instead of integers as subscript values. Unlike indexed arrays, you must declare a variable to be an associative array, using the `-A` option of the `typeset` command, before you can use the variable with strings as subscripts.

If you try to use a string as a subscript without declaring a variable as an associative array, the shell will treat the subscript as an arithmetic expression, as shown in the previous exercise.

Enter a command that declares the variable names *venus* and *mars* as associative arrays.

a) What command did you use?

Enter the following commands:

```
venus[domain]=.cs.qc.edu
venus[address]=149.4.44.101
venus[building]="Science Building"
venus[room]=A-219
print venus${venus[domain]} is in ${venus[building]},\
room ${venus[room]}.
```

b) What printed?

Enter the following command:

```
print mars${mars[domain]} is in ${mars[building]}, \
room ${mars[room]}.
```

c) What printed this time?

Enter the following commands:

```
print venus has ${#venus[@]} elements and mars has \
${#mars[@]} elements.
print ${venus[@]}
print ${!venus[@]}
print ${!venus}
```

d) What do `${#venus[@]}` and `${#mars[@]}` print?

---

e) What does `${venus[@]}` print?

---

f) What does `${!venus[@]}` print?

---

g) What does `${!venus}` print?

____

____

Enter the following commands:

```
venus[an arbitrary string]=hello
print \"${venus[an arbitrary string]}\"
print \"${venus[An arbitrary string]}\"
```

h) What printed?

____

____

6.2.3 USE COMPOUND VARIABLES AND DISCIPLINE FUNCTIONS

We'll start by looking at ways that compound variables and associative arrays are similar. To do that, enter the following commands:

```
typeset pluto
pluto=(domain=.cs.qc.edu \
       address=149.4.44.109 \
       building="Science Building" )
pluto.room=A-219
print $pluto
print pluto${pluto.domain} is in ${pluto.building}, \
      room ${pluto.room}.
```

a) How do you access the elements of the compound variable, *pluto,* compared with the associative array, *venus*?

____

____

Now, let's start looking at the things you can do with compound variables that have no equivalent in associative arrays. First of all, you can have an arbitrary number of parts in a compound variable, which are organized hierarchically. The terminology is that you call the left part of a compound variable the *parent* of all the parts to the right, and the right parts are called *children* of the part to the left.

FOR EXAMPLE

Assume some of your workstations use IP addresses, others use IPX, and others use IPV6, each with a different format for the address information.

Enter the following commands to set up *pluto*'s address type, its IP address, and its subnet mask:

```
pluto.address=IP
pluto.address.ip=149.4.44.109
pluto.address.mask=255.255.255.0
```

b) What is *address* the child of?

____

____

c) What is *address* the parent of?

____

____

d) What is the value of *pluto.address*?

____

____

You can also create function definitions that *look like* compound variables, called *discipline functions*. They allow you to write functions that will automatically be run any time something "interesting" is done with a variable. The shell lets you define any of three discipline functions, get, set, and unset, for all shell variables. (There is a mechanism for using additional ones beyond these three, but that is beyond the scope of this workbook.) Although discipline functions are not really related to to compound variables, the shell provides some compound variables that you can use when you write discipline functions.

To see how discipline functions work, enter the following code into a file named ~/fun/pluto_stuff and dot the file:

```
#  pluto.set -- Discipline functions for pluto.

function pluto.set {
  print -- "${.sh.name}" was set to "${.sh.value}"
  }

function pluto.get {
  print -- "${.sh.name}" was referenced.
  .sh.value=${.sh.name:-"a default value"}
  }

function pluto.unset {
  print -- "${.sh.name}" has been unset.
  }
```

Now enter the following commands:

```
unset pluto
pluto=hello
print -- This is pluto: \"$pluto\"
pluto.address="123 Main Street"
```

e) Under what conditions are the three discipline functions executed by the shell?

____

____

f) What are the values of the compound variables *.sh.name* and *.sh.value* when a discipline function is run?

g) Does the shell run discipline functions when something happens to compound variables?

LAB 6.2 ANSWERS

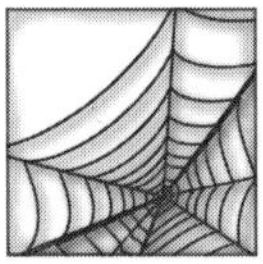

This section gives you some suggested answers to the questions in Lab 6.2, with discussion related to those answers. Your answers may vary, but the most important thing is whether or not your answer works. Use this discussion to analyze differences between your answers and those presented here.

If you have alternative answers to the questions in this exercise, you are encouraged to post your answers and to discuss them at the companion web site for this book, located at:

```
http://www.phptr.com/phptrinteractive/
```

6.2.1 ANSWERS

```
days[0]=Sunday days[1]=Monday days[2]=Tuesday
days[3]=Wednesday
days[4]=Thursday days[5]=Friday days[6]=Saturday
```

a) What is the name of the array variable?

Answer: The name of the array variable is days.

You don't have to do anything special to start working with array variables. Just put a subscript inside square brackets after the variable name in an assignment.

b) How could you print the value of array element 5?

Answer: Reference the array element using the ${ ... } construct. Your interaction should look like the following:

```
[6081]: print ${days[5]}
Friday
[6082]:
```

Be sure to put both the variable name and the subscript inside the braces.

The first element of an array has a subscript number of zero. Be sure to keep the ordinal position (first) and the subscript number of the element (`0` *) straight.*

c) What happens if you try to print the value of *days[7]*?

Answer: Your interaction should look like the following.

```
[6082]: print Element 7 is: ${days[7]}.
Element 7 is: .
[6083]:
```

No value has been assigned to position 7, so nothing prints. Referencing an uninitialized element of an array is like referencing any uninitialized variable: the shell does not consider the reference to be an error (unless you have set the shell's `nounset` option), and substitutes the empty string as the value.

d) What happens if you try to print the value of *days[4096]*?

Answer: Your interaction should look like the following:

```
[6083]: print ${days[4096]}
ksh: days: subscript out of range
[6084]:
```

The largest subscript value you can use is 4095.

e) What happens if you try to use -1 as a subscript?

Answer: Your interaction should look like the following:

```
[6084]: print ${days[-1]}
ksh: days: subscript out of range
[6085]:
```

The smallest subscript value you can use is zero.

f) What happens if you use 3.7 as a subscript?

Answer: Your interaction should look like the following:

```
[6085]: print ${days[3.7]}
Wednesday
[6086]:
```

It's all right to use a noninteger as the value of a subscript, but the shell silently converts it to an integer by *truncating* the number. The fraction part is dropped without any rounding. In the present case, the result is the same as if you printed `${days[3]}` as your reference.

g) What happens if you print a reference to *days* without using any subscript?

Answer: Your interaction should look like the following:

```
[6086]: print ${days}
Sunday
[6087]:
```

If you reference an array without any subscript, you get the value of the first element of the array. This flexibility works the other way around, too: If you already have a scalar variable (that's the name for a variable that isn't an array), you can turn it into an array just by using subscripts to give values to other elements of the array. The value you assigned to the scalar will remain as the value of element number zero.

You can treat the same variable as either a scalar or as an array. This can be convenient, but doing so makes programs hard to understand. Don't use the same variable name as both a scalar and as an array in the same function or script.

h) What happens if you use the string, `hello`, as a subscript?

Answer: You could find using an interaction like the following:

```
[6087]: print ${days[hello]}
Sunday
[6088]:
```

You could also have enclosed `hello` in quotes (either single or double) with the same effect: If you try to use a string where the shell expects you to put a number and the string is not the name of a variable that has been assigned a numeric value, the shell treats the string as the number zero.

However, there is nothing about `hello`, even if you put it in quotes, that makes it unequivocally a string; it could be the name of another variable whose value you want to use as a subscript.

Assign the value *5* to a variable named *TGIF*.

i) How can you use the value of *TGIF* to print the value of the sixth element of *days?*

Answer: Your interaction should look something like the following:

```
[6088]: TGIF=5
[6089]: print ${days[TGIF]}
Friday
[6090]:
```

Friday is the value of *days[5].*

The only difference between `hello` in the previous question and *TGIF* in this question is that line 6088 assigns a value to *TGIF* before using it as a subscript, whereas *hello* was never assigned a value.

The shell "knows" that there must be a number inside the square brackets, so if you give it a string, it automatically checks to see whether the string can be used as the name of a variable and, if so, whether the variable's value can be used as a number. You don't have to use a dollar sign to tell the shell to evaluate the variable.

> *What you write inside the square brackets of a subscript is called an* arithmetic expression. *The rules for writing arithmetic expressions were covered in Exercise 6.1.2.*

Print the value of `days` using `@` as the subscript.

j) What did the shell print?

Answer: Your interaction should look like the following:

```
[6090]: print ${days[@]}
Sunday Monday Tuesday Wednesday Thursday Friday
  Saturday
[6091]:
```

Just as the at sign (`@`) refers to a list of all the parameters passed to a function or script when used as a variable name inside a function or script, it also refers to a list of all the elements of an array when used as a subscript for the array.

Enter the following command:

```
print ${#days[@]}
```

k) What number was printed, and how does it relate to the array, `days`?

Answer: Your interaction should look like the following:

```
[6091]: print ${#days[@]}
7
[6092]:
```

The `${# ... }` construction is a type of *parameter expansion*, which is a topic that will be covered in Chapter 10, "Patterns, Expansions, and Substitutions." This particular expansion gives the length of what follows the sharp sign(#) in this case the number of elements in the array.

You can also use `${# ... }` to get the length of a string. For example, the shell would evaluate `${#days[0]}` as 6 because there are six letters in Sunday.

Enter the following commands:

```
weekend[0]=6 weekend[1]=0
print There are ${#weekend[@]} \
days in the weekend.
print They are ${days[${weekend[0]}]} \
and ${days[${weekend[1]}]}.
```

l) Explain the output of the first `print` command.

Answer: Your interaction should look like the following:

```
[6092]: weekend[0]=6 weekend[1]=0
[6093]: print There are ${#weekend[@]} \
days in the weekend.
There are 2 days in the weekend.
[6094]: print They are ${days[ weekend[0] ]} and \
${days[ weekend[1] ]}.
They are Saturday and Sunday.
[6095]:
```

The array `weekend` has two elements, so the message prints the number 2 in place of `${#weekend[@]}`.

m) Explain the output of the second `print` command.

Answer: Elements zero and one of the array weekend *have the values 6 and 0, so the strings* `Saturday` *and* `Sunday` *are printed.*

There are two points to note here. The first one is that you can use a reference to an array element as a subscript for another array. The second one is that the rules for arithmetic expressions, which determine what you can write as a subscript, allow you to put extra spaces inside the expression. They aren't needed, but the spaces on each side of `weekend[0]` and `weekend[1]` make it easier to read the code.

Arithmetic expressions allow you to drop the dollar sign and braces for referencing variables and to insert spaces around variable names. Judicious use of spaces makes your code much easier to read.

Assign the value `Birthday` to *days[31]* and assign the empty string to *days[99]*.

n) What happens if you print `${days[@]}` and `${#days[@]}` now?

Answer: Your interaction should look like the following:

```
[6095]: days[31]=Birthday days[99]=
[6096]: print ${days[@]}
Sunday Monday Tuesday Wednesday Thursday Friday \
Saturday Birthday
[6097]: print ${#days[@]}
9
[6098]:
```

The shell keeps track of which elements of an array have been assigned values and which ones have not. Elements 0 through 6, 31, and 99 have been assigned values, so the value printed for `${#days[@]}` is 9. Printing all the elements of the array shows only the values of the elements that have been assigned non-empty strings or numerical values.

6.2.2 ANSWERS

Enter a command that declares the variable names `venus` and `mars` as associative arrays.

a) What command did you use?

Answer: You should have entered the following command:

```
[6098]: typeset -A mars venus
```

You could have entered the variable names in the opposite order, or you could have used two separate `typeset` commands. In either event, you must use the `-A` option on the `typeset` command to make the variables associative arrays.

Enter the following commands:

```
venus[domain]=.cs.qc.edu
venus[address]=149.4.44.101
venus[building]="Science Building"
venus[room]=A-219
print venus${venus[domain]} is in ${venus[building]},\
room ${venus[room]}.
```

b) What printed?

Answer: Your interaction should look like the following:

```
[6099]: venus[domain]=.cs.qc.edu
[6100]: venus[address]=149.4.44.101
[6101]: venus[building]="Science Building"
[6102]: venus[room]=A-219
[6103]: print venus${venus[domain]} is in \
${venus[building]}, room ${venus[room]}.
venus.cs.qc.edu is in Science Building, room A-219.
[6104]:
```

A common use for associative arrays is to hold a set of related values for some object, in this case a computer workstation.

You will see in the next exercise that compound variables *can be used to do many of the same things as associative arrays, such as holding a set of related values for some object. You can use whichever one is easier to work with for your particular application.*

Enter the following command:

```
print mars${mars[domain]} is in ${mars[building]}, \
room ${mars[room]}.
```

c) What printed this time?

Answer: Your interaction should look like the following:

```
[6105]: print mars${mars[domain]} is in
  ${mars[building]}, room ${mars[room]}.
mars is in , room .
[6106]:
```

Because nothing was assigned to any of the elements of the mars array, the message has blanks wherever there is a reference to any element of the array.

Enter the following commands:

```
print venus has ${#venus[@]} elements and mars has \
${#mars[@]} elements.
print ${venus[@]}
print ${!venus[@]}
print ${!venus}
```

d) What do `${#venus[@]}` and `${#mars[@]}` print?

Answer: Your interaction should look like the following:

```
[6106]: print venus has ${#venus[@]} elements and mars\
has ${#mars[@]} elements.
venus has 4 elements and mars has 0 elements.
[6107]: print ${venus[@]}
149.4.44.101 A-219 .cs.qc.edu Science Building
[6108]: print ${!venus[@]}
address room domain building
[6109]: print ${!venus}
venus
[6110]:
```

Just as for indexed arrays, the `${# ... }` construct evaluates to the number of elements of an associative array that have been initialized.

e) What does `${venus[@]}` print?

Answer: The values of all the initialized elements of the associative array.

The shell prints this list of values in just the same way as when you have it evaluate `${ ...[@]}` for an indexed array. Note, however, that the values are not listed in any obvious sequence.

f) What does `${!venus[@]}` print?

Answer: The names of the subscripts that have been used to assign values to elements of the array.

Note that the names of the subscripts are printed in the same sequence as the sequence in which the values were printed above. However, the sequence is neither alphabetical nor the sequence in which the subscripts were first used. The shell performs a calculation on each subscript used with an associative array to make it efficient to locate any element.

g) What does `${!venus}` print?

Answer: It prints the name of the variable.

This may not seem too useful a feature; in this case, it really isn't. On the other hand, if you have used a variable as a name reference for another variable (Exercise 6.1.1), this construct will tell you the other variable's name.

Enter the following commands:

```
venus[an arbitrary string]=hello
print \"${venus[an arbitrary string]}\"
print \"${venus[An arbitrary string]}\"
```

h) What printed?

Answer: Your interaction should look like the following:

```
[6110]: venus[an arbitrary string]=hello
[6111]: print \"${venus[an arbitrary string]}\"
"hello"
[6112]: print \"${venus[An arbitrary string]}\"
""
[6113]:
```

If you read this code without actually typing it in, you might miss the difference between the two subscript values (the capital *A* at the beginning of the second subscript). But the shell doesn't miss the difference: The string you use to assign a value to an associative array element has to be exactly the same in terms of spacing and capitalization as the string you use to reference the same array element later.

6.2.3 Answers

To do that, enter the following commands:

```
pluto=(domain=.cs.qc.edu \
       address=149.4.44.109 \
       building="Science Building" )
pluto.room=A-219
print $pluto
print pluto${pluto.domain} is in ${pluto.building}, \
room ${pluto.room}.
```

a) How do you access the elements of the compound variable, *pluto*, compared with the associative array, *venus?*

Answer: Your interaction should look like the following:

```
[6113]: typeset pluto
[6114]: pluto=(domain=.cs.qc.edu \
               address=149.4.44.109 \
               building="Science Building" )
[6115]: pluto.room=A-219
[6116]: print $pluto
(    building='Science    Building'    room=A-219    \
address=149.4.44.109 domain=.cs.qc.edu )
[6117]: print pluto${pluto.domain} is in \
  ${pluto.building}, room ${pluto.room}.
pluto.cs.qc.edu is in Science Building, room A-219
[6118]:
```

The first difference is that, you have to declare *pluto* using a `typeset` command (or by assigning a value to it), but you don't use any option to indicate that *pluto* is a compound variable. (You had to use `typeset -A` for associative arrays.)

The second difference is that compound variables use "dot notation" to indicate which element of a compound variable you want to work with instead of subscript notation. The element name is separated from the variable name by a dot (.) instead of being inside square brackets (`[]`). In line 6115, we used dot notation to set the value of *pluto.room*, and in line 6117 we used dot notation to reference each of the elements of *pluto* individually. Line 6114 shows a convenient way to initialize several elements of *pluto* in one command. If you use this syntax, you don't need to declare *pluto* ahead of time with a `typeset` command. Line 6116 shows that you can reference the entire compound variable using just the "root" part of the name.

You could use any string you wanted as a subscript for an associative array, but all the parts of a compound variable's name must follow the normal rules for variable names; there cannot be any embedded spaces or tabs. You could not write `pluto."an arbitrary string"=hello`*, for example.*

Note that we said "all the parts of a compound variable's name" rather than "both parts" in the Tip. That's going to be the next difference between compound variables and associative arrays that you will look at.

```
pluto.address=IP
pluto.address.ip=149.4.44.109
pluto.address.mask=255.255.255.0
```

b) What is `address` the child of?

Answer: It is the child of pluto.

The variable *pluto* is the parent of *address*, and *address* is the child of *pluto.*

c) What is *address* the parent of?

Answer: It is the parent of both ip *and* mask.

A parent can have any number of children. In this case, *address* has two children. You can also think of *ip* and *mask* as "grandchildren" or, more generically, as "descendants" of *pluto*, and you can call *pluto* an "ancestor" of *ip* and *mask*.

d) What is the value of *pluto.address?*

Answer: The value of pluto.address *is* `IP`.

You could use the following interaction to verify this answer:

```
[6118]: pluto.address=IP
[6119]: pluto.address.ip=149.4.44.109
[6120]: pluto.address.mask=255.255.255.0
[6121]: print ${pluto.address}
IP
[6122]:
```

Now enter the following commands:

```
unset pluto
pluto=hello
print -- This is pluto: \"$pluto\"
pluto.address="123 Main Street"
```

e) Under what conditions are the three discipline functions executed by the shell?

Answer: Your interaction should look like the following:

```
[6122]: . ~/fun/pluto_stuff
[6123]: unset pluto
pluto has been unset.
[6124]:pluto=hello
pluto was set to "hello"
[6125]:print -- This is pluto: \"$pluto\"
pluto was referenced
This is pluto: "a different value"
[6126]:pluto.address="123 Main Street"
[6127]:
```

From line 6123 you can see that the `unset` discipline function is run whenever the variable is unset; line 6124 shows that the `set` discipline function is run when the variable is assigned a value, and line 6125 shows that the `get` discipline function is called whenever the variable is referenced.

f) What are the values of the compound variables *.sh.name* and *.sh.value* when a discipline function is run?

Answer: The name of the variable is the value of .sh.name, *and the value is the value of* .sh.value.

As the interactions show, you can always determine the name of the variable being set, unset, or referenced using the special compound variable named *.sh.name*. Note that this variable name starts with a dot, which makes it impossible for you to use as your own variable name; only the shell can assign a value to it.

The compound variable named *.sh.value* can be used it two different ways. In the `set` discipline function, you can use it to find out the value being assigned to the variable. In the `get` discipline function, you can assign a value to this compound variable, and that will become the value that the shell actually assigns to the original variable, regardless of the value specified in the original assignment.

g) Does the shell run discipline functions when something happens to compound variables?

Answer: Not unless you explicitly define a discipline function for the fully qualified compound variable name.

Line 6126 shows that no discipline function is called for descendants of the parent variable for which a discipline function is defined. If you want to, you can explicitly create discipline functions for descendants, though. For example, if you had defined a function named `pluto.address.set`, line 6126 would have caused it to be run.

LAB 6.2 SELF-REVIEW QUESTIONS

To test your progress, you should be able to answer the following questions:

1) What will the following command, without declaring *a* in any way, do?
`a[-3]=5`
a) _____It will print an error message because *a* was not declared as an array.
b) _____It will print an error message because -3 is not a valid subscript value.

c) ______It will make *a* into an associative array and use -3 as a subscript.
d) ______It will put 5 into position -3 of the indexed array, *a*.
e) ______It will print an error message because -3 is not a number.

2) What will the following sequence of commands do?

```
typeset -A a
a[-3]=5
```

a) ______It will print an error message because *a* was not declared as an array.
b) ______It will print an error message because -3 is not a valid subscript value.
c) ______It will make *a* into an associative array, and use "-3" as a subscript.
d) ______It will put 5 into position -3 of the indexed array, *a*.
e) ______It will print an error message because -3 is not a number.

3) What will the following commands do?

```
integer a
a[3]=Howdy!
```

a) ______It will assign the string `Howdy`! to element number 3 of the array *a*.
b) ______It will assign the value zero to element number 3 of the array `a`.
c) ______It will print an error message because `Howdy`! is not a valid arithmetic expression.
d) ______It will assign 3 to associative array `a` using `Howdy` as the subscript.
e) ______It will print "Error: Howdy must always be followed by "partner.""

4) What is the difference between the following two commands?

```
print $a[3]
print ${a[3]}
```

a) ______Nothing, they both print the value of element number 3 of the array *a*.
b) ______The first one prints the value of element number 3, but the second one prints an error message because you can't use braces with arrays.
c) ______The first one prints the value of *a* followed by `[3]` but the second one prints the value of element number 3.

d) _____Nothing; they both print error messages because 3 is not a valid subscript.

e) _____Nothing; they both print error messages because *a* was not declared as an array.

5) What do the following commands do?

```
node="Bourne Shell"
node.child1="KornShell"
node.child2="Bourne-again Shell"
```

a) _____They print error messages because you can't put dots inside variable names.

b) _____They print error messages because *node.child1* and *node.child2* should be assigned values *before node* is assigned a value.

c) _____They make a compound variable named `node`, with two member variables, named *child1* and *child2*.

d) _____They make an associative array named *node*, with two elements that are accessed using subscript strings *child1* and *child2*.

e) _____They make an associative array named *node*, with two elements that are accessed using subscript strings `KornShell` and `Bourne-again Shell`.

Quiz answers appear in Appendix A, Section 6.2.

CHAPTER 6

TEST YOUR THINKING

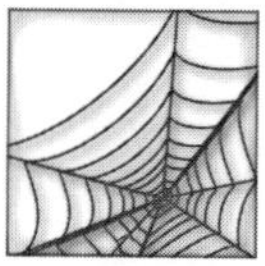

The projects in this section are meant to have you utilize all of the skills that you have acquired throughout this chapter. The answers to these projects can be found at the companion web site to this book, located at:

`http://www.phptr.com/phptrinteractive/`

Visit the web site periodically to share and discuss your answers.

1) Write a function named `init_bd` that puts the names of chess pieces into a 64-element array named *bd*, representing the layout of a chess board at the beginning of a game. Piece names begin with *w* for white or *b* for black, followed by *p* for pawn, *r* for rook, *b* for bishop, *q* for queen, and *K* for king. Use two dashes for empty squares. Write a function named `show_bd` that prints the array, 8 elements per line of output. Run `init_bd`, then run `show_bd`. Your output should look like the following:

```
br bk bb bq bK bb bk br
bp bp bp bp bp bp bp bp
-- -- -- -- -- -- -- --
-- -- -- -- -- -- -- --
-- -- -- -- -- -- -- --
-- -- -- -- -- -- -- --
wp wp wp wp wp wp wp wp
wr wk wb wq wK wb wk wr
```

2) Think of the chessboard as 8 rows, numbered 1–8 from bottom to top, with 8 columns numbered 1–8 from left to right. Write a function named `move_pc` that receives two arguments. The first is a compound variable with members named *row* and *col* that locates a piece to be moved. The second is another compound variable, also with members named *row* and *col*, that locates a square that a piece is to be moved to. The `move_pc` function should update the *bd* to reflect the move requested. (The function has to translate the *row* and *col* values into numbers between 0 and 63. Visit the web

site if you have trouble figuring out the arithmetic expression that will do this.) The following would be a possible interaction you could have with your functions:

```
[6128]: init_bd
[6129]: from.row=1 from.col=7 to.row=3 to.col=6
[6130]: move_pc from to
[6131]: show_bd
br bk bb bq bK bb bk br
bp bp bp bp bp bp bp bp
-- -- -- -- -- -- -- --
-- -- -- -- -- -- -- --
-- -- -- -- -- -- -- --
-- -- -- -- -- wk -- --
wp wp wp wp wp wp wp wp
wr wk wb wq wK wb -- wr
[6132]:
```

3) Write a function named `reminder` that takes two arguments. The first one is a string specifying a date or time, and the second one is a string containing a message. Write a second function named `todo` that takes a date or time string as an argument and prints the date/time string and its associated message. The following would be a possible interaction you could have with your functions:

```
[6132]: reminder 4:15 "Get a snack."
[6133]: reminder 4:30 "Drink some coffee."
[6134]: todo 4:15
4:15: Get a snack.
[6135]: todo 5:30
5:30:
[6136]: todo 4:30
4:30: Drink some coffee.
[6137]:
```

CHAPTER 7

BASIC TESTS

There will be a test on this next Tuesday.

Chapter Objectives

In this chapter, you will learn about:

Scripts and functions would have pretty limited usefulness if they could only run a fixed list of commands each time they are run. In this chapter, you will learn the `if` built-in commands provided by the KornShell for controlling which commands get executed based on the outcomes of various tests. You will also learn to use the double-bracket operator (`[[ ... ]]`) to make those tests. By the end of this chapter, you can start writing "real" programs that make decisions about which commands to run as they execute.

You use the commands in this chapter and the next to implement *control structures*, in which you group other commands in ways not covered in Chapter 2, "Command Line Syntax." Each type of control structure consists of two or more built-in commands (a *compound command*) that mark the parts of the control structure, as well as other commands (of any type) that make up the *body* of the control structure. For example, the first compound command you will look at has at least three parts: `if`, `then`, and `fi`. We will use the term *statement* to refer to an entire control structure, including both the compound command that marks the parts of the structure and the other commands that are the subjects of the control structure.

LAB 7.1

LAB 7.1

THE `if` COMMAND

LAB OBJECTIVES

After this lab, you will be able to:

- ✓ Write a Simple `if, then, ... else` Statement
- ✓ Use `if` to Test the Outcome of External Commands
- ✓ Use an Alternative Way to Test a Command

This first control statement follows very closely the way we talk about decision making in everyday life. "*If* something is true, *then* I will do one thing, *else* I will do another thing." For the `if` command, *something is true* means *execute some commands and test whether the exit code of the last one is true*. Likewise, *I will do one thing* and *I will do another thing* both mean *execute some commands*. That is, with the `if` command, you test the result of executing one set of commands to decide which of two other sets of commands to execute.

SYNTAX DIAGRAMS

The previous paragraph gives an informal sense of what an `if` command does, but it doesn't tell you all the details about how to write an `if` command, and it doesn't tell you about the variations that you can use when writing `if` commands. All that detailed information can be expressed very concisely using a table called a *syntax diagram*. Once you know how to read the syntax diagram for a command, you will have all the information you need to be able to use the command in any situation you desire.

You already saw a form of syntax diagram in the "syntax synopsis" introduced in Lab 2.1, "Command Parts"; syntax diagrams are just another form for the same information.

FOR EXAMPLE

To show you how syntax diagrams work, here is the one for the `if` command, followed by an explanation. This syntax diagram has line numbers in the left column to make it easier to talk about the diagram itself. We will not bother to number the lines in future syntax diagrams.

```
1.    if          Command ...
2.    then        Command ...
3.    [ elif      Command ...
4.      then      Command ... ]
5.      ...
6.    [ else      Command ... ]
7.    fi
```

- Line 1 shows that an `if` command starts with the `if` keyword, followed by any number of commands. (ellipses (...) after `Command` means you can have any number of additional commands after the first one.)
- The second line says that after the `if` command line, there must be a command that starts with the `then` keyword, again followed by any number of commands.
- Lines 3 and 4 are inside square brackets, which means that they are optional. If you want to, you may put in a command starting with the `elif` keyword, followed by any number of commands. If you do use `elif`, it must be followed by a command that starts with the `then` keyword, followed by any number of commands.
- Line 5 uses ellipses to show that what precedes it (i.e., lines 3 and 4) may be repeated any number of times. In this case, "any number of times" might be zero because of the square brackets around lines 3 and 4.

- Line 6 is also optional, as indicated by the square brackets around it. It shows that after the `then` part and any `elif` parts, you can start a command with `else`, followed by any number of commands.
- The last line shows that there has to be a `fi` (that's *if* spelled backward) to mark the end of an `if` command.

There are several points to make about this syntax diagram. The first point is that the phrase *any number of commands* means *"one or more complete command lines."* You can write anything that would be a valid command line, including command sequences, pipelines, and the other types of command lines introduced in Chapter 2, "Command Syntax," *including other* `if` *commands and any of the other control structure commands you will be learning.*

The ability to put command sequences, command groups, and other control structures inside the parts of a control structure is extremely powerful. However, this feature also lets you write very complex programs. Beginning programmers tend to produce more complex programs than do more advanced programmers, who learn how to write efficient programs that are easy to understand. Strive to make your programs simple. If your code starts to get complex, think about how to write it more simply.

The next point is that there *must* be an `if`, a `then`, and a `fi`—in that sequence.

If there is an `else`, it must be the last part of the `if` structure before the `fi`.

The `elif` keyword is a contraction for *else if.* I've included it in the syntax diagram for completeness, but if you need the logical feature it provides, you can often accomplish the same thing more clearly and at least as efficiently by using the `case` command introduced in Chapter 9, "The `Case` and `Select` Commands."

Avoid `elif`. It can lead to programs that are very hard to understand, debug, and modify. If you can, use `case` statements instead.

LAB 7.1 EXERCISES

7.1.1 WRITE A SIMPLE `if, then, ... else` STATEMENT

This exercise uses the KornShell's built-in commands, `print`, `true`, and `false`. If you are not comfortable with these commands, you should review Chapter 2, "Command Syntax," where they were introduced.

Look at the following commands and see if you can predict what will be printed:

```
if   true
then print yes
else print no
fi
```

a) Type in these commands. What printed, and why?

____

____

Now, look at the following commands and see if you can predict what will be printed:

```
if   true && false
then print ok 1
     print ok 2
     print ok 3
else print not ok 1
     print not ok 2
fi
```

b) Type in these commands. What printed, and why?

____

____

c) How does the indention affect what gets executed?

---

d) What advantage is there to indenting the code as shown?

Now, look at the following commands and see if you can predict what will be printed:

```
if   false
     false
     true
then print ok
else print not ok
fi
```

e) Type in these commands. What printed, and why?

---

f) What would happen if you reversed the second and third command lines?

Predict what the following commands will print:

```
if   print hello ||
     print there
then print again
fi
```

g) Type in these commands. What printed, and why?

7.1.2 USE `if` TO TEST THE OUTCOME OF EXTERNAL COMMANDS

So far you have used `true`, `false`, and `print` commands to decide whether to execute the `then` or the `else` part of an `if` statement. Fortunately, `if` is a lot more useful than that.

In this exercise, you will practice using `if` to test the results of some of the other commands you have already seen. As you go on, you will learn more commands that are commonly tested using `if`, as well as other uses for this versatile command.

Write a script named `s712a` that prints the message, "Option -a was set" if the `-a` option was given on the command line. There are a number of ways you could do this; your script is to use an `if` statement to test the exit code of a `getopts` command.

a) What does your script look like?

b) What happens when you test your script?

The `grep` command sets its exit code to *true* if it finds the string you want to search for and sets it to *false* if it does not find the string.

Create the following script in your `bin` directory:

```
# s712b -- Tell if the user typed the name of a month.

if    grep -i "^$1\$" Months > /dev/null
then  print -- "$1 is the name of a month. "
else  print -- "\"$1\" is not the name of a month."
fi
```

c) What file name should you have used for this script, and why?

Consult your documentation for the `grep` command if you don't know the answers to the next two questions.

d) What does the `-i` option do?

e) What do `^` and `\$` around `$1` do?

---

f) Why is it necessary to put `^$1\$` inside quotes in the `grep` command?

---

g) Why is the output of the `grep` command redirected to `/dev/null`?

---

h) Why is `--` put on both `print` commands?

---

i) Why is `\"` put on each side of `"$` in the second `print` command, but not the first one?

7.1.3 Use an Alternative Way to Test a Command

The `if` statement is a very clear way to test the outcome of a command, but there is another way of doing the same thing that you should be familiar with.

Consider the following script:

```
# s713 -- Tell if the user typed the name of a month
grep "^$1\$" Months > /dev/null || print -- "$1 is not
  the name of a month."
```

a) Explain how this script works.

7.1.4 NEST `if` STATEMENTS

You can put one `if` statement "inside" another one, which is known as *nesting*. The result can get confusing, but simple nesting can be fairly clear to follow.

Be sure you still have the `days` file from Exercise 3.1.3, "Pipelines" (or create it again), and run the following script:

```
# s714 -- Demonstrate nested if statements
if     grep -i "^$1\$" Months > /dev/null
then   print -- "$1" is the name of a month.
else   if     grep -i "^$1\$" days > /dev/null
       then   print -- "$1" is the name of a day.
     else   print -- \""$1"\" is neither a month nor a day.
       fi
fi
```

a) What happens if you give the name of a month as a parameter?

---

b) What happens if you give the name of a day of the week?

---

c) What happens if you give something else?

d) Under what condition is the second `if` executed?

e) Which `if` does the first `fi` go with?

f) How could this script be changed to use `elif`?

LAB 7.1 ANSWERS

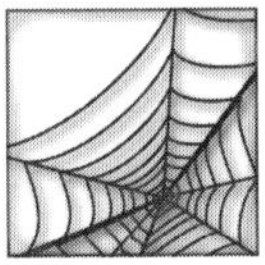

This section gives you some suggested answers to the questions in Lab 7.1, with discussion related to those answers. Your answers may vary, but the most important thing is whether or not your answer works. Use this discussion to analyze differences between your answers and those presented here.

If you have alternative answers to the questions in this exercise, you are encouraged to post your answers and to discuss them at the companion web site for this book, located at:

`http://www.phptr.com/phptrinteractive/`

7.1.1 ANSWERS

```
if   true
then print yes
else print no
fi
```

a) Type in these commands. What printed, and why?

Answer: The word yes was printed. Your interaction should look like the following:

```
[7000]: if   true
> then print yes
> else print no
> fi
yes
[7001]:
```

As soon as you type the first line, the shell recognizes that it is part of an *if, then* structure, and it uses the continuation prompt string (by default, >) to tell you to enter the remaining lines of the command. As soon as you type `fi`, the shell recognizes the end of the compound `if` command and runs it. The `if` command is followed by a `true` command, which sets its exit code to *true*, and the shell knows it should execute the commands following the `then`, which it does, resulting in the output shown.

```
if   true && false
then print ok 1
     print ok 2
     print ok 3
else print not ok 1
     print not ok 2
fi
```

b) Type in these commands. What printed, and why?

Answer: The two "not ok" messages printed. Your interaction should have looked like the following:

```
[7001]: if   true && false
> then print ok 1
>      print ok 2
>      print ok 3
> else print not ok 1
>      print not ok 2
> fi
```

```
not ok 1
not ok 2
[7002]:
```

Again, the shell issues the continuation prompt until you type the `fi` that marks the end of the `if` (or make a mistake!), then it executes the statement from the beginning. In this case, it has to execute two commands joined by `&&`, producing a result of *false*. Therefore, it executes the commands between the `else` and the `fi`.

c) How does the indention affect what gets executed?

Answer: It doesn't. You could have gotten the same results by typing everything at the beginning of each line, like the following interaction:

```
[7002]: if true && false
> then print ok 1
> print ok 2
> print ok 3
> else print not ok 1
> print not ok 2
> fi
not ok 1
not ok 2
[7003]:
```

The problem is that this format makes it hard to see which commands are doing the controlling (the `then`, `else`, and `fi` commands) and which ones are being controlled (the `print` commands).

d) What advantage is there to indenting the code as shown?

Answer: It makes the code easier to read.

Don't forget that there are always at least two readers of your code—the computer, of course, but also anyone who wants to see what your program does. Make it easy for people to read your code. You'll be especially appreciative when you have to do it yourself!

```
if   false
     false
     true
then print ok
else print not ok
fi
```

e) Type in these commands. What printed, and why?

Answer: The "ok" message printed. Your interaction should look like the following:

```
[7003]: if   false
>            false
>            true
> then print ok
> else print not ok
> fi
ok
[7004]:
```

In this example, the `if` command is followed by three independent commands, *all* of which are run. The exit code of the *last* one (`true` in this case) determines whether the `then` or the `else` command group is run. In this case, the `then` group executes, printing the "ok" message.

f) What would happen if you reversed the second and third command lines?

Answer: The "not ok" message would print. Your interaction should look like the following:

```
[7004]: if   false
>            true
>            false
> then print ok
> else print not ok
> fi
not ok
[7005]:
```

Now the last command in the `if` group is `false`, so the `else` statement group executes.

```
if   print hello ||
     print there
then print again
fi
```

g) Type in these commands. What printed, and why?

Answer: The lines, "hello" and "again" print, but not "there." Your interaction should look like the following:

```
[7005]: if   print hello ||
>       print there
> then print again
> fi
hello
again
[7006]:
```

The `print there` command does not run because it is joined to the `print hello` command with the || (logical *or*) operator. The fact that the two `print` commands are entered on separate lines does not make them separate commands. Rather, they are a command *group*, as defined in Chapter 2, "Command Syntax." The "there" was not printed because of the rule for evaluating commands using the || operator: If the first command results in *true* (and `print` commands always do return *true*), the shell does not run the second command because *true* || *X* is *true*, regardless of the value of *X*. Then, because the result of the || operator was *true*, the `then` command was run, resulting in "again" being printed.

The previous question shows that applying a number of simple principles can require a very complex analysis. However, you can do it if you look at all the simple parts systematically.

7.1.2 ANSWERS

a) What does your script look like?

Answer: The following script will work:

```
# a  s712 -- Print a message if option a is set.
if    getopts a optletter
then  print Option -a was set.
fi
```

The first line of this script is a comment. Once you put a pound sign (#) on a line (if it isn't part of something such as `$#` for referencing the number of parameters, or in a single-quoted string, etc.), the shell ignores anything else on the line after the pound sign, so you can write comments after it that will help people understand your program.

Always put a comment line giving the name of the script and a statement of what it does at the beginning of all the scripts you write.

The script uses `if` to test the results of running the `getopts` command with (`a`) as the option list. If the `getopts` command has a *true* exit code, the `print` command executes; otherwise, it is skipped.

b) What happens when you test your script?

Answer: You should have written and tested your script using an interaction like the following:

```
[7006]: vi bin/s712a
[7007]: chmod +x bin/s712a
[7008]: s712 -a hello
Option -a was set.
[7009]: s712a hello
[7010]: s712a -b
s712: -b: unknown option
Option -a was set.
[7011]:
```

Command lines 7006 and 7007 represent the commands you used to create the script and make it executable, then lines 7008 and 7009 verify that the script prints the message if the `-a` option is given on the command line, and it does not print anything if the `-a` option is not given on the command line. However, line 7010 shows that the script also prints the message if the user gives an invalid option (`-b`)! Because `getopts` returns *true*, even if the option it finds is invalid, this script has no way to differentiate between the `-a` option and any other. The next lab shows a way to deal with this problem.

Always test your programs carefully before assuming they are correct!

c) What name should you have used for this script, and why?

Answer: The script should be in a file named `~/bin/s712b`.

There are two reasons for this. The first is that the script has to be in your `~/bin` directory in order to be in the shell's search path, and the second is that the comment indicates that the name of the script is `s712b`, so that should be the name of the executable file.

d) What does the `-i` option do?

Answer: It tells `grep` to ignore the case of the characters as it looks for lines containing the given pattern.

By using this option, you can have "January" in the `Months` file match "january" or "January" (or "JAnuary," or however the user capitalizes it) on the command line.

e) What do `^` and `\$` around `"$1"` do?

Answer: They "anchor" the pattern so that it must occur as the only characters on a line.

The caret (^) says that the command line argument must appear at the beginning of a line, and the dollar sign says the argument must appear at the end of a line. If it has to be at both the beginning and the end of a line, it must be the only thing on the line, which is the structure of the `Months` file you wrote for Chapter 2, "Command Syntax." If you didn't provide this "anchoring" information, the user could type part of the name of a month, for example, "marc," and `grep` would match it to the line containing "March."

Be careful when you make up the pattern part of a `grep` command; it's easy to get unintended results.

The version of `grep` that you have may support the `-w` option to match "words" or allow you to enclose the pattern inside angle brackets (< and >) to indicate that you want to match words. Be sure to quote the angle brackets so the shell doesn't interpret them as redirection symbols. These word options are very useful for searching files with multiple words on a line.

f) Why is it necessary to put `^$1\$` inside quotes in the `grep` command?

Answer: They prevent embedded spaces in variable 1 from "breaking" the script.

Imagine what happens if the user types this command:

```
s712b "January February"
```

Inside the script, a reference to the variable *1* will include a space in the middle. If the reference is not enclosed in quotes, the `grep` command, after the reference is evaluated by the shell, will look like the following command:

```
grep ^January February$ Months
```

This command tells `grep` to look for "January" at the beginning of any line in the two files named `February$` and `Months`, which is clearly not at all what you want to do.

Kids say the darndest things!

Art Linkletter

Users do too!

Anonymous

Always write your code so that it behaves "reasonably," no matter what the user types.

g) Why is the output of the `grep` command redirected to `/dev/null`?

Answer: So the user doesn't see it.

The `grep` command writes all lines that match your pattern to *stdout*. For this script, you want to print your own message rather than show the user the matching line. The special file named */dev/null* accepts anything you send to it—and silently discards it.

h) Why is `--` put on both `print` commands?

Answer: So the program doesn't break if the user puts options on the command line.

This is another example of "defensive programming." Consider the possibility that the user types the following command line:

```
s712b -a
```

When the `print` command (it will be the second one) is executed, the shell will substitute `-a` for the reference to the variable *1*, and the command without the double dashes would look like the following:

```
print "-a" is not the name of a month.
```

Remember, the shell removes quotes before running a command, so the print command receives the `-a` (without any quotes) as its first parameters, and it looks like an option parameter because it starts with a dash. Because `-a` is not a valid option for `print`, the user will get an error message from `print` instead of the message from your script.

Always write your code so that it behaves "reasonably," no matter what the user types! (I know, you already saw this advice, but it's important.)

i) Why is `\"` put on each side of `"$` in the second `print` command, but not the first one?

Answer: So anything the user types that is not the name of a month will be inside quotes.

Consider the following possible command line:

```
s712b
```

If the quotes were not there, the user would see a message like the following:

```
is not the name of a month.
```

With the quotes, the message is much clearer:

```
"" is not the name of a month.
```

Always write your code so that it behaves "reasonably," no matter what the user types!!

7.1.3 ANSWERS

```
# s713 -- Tell if the user typed the name of a month
grep "^$1\$" Months > /dev/null || print -- "$1" is
  not the name of a month.
```

a) Explain how this script works.

Answer: It uses the `||` operator to group the `grep` and the `print` commands.

If the `grep` commands does find the argument in `Months`, its exit code will be *true*, and the shell will not execute the `print` command. However, if the `grep` command fails, its exit code will be *false,* and the shell will execute the `print` command.

Using `||` instead of `if` in this situation is a popular programming technique because `||` is more concise to write. Even if you don't care to use it yourself, you should recognize it as a common "programming idiom" that you are likely to see in other people's scripts.

7.1.4 ANSWERS

a) What happens if you give the name of a month as a parameter?

Answer: The month name is printed, followed by the message, "is the name of a month."

The first `grep` command will have an exit code of *true,* so the first `then` will be executed, giving the "month" message.

b) What happens if you give the name of a day of the week?

Answer: The day's name is printed, followed by the message, "is the name of a day."

The first `grep` command will fail (that is, its exit code will be *false*), so the first `else` will be executed, giving the "day" message.

c) What happens if you give something else?

Answer: Whatever the user typed will be printed inside quotes, followed by the "is neither" message.

Both the first and second `grep` commands will fail, so the second `else` will be executed, giving the "neither" message.

d) Under what condition is the second `if` executed?

Answer: It will be executed if the first `if`*'s* `else` *is executed.*

The reason the second `grep` executed was that the first `else` executed.

e) Which `if` does the first `fi` go with?

Answer: The first `fi` *goes with the* second `if`.

This structure is where the name nested *comes from: The entire second* `if` *statement has to be nested entirely inside the first* `if` *statement.*

f) How could this script be changed to use `elif`?

Answer: Change the `else    if` *on the fourth line to* `elif` *and eliminate the first* `fi`*. The script should then look like the following:*

```
# s714a -- Use elif to avoid nested if.
if      grep -i "^$1\$" Months > /dev/null
then    print -- "$1" is the name of a month.
elif    grep -i "^$1\$" Days > /dev/null
then    print -- "$1" is the name of a day.
else    print -- \""$1"\" is neither a month nor a day.
fi
```

Notice the change in indentation in this code, too. Now there is no nested `if`, just one long `if` statement with two `then`s. Some people find this coding style clearer than nested `if` statements. As you will see, using the `case` statement lets you avoid making the choice.

LAB 7.1 SELF-REVIEW QUESTIONS

To test your progress, you should be able to answer the following questions:

1) Every `if` command must be followed by a `then` command.

a) _____True
b) _____False

2) There can be multiple `then` commands for one `if` command.

a) _____True
b) _____False

3) Every `if` command must be followed by one or more `else` commands.

a) _____True
b) _____False

4) Every `if` command must be followed by one `fi` command.

a) _____True
b) _____False

5) What's wrong with the following code?

```
if      ls -l junk > /dev/null
then    print There is junk.
else    print There is no junk.
fi
```

a) _____Nothing. It will print one of the two messages, depending on whether there is a file or directory named `junk` or not.
b) _____It's illegal to redirect the output of an `if` command.
c) _____It's illegal to redirect the output of an `ls` command.
d) _____The `else` line should come before the `then` line.
e) _____`fi` is spelled wrong.

6) What is the difference between the following two pieces of code:

First:

```
if      cmd-1
then    if      cmd-2
        then    print yes
        fi
fi
```

Second:

```
cmd-1 && cmd-2 && print yes
```

a) _____The first one is simpler.
b) _____The first one will never print "yes," but the second one might.
c) _____The second one will never print "yes," but the first one might.
d) _____They will both print "yes" if and only if `cmd-1` and `cmd-2` both have *true* exit codes.
e) _____The first one won't work because the nesting is wrong.

Quiz answers appear in Appendix A, Section 7.1.

LAB 7.2

THE [[COMMAND...]] OPERATOR

LAB OBJECTIVES

After this lab, you will be able to:

- ✓ Use `[[ ... ]]` in an `if` Statement
- ✓ Use `[[ ... ]]` Instead of `if`
- ✓ Write Logical Expressions

The purpose of the double-bracket operator (`[[ ... ]]`) is to generate an exit value that can be tested, and for this reason it is sometimes called the *test command.* In fact, it replaces an older built-in command, `test`, and an equivalent, single-bracket (`[`) command. You may find those other two commands in older scripts, and they continue to be supported by the KornShell but are no longer needed except for backward compatibility. The double-bracket command operator does everything they did, and more.

Because the purpose of `[[ ... ]]` is to generate an exit value, it is always used with an `if` statement or other shell construct that depends on exit values, such as the `&&` and `||` grouping operators.

The `[[ ... ]]` operator allows you perform a large number of tests that allow your scripts and functions to react intelligently to their environment. You can use the double-bracket to find out about files, directories, I/O devices, FDs, and shell options. Many of these tests wouldn't make sense at this point unless you are already a UNIX expert, and some of the items will not be covered in this book, but a complete list of the things you can test is given in Appendix B, "Command Summary."

LAB 7.2 EXERCISES

7.2.1 USE `[[ ... ]]` IN AN `if` STATEMENT

This exercise deals with the syntax of the `[[ ... ]]` operator. Every test starts with the opening double brackets, a *test expression*(indicated by the ellipses), and a pair of right brackets (`]]`) that end the expression.

For this Exercise, we will use the `-e` test to find out whether a file exists.

Put the following script in your `bin` directory:

```
# s721 -- Test whether a file exists or not
if      [[ -e "$1" ]]
then    print -- "$1 does exist."
else    print -- "\"$1\" does not exist."
fi
```

The shell knows that what is inside a `[[ ... ]]` *has to be a test expression, and does not do token splitting on what is inside. The quotes around* `$1` *could safely have been left off, even if there were spaces inside the value of parameter 1.*

Run this script twice using the following command lines:

```
s721 ~/.kshrc
s721 the_name_of_a_file_that_does_not_exist
```

You can change the parameters in the two commands, provided that the first one names a file that *does* exist and the second one names a file that does *not* exist.

a) Does this script correctly tell whether a file exists?

Now run the following command:

```
s721 ~/bin
```

b) What happens if you give `s721` the name of a directory instead of the name of a file?

Change `s721` so it contains the following commands:

```
# s721 -- Test a file or directory
if      [[ -e "$1" ]]
then    if      [[ -f "$1" ]]
        then    print -- "$1 is a regular file."
        elif    [[ -d "$1" ]]
        then    print -- "$1 is a directory."
        fi
else    print -- "\"$1\" does not exist."
fi
```

c) Explain what happens if you run this version of the script with the name of a file as the parameter.

d) Explain what happens if you run the script with the name of a directory as the parameter.

e) Explain what happens if you run the script with a parameter that is the name of neither a file nor a directory.

7.2.2 USE `[[... ]]` INSTEAD OF `if`

You can use the double-bracket operator as a command to replace simple `if` statements—ones that consist only of `if`, `then`, and `fi`.

If you recall that the grouping operators (`&&` and `||`) work by testing exit codes, you can see that the following two commands are equivalent:

FOR EXAMPLE

The following command line

```
if [[ -e a_file ]] then print a_file exists; fi
```

is equivalent to the following:

```
[[ -e a_file ]] && print a_file exists
```

The first command line could also have been written on three command lines, but this "one-liner" format is convenient to use for simple `if` commands.

a) What does the following command line accomplish:

```
[[ -e a_file ]] || print a_file does not exist!
```


You can also use brace-grouping (Lab 3.2, "Command Groups"), along with the double-bracket command, to mimic more than just the simple `if` structure of the previous example.

Type the following function definition into a file named `~/fun/f722`:

```
# f722 -- Use [[ instead of if
function f722 {
  [[ -e "$1" ]] && {
       [[ -f "$1" ]] && {
            print "$1" is a regular file.
            return
            }
       [[ -d "$1" ]] && {
            print "$1" is a directory.
            return
            }
       }
  print \""$1"\" does not exist.
  }
```

b) What do the `return` commands do?

c) How does the logic of this function differ from the logic of `s714` from the previous lab?

d) Could this program have been written as a script instead of as a function?

7.2.3 WRITE LOGICAL EXPRESSIONS

So far, you have discovered what the unary operators, `-d`, `-e`, and `-f` do. For this exercise, you will use some other unary operators, plus some *binary* operators that compare two things. The following table, which is extracted from Appendix B, "Command Summary," lists the operators, also called *testing primitives*, that you will use here:

`-d` *name*	*name* is the name of a directory.
`-e` *name*	*name* is the name of a file or directory that exists.
`-f` *name*	*name* is the name of a regular file.
`-r` *name*	*name* is a file or directory that the user can read.
`-w` *name*	*name* is a file or directory that the user can write.
`-x` *name*	*name* is a file that the user can execute or the name of a directory the user can browse.
`-o` *name*	*name* is a shell option that is currently set.
string1 `==` *string2*	*string1* is the same as *string2*
string1 `!=` *string2*	*string1* is not the same as *string2*
name 1 `-nt` *name2*	The file *name1* was modified more recently than ("is newer than") the file *name2,* or there is no file *name2.*
name1 `-ot` *name2*	The file *name1* was modified before ("is older than") the file *name2,* or there is no file *name2.*

You can use the `&&` and `||` operators that you have already seen for command grouping in test expressions.

FOR EXAMPLE

You could use the following function to test whether a parameter is the name of a regular file that is also readable:

```
# f723 -- Test if parameter 1 is a readable regular file
function f723 {
  [[ -f "$1" && -r "$1" ]] && {
    print -- "$1 is a readable regular file."
    return
    }
  print "\"$1\" is not a readable regular file."
  }
```

In this example, the `&&` operator is used twice. Inside the double brackets, it performs a logical "and" between the `-f` and `-r` tests; the second time it is used in the way you have already seen (Lab 3.2, "Command Groups") to perform a logical "and" between the double bracket command and the print/return command group inside the braces.

The two uses work just about the same way, with the shell using *true/false* values to decide how much work to do. The double bracket command has a *true* exit code if both the `-f` *and* `-r` tests are true.

As with `&&` used for command grouping, the shell evaluates the right-hand side of a `&&` only if the left-hand side's result is *true*.

If you are not familiar with the ideas of file modification times or the permission bits that UNIX systems associate with files (read, write, execute), you should consult your documentation. Likewise, if you are running the KornShell on a non-UNIX system that does not have similar file system capabilities, the tests used in this exercise may not work for you. For example, U/WIN running with a FAT file system cannot mimic all these features, although U/WIN does fine with an NTFS file system.

Put `f723` in your `fun` directory, and run the following commands:

```
f723 ~/.kshrc
f723 ~/bin
f723 "A figment of your imagination"
```

a) Explain the output of these commands.

There are two other pieces of syntax that you can use when you construct an expression for the double-bracket command. The first one is parentheses (`()`), which you can use to group tests in much the same way as you used them to group commands in Lab 3.2, "Command Groups." The second one is the exclamation mark (`!`), which logically negates whatever follows it.

Run the following command:

```
[[ ! (-d ~/bin && -r ~/bin && -w ~/bin && -x ~/bin) ]] ||
print \~/bin is good
```

There has to be a space after the `[[`*, after the exclamation mark, and on both sides of the* `]]`*, but you don't have to put spaces around the parentheses.*

b) What is the value of the expression inside the parentheses?

---

c) What is the result of the double-bracket command?

---

d) Is the message, "~/bin is good" appropriate?

Run the following sequence of commands to see how to use the -o testing primitive to find out whether a shell option is set:

```
set -o noclobber
[[ -o noclobber ]] && print noclobber is set
set -o | grep noclobber
set +o noclobber
[[ -o noclobber ]] && print noclobber is set
set -o | grep noclobber
```

e) What does the sequence of commands here show about the -o testing primitive?

Strings and patterns are so important in shell programming that they will be covered separately in Chapter 10 "Patterns, Expansions, and Substitutions." However it's hard to avoid using them, so type the following commands as your introduction now to the way you can use the == and != testing primitives with simple strings:

```
[[ hello == "hello" ]] && print The strings are equal.
[[ hello != "good-bye" ]] && print The strings are not \
equal.
```

Early versions of the shell used a single equal sign (=) to test whether two strings are equal, and the current version of the KornShell *still recognizes it. However, you should always use the double equal sign in the scripts and functions you write because the single equal sign may not be supported for string comparisons in the future.*

f) Did both messages print, and why?

g) Do you have to put quotes around something to make it into a string?

FOR EXAMPLE

UNIX file systems keep track of a wealth of information about files and directories, and the KornShell provides testing primitives for the items that are most useful for shell programs. For example, if you have two files and you want to know which one you edited most recently, you could print its name using the following function:

```
# newer -- Print the name of the more recently edited
  of two files.
function newer {

  [[ -f $1 ]] ||     { print -- \""$1"\" is not a file!
                        return 1
                        }
  [[ -f $2 ]] ||     { print -- \""$2"\" is not a file!
                        return 1
                        }
  [[ $1 -nt $2 ]] &&  { print -- $1
                          return 0
                          }
  print $2

  }
```

h) What do the first two double-bracket commands do?

____

____

i) Why do the `return` commands have numbers after them?

____

____

j) What happens if the two files were both modified at the same time?

____

____

You can use the `touch` command to simulate editing a file. If you give the name of a file to this command, it will change the last modified time of the file to whatever the time and date are at that moment, or will create the file if it does not exist.

You can also use output redirection as a command by itself to create a file easily; but unlike `touch`, `>` *will truncate a file's contents if the file already exists.*

Enter function `newer` in your `~/fun` directory and run the following commands to test it:

```
touch a
touch b
newer a b
touch a
newer a b
```

k) What is the output of the two `newer` commands?

l) Does it matter in which order the file names are given on the `newer` command line?

m) What does the following command line do?

```
newer a b > /dev/null || print Problem!
```

LAB 7.2 ANSWERS

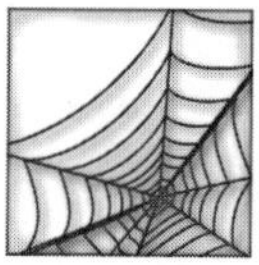

This section gives you some suggested answers to the questions in Lab 7.2, with discussion related to those answers. Your answers may vary, but the most important thing is whether or not your answer works. Use this discussion to analyze differences between your answers and those presented here.

If you have alternative answers to the questions in this exercise, you are encouraged to post your answers and to discuss them at the companion web site for this book, located at:

http://www.phptr.com/phptrinteractive/

7.2.1 ANSWERS

Run the given script twice, using the following command lines:

```
s721 ~/.kshrc
s721 the_name_of_a_file_that_does_not_exist
```

a) Does this script correctly tell whether a file exists?

Answer: Yes it does. Your interaction should look like the following:

```
[7011]: s721 ~/.kshrc
.kshrc does exist.
[7012]: s721 the_name_of_a_file_that_does_not_exist
"the_name_of_a_file_that_does_not_exist" does not exist.
[7013]:
```

The (-e) primitive is called a *unary operator* because it is followed by *one* operand, a name that is checked to see whether it is the name of an existing file.

b) What happens if you give s721 the name of a directory instead of the name of a file?

Answer: If the directory does exist, the script will say so, as the following interaction shows:

```
[7013]: s721 ~/bin
/home/vickery/bin does exist.
[7014]:
```

So, -e does not distinguish between files and directories—it simply tests for the existence of either one.

Note that the shell has performed "tilde expansion" by substituting the actual pathname of my home directory for the ~/ before bin. Naturally, your home directory is not the same as mine, so the pathname you see will be different.

```
# s721 -- Test a file or directory
if      [[ -e "$1" ]]
then    if      [[ -f "$1" ]]
        then    print -- "$1" is a regular file.
        elif    [[ -d "$1" ]]
        then    print -- "$1" is a directory.
        fi
else    print -- \""$1"\" does not exist.
fi
```

c) Explain what happens if you run this version of the script with the name of a file as the parameter.

Answer: The script prints the "is a regular file" message. Your interaction should look like the following:

```
[7014]: s721 ~/.kshrc
/home/vickery/.kshrc is a regular file.
[7015]:
```


The `-e` test succeeds, so the nested if is executed. Its `-f` test also succeeds, and the "regular file" message prints. The `elif` is skipped because the corresponding `if` (the nested `if`) succeeded, so the "is a directory" message does not print. Finally, the `else` is skipped because the first `if` succeeded, so the "does not exist" message does not print.

Nested `if` statements, especially with `else` statements, can give you a headache. Using `elif` instead of `else ... if` can reduce the pain to a dull throb.

d) Explain what happens if you run this version of the script with the name of a directory as the parameter.

Answer: The script prints the "is a directory" message. Your interaction should look like the following:

```
[7015]: s721 ~/bin
/home/vickery/bin is a directory.
[7016]:
```

The `-e` test succeeds, so the nested `if` is executed. Its `-f` test fails, so the "regular file" message does not print. The `elif` is executed because the corresponding `if` (the nested `if`) failed, and the `-d` test succeeds, and the "is a directory" message does print. Finally, the `else` is skipped because the first `if` succeeded, so the "does not exist" message does not print.

e) Explain what happens if you run the script with a parameter that is the name of neither a file nor a directory.

Answer: The "does not exist" message prints. Your interaction should look something like the following:

```
[7016]: s721 "A figment of your imagination"
"A figment of your imagination" does not exist.
[7017]:
```

The imaginary file name is in quotes because it contains embedded spaces. You could have used any name you wanted, provided it was not the name of a file or directory.

The `-e` test fails, so the nested `if` is skipped entirely, and neither the "is a file" nor the "is a directory" message prints. However, the `else` is not skipped because the first `if` failed, so the "does not exist" message prints.

7.2.2 ANSWERS

a) What does the following command line accomplish?

```
[[ -e a_file ]] || print a_file does not exist!
```

Answer: It prints the "does not exist" message if `a_file` is the name of neither a file nor a directory (or one of the myriad other I/O, communication, or other mechanisms that masquerade as files and directories on UNIX systems).

To understand the logic of this command line, you need to recall that the `||` operator causes the right side to be executed only if the left side fails—that is, if the left side's exit code is *false.*

b) What do the `return` commands do?

Answer: If they are executed, they cause the function to stop executing.

A script or function can contain any number of `return` statements. As shown in this example, they can be used to skip over parts of the program that you don't want to execute.

Using `return` commands can make a program's logic difficult to follow. There are often clearer ways to structure your code.

c) How does the logic of this function differ from the logic of `s714` from the previous lab?

Answer: It accomplishes exactly the same thing.

Perhaps the following "pseudo-code" will make the parallels clearer:

```
[[ X ]] && { Y } || { Z }
```

is equivalent to

```
if [[ X ]] then { Y } else { Z } fi
```

In the code we are looking at, `Z` is a single command, the one that prints the "does not exist" message, so the braces around it are omitted because there is no need to "group" a single command.

That takes care of the outer `if` statement. The inner one, the `Y` part of the code shown here, is a bit more complex. We'll use lowercase letters to differentiate between the following pseudo-code and the code we just looked at.

```
[[ w ]] && { x ; return }
[[ y ]] && { z ; return }
```

is equivalent to

```
if   [[ w ]] then x
elif [[ y ]] then z
fi
```

Watch out! The `return` statement takes you out of whatever program you are running, but if you use it from the command line, where no script or function is running, it will take you out of your interactive session with the shell and log you off!

d) Could this program have been written as a script instead of as a function?

Answer: Yes it could. Scripts and functions work the same way.

The script version would look like the following:

```
# s722 -- Use [[ instead of if -- script version
  [[ -e "$1" ]] && {
      [[ -f "$1" ]] && {
          print "$1" is a regular file.
          return
          }
      [[ -d "$1" ]] && {
          print "$1" is a directory.
          return
          }
      }
  print \""$1"\" does not exist.
```

7.2.3 ANSWERS

```
f723 ~/.kshrc
f723 ~/bin
f723 "A figment of your imagination"
```

a) Explain the output of these commands.

Answer: Your interaction should look like the following:

```
[7017]: f723 ~/.kshrc
.kshrc is a readable regular file.
[7018]: f723 ~/bin
"/home/vickery/bin" is not a readable regular file.
[7019]: f723 "A figment of your imagination"
"A figment of your imagination" is not a readable reg-
  ular file.
[7020]:
```

The first command on line 7017 is the only one of the three commands that names something that is both a regular file *and* is readable. Line 7018 names a directory, which is readable but not a regular file, and line 7019 names something that (presumably) does not exist at all. You might want to experiment with this function by creating a regular file that is not readable to test it more completely.

Run the following command:

```
[[ ! (-d ~/bin && -r ~/bin && -w ~/bin && -x ~/bin) ]] \
|| print \~/bin is good
```

b) What is the value of the expression inside the parentheses?

Answer: The expression will be true only if `~/bin` *is a directory and the user has permission to read, write, and browse it. Your interaction should look like the following:*

```
[7020]:[[ ! (-d ~/bin && -r ~/bin && -w ~/bin && -x \
~/bin) ]] || print \~/bin is good
/home/vickery/bin is good
[7021]:
```

If the message prints, your account is set up with a `bin` directory under your home directory and you can read, write, and browse it, as configured in Chapter 1, "Setting Up." If the message doesn't print, there is a problem, and the following questions might help you analyze it.

c) What is the result of the double-bracket command?

Answer: The result of the double bracket command is the opposite of the result of the expression inside the parentheses, because of the exclamation mark.

Note that the exclamation mark applies to the result of evaluating *all* the tests inside the parentheses. All four of the inner tests must be *true* for the exclamation mark to make the double-bracket return *false*.

Always put a space or open parentheses after an exclamation mark or you will get a syntax error from the shell.

d) Is the message "/home/vickery/bin is good" appropriate?

Answer: Yes, assuming that "good" means that the directory exists and that the user can read, write, and browse it. (Substitute the pathname of your own home directory, of course.)

If everything inside the parentheses is *true*, the double bracket will return *false*, so the shell will run the `print` command because of the rule for evaluating `||` in command groups.

```
set -o noclobber
[[ -o noclobber ]] && print noclobber is set
set -o | grep noclobber
set +o noclobber
[[ -o noclobber ]] && print noclobber is set
set -o | grep noclobber
```

e) What does this sequence of commands show about the `-o` testing primitive?

Answer: It evaluates to true *or* false*, depending on whether the named option is set.*

You saw how to turn the `noclobber` option on and off in Chapter 2, "Command Syntax," and you saw how to use `grep` to search for items in the output of a `set` command in Chapter 4, "Simple Variables." This exercise extends those two techniques to pipe the output of `set -o`, which lists the settings of all the shell options, including `noclobber`, to `grep noclobber` to see the setting of just that one option. The idea here is to look at the same information two different ways to make sure each command does what we expect it to.

```
[[ hello == "hello" ]] && print The strings are equal.
[[ hello != "good-bye" ]] && print The strings are not \
equal.
```

f) Did both messages print, and why?

Answer: Both messages printed because both tests were successful.

You can put strings inside quotes or not, so *hello* is the same as *"hello"*. However, *hello* is not the same as *good-bye,* so the test for inequality succeeded, too.

This question brings up a technical issue that will be dealt with in Chapter 10, "Patterns, Expansions, and Substitutions." The item on the right side of these two primitives has to be in quotes to guarantee that it is treated as a string rather than as a pattern. *However, in this particular instance, the quotes are not really needed because* hello *does not contain any of the special characters used in patterns. The full implications of this distinction will have to wait until we cover patterns.*

g) Do you have to put quotes around something to make it into a string?

Answer: No, not necessarily.

However, by now you should be familiar enough with the way the shell processes command lines to realize that you *would* have to use quotes if you wanted to put a space inside a string because spaces are what the shell uses to tell where various tokens begin and end. If you want to have a string, it has to be a token, so any spaces inside it have to be quoted.

h) What do the first two double-bracket commands do?

Answer: They make sure the two files exist before proceeding.

There is no point in comparing two files' modification times if they don't both exist. The results would be confusing to the user.

i) Why do the `return` commands have numbers after them?

Answer: To set the exit code returned by the function.

A function's exit code is zero if it terminates "normally." You can explicitly set the value using `return` statements; any value other than zero is interpreted as *false,* meaning the function did not terminate normally. You have already seen many examples of testing exit codes throughout this workbook. Now you know how to set these codes from inside your functions and scripts.

j) What happens if the two files were both modified at the same time?

Answer: The name of the second one would print.

The third double bracket command prints the first file's name if it is newer than the second one. Otherwise (that is, if the second one is newer than the first or if they are equally old), the name of the second one prints.

k) What is the output of the two `newer` commands?

Answer: The first one prints `b` *and the second one prints* `a`.

By touching `b` after touching `a`, you make `b` the newer file, and its name is printed the first time. Touching `a` the second time simulates an operation like editing the file and it then becomes the newer one.

l) Does it matter in which order the file names are given on the `newer` command line?

Answer: No.

The exception to this, however, is if both files have the same modification times. In this situations, the second one is the one that will have its name printed.

m) What does the following command line do?

```
newer a b > /dev/null || print Problem!
```

Answer: It prints "Problem!:" if either file `a` *or file* `b` *does not exist, but it does not print either of the "is not a file" messages from the function.*

This code illustrates how the exit codes on the `return statements in the newer` function can interact with commands that use the function.

LAB 7.2 SELF-REVIEW QUESTIONS

To test your progress, you should be able to answer the following questions:

1) The `&&` and `||` operators can be used only to group commands, not inside the double-bracket command.

a) _____True
b) _____False

2) Which of the following tests will be *true* if `it` is a directory that can be written?

a) _____`[[ ! -d it -x it ]]`
b) _____`[[ -d it && -w it ]]`
c) _____`[[ (-d && -w) it ]]`
d) _____`[[ ! ( -w it -x it ) ]]`
e) _____`[[ -wd it ]]`

3) What will print after running the following commands?

```
touch a
touch b
if      [[ a -nt b ]]
then    print a
else    print b
fi
```

a) _____a
b) _____b
c) _____c
d) _____ab
e) _____a -nt b

4) Which test will be true in a function that is run with `/usr/bin` as the second parameter?

a) _____`[[ second == parameter ]]`
b) _____`[[ $2 -ot /usr/bin ]]`
c) _____`[[ /usr/bin == "$2" ]]`
d) _____`[[ "/usr/bin" eq "$2" ]]`
e) _____`second.equals( "/usr/bin");`

Quiz answers appear in Appendix A, Section 7.2.

CHAPTER 7

TEST YOUR THINKING

The projects in this section are meant to have you utilize all of the skills that you have acquired throughout this chapter. The answers to these projects can be found at the companion Web site to this book, located at:

`http://www.phptr.com/phptrinteractive/`

Visit the web site periodically to share and discuss your answers.

1) Write a script that prints all the information available about a command line argument (whether it is a file, a directory, or does not exist), using `||` instead of `&&`, as in `f722`.

2) Write a script that verifies that there are exactly two parameters and that the first one is the name of a writeable directory before proceeding. Then, if the second parameter is the name of a file that is already in the named directory, make a backup copy of the file. If the file does not yet exist in the directory, create a new (empty) file with that name. (Lab 5.2, "Processing Option Parameters," covered the parameter processing techniques you will need to use here.)

C H A P T E R 8

LOOPS

No hinge nor loop to hang a doubt on.

Othello, Act 3 Scene 3.

CHAPTER OBJECTIVES

In this chapter, you will learn about:

The testing facilities you saw in the previous chapter are useful elements in themselves, but you may have noticed that you haven't started doing "real work" yet. We've mostly used `print` statements to see how the test operations work, but you will generally want your scripts and functions to do more than just print out messages. Once you have learned to use the control structures from the following labs, you will indeed be able to write programs that can automate tasks for you. You will see that the examples from here on include a richer use of conventional commands, a larger use of variables to keep track of what is happening in your programs, and a heavy reliance on loops and advanced testing structures to hold everything together.

So, get ready! What follows is the good stuff.

LAB 8.1

LOOPS: `while` AND `until`

LAB OBJECTIVES

After this lab, you will be able to:

- ✓ Use `while` to Repeat Commands
- ✓ Use `break` and `continue` to Manage a Loop
- ✓ Use `until`, a Variant of `while`

A *loop* is a set of commands that gets executed more than once. Every loop has markers to indicate where the loop starts and ends, and some testing mechanism that decides how many times the commands inside the loop will be executed.

The two types of loops you will learn about in this lab, called `while` and `until`, nearly identical syntax diagrams:

`while`

`Command` ... This is the *loop test,* the commands to decide whether or not to execute the loop body.

`do`

`Command` ... This is the *loop body,* the commands inside the loop.

`done`

until

`Command` ... This is the *loop test,* the commands to decide whether or not to execute the loop body.

do

`Command` ... This is the *loop body,* the commands inside the loop.

done

Execution of either type of loop proceeds as follows: First, the shell executes all the commands in the *loop test,* resulting in a *true/false* value that is used to decide whether or not to execute the commands in the *loop body.* After the loop body is executed and the `done` command is reached, the shell returns to the `while` or `until` command (called the *top of the loop* because it is at the beginning), and executes all the commands in the loop test again to decide whether or not to execute the loop body again. This cycle can repeat forever, but normally, something eventually happens in the loop body that makes the loop test fail, and the shell then skips to the first command after the `done` and resumes execution from there.

LAB 8.1 EXERCISES

8.1.1 USE `while` TO REPEAT COMMANDS

The `while` loop executes the loop body if the loop test results in a value of *true*. (You might be able to guess how this differs from the operation of the `until` loop.)

In this exercise, we will use the exit code of a single `getopts` command for the loop test, and inside the loop body we will set the values of some variables to keep track of the command line options passed to a script.

You can put any number of commands in the loop test, but most of the time, there is just one because it is easier to understand the logic that way. When there is more than one command in the loop test, the shell takes the exit code of the last one as the value of the entire loop test.

There has to be at least one command in both the loop test and the loop body.

Enter the following function in your `fun` directory:

```
#    f811 -- Process option parameters

#    The variables a_opt, b_opt, and c_opt will be
  either empty
#    strings or the string "on", depending on the
  command line,
#    when this function terminates.

function f811 {

#    Initialize all option variables to empty strings.

    a_opt=
    b_opt=
    c_opt=

#    Loop through command line option parameters

    while   getopts abc optletter
    do      [[ $optletter == "a" ]] && a_opt=on
            [[ $optletter == "b" ]] && b_opt=on
            [[ $optletter == "c" ]] && c_opt=on
    done

    }
```

Until now, it really didn't matter whether you wrote functions or scripts, but starting with this one, it does make a difference. If you were to rewrite this function as a script, the variables `a_opt`*, etc. would not be "visible" from your interactive command line. This topic was covered in Lab 6.1.4, "Control the Scope of Variables."*

Now run the following commands:

```
f811 -ac
print a is \'$a_opt\', b is \'$b_opt\',c is \'$c_opt\'
```

a) What was printed?

b) How many times was the loop body executed?

c) How many commands are in the loop body?

d) What was the total number of commands executed when you ran `f811`?

e) What would be the total number of commands executed if you ran the following command line?
`f811 -abcabc`

8.1.2 USE break AND continue TO MANAGE A LOOP

It may have occurred to you that f811 is inefficient because it executes all three double-bracket commands every time the loop executes. If the first double-bracket command is *true*, it is a waste of time to execute the second and third.

Keep your thinking about efficiency in perspective. You are about to spend more time making a function more efficient than will ever actually be saved, even if you run the function a million times.

Sometimes it's not just inefficient to execute all of the commands in a loop's body, it may be logically wrong. This exercise will show two ways to "short-circuit" a loop that you might use either for efficiency or for logical correctness.

The first command is continue. When the shell encounters this command in a loop, it skips all the remaining commands in the loop body and runs the loop test commands again. Some people like to think of this as jumping to the done command, which in turns takes you back to the top of the loop to test whether to start a new iteration or not.

Here is f811, modified to use continue to skip double-bracket commands that aren't needed. This is not a very realistic use for continue because this particular function would be more naturally implemented using a case statement, but you won't see that until Chapter 10, "The case and select Statements." However, this function does show you how continue works.

```
#   f812 -- Process option parameters; use continue
#           when match is found.

#  The variables a_opt, b_opt, and c_opt will be
#  either empty strings or the string "on", depending
#  on the command line, when this function terminates.

function f812 {
```

```
#   Initialize all option variables to empty strings.

    a_opt=
    b_opt=
    c_opt=

#   Loop through command line option parameters

    while   getopts abc optletter
    do      [[ $optletter == "a" ]] &&  {
                                        a_opt=on
                                        continue
                                        }
            [[ $optletter == "b" ]] &&  {
                                        b_opt=on
                                        continue
                                        }
            [[ $optletter == "c" ]] &&  {
                                        c_opt=on
                                        continue
                                        }
    done

    }
```

a) What commands will be executed if the following command line is entered?

`f812 -a`

b) How many commands will be executed if the following command line is entered?

`f812 -abcabc`

The `break` command is similar to `continue`, in that it causes the remaining commands in the loop body to be skipped, but it completely exits the loop instead of returning to the top for another loop test. It takes its name from the fact that it "breaks out" of the loop.

Put a `break` command between the last double-bracket command and the `done` command in `f812`. The last few lines will look like this:

```
[[ $optletter == "c" ]] &&  {
                                        c_opt=on
                                        continue
                                        }
            break
    done

    }
```

Now run the following command lines:

```
f812 -adbc
print a is \'$a_opt\', b is \'$b_opt\',c is \'$c_opt\'
. ~/fun/f812
f812 -adbc
print a is \'$a_opt\', b is \'$b_opt\',c is \'$c_opt\'
```

c) What is the reason for the "dot" command on the third line?

____

____

d) Explain the difference in the output from the two `print` commands.

____

____

____

____

8.1.3 *USE* `until`*, A VARIANT OF* `while`

Did you guess how `while` and `until` are related? The body of a `while` loop is executed if the test part is *true*, but for `until`, the body is executed if the test part is *false*.

a) Why is the `until` statement not really a necessary part of the shell?

____

____

b) If it's not really needed, why is `until` included?

____

____

c) What does the following function print?

```
function u {
until [[ "$1" == "" ]]
do    print -- "$1"
      shift
done
}
```

____

____

LAB 8.1 ANSWERS

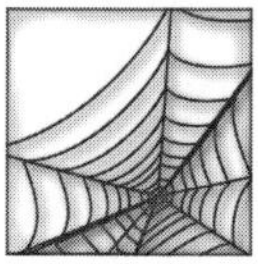

This section gives you some suggested answers to the questions in Lab 8.1, with discussion related to those answers. Your answers may vary, but the most important thing is whether or not your answer works. Use this discussion to analyze differences between your answers and those presented here.

If you have alternative answers to the questions in this exercise, you are encouraged to post your answers and to discuss them at the companion web site for this book, located at:

http://www.phptr.com/phptrinteractive/

8.1.1 ANSWERS

After entering the given function into your `~/fun` directory, run the following commands:

```
f811 -ac
print a is \'$a_opt\', b is \'$b_opt\',c is \'$c_opt\'
```

a) What was printed?

Answer: Your interaction should look like the following:

```
[8000]: f811 -ac
[8001]: print a is \'$a_opt\', b is \'$b_opt\',c is \
\'$c_opt\'
a is 'on', b is '', c is 'on'
[8002]:
```

You can experiment with different sets of option parameters for the `f811` command line. In all cases, the variables `a_opt`, and so forth should be set to the string `on` or to the empty string, depending on what options you gave on the command line.

The reason for using the empty string as the value when an option is not set is that you can test for it easily. Inside a double-bracket command, an empty string has a value of false *and any other string has a value of* true, *so the following command will print a message if* `a_opt` *has a value that is anything other than the empty string (such as on) and won't print anything if its value is the empty string:*

```
[[ $a_opt ]] && print a is set.
```

b) How many times was the loop body executed?

Answer: Twice, once for each option parameter on the command line.

The `getopts` command was executed three times. The first two times, its exit value was *true*, and the loop body was executed. But the third time, there were no more command line options, so `getopts` returned *false*, the shell jumped to the next command after the `done`, and the function terminated.

c) How many commands are in the loop body?

Answer: Six, the three double-bracket commands and the three assignment commands.

However, no more than one of the three assignment commands would be executed each time the loop body is processed, because `optletter` would have just one value each time. (If the user enters an invalid option letter on the command line, none of the assignment commands will be executed.)

d) What was the total number of commands executed when you ran `f811`?

Answer: 14, not counting `while`, `do`, *and* `done` *as commands.*

You can figure out the number of commands as follows:

3	The three assignments before `while`.
3	The `getopts` command, which has an exit code of *true* twice, and then *false* once.
6	The three double-bracket commands, each of which is executed twice.
2	One of the assignment commands each time the loop body was executed.
14	Total

e) What would be the total number of commands executed if you ran the following command line?

`f811 -abcabc`

Answer: 34 commands.

You can figure out the number of commands as follows:

3	The three assignments before `while`.
7	The `getopts` command, which has an exit code of *true* six times, then *false* once.
18	The three double-bracket commands, each of which is executed six times.
6	One of the assignment commands each time the loop body was executed.
34	Total

There are two points to understand from this question. The first is the relatively minor point that the user can repeat option parameters and `getopts` does not consider this to be an error, or even unusual. The second is that it takes time to execute commands, and loops typically affect the execution times of scripts and functions: You have to multiply the number of commands in the test and body parts by the number of times the loop is executed. This multiplicative effect becomes very significant if a loop is executed many times.

Whenever possible, put commands outside loops instead of inside them; the performance improvements can be dramatic.

8.1.2 Answers

a) What commands will be executed if the following command line is entered?

```
f812 -a
```

Answer: The following commands will be executed:

```
a_opt=
b_opt=
c_opt=
getopts abc optletter
[[ $optletter == "a" ]]
a_opt=on
getopts abc optletter
```

After assigning `on` to `a_opt`, execution of the loop body terminates, and the next loop test is executed immediately, skipping the remaining two double-bracket commands in the loop body.

b) How many commands will be executed if the following command line is entered?

```
f812 -abcabc
```

Answer: 28 commands.

You can figure out the number of commands as follows:

3 The three assignments before `while`.

7 The `getopts` command, which has an exit code of *true* six times, then *false* once.

6 The first double-bracket command, which is executed every time.

4 The second double-bracket command, which is executed only if `optletter` is not *a*.

2 The third double-bracket command, which is executed only if `optletter` is nether *a* nor *b*.

6 One of the assignment commands each time the loop body was executed.

28 Total

Assuming the shell spends no time executing the `while`, `do`, `done`, and `continue` commands, this analysis shows a speedup of 1.21, compared with the version without the `continue` statements. Of course, the assumption that the control statements take no time to execute is not totally realistic; you will see later in this chapter how to determine just how long they do take.

The speedup of a program is given by the ratio of the time to execute it before an improvement is made, divided by the time to execute it after the improvement is made. If you subtract 1 and multiply by 100, you get a "percent faster" measure. (`f812` is 21 percent faster than `f811`.) Using the number of commands as a measure of the time to execute a program is not totally accurate because commands don't all take the same amount of time to run.

Of course, this whole analysis is based on just one of the possible ways the user might have typed the command line.

```
f812 -adbc
print a is \'$a_opt\', b is \'$b_opt\',c is \'$c_opt\'
. ~/fun/f812
f812 -adbc
print a is \'$a_opt\', b is \'$b_opt\',c is \'$c_opt\'
```

c) What is the reason for the "dot" command on the third line?

Answer: To redefine the function.

The first time the function is run, it still has the old definition, without the `break` command. As described in Chapter 1, "Setting Up," the shell will find a function definition in your `~/fun` directory the first time you use it, but it does not automatically update the definition even if you update the file, so you have to use the "dot" command to get the shell to read the modified function definition. The reason the two `print` commands have different outputs is that they follow executions of two different versions of the function.

d) Explain the difference in the output from the two `print` commands.

Answer: Your interaction should look like the following:

```
[8002]: f812 -adbc
ksh: f812: -d: unknown option
[8003]: print a is \'$a_opt\', b is \'$b_opt\',c is \
\'$c_opt\'
a is 'on', b is 'on',c is 'on'
[8004]: . ~/fun/f812
[8005]: f812 -adbc
ksh: f812: -d: unknown option
[8006]: print a is \'$a_opt\', b is \'$b_opt\',c is \
\'$c_opt\'
a is 'on', b is '',c is ''
[8007]:
```

Without the `break` command, all the options were turned on, but with the `break` command, the function broke out of the loop before processing the `b` and `c` options.

In both forms of the function, `getopts` printed an error message when it encountered the `d` in the option parameter, which is not in the list of valid options. Note that despite the error, `getopts` sets a *true* exit code, so you can continue processing additional options if you want to.

Some programs just print a warning message and continue to run if they find an invalid option letter, in the name of being "user-friendly." It's better to assume that an invalid option letter means the user either mistyped the command line or doesn't know how to use the command, and to stop execution before doing something the user didn't intend.

The modified version of the function executes the `break` only if none of the double-bracket commands succeeds. (If any one was *true*, the corresponding `continue` command would cause the `break` to be skipped.)

8.1.3 Answers

a) Why is the `until` statement not really a necessary part of the shell?

Answer: Because it is equivalent to a `while` statement with an exclamation mark in front of the test.

You saw the use of an exclamation mark to negate the truth value of the expression inside the double-bracket command in the previous lab. You can also use it to negate the truth value of a command's exit value.

FOR EXAMPLE

The following statements are equivalent:

```
while   cmd-a
do      cmd-b
done
```

and

```
until   ! cmd-a
do      cmd-b
done
```

b) If it's not really needed, why is `until` included?

Answer: Sometimes it's more natural to express what you want to do using `until` *instead of* `while`.

If you can express what you want to do in a natural way, you are less likely to make a mistake doing it, and other people are more likely to understand your program.

c) What does the following function print?

```
function u {
until [[ "$1" == "" ]]
do    print -- "$1"
      shift
done
}
```

Answer: It tries to print all of its command line option, but illustrates a common programming error!

The program repeatedly tests the parameter variable `1`, prints it if it is not empty, and shifts the next parameter into position number `1` for the next test. Normally, this works because a variable that has not been initialized has the same value as the empty string.

The function does not print all the command line options if the user explicitly types an empty string as an option, like the following interaction:

```
[8007]: u hello "" there
hello
[8008]:
```

If you want to print *all* the command line options using `until`, the function should look like the following:

```
function u {
until       [[ ! "$1" ]]
do          print -- "$1"
done
}
```

However, it is arguably more natural to do this using `while`:

```
function u {
while       [[ "$1" ]]
do          print -- "$1"
done
}
```

LAB 8.1 SELF-REVIEW QUESTIONS

To test your progress, you should be able to answer the following questions.

1) What are the commands between the `while` and the `do` called?
   a) _____The loop body
   b) _____The loop boundary
   c) _____The loop banner
   d) _____The loop banana
   e) _____The loop test

2) What are the commands between the `do` and the `done` called?
   a) _____The loop test
   b) _____The loop top
   c) _____The loop tail
   d) _____The loop tangerine
   e) _____The loop body

3) Any `while` loop can be converted to an `until` loop by negating the test using an exclamation mark.
   a) _____True
   b) _____False

4) Which statement causes the shell to jump to the statement immediately *after* the loop?
   a) _____break
   b) _____continue
   c) _____skip
   d) _____jump
   e) _____exit

5) Which statement causes the shell to jump immediately to the first statement in the test part of the loop?
   a) _____break
   b) _____continue
   c) _____skip
   d) _____jump
   e) _____exit

6) What does the following function do:

```
function q6 {
  until       [[ ! "$1" ]] || grep "$target" "$1" \
  > /dev/null
  do          shift
  done
  if          [[ "$1" ]]
  then        print -- Found "$target" in "$1"
  else        print -- Did not find "$target"
  fi
  }
```

a) _____It prints an error message because you cannot use || in the loop test.

b) _____It prints the name of each command line parameter.

c) _____It prints the name of the first file named on the command line that that contains whatever string is the value of a variable named `target`.

d) _____It prints the "Did not find" message if the value of `target` is not one of the files given as a command line option.

e) _____It prints an error message because the double-bracket command on the `if` statement does not use a logical primitive.

Quiz answers appear in Appendix A, Section 8.1.

LAB 8.2

LAB 8.2

LOOPS: LIST AND ARITHMETIC FOR

LAB OBJECTIVES

After this lab, you will be able to:

- ✓ Use `for` to Work with a List of Values
- ✓ Use `for` to Count Iterations

The `for` loop is one of the workhorses of shell programming. Do you want to do something with some or all of the files in a directory? Use a `for` loop. You will find many ways to use `for` loops, but being able to execute a set of commands for different files is so common that this lab will use that type of operation to introduce you to the mechanics of `for` loops.

The KornShell has two types of `for` loops. The first one is used for working with lists, such as the names of files, and the second one, which is based on the `for` loop provided by C, C++, and Java, is used to count the number of iterations. Both are very powerful, and both have structures that look just like `while` and `until`, except that they start with `for`:

for

`Command` . . . This is the *loop test,* the commands to decide whether or not to execute the loop body.

do

`Command` . . . This is the *loop body,* the commands inside the loop.

done

The *loop test* is what differentiates the two `for` loops from each other, and the `for` loops from the `while/until` loops you saw in the previous lab. The `for` loops both use the loop test to introduce a variable called the *control variable* because it controls how many times to repeat the loop. The control variable, which can be any simple variable you choose to use for that purpose, is automatically assigned a different value for each iteration of the loop, and the loop test is used to tell the shell what values you want to use.

LAB 8.2 EXERCISES

8.2.1 USE `for` TO WORK WITH A LIST OF VALUES

You have already seen lists of values when you saw command line options being passed as the values of a set of parameters named *1*, *2*, *3*, and so forth, in a function or script. You can create lists of values other ways, but let's start by using a `for` loop to *iterate over* the parameter list in a function.

The phrase to "iterate over a list" means to execute a loop with the control variable taking on the value of a different item in the list each time through the loop.

Enter the following code as function `f821`:

```
# f821 -- Iterate over the elements of the parameter
# variables

function f821 {

  for   param in "$@"
  do    print The parameter is: \"$param\"
  done

  }
```

a) What is the name of the control variable of this `for` loop?

____

____

b) What is the *loop test* part of this `for` loop?

c) What is the word `in` after the control variable name?

d) What is the list that this loop iterates over?

e) What is the *loop body* part of this `for` loop?

f) What prints if you run the following command?

```
f821 Tippy canoe, "and Tyler too!"
```

g) What happens if you remove the quotes from the `$@` in the loop test and run the same command again?

You can write out the list that you want to iterate over. Try it by running the following command line:

```
for p in a b c ; do print $p ; done
```

h) What is the name of the control variable for this loop?

i) What is the list that this loop iterates over?

j) What prints when you run this command line?

8.2.2 USE `for` TO COUNT ITERATIONS

The second type of `for` loop sets the control variable to a sequence of *numeric values*.

If you already know C, C++, or Java, you can write this kind of `for` *loop just the way you already know, except that the KornShell* `for` *loop uses double parentheses instead of single parentheses.*

■ FOR EXAMPLE

Let's start with a loop that prints the numbers 0–9:

```
for (( i=0; i<10; i++ )) do print $i ; done
```

Double parentheses introduce *arithmetic commands* in general, and a special form of arithmetic command used just in `for` loops in this case. (You may recall that we made up a rule about putting a space after an open parentheses for command grouping in Chapter 2, "Command Syntax"; the reason for that was so you wouldn't accidentally start an arithmetic command if you tried to nest command groups.)

You don't have to put a dollar sign in front of variable references inside arithmetic commands.

a) What is the control variable in the example?

The loop test in an arithmetic `for` has three parts, separated by two semicolons (`;`). In left-to-right order, they are:

- The *initialization* part, which assigns the value to the control variable that will be used for the first iteration of the loop. In the example, the number zero (`0`) is assigned to the control variable, `i`. You can have multiple initializations in the initialization part if you separate them with commas.
- The *termination test* part, which consists of an expression that gives a *true/false* value. You usually use the numeric comparison operators (`<`, `<=`, `!=`, `==`, `>=`, `>` for *less than, less than or equal, not equal, equal, greater than or equal,* and *greater than,* respectively), but you can do any arithmetic calculation, with a result of zero meaning *false* and any nonzero result meaning *true.* The termination test is performed before each iteration of the loop, and the loop body is executed if the result of the test is *true.* In the example, the loop is executed as long as the variable `i` has a value less than 10.
- The *loop expression* is any arithmetic expression you would like to calculate at the end of each iteration. Most always, it is an expression that computes a new value for the control variable. In the example, we added 1 to the control variable using the *postincrement operator* (++). A complete list of arithmetic operators is in Appendix B, "Built-In Command."

Each of the three parts of the arithmetic expression is optional; only the semicolons are required.

Consider the following command line:

```
for (( i=10; i>0; i-- )) do print "$i \c" ; done ; \
print Bang!
```

b) What is the initialization part?

______

______

c) What is the termination test part?

______

______

d) What is the loop expression?

______

______

e) What would the command line print?

______

______

f) What would the following command line print?

```
for (( i=10; i-- > 0; )) do print $i ; done; print Bang!
```

______

______

We will use arithmetic `for` loops to help us measure the efficiency of our code. The shell provides a command prefix called `time` that you can put in front of any command, and the shell will report the amount of time the command took to run once it completes. Many commands run too fast to be timed accurately because the clock used by the time command usually has a resolution of several milliseconds (1 millisecond, or msec, is 0.001 second), and many commands can execute in as little as a few microseconds (1 microsecond, or µsec, is 0.000001 second).

Run the following command line:

```
time for (( i=0; i<1000; i++ )) do : ; done
```

That's a colon followed by a semicolon between `do` *and* `done`.

g) What does the colon (:) command do?

____

____

h) How much "real" time did it take to run this command line?

____

____

i) Do you get the same results if you run this command several times?

____

____

j) How long does it take to execute *one* iteration of an empty loop on your computer?

____

____

LAB 8.2 ANSWERS

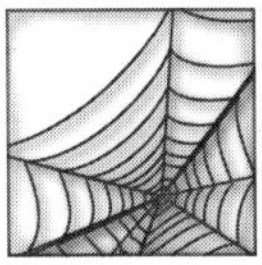

This section gives you some suggested answers to the questions in Lab 8.2, with discussion related to those answers. Your answers may vary, but the most important thing is whether or not your answer works. Use this discussion to analyze differences between your answers and those presented here.

If you have alternative answers to the questions in this exercise, you are encouraged to post your answers and to discuss them at the companion web site for this book, located at:

`http://www.phptr.com/phptrinteractive/`

8.2.1 ANSWERS

a) What is the name of the control variable of this `for` loop?

Answer: The control variable is named `param`.

You can use any simple variable name you like for the control variable. This name is an abbreviation for parameter. Each time through the loop, this variable will be assigned the value of the next element in the list being iterated over.

b) What is the *loop test* part of this `for` loop?

Answer: The loop test part is `in "$@"`.

The loop test part of this type of `for` loop consists of the keyword `in` followed by the list of values to be iterated over. When there are no more values in the list, the test fails, and the shell skips to the next statement after the done.

c) What is the word `in` after the control variable name?

Answer: It is a keyword, *a piece of syntax that tells which type of* `for` *loop this is.*

The next token after `for` must be either `in`, the start of an arithmetic expression (see next exercise), or the keyword `do`.

If the next token after `for` *is* `do`*, it means the loop test is omitted, and the shell automatically uses exactly the same loop test as we did in this function (*`in "$@"`*). You might want to try running this alternate form of* `f821` *just to verify it.*

d) What is the list that this loop iterates over?

Answer: It iterates over the values of the command line parameters, whatever they might be.

We covered the special symbol (`@`) and how to reference it (`$@`) in Exercise 5.1.3, "Related Parameter Variables `(#@*)`."

e) What is the *loop body* part of this `for` loop?

Answer: The loop body is the `print` *command.*

Everything between `do` and `done` is the loop body. You can have any number of commands there.

f) What prints if you run the following command?

```
f821 Tippy canoe, "and Tyler too!"
```

Answer: Your interaction should look like the following:

```
[8008]: f821 Tippy canoe, "and Tyler too!"
The parameter is: "Tippy"
The parameter is: "canoe,"
The parameter is: "and Tyler too!"
[8009]:
```

There are three command line parameters, so the loop iterates three times. The first time, `param` is set to the value of the first parameter, *Tippy*, the second time it is set to the value of the second parameter, *canoe,*, and the last time it is set to the value of the third one, which is the entire quoted phrase, *and Tyler too!*.

g) What happens if you remove the quotes from the `$@` in the loop test and run the same command again?

Answer: Your interaction should look like the following:

```
[8009]: f821 Tippy canoe, "and Tyler too!"
The parameter is: "Tippy"
The parameter is: "canoe,"
```

```
The parameter is: "and"
The parameter is: "Tyler"
The parameter is: "too!"
[8010]:
```


The quotes are needed so that parameters with embedded blanks will be treated as single parameters instead of separate ones.

```
for p in a b c ; do print $p ; done
```

h) What is the name of the control variable for this loop?

Answer: The control variable is `p`.

There can be just one variable name between `for` and `in`.

It's fine to use meaningless variable names when you are writing interactive commands, but be sure to use meaningful names in scripts, where people need clues to help understand the logic of your code.

i) What is the list that this loop iterates over?

Answer: The one-letter strings, `a`, `b`, *and* `c`.

The list can be as long as you like. Often, it will be a list of file names or directories, but it could be dates, the names of cities, e-mail addresses, or anything else you find useful.

j) What prints when you run this command line?

Answer: Your interaction should look like the following:

```
[8010]: for p in a b c ; do print $p ; done
a
b
c
[8011]:
```

Naturally, you won't print out the values of a list that you just typed in very often! Nonetheless, as you get comfortable with `for` loops, you will find that it is convenient to run them interactively. Most often, however, your interactive loops will use a list that the shell generates for you, such as a list of all the files in a directory. You will see how to use the shell to generate many useful lists using wildcards and patterns in Chapter 10, "Patterns, Expansions, and Substitutions."

8.2.2 ANSWERS

a) What is the control variable in the example?

Answer: The name of the control variable is i.

Because the control variable of an arithmetic `for` is often used as the subscript of an array, there is a long-standing convention to use names like `i`, `j`, and `k`.

Variable names like `i`, `j`, and `k` may seem to violate the principle that you should use meaningful variable names, but they don't. "Everyone" knows that they are convenient names for the control variables of arithmetic `for` loops. As long as you use them this way, they are fine to use.

Consider the following command line:

```
for (( i=10; i>0; i-- )) do print "$i \c" ; done ; \
print Bang!
```

b) What is the initialization part?

Answer: `i=10`

This sets `i` to an initial value of *10.*

c) What is the termination test part?

Answer: `i>0`

The loop body will be repeated as long as `i` is greater than zero.

d) What is the loop expression?

Answer: `i--`

After each iteration, `i` will be postdecremented. Thus, at the end of the first iteration, `i` will be reduced from 10 to 9, and so forth.

e) What would the command line print?

Answer: Your interaction should look like the following:

```
[8011]: for (( i=10; i>0; i-- )) do print -n "$i";
  done ; print Bang!
10 9 8 7 6 5 4 3 2 1 Bang!
[8012]:
```

First, there is a little trick here: The `-n` tells `print` not to go to a new line after printing.

You can go through a loop "backward" by constructing the initialization part to start at a high number—the test will be *true* while the value is greater than zero (or some other value)—and decrementing the control variable at the end of the loop, in this case by using the *postdecrement* operator, (--).

f) What would the following command line print?

```
for (( i=10; i-- > 0; )) do print $i ; done; \
print Bang!
```

Answer: Not exactly what you might think! Your interaction should look like the following:

```
[8012]: for (( i=10; i-- > 0; )) do print $i ; done; \
print Bang!
9 8 7 6 5 4 3 2 1 0 Bang!
[8013]:
```

This loop puts the code for decrementing the control variable into the code for the loop test and eliminates the loop expression. Now the loop test subtracts 1 from `i` using the postdecrement operator and compares `i` to zero. The result is "off by 1" compared with the previous loop for two reasons:

1. The control variable in this loop is decremented in the loop test, which is done *before* the loop body executes, so the value printed the first time through the loop is *9* instead of *10*.
2. The postdecrement operator subtracts 1 from the variable *after* its value is used in the expression. (That's why it's called *post*decrement.) So the loop is executed with a value of zero even though the test is for a value greater than zero. For the last iteration, the value of `i` starts at 1, which is

greater than zero, in evaluating the greater-than operator, but the value is then decremented to zero before the loop body executes.

Run the following command line:

```
time for (( i=0; i<1000; i++ )) do : ; done
```

g) What does the colon (:) command do?

Answer: Nothing! It is the shell's "do-nothing" built-in command.

The colon command (:) actually does do something: It always sets its exit code to *true,* like the `true` command you have already seen. You can use the following command as a do-nothing command, too:

```
print "\c"
```

The idea in this loop is to see how long it takes the shell to run an "empty" loop. You can then use that value as the baseline for comparing how long it takes to execute loops containing the commands you are actually interested in timing. You can subtract out the baseline value to get the time spent executing the command(s) you are interested in.

h) How much "real" time did it take to run this command line?

Answer: It depends on how fast your computer is! Your interaction should look something like the following:

```
[8013]: time for (( i=0; i<1000; i++ )) do : ; done

real    0m0.23s
user    0m0.00s
sys     0m0.00s
[8014]:
```

The shell prints the execution time for the entire command, broken down into three parts. The "real" part (0.23 seconds on my computer) is the number we are interested in (although it might include time the computer spent doing work for other users in a timesharing system). The other two lines show how much time was spent executing the code inside the commands being timed (user time) and how much time was spent executing code inside the operating system's kernel. C, C++, and Java programmers are often interested in the latter two values because they can tune their programs' performances based on them, but shell programmers don't have the resources available to do that sort of thing. (The values shown here 0.00 seconds for user and system times may be anomalies outside the scope of this book.)

i) Do you get the same results if you run this command several times?

Answer: Probably not.

The resolution of the clock used for timing things on most UNIX systems is 0.01 second (10 msec), although compiled programs often have access to timers with finer resolution. Because 10 msec is course-grained, compared with the time it takes to execute a command, you typically have to run timing tests several times and average the results to get meaningful numbers.

j) How long does it take to execute *one* iteration of an empty loop on your computer?

Answer: For my computer, it was 230 μsec.

If it took 0.23 seconds to execute 1,000 iterations, it took 0.23/1000 or 0.00023 seconds, to execute one iteration, on average.

LAB 8.2 SELF-REVIEW QUESTIONS

To test your progress, you should be able to answer the following questions:

1) The list part of a `for` loop must be generated by the shell.

a) _____True
b) _____False

2) How many times will the following loop execute?

```
for x in 1 2 3 4 5 I caught a fish alive ; do : ; done
```

a) _____None, because the double parentheses are missing.
b) _____None, because the loop body is missing.
c) _____None, because `x` is not a valid control variable name.
d) _____5 times.
e) _____10 times.

3) If `x += 2` means to add 2 to the value of `x` (which it does mean), which of the following loops prints the odd integers between 1 and 99?

a) _____`for ((x=0; x<100; x += 2 )) do print $x ; done`

b) _____`for ((x=1; x<100; x += 2 )) do print $x ; done`
c) _____`for ((x=0; x<99; x += 2 )) do print $x ; done`
d) _____`for ((x>0; x=99; x += 2 )) do print $x ; done`
e) _____`print(odd from 1 to 99)`

4) If the test part of an arithmetic `for` is left out, the shell assumes its value is *true*. How could such a loop end?
a) _____You could put a `break` command someplace inside the loop body.
b) _____You could put a `continue` command someplace inside the loop body.
c) _____You could put a `stop` command someplace inside the loop body.
d) _____You could combine the test part in the initialization part.
e) _____You could put the loop body outside the loop.

5) Why are loops used to time the execution of commands?
a) _____To make it more complicated.
b) _____To make it simpler.
c) _____Because the resolution of the `time` prefix is too coarse to measure a single execution of many commands.
d) _____Because commands do more work if they are inside loops.
e) _____To separate real time from user and system time.

Quiz answers appear in Appendix A, Section 8.2.

CHAPTER 8

TEST YOUR THINKING

The projects in this section are meant to have you utilize all of the skills that you have acquired throughout this chapter. The answers to these projects can be found at the companion web site to this book, located at:

`http://www.phptr.com/phptrinteractive/`

Visit the Web site periodically to share and discuss your answers.

1) Write a script that synchronizes two directories, which are given as command line parameters. Verify that there are exactly two parameters on the command line, and that they both exist, and can be written to before proceeding. The idea is to make both directories contain all the same files. If the same file exists in both directories, copy the newer one over the older one.

Hint: The command `for f in ~/bin/*` *will iterate over all the files in the user's* `bin` *directory.*

Optional: a)If one of the directories does not exist, create it if the shell variable `CREATE_DIRECTORIES` is set.

b)Add an option parameter, `-c`. If it is present, confirm overwriting files by asking the user whether it is all right to do so. (You will have to use `select`, covered in Chapter 9, "The `case` and `select` Commands," or `read`, covered in Chapter 11, "Input/Output and Trap Processing," to input the user's choice.)

2) Compare the execution times of the built-in and external `print` commands. Use `print "\c"` to make the `print` command print nothing. How much faster is the built-in version?

CHAPTER 9

THE `case` AND `select` STATEMENTS

Take one from Column A and two from Column B

CHAPTER OBJECTIVES

In this chapter, you will learn about:

This chapter covers two commands, `case` and `select`, which are "advanced," in the sense that there is a bit more to master in order to use them, compared with the basic tests and loops covered in the previous chapter. They are very powerful, but as you will see, they deserve a prominent place in any shell programmer's box of "basic tools."

LAB 9.1

THE case AND select STATEMENTS

LAB OBJECTIVES

After this lab, you will be able to:

- ✓ Use the case Command
- ✓ Use the select Command
- ✓ Work with select Details

The two commands in this lab are often used together, yet they have totally different uses. The `case` command is one you will use a lot once you master it because it simplifies doing things that would otherwise require complex `if-elif` constructions. It's also very efficient compared to the equivalent `if` structures. The `select` command, on the other hand, is an easy way to set up menus for interacting with a user. The relationship between the two is that you typically use a `case` command in the body of a `select` command to process the user's menu selection.

The syntax for the two commands looks like the following:

case *value* **in**

[*pattern* [| *pattern*] ...)   Command ... **;;**

[*pattern* [| *pattern*] ...)   Command ... **;&**

. . .

esac

select *name* **in** *list*

do

`Command ...` This is the *select body,* where you typically put a `case` command.

done

For the `case` command, *value* is the value you want to test, normally a reference to a variable. The keyword `in` is followed by any number of *pattern tests,* each of which is followed by a set of one or more commands that are executed if the value of the variable being tested matches one of the patterns in the pattern test. If a command list ends with a double-semicolon (`;;`), the `case` command terminates when the last command in the list finishes, and the shell jumps to the next command after the `esac`. However, if the list ends with semicolon-ampersand (`;&`), the `case` command executes commands until it completes a command list that ends with a double-semicolon.

The (`;&`) form is seldom used. It tends to make a program's logic "tricky."

For the `select` command, *list* is a list of strings that will be displayed to the user as a menu from which to choose. The shell displays the list and waits for the user to make a selection from the items displayed. When the user makes a selection, the shell assigns the item selected as the value of the variable given as the *name* and executes the commands inside the *body.* As the syntax diagram points out, you almost always use a single `case` in the select body, with one pattern test for each of the items in the menu list.

LAB 9.1 EXERCISES

9.1.1 USE THE case COMMAND

In this exercise and the next, you will work with a realistic model of a shell program, with a `case` command at its heart. We will assume there are three functions and that you want your script to execute one of them, with the one to be executed determined by the value of a variable named *which_one*. If *which_one* is *a*, the program is to execute a function named `f911_a`. If *which_one* is *b*, the program is to execute a function named `f911_b`, and likewise for the value *c* and the function named `f911_c`.

To start, create three function definitions in a file named `f911` in your `~/fun` directory. The file should look like the following:

```
#   f911      Some functions that print
#             their names when executed.
function f911_a {
  print This is f911_a executing.
  }

function f911_b {
  print This is f911_b executing.
  }

function f911_c {
  print This is f911_c executing.
  }
```

Now, you need the script, which you should put in a file named `s911` in your `~/bin` directory. The script should look like the following:

```
#   s911   Invoke each function, using command line
#          parameters to decide which ones to invoke,
#          and in what order.

#   Define each of the functions for this script
. ~/fun/f911

#     Iterate over the command line parameters
```

```
for    fun in "$@"
do     case   $fun in
         a)   f911_a ;;
         b)   f911_b ;;
         c)   f911_c ;;
         *)   print -- $0: "$fun": Unrecognized
                parameter. 1>&2;;
       esac
done
```

Now run the following command line and observe the results:

```
s911 a b b c delta a "bad news"
```

a) What was printed?

____

____

____

____

____

____

____

b) What does the "dot" command do at the beginning of the script?

____

____

c) What is the first *pattern* in the `case` command?

____

____

d) What is the last *pattern*, and what do you think it means?

---

e) What is the reference to the variable `0` in the `print` command for?

---

f) What is the reason for `1>&2` at the end of the `print` command?

Run the following command after you have run script `s911`:

```
functions | more
```

g) Are the functions `f911_a`, `f911_b`, and `f911_c` defined?

9.1.2 USE THE select COMMAND

For this exercise, we'll modify `s911` so that the user gets to select which function to run interactively. Here is `s912`, which you should enter in your `~/bin` directory:

```
#   s912        Interactive version of s911, using
#               select.

# Define each of the functions for this script
  . ~/fun/f911
```

```
# Set up the prompt for the menu
  PS3="Select a function to run: "

# Display the menu, and get the user's selection
  select choice in f911_a f911_b f911_c
  do    case   $choice in

            f911_a)    f911_a
                       break ;;
            f911_b)    f911_b
                       break ;;
            f911_c)    f911_c
                       break ;;

            *)    print -u2 -- Invalid choice.\
                             Enter 1, 2, or 3.

        esac
  done
```

Now run the command s912. Don't bother to enter any command line parameters; this is an interactive script.

a) What does the menu look like?

____

____

b) What is the variable PS3?

____

____

c) Does the user type in a number or the name of a function to select a function?

____

____

d) Is `choice` set to the number the user typed, or to the value of one of the items in the menu list?

e) What happens if the user makes an invalid selection?

f) What happens if the user presses Enter in response to the prompt?

g) What happens if the user presses `Ctrl-D` (`^D`) in response to the prompt?

h) What is the purpose of the `break` commands?

i) Name two commands that would cause the `select` command to terminate by ending the whole script.

9.1.3 WORK WITH select DETAILS

In the previous exercise you worked with `select` in the "standard" way. This exercise gives you some practice using `select`'s default prompt and introduces you to using an `if` command instead of `case` in the body of a `select` command.

Enter the following command lines:

```
select choice in a b;
do  if [[ $choice == "a" ]] then
        print ok
        break
    fi
done
```

a) What prompt string is used?

____

____

b) What happens if you enter 2 as your selection?

____

____

c) What happens if you enter 1 as your selection?

____

____

d) Is it necessary to put a `case` command inside every `select` command?

____

____

LAB 9.1 ANSWERS

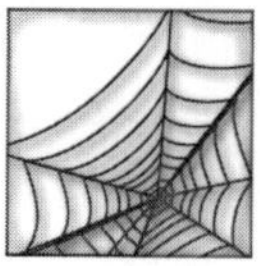

This section gives you some suggested answers to the questions in Lab 9.1, with discussion related to those answers. Your answers may vary, but the most important thing is whether or not your answer works. Use this discussion to analyze differences between your answers and those presented here.

If you have alternative answers to the questions in this exercise, you are encouraged to post your answers and to discuss them at the companion web site for this book, located at:

`http://www.phptr.com/phptrinteractive/`

9.1.1 ANSWERS

Now run the following command line and observe the results:

```
s911 a b b c delta a "bad news"
```

a) What was printed?

Answer: Your interaction should look like the following:

```
[9000]: s911 a b b c delta a "bad news"
This is f911_a executing.
This is f911_b executing.
This is f911_b executing.
This is f911_c executing.
s911: delta: Unrecognized parameter.
This is f911_a executing.
s911: bad news: Unrecognized parameter.
[9001]:
```

This is a pretty thorough test of the script and the functions, although you should feel free to experiment with different command lines if it's not clear what the program is doing. Here are some observations you should make based on the output:

- You can invoke each function by putting its associated letter on the `s911` command line.

- Each function can be run any number of times in any order; the order is determined by the order of the letters on the command line.
- If a parameter is something other than "a", "b", or "c," the program prints an error message, but it continues to process the other command line parameters after that.

b) What does the "dot" command do at the beginning of the script?

Answer: It gets the shell to read and remember the three function definitions.

The shell automatically "dots" a function definition file the first time you run a function, provided the definition file has the same name as the function and provided the file is in your `FPATH`. However, in this case, we have adopted the common strategy of putting several small but related functions into one definition file, and have given the file a name that doesn't match any of the function names. To have the functions defined inside the script, we explicitly dot the file that holds the three function definitions.

If you are familiar with the UNIX `ln` command, you could link three files named `f911_a`, `f911_b`, and `f911_c` to the "real" file, `f911`. Then the shell would read all three definitions the first time any of them is referenced and you would not have to dot `f911`.

c) What is the first *pattern* in the `case` command?

Answer: It's the letter "a."

Patterns are covered in Chapter 10, "Patterns, Expansions, and Substitutions," but we will explain some simple ones as we go along here. In this case, the pattern is simply a string. It doesn't have to be a single letter; we just did that in this case (pardon the pun) to make the command line easy to type. If you want the same command list executed if the *value* matches any of several patterns, you could put them all before the close parentheses, separated by vertical bar (|) symbols.

FOR EXAMPLE

If you wanted to let the user type an upper or lowercase "a" or the word *alpha* to run `f911_a`, you could have used the following line in place of the first one in the case body:

```
a | A | alpha )      f911_a ;;
```

d) What is the last *pattern*, and what do you think it means?

*Answer: The last pattern is an asterisk (*). I think it matches any value.*

Your answer is technically "correct," even if you didn't think what I think. But *now* you *know* what it means!

The asterisk pattern is the standard thing to use as the last "leg" of a `case` command. If none of the previous legs is matched, this one is guaranteed to get executed, and you can use it (as in this script) to print an error message and to take whatever other action might be appropriate, possibly such as exiting the script using an `exit` or `return` command.

e) What is the reference to the variable *0* in the `print` command for?

Answer: It prints the name of the script.

This print command is an example of the standard format for UNIX error messages.

f) What is the reason for `1>&2` at the end of the `print` command?

Answer: This causes the output of the `print` *command to be redirected to* stderr.

The `print` command writes to *stdout,* but if the user redirects the output of the script away from the screen, he or she won't see any of the error messages from this `print` command, so *stdout* (*fd* number 1) is redirected to the same place as (`>&`) *stderr* (*fd* number 2), as covered in Chapter 2, "Command Syntax."

The `print` *command has an option,* `-u`*, that tells what fd to print to, so the following line of code would also print the message to stderr:*

```
*)     print -u2 -- $0: "$fun":\
                         Unrecognized parameter.
```

g) Are the functions `f911_a`, `f911_b`, and `f911_c` defined?

Answer: No, they are not!

The `functions` built-in command lists all defined functions, but the three that you have been using are not in the list. (If they are, it means you "dotted" the definition file from the command line at some point.) Functions defined inside a script are not automatically known outside the script, and vice versa. So you don't see the function definitions at the interactive command level.

9.1.2 ANSWERS

Now run the command `s912`. Don't bother to enter any command line parameters; this is an interactive script.

a) What does the menu look like?

Answer: The menu part of the output should look like the following:

```
1) f911_a
2) f911_b
3) f911_c
```

There is one line for each of the items in the list on the `select` command line, showing a number, a parenthesis, and the value of the list item.

b) What is the variable `PS3`?

Answer: It is the prompt string the shell prints after displaying the menu.

The prompt string should be descriptive enough so the user knows what to do when he or she sees it. Once you assign a value to `PS3`, it will be used for all succeeding `select` commands in the script unless you change it.

c) Does the user type in a number or the name of a function to select a function?

Answer: A number.

The left side of the menu tells the user what numbers to type, and the right side should be descriptive text telling the user what each number selects. In our script, we assume the user knows what things such as `f911_a` mean. Normally, you would provide more descriptive values for the elements of the list.

d) Is `choice` set to the number the user typed, or to the value of one of the items in the menu list?

Answer: It is set to the value of one of the items in the menu list.

The user has to type in a number, but the control variable is set to the corresponding value.

e) What happens if the user makes an invalid selection?

Answer: The `print` command is executed, so the error message is printed, and the prompt is shown again.

If you don't supply a "default" leg for the case statement (the one with the asterisk pattern), there will be no error message. The shell does *not* print an error message on its own. It just repeats the prompt and waits for the user to enter another selection.

f) What happens if the user presses Enter in response to the prompt?

Answer: The shell shows the menu over again.

If the user types an invalid choice, the shell simply redisplays the value of `PS3`, but if the user responds with a blank line, the shell redisplays the whole menu list before showing `PS3` again.

g) What happens if the user presses Ctrl-D (`^D`) in response to the prompt?

Answer: The user is returned to the normal command prompt.

Ctrl-D is the way to indicate "end of file" to programs that read input from the keyboard. (Watch out; if you type it when the shell is trying to read a command interactively, it will log you off!) Inside a `select` command, it causes the command to terminate, and the shell executes the next command after `done`. In this script, there are no commands after `done`, so the script terminates, and you get another command prompt from the shell.

h) What is the purpose of the `break` commands?

Answer: They terminate the `select` *command.*

Once the user makes a valid selection, the program runs the selected function. In each case, the next command is a `break` command, which terminates `select`. Then, because there are no more commands in the script after `done`, the script terminates, and you get another command prompt from the shell again.

i) Name two commands that would cause the `select` command to terminate by ending the whole script.

Answer: `exit` *and* `return`

These commands immediately terminate the script or function they are in, so they will take you out of the `select` command. Either one could have been used in place of the `break` commands in this script because there is nothing else in the script after `select`, but you would use `break` if there were more commands in the script that you wanted to execute after `select` completes.

9.1.3 ANSWERS

Run the following command lines:

```
select choice in a b;
do if [[ $choice == "a" ]] then
        print ok
        break
     fi
done
```

a) What prompt string is used?

Answer: A number sign followed by a question mark. Your interaction with this command line might look like the following (depending on what you type in response to the prompt):

```
[9001]: select choice in a b;
> do  if [[ $choice == "a" ]] then
>           print ok
>           break
>       fi
```

```
> done
1) a
2) b
#? 2
#? 3
#? hello
#? 1
ok
[9002]:
```

This rather terse command line prompts you to select between "a" and "b." It also shows the default value for *PS3,* a pound sign followed by a question mark.

b) What happens if you enter 2 as your selection?

Answer: As the previous interaction shows, the shell does nothing but issue another prompt.

This behavior is because the body of the `select` statement is an `if` statement that checks only if the user selected "a" (by typing a 1) and ignores anything else the user selects. As the next two selections (*3* and *hello*) illustrate, the user can make erroneous selections too, and nothing happens if you don't write code to handle those cases; the shell just reissues the prompt.

c) What happens if you enter *1* as your selection?

Answer: The message "ok" prints, and the shell prompts for another command.

This behavior is also illustrated at the end of the previous interaction. The "ok" prints because of the `print` command before the `break` command.

d) Is it necessary to put a `case` command inside every `select` command?

Answer: No.

This is the point of the interaction you just looked at: You can program anything you want inside the `select` command, it's just that the most common thing to use is a single `case` command with one leg for each of the menu items, plus a default case to handle invalid selections.

LAB 9.1 SELF-REVIEW QUESTIONS

To test your progress, you should be able to answer the following questions:

1) What does the following line do inside a `case` statement?

```
x | xx | xxx)  print oh! ;;
```

a) _____Nothing, because you can't have more than one pattern before the parentheses.
b) _____Nothing, because you have to use left parentheses before you use right parentheses.
c) _____It always prints *oh!*.
d) _____It never prints *oh!*.
e) _____It prints *oh!* if the value of the control variable is x, xx, or xxx.

2) What is the pattern, *), used for in a `case` statement?
a) _____Nothing, it is never used.
b) _____It marks the beginning of the list of patterns.
c) _____It marks the end of the list of patterns.
d) _____It matches any value and may be used after all valid values have been tested to detect errors, unexpected values, or values that can be handled in some default way.
e) _____It is used to tell the shell that an error has occurred.

3) How many patterns can you have for one command list in a `case` statement?
a) _____None.
b) _____One.
c) _____Two.
d) _____Three.
e) _____Any number greater than zero.

4) How many command lists can you have in a `case` statement?
a) _____None.
b) _____One.
c) _____Two.
d) _____Three.
e) _____Any number greater than zero.

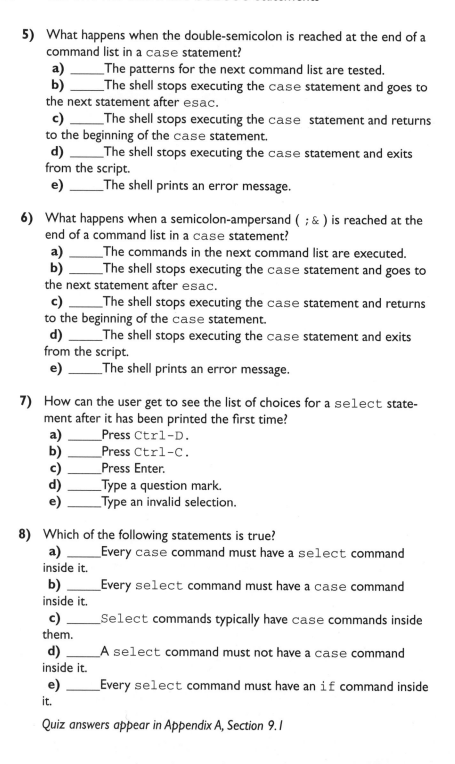

5) What happens when the double-semicolon is reached at the end of a command list in a `case` statement?
   a) _____The patterns for the next command list are tested.
   b) _____The shell stops executing the `case` statement and goes to the next statement after `esac`.
   c) _____The shell stops executing the `case` statement and returns to the beginning of the `case` statement.
   d) _____The shell stops executing the `case` statement and exits from the script.
   e) _____The shell prints an error message.

6) What happens when a semicolon-ampersand (`;&`) is reached at the end of a command list in a `case` statement?
   a) _____The commands in the next command list are executed.
   b) _____The shell stops executing the `case` statement and goes to the next statement after `esac`.
   c) _____The shell stops executing the `case` statement and returns to the beginning of the `case` statement.
   d) _____The shell stops executing the `case` statement and exits from the script.
   e) _____The shell prints an error message.

7) How can the user get to see the list of choices for a `select` statement after it has been printed the first time?
   a) _____Press `Ctrl-D`.
   b) _____Press `Ctrl-C`.
   c) _____Press Enter.
   d) _____Type a question mark.
   e) _____Type an invalid selection.

8) Which of the following statements is true?
   a) _____Every `case` command must have a `select` command inside it.
   b) _____Every `select` command must have a `case` command inside it.
   c) _____`Select` commands typically have `case` commands inside them.
   d) _____A `select` command must not have a `case` command inside it.
   e) _____Every `select` command must have an `if` command inside it.

Quiz answers appear in Appendix A, Section 9.1

CHAPTER 9

TEST YOUR THINKING

The projects in this section are meant to have you utilize all of the skills that you have acquired throughout this chapter. The answers to these projects can be found at the companion web site to this book, located at:

`http://www.phptr.com/phptrinteractive/`

Visit the web site periodically to share and discuss your answers.

1) Write a program that accepts exactly two numbers as command line options, then uses a `select` statement to ask the user whether to add, subtract, multiply, or divide them. After the user makes his or her choice, display the result. Include a fifth choice, *quit*, for exiting the program.

2) Add the feature to your program for Question 1 that the user may enter either one or two numbers as command line arguments. If the user enters two numbers, it behaves as before, but if the user enters just one number, the menu asks the user which of several arithmetic functions, such as square root and trigonometric functions, the user wants to compute.

3) Rewrite `s912` without using a `case` statement. This would be a very silly thing to do in the real world, but is a very instructive exercise.

CHAPTER 10

PATTERNS, EXPANSIONS, AND SUBSTITUTIONS

Though this be madness, yet there is method in't.

Hamlet, Act 2 Scene 2.

Chapter Objectives

In this chapter, you will learn about:

Once the shell has read a command line and has broken it into a set of individual commands (see Chapter 2, "Command Line Syntax"), it performs several very powerful operations on the tokens that make up the command's name and parameters. These operations are performed in the following sequence: *alias substitution, message substitution, tilde expansion, command substitution, parameter expansion, arithmetic expansion, field splitting, pathname expansion, and quote removal*. As you can see from the list of chapter objectives, this chapter deals with several of these operations in the order in which the shell performs them on a command. We won't cover alias substitution, message substitution, tilde expansion, or quote removal, because you've either already seen them or they are outside the scope of this workbook. Field splitting will be covered in the next chapter (Chapter 11, "I/O and Trap Processing").

LAB 10.1

PATTERNS

LAB OBJECTIVES

After this lab, you will be able to:

- ✓ Use Asterisk (*) to Match Zero or More Characters
- ✓ Use the Question Mark (?) to Match a Single Character
- ✓ Use Square Brackets ([]) to Match Character Sets
- ✓ Work with Subpatterns

Patterns have to do with strings of characters. Sometimes patterns are used to describe sets of strings that you want to *match* a given string, and sometimes patterns are used to describe sets of strings that you want to *generate* in some way. The KornShell uses patterns in four different situations:

1. In `case` statements, the items before the `)` character are patterns that describe the sets of strings that the control value must *match* in order for the associated command list to be executed. As you saw in Chapter 9, "The `case` and `select` Statements," you can specify multiple patterns, separated by | symbols in one leg of a `case` statement, and the command list will be executed if the control value matches any one of the patterns. You also saw that a pattern can be as simple as a string. In this lab, you will learn how to construct more elaborate patterns.

2. In *double-bracket* tests, the right side of a double-equal (==) or not-equal (!=) is a pattern unless it is enclosed in quotes. With quotes, the shell treats the right side as a string instead of as a pattern. If you don't use the special pattern symbols described in this lab, strings and patterns are the same. If you do use a pattern, you can test whether a string (the left side) *matches* any one of the strings described by the pattern on the right side.
3. In *parameters* that you are passing to a command, you can use patterns to *generate* lists of file names that have characteristics you are interested in. You have undoubtedly seen the form of this called *wildcard expansion*, such as using an asterisk (*) to generate the names of all the files and subdirectories in the current directory. This use of patterns is what was meant by the term *pathname expansion* in the introduction to this chapter.
4. Patterns are also used in *substring expansion*, which will be covered later in this chapter. In fact, the reason for introducing patterns at this point is that we could deal with the first three items without saying too much about patterns, but we can't talk about substring expansion at all until you understand patterns more fully.

The KornShell's pattern features are related to the idea of *regular expressions* used elsewhere, such as in the `grep` command and inside editors. However, KornShell patterns are different from these regular expressions, and you shouldn't assume you already know about patterns if you already know about `grep`-style regular expressions. Likewise, what you learn here will help you understand other regular expressions better, but it would be a mistake to think that you understand all regular expressions after you finish this chapter.

LAB 10.1 EXERCISES

10.1.1 USE ASTERISK (*) TO MATCH ZERO OR MORE CHARACTERS

This exercise uses pathname expansion to look at the use of the shell's asterisk (`*`) character for pattern substitution.

Start by making a directory to use just for this Lab. You will be creating and deleting files, and it's a good idea to do the exercises in a place where you won't accidentally affect the "real" files on your computer.

Run the following commands:

```
mkdir Lab10.1
cd Lab10.1
touch a b c d e a.b b.c c.d d.e
ls *
print *
```

a) What is the difference in output between the `ls` and the `print` commands?

____

____

Run the following commands:

```
ls abc *
print abc *
```

b) What do these two commands print?

____

____

Run the following command:

```
print *.*
```

c) How does the output of this command differ from the output of the `print` command in Question a?

____

____

Run the following commands:

```
print *b
print b*
print *b*
```

d) Explain the output from these three commands.

____

____

Enter the following script, and run it:

```
# s1011 Asterisks
for f in *
do    case $f in
        a*)       print "$f\tMatches a*."          ;;
        *.*)      print "$f\tHas a dot in it."     ;;
        *b*)      print "$f\tHas a b in it."       ;;
        *d | *e)  print "$f\tEnds with a d or e."  ;;
        *)        print "$f\tIs something else."   ;;
      esac
done
```

e) What does the `\t` in each `print` command do?

____

____

f) How many lines of output were there?

____

____

g) What is the value of f the first time through the loop?

h) What would print if the first print command's message was not in quotes?

i) What is the difference between the outputs for files a.b and b.c?

j) What is the difference between the outputs for files d and d.e?

Now enter the following commands:

```
for f in *
do [[ $f == *.* ]] &&
  print "$f\tHas a dot in its name.".
done
```

k) How many lines print?

Repeat the previous commands but switch around the $f and the *.* in the double bracket command.

l) What printed this time?

10.1.2 USE QUESTION MARK (?) TO MATCH A SINGLE CHARACTER

The asterisk pattern matches any number of characters, including none. If you want to have a single character somewhere in a pattern, use a question mark.

With the same file in your current directory as in the previous exercise, run the following command:

```
print ?
```

a) What printed?

Run each of the following commands:

```
print ??
print ???
print ??e
```

b) What is the difference between the outputs of the first two commands?

---

c) What is the difference between the outputs of the second two commands?

____

____

Run the following three commands:

```
print ?
print *?
print ?*
```

d) What is the difference between the outputs of the first two commands?

____

____

e) What is the difference between the outputs of the second two commands?

____

____

10.1.3 Use Square Brackets ([]) to Match Character Sets

If you have particular letters that you want to match, you can put them inside square brackets.

Still working the directory Lab 10.1, run the following command:

```
print [abcd]*
```

a) What printed?

If you don't want to list all the letters in a contiguous range, you can use a dash inside the square brackets.

Run the following commands:

```
print [a-e]
print [d-z]*
```

b) What is the difference between the outputs of these two commands?

You can complement the meaning of square brackets by using an exclamation mark as the first character inside the square brackets.

To see this behavior, run the following command:

```
print [!ab]*
```

c) What printed?

You can also specify *classes* of characters that you want to match inside square brackets. There are a dozen of these classes listed in Appendix B, "Built-In Command," here we will look at just the "alpha" and "digit" classes. There is another class, "alphanumeric," that could be used to accomplish the same thing, but for this exercise, we'll practice using these two classes to look for file names that consist of either a digit or a letter.

To do this, run the following commands:

```
for ((i=1; i<6;i++)) do touch $i ; done
print [[:alpha:][:digit]]
```

d) What did the first command do?

---

e) Is there a double-bracket command in the second line?

---

f) What printed?

Finally, run the following commands:

```
print [a\-e]
print [!\!]*
```

g) What was the output?

10.1.4 Work with Subpatterns

Subpatterns let you put patterns inside patterns. This may seem like an arcane thing to do at first, but you will find that subpatterns let you solve a lot of common problems in very natural way. Subpatterns are patterns that you surround with parentheses and precede with one of five character codes:

!(...)	The subpattern must occur zero times. (Must *not* occur.)
?(...)	The subpattern must occur exactly zero or once.
*(...)	The subpattern may occur zero or more times.
@(...)	The subpattern must occur exactly once.
+(...)	The subpattern must occur once or more times.

You will see that patterns are used with variables as well as with file names later in this chapter, but for now we'll continue to work with file names. However, you will need some longer file names than the ones used above to get an idea of how subpatterns work.

So remove all the files in your `Lab10.1` directory and run the following commands to create a set of file names to work with:

```
for prefix in re un ""
do  for root in read reread
    do  for suffix in ed ing
        do > $prefix$root$suffix
        done
    done
done
```

The third `do` *command could have used the* `touch` *command instead of output redirection to accomplish the same thing, as follows:*

```
touch $prefix$root$suffix
```

The `touch` *command is slower to run and takes more characters to type but will not destroy the contents of a file if it already exists.*

a) How many files did these commands create?

____

____

Run the following two commands:

```
print !(un*)
print !(un)*
```

b) What printed, and why?

Run the following commands:

```
print ?(re)read*
print +(re)read*
print @(re)read*
print *(re)read*
```

c) What printed, and why?

LAB 10.1 ANSWERS

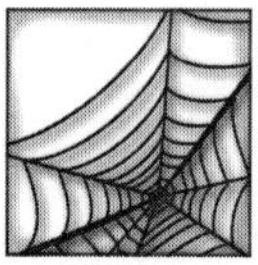

This section gives you some suggested answers to the questions in Lab 10.1, with discussion related to those answers. Your answers may vary, but the most important thing is whether or not your answer works. Use this discussion to analyze differences between your answers and those presented here.

If you have alternative answers to the questions in this exercise, you are encouraged to post your answers and to discuss them at the companion web site for this book, located at:

http://www.phptr.com/phptrinteractive/

10.1.1 Answers

a) What is the difference in output between the `ls` and the `print` commands?

Answer: Your interaction should look like the following:

```
[10000]: mkdir Lab10.1
[10001]: cd Lab10.1
[10002]: touch a b c d e a.b b.c c.d d.e
[10003]: ls *
a      a.b    b      b.c    c      c.d    d      d.e    e
[10004]: print *
a a.b b b.c c c.d d d.e e
[10005]:
```

Only the number of spaces between the file names is different. The `ls` command spaces the file names so they will line up in columns if there are too many names to fit on one line, but the `print` command prints each of its parameters separated by a single space.

Be sure you understand that the shell, not the commands, is processing the asterisks. In both command lines, the shell is expanding the asterisk to be a list of file names that match the pattern, "zero or more characters." The `ls` command verifies that each of the parameters passed to it really is the name of a file, then prints its name. The `print` command just prints whatever the values of its parameters are.

```
ls abc *
print abc *
```

b) What do these two commands print?

Answer: Your interaction should look like the following:

```
[10005]: ls abc *
abc: no such file or directory
a      a.b    b      b.c    c      c.d    d      d.e    e
[10006]: print abc *
abc a a.b b b.c c c.d d d.e e
[10007]:
```

This interaction shows that `ls` looks at each of its parameters to make sure they are all valid file names—which `abc` is not, in this case. The `print` command, however, just prints whatever parameters you give it, whether they are file names or not.

```
print *.*
```

c) How does the output of this command differ from the output of the print command in Question a?

Answer: Your interaction should look like the following:

```
[10007]: print *.*
a.b b.c c.d d.e
[10008]:
```

This command prints the file names that have a dot in them, whereas the other one printed *all* file names.

The idea that a dot is just another character that may or may not be present (or may be present multiple times) in any particular UNIX file name is sometimes a point of confusion for people coming from a DOS/Windows background, where a dot is significant because it introduces the extension that identifies the type of file. UNIX programs often look at a file's extension to decide what to do with it but not, for example, to find out whether a file is executable.

```
print *b
print b*
print *b*
```

d) Explain the output from these three commands.

Answer: Your interaction should look like the following:

```
[10008]: print *b
a.b b
[10009]: print b*
b b.c
print *b*
a.b b b.c
[10010]:
```

The first command prints the names of the files that *end* with `b`. This includes `a.b`, which has *two* characters before the final `b`, and `b`, which has *no* characters before the final `b`.

The important point here is that the asterisk matches any number of characters, including none.

The second command prints all file names that start with `b`, followed by zero or more characters, so this pattern matches the file named `b` again, as well as `b.c`. Finally, the last command matches any file name that has a `b` anywhere in it, which includes all three of the different file names printed by the previous two commands.

Enter the `... script [s1011]`, and run it:

e) What does the `"\t"` in each `print` command do?

Answer: After you have set up the script, your interaction should look like the following:

```
[10010]: s1011
a       Matches a*.
a.b     Matches a*.
b       Has a b in it.
b.c     Has a dot in it.
c       Is something else.
c.d     Has a dot in it.
d       Ends with a d or e.
d.e     Has a dot in it.
e       Ends with a d or e.
[10011]:
```

The `\t` is an ANSI C string, which you may not have seen before. This one contains the code for a <Tab>, which causes the right side of the messages to line up, making them easier to read. It has to be inside quotes to be recognized as a <Tab> code.

f) How many lines of output were there?

Answer: There are nine lines of output.

There are also exactly nine files in the directory. The idea is to see that the asterisk pattern in the `for` command *generates* a list of all the file names in the directory. The `case` statement then *matches* each file name to exactly one of the patterns shown there, resulting in one line of output for each file.

g) What is the value of `f` the first time through the loop?

Answer: It's `a`.

This file name matches two of the patterns in the case statement—the first and the last ones—but the first one is the one that gets printed. Once it reaches the double-semicolon after that `print` command, the shell terminates that execution of the `case` statement and does not try to match the `a` to any of the other patterns.

h) What would print if the first `print` command's message was not in quotes?

Answer: The output for just the first iteration would look like the following:

```
atMatches a a.b.
```

As you can see, the `\t` prints as the letter `t` instead of as a `<Tab>`, and the names of all files that match the `a*` pattern are printed instead of the characters `a*`.

Putting quotes (either single or double) around characters makes the shell treat the characters as a string, even if they contain pattern characters, such as asterisks.

i) What is the difference between the outputs for files `a.b` and `b.c`?

Answer: The output lines for these two files look like the following:

```
a.b     Matches a*.
b.c     Has a dot in it.
```

Both files have dots and `b`s in their names, yet they match different patterns because `a*` is the first pattern that `a.b` matches in the `case` statement, whereas `*.*` is the first pattern that `b.c` matches. If you changed the order of the legs of the `case` statement, you would get different outputs.

Be careful to arrange the sequence of patterns in your `case` *statements; if a value matches more than one pattern, only the command list for the first matching pattern will be executed.*

One reason the `;&` *command list terminator isn't used much is that the shell does not do any more pattern matching once it finds the first match. If you terminate a command list with* `;&`*, the shell then executes every succeeding command list, whether the control value matches succeeding patterns or not, until it comes to a* `;;` *or the* `esac`.

j) What is the difference between the outputs for files `d` and `d.e`?

Answer: The output lines for these two files look like the following:

```
d       ends in d or e.
d.e     has a dot in it.
```

The point of this question is to make sure you understand the *or* (|) separator in the patterns in the fourth leg of the `case` statement. The `d` matches the `*d` part, so that's a match, even though it doesn't match the `*e` part.

Now enter the following commands:

```
for f in *
do [[ $f == *.* ]] && print "$f\tHas a dot in its name."
done
```

k) How many lines print?

Answer: The following four lines should print:

```
a.b     Has a dot in its name.
b.c     Has a dot in its name.
c.d     Has a dot in its name.
d.e     Has a dot in its name.
```

This code illustrates the use of a pattern on the right side of a double-bracket command's double-equal operator. It matches just the four file names that have a dot in them.

Repeat the previous commands but switch the `$f` and the `*.*` in the double-bracket command.

l) What printed this time?

Answer: Your interaction should look like the following:

```
[10011]: for f in *
> do [[ *.* == $f ]] && print "$f\tHas a dot in its name."
> done
[10012]:
```

In case you missed it, *nothing* printed! That's because the pattern has to be on the right side of the double-equal (or not-equal) operator in double-bracket commands. If you put what looks like a pattern on the left side, the shell treats it as a string, the same as putting it in quotes.

10.1.2 ANSWERS

```
print ?
```

a) What printed?

Answer: Your interaction should look like the following:

```
[10012]: print ?
a b c d e
[10013]:
```

The shell generated a list of all the single-character file names, and that's what the `print` command printed.

Run each of the following commands:

```
print ??
print ???
print ??e
```

b) What is the difference between the outputs of the first two commands?

Answer: The first two output lines should look like the following:

```
[10013]: print ??
??
[10014]: print ???
```

```
a.b b.c c.d d.e
[10015]:
```

That is, two questions marks print as two question marks, but three question marks expand to all the file names with exactly three characters in them. You might expect that two question marks should expand to nothing because there are no file names that match that pattern. However, think about the difference between the following two `ls` commands:

```
ls
ls "??"
```

The first one is what you would get if you typed `ls ??` with no two-character file names in the directory and the shell substituted nothing; `ls` would print the names of *all* files in the directory. The second one is what you get with the shell's actual behavior. The double question mark is passed as a parameter to the `ls` command, which prints out the following error message:

```
ls: ??: not found
```

There may be situations where the "expected" behavior would be better, but this is the way the shell works.

c) What is the difference between the outputs of the second two commands?

Answer: The outputs look like the following:

```
[1014]: print ???
a.b b.c c.d d.e
[1015]: print ??e
d.e
[1016]:
```

Both patterns generate lists of three-character file names, but the last one has the added constraint that the file name must end in `e`. A pattern equivalent to the last one would be `???&*e`, but you can't use it for parameter expansion because the shell interprets the ampersand to mean "run the command to left asynchronously" as discussed in Chapter 2,

"Command Syntax." You will see how to write this type of pattern in Exercise 10.1.4, "Work with Subpatterns."

10.1.3 ANSWERS

Run the following command:

```
print [abcd]*
```

a) What printed?

Answer: Your interaction should look like the following:

```
[1016]: print [abcd]*
a a.b b b.c c c.d d d.e
[1017]:
```

That's a list of all the file names that start with one of the letters a through d, followed by zero or more additional characters. Note that the file named e is not listed because its name does not start with one of the letters inside the square brackets.

Run the following commands:

```
print [a-e]
print [d-z]*
```

b) What is the difference between the outputs of these two commands?

Answer: Your interaction should look like the following:

```
[1017]: print [a-e]
a b c d e
[1018]: print [d-z]*
d d.e e
[1019]:
```

The first command prints all the one-character names consisting of a letter in the range a-e. This matches exactly the five single-character file names in the directory. The second command asks for all the file names that start with a letter in the range d-z, followed by any number of letters. In this case, there are the three file names shown.

Just because you specify a range of characters, such as `d-z`*, it doesn't mean you will necessarily match all of them.*

In this question, `d` matched twice, `e` matched once, and all the other letters from `f` to `z` didn't match at all. As long as there is at least one match, the shell will generate a list for you instead of using the pattern itself as the list, as you saw earlier.

To see this behavior, run the following command:

```
print [!ab]*
```

c) What printed?

Answer: Your interaction should look like the following:

```
[1019]: print [!ab]*
c c.d d d.e e
[1020]:
```

This command printed all the file names that do *not* start with `a` or `b`.

```
for ((i=1; i<6;i++)) do touch $i ; done
print [[:alpha:][:digit]]
```

d) What did the first command do?

Answer: It created six files, named `1, 2, 3, 4, 5,` *and* `6`.

You could have accomplished the same thing with six `touch` commands or with the following command, which is easier to type but doesn't help you review the arithmetic `for` loop!

```
touch -- 1 2 3 4 5 6
```

The idea here is to create some file names with digits in their names.

e) Is there a double-bracket command in the second line?

Answer: No.

A double-bracket command has to have a space after the two opening brackets, but this one doesn't. Besides, you can't print a command, so even if you put what looks like a real double-bracket command in a `print` command, the shell will just pass the characters to `print`.

What this is, is a pattern that uses character classes.

f) What printed?

Answer: Your interaction should look like the following:

```
[1020]: print [[:alpha:][:digit:]]
1 2 3 4 5 6 a b c d e
[1021]:
```

That is, all single-character file names get printed, provided that the character is either alphabetic or a digit.

Watch the spacing inside the square brackets. There can't be any spaces unless you want your pattern to match a space character. In that case, you can either put in a space with a backslash (\ ) to quote it, or use the `[:space:]` *character class, which matches space,* `<tab>`*, and various other "whitespace" characters.*

Finally, run the following commands:

```
print [a\-e]
print [!\!]*
```

g) What was the output?

Answer: Your interaction should look like the following:

```
[1021]: print [a\-e]
a e
[1022]: print [!\!]*
1 2 3 4 5 6 a a.b b b.c c c.d d d.e e
[1023]:
```

The command line 1021 shows that you can remove the special meaning of the dash by quoting it with a backslash inside the square brackets. If there had been a file named `-` (never a good idea because it's tricky to remove), its name would have been printed, as well as the names `a` and `e`.

10.1.4 ANSWERS

```
for prefix in re un ""
do  for root in read reread
    do  for suffix in ed ing
        do touch -- $prefix$root$suffix
        done
    done
done
```

a) How many files did these commands create?

Answer: Ten.

The `touch` command was executed twelve times, but only ten different files were actually created. The outermost loop sets `prefix` to each of three different values (*re, un,* and the empty string). For each of these three values, the middle loop sets `root` to each of two different values (*read* and *reread*), which means the innermost loop is executed 3 x 2 = 6 times. The innermost loop iterates over two different values (*ed* and *ing*), so the innermost command is executed 3 x 2 x 2 = 12 times. However, two of the twelve combinations are not unique: "rereaded" prefixed with "" is the same as "readed" prefixed with "re," and likewise for "rereading."

Run the following two commands:

```
print !(un*)
print !(un)*
```

b) What printed, and why?

Answer: Your interaction should look like the following:

```
[1023]: print !(un*)
readed    reading    rereaded    rereading    rerereaded
  rerereading
[1024]: print !(un)*
readed reading rereaded rereading rerereaded
rerereading unreaded unreading unrereaded unrereading
[1025]:
```

The first command prints all the file names that do not start with "un," but the second one prints *all* the file names. The asterisk outside the subpattern's parentheses in line 1024 tells the shell to accept anything other than "un," *including the empty string,* followed by anything, *including "un."*

Asterisks match anything, *including* nothing!

Run the following commands:

```
print ?(re)read*
print +(re)read*
print @(re)read*
print *(re)read*
```

c) What printed, and why?

Answer: Your interaction should look like the following:

```
[1025]: print ?(re)read*
readed reading rereaded rereading
[1026]: print +(re)read*
rereaded rereading rerereaded rerereading
[1027]: print @(re)read*
rereaded rereading
[1028]: print *(re)read*
readed   reading   rereaded   rereading   rerereaded   \
rerereading
[1029]:
```

Line 1025 prints each file name that starts with zero or one occurrences of "re," followed by "read," so it prints "readed" and "reading," as well as the same two words prefixed by "re," but it does not print the names that start with "rere."

Line 1026 matches one or more occurrences of "re," followed by "read," so it prints everything that starts with "reread," which eliminates "readed," "reading," and all the "un" words.

Line 1027 matches exactly one occurrence of "re," followed by "read," so it prints the two names shown, but not words that start with "read," "rere," or "un."

Finally, line 1028 matches zero or more occurrences of "re" followed by "read," so it prints everything except the "un" words.

LAB 10.1 SELF-REVIEW QUESTIONS

To test your progress, you should be able to answer the following questions.

1) What does the pattern `**` match?

a) _____Anything followed by anything, which is the same as zero or more characters.
b) _____One or more characters, but not zero characters.
c) _____Exactly two characters, but not zero or one characters.
d) _____Any two punctuation marks, but not two letters.
e) _____All empty subdirectories.

2) What does the pattern `*.c` match?

a) _____Any string with a dot before a `c`.
b) _____Any string ending with a `c`, provided that there is at least one character before it.
c) _____Any string ending with `.c`, provided that there is at least one character before the dot.
d) _____Any string ending with `.c`, including `.c` by itself.
e) _____Any string ending with `.c`, provided that all preceding characters are letters, not digits.

3) Which of the following patterns will match all strings that end with a dot, followed by exactly 3 characters?

a) _____`8.3`
b) _____`*.3`
c) _____`*.[3]`
d) _____`*.???`
e) _____`?.***`

4) Which of the following patterns could be used to match the string "`hello`"?

a) _____`???????`
b) _____`?`
c) _____`*a*`
d) _____`h*ll`
e) _____`*ll*`

5) What does the following code print?

```
for f in *
do    [[ $f == *[[:digit:]]* ]] &&
  case $f in
    *[:alpha:]) print $f ;;
  esac
done
```

a) _____An error message, because you can't have `esac` inside a `for` statement.
b) _____The names of all the files in the directory.
c) _____The names of all the files in the directory that end with `:alpha:`.
d) _____Nothing, because you can't have colons in a file name.
e) _____The names of all the files in the directory that contain at least one digit and that end with a letter.

6) Which of the following commands would do the same thing as the code for Question 5?

a) _____`print *.*`
b) _____`print *[12345]*`
c) _____`print *[[:digit:]]*[[:alpha:]]`
d) _____`print *:digit:*:alpha:`
e) _____None of the above.

7) Which of the following patterns would match the following description: All names that do not start with a digit, but that have at least three digits in them, separated from each other by one or more letters.

a) _____`[a-z]_[1*2*3]`
b) _____`[![:digit:]]*[[:digit:]]+([[:alpha:]])[[:digit:]]+([[:alpha:]])[[:digit:]]*`
c) _____`!([[:digit:]])*[[:digit:]]+([[:alpha:]])[[:digit:]]+([[:alpha:]])[[:digit:]]*`
d) _____`[![:digit:]]*[[:digit:]]@([[:alpha:]])[[:digit:]]@([[:alpha:]])[[:digit:]]*`
e) _____There is no way to construct such a pattern.

8) Subpatterns are used only at the beginning of patterns.

a) _____True
b) _____False

Quiz answers appear in Appendix A, Section 10.1.

LAB 10.2

COMMAND SUBSTITUTION

LAB OBJECTIVES

After this lab, you will be able to:

- ✓ Use Command Substitution for the Value of a Variable
- ✓ Use Command Substitution for the Value of a Parameter

You already know that a command sets an exit code, a number that is normally interpreted as a *true/false value* (0 or not-0, respectively) that you can test to see whether the command was "successful." You also know that commands normally write messages to *stdout,* which you can redirect to a file if you want to save it. In this lab, you will see how to use the messages that a program writes to *stdout* as values that can be assigned to variables or passed as parameters to scripts. The exercises will suggest some ways that this capability can be used; once you have mastered the concept, you will find a surprising number of situations where this is a valuable tool.

Lab 10.2 Exercises

10.2.1 Use the Output of a Command as the Value of a Variable

To introduce the idea of command substitution, try running the following commands:

```
NOW=$(date)
print -- $NOW
```

a) What is the value of the variable *NOW*?

b) What is the difference between `$(date)`, `${date}`, and `$date`?

It's common to use files to keep track of things on UNIX systems, and command substitution using `cat` commands is a common way to capture the contents of a file as a variable's value.

To see this sort of operation in action, run the following script:

```
# s1021 -- Demonstrate command substitution.

last_time=$(cat timestamp 2>/dev/null)
date >| timestamp

 [[ $last_time != "" ]] || last_time=never

cat << END

 Hello!

```

```
12)  It is now $(date).
13)  This script was last run $last_time.
14)
15)END
```


c) What does this script display the first time you run it?

---

d) What does it display the second time you run it?

---

e) What is the reason for `2>/dev/null` on line 3?

---

f) What would be the difference between the following two versions of line 3?

```
last_time=$(cat timestamp 2>/dev/null)
last_time=$(cat timestamp) 2>/dev/null
```

---

g) What does line 4 do?

---

h) What does line 6 do?

____

____

10.2.2 Use Command Substitution for the Value of a Parameter

Here is the first part of a script that illustrates using the same kind of command substitution as in the previous exercise, as well as providing a parameter to another command (line numbers are not part of the script):

```
1)  # s1022 -- Verify editing access to reports.

2)  #  Usage: s1022 [report_name]
3)  #  Where "report_name" is the name of a text file to start or continue
4)  #  editing.  The user may not start a new report until a previous one
5)  #  has been completed.


6)  #  Check the report name supplied by the user, if there is one.

7)  current_report=$(cat ~/.s1022_current_report 2>/dev/null)

8)  case $# in

9)  0)   [[ $current_report == "" ]] && {
10)      print -u2 You must give the name of a new report to start editing.
11)         return 1
12)         }
13)      ;;

14) 1)   [[ $current_report != "" && $current_report != "$1" ]] && {
15)         cat << END 1>&2
16) You are already working on "$current_report", so you may not
17) start a report named "$1".
18) If this is not correct, remove the file ~/.s1022_current_report.
19) END
20)         return 1
21)         }
22)      print -- $1 >| ~/.s1022_current_report
```

```
       ;;

*)  print -u2 Usage: s1022 [report name]
    return 1
    ;;

esac

#   Now edit the report ...
vi -- "$(cat ~/.s1022_current_report)" 1>/dev/tty
```

a) What happens the first time you run the script if you do not provide a file name?

b) What happens if you run the script with a file name, and there is no file named `~/.s1022_current_report`?

c) What happens if you run the script and do not provide a file name but have already run it once with a file name?

d) What happens if you run the script with a file name that is not the same as the contents of `~/.s1022_current_report`?

e) Why are there quotes around the command substitution of the `vi` command?

f) Why is the output of the `vi` command redirected?

g) How could you modify this script so it would use the user's preferred editor instead of always using `vi`?

LAB 10.2 ANSWERS

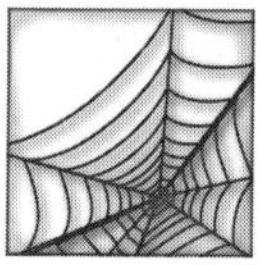

This section gives you some suggested answers to the questions in Lab 10.2, with discussion related to those answers. Your answers may vary, but the most important thing is whether or not your answer works. Use this discussion to analyze differences between your answers and those presented here.

If you have alternative answers to the questions in this exercise, you are encouraged to post your answers and to discuss them at the companion web site for this book, located at:

`http://www.phptr.com/phptrinteractive/`

10.2.1 ANSWERS

a) What is the value of the variable *NOW*?

Answer: The value of the variable is the output of the `date` *command. Depending on the moment that you ran the commands, your interaction should look something like the following:*

```
  [1029]: NOW=$(date)
[1030]: print -- $NOW
Mon Jan 20 20:20:20 EDT 2020.
[1031]:
```


Putting the command inside `$( ... )` triggers the shell's command substitution mechanism. It runs the command, capturing whatever the command writes to *stdout*, and substitutes that as the value of `$( ... )`.

b) What is the difference between `$(date)`, `${date}`, and `$date`?

Answer: The first causes the shell to do command substitution, but the second and third cause it to do variable substitution.

In the command substitution, `date` is the name of a command. You could use any command name here, including the name of one of your scripts or functions. In the variable substitutions, `date` is the name of a variable.

You can use the name of a command as the name of a variable, as in this example, but it's not a good practice because it can be confusing to people who read your programs.

c) What does this script display the first time you run it?

Answer: Your interaction should look something like the following:

```
[1031]: s1021

  Hello!

  It is now Wed Aug  5 11:57:00 EDT 1998.
  This script was last run never.

[1032]:
```

The *here document* uses command substitution in the "It is now" message and uses variable substitution in the "This script was" message. The variable `last_time` has the value *never*, which is appropriate for the first time the script is run.

d) What does it display the second time you run it?

Answer: Your interaction should look something like the following:

```
[1032]: s1021

  Hello!

  It is now Wed Aug  5 12:00:00 EDT 1998.
  This script was last run Wed Aug  5 11:57:00 EDT 1998.

[1033]:
```

The "It is now" message has been updated to the current date and time, and the "This script was" message shows the date and time that the script was last run.

e) What is the reason for `2>/dev/null` on line 3?

Answer: It redirects stderr *to the null device so it won't appear on the screen.*

The first time you run the script, the `timestamp` file does not exist, and the `cat` command will issue an error message when it can't find it. For this script, a missing `timestamp` file is a normal event that we have anticipated, so we get rid of the error message by sending it to oblivion.

f) What would be the difference between the following two versions of line 3?

```
last_time=$(cat timestamp 2>/dev/null)
last_time=$(cat timestamp) 2>/dev/null
```

Answer: The first one (the one used in the script) sends any error messages from the `cat` *command to* `/dev/null`*, whereas the second one sends any error messages from the assignment command to* `/dev/null`.

You can see from this code that it is all right to put I/O redirection inside the parentheses used for command substitution, and the shell performs the redirection while running the command. The second line will not redirect the error message from the `cat` command, which could confuse a user.

Housekeeping files, such as `s1021's timestamp`, normally should not be put in the current directory as in this example because you never know what directory the script will be run from. It's better to pick a known location in the file system for such files, perhaps in the user's home directory, in which case it's a good idea to make them hidden (put a dot at the beginning of the file name) so they don't clutter up normal directory listings. Most UNIX systems provide a `/tmp` directory that you can use for such files, too. However, all users on the system share the `/tmp` directory, which can cause problems if two users run the script at the same time. You can use `$$` in such file's names to create file names that are unique to a user's shell process.

g) What does line 4 do?

Answer: It runs the `date` command, with the output redirected to the `timestamp` file.

Note that this is *not* command substitution—it is just the regular execution of a command from within a script. The >| redirection guarantees that the timestamp file will be written, even if it exists and the user has the `noclobber` option set.

h) What does line 6 do?

Answer: It tests whether the `last_time` variable has been assigned a nonempty string value, and sets it to never *if not.*

If the `timestamp` file does not exist (such as the first time the script is run), the output of the first `cat` command will be nothing, and the shell will assign the empty string value to `last_time`.

10.2.2 ANSWERS

a) What happens the first time you run the script if you do not provide a file name?

Answer: Your interaction should look like the following:

```
[1033]: s1022
You must give the name of a new report to start
  editing.
[1034]:
```

The first pattern of the case statement, line 9, matches a value of zero for the `$#` reference to the number of command line parameters. The double-bracket command then tests whether the `current_report` variable was set to a nonempty string by the assignment using command substitution on the eleventh line. If `current_report` is the empty string, the error message is printed. The return command on line (11) then exits the script, setting the exit code to 1, indicating that the command "failed."

b) What happens if you run the script with a file name, and there is no `~/.s1022_current_report` file?

Answer: The editor starts up, editing the file named on the command line.

This is the normal way to start working on a new report. The second pattern of the case statement, line 14, matches the value of one for the `$#` reference to the number of command line parameters. The first test in the double bracket will fail, because `current_report` will, in fact, be the empty string, so the command group in braces will be skipped, and the `print` command on line 22 will write whatever file name the user specified as the parameter to the script to the contents of `~/.s1022_current_report`. Note the double dash in the print command, to manage the situation in which the user gives a file name that starts with a dash.

Try to anticipate the things a user might do that would "break" your programs, such as using file names that start with a dash or contain embedded whitespace, and take reasonable precautions. Don't assume that you will be the only one to use your programs and that you will always type the "correct thing."

On the other hand, don't get carried away with testing for every strange "wrong thing" a user might type.

c) What happens if you run the script and do not provide a file name but have already run it once with a file name?

Answer: The editor starts up, editing the file named previously.

The zero-parameter case, line (9), fails the double-bracket test because `current_report` will be a non-empty string, so the shell jumps to the next command after the `esac`, which starts up the editor.

d) What happens if you run the script with a file name that is not the same as the contents of `~/.s1022_current_report`?

Answer: You get a long error message. Your interaction should look something like the following:

```
[1034]: s1022 "Bad Report"
You are already working on "Good Report", \
so you may not start a report named "Bad Report".
If this is not correct, remove the file
  ~/.s1022_current_report.
[1035]:
```

In this situation, the second test in the double-bracket command on line 14 fails, and the here document gets copied to *stderr.* (Note the `1>2&` to redirect the `cat`'s *stdout* to *stderr* on line (22).) Because there is no reasonable way to proceed in this situation, the script then returns with an exit code of 1 on line (20).

e) Why is the output of the `vi` command redirected?

Answer: Because if the user redirects the output of the script, the screen display of the editor would get lost.

The editor's *stdout* is redirected to a "file" named `/dev/tty`, which is the file name you can almost always use to get to the user's terminal window, no matter what is redirected where. Using the actual device reference instead of *stdout* or *stderr* is generally not a good idea, but is justified in this case because the user's console would otherwise appear to "lock up" if the script was run with both *stdout* and *stderr* redirected to a file.

f) How could you modify this script so it would use the user's preferred editor instead of always using `vi`?

Answer: You could use a reference to the shell variable, `EDITOR`*, if it is set.*

There is a possible problem with this approach, however. As described in Chapter 1, "Setting Up," the shell uses this variable to tell it what command-line editing style to use, but its value does not necessarily name an installed editor. For example, you may have set `EDITOR` to *emacs*, but still prefer to use `vi`, `vim`, or some other editor for editing files. The "proper" approach to this problem is considered in the Test Your Thinking exercises at the end of the chapter.

LAB 10.2 SELF-REVIEW QUESTIONS

To test your progress, you should be able to answer the following questions.

1) What would be a good name for the `timestamp` file used by `s1021`?

a) _____`timestamp`
b) _____`~/.s1021_last_time`
c) _____`/timestamp`
d) _____`date`
e) _____`ksh`

2) Will the time and date displayed by `s1021` in the "It is now" message always agree, to the second, with the time and date displayed in the "This script was last" message the next time `s1021` is run? *Hint:* Choice *a)* is wrong!

a) _____Yes, always. No doubt about it. Definitely. There is no way they could be different.
b) _____No, because the "This script was last" message always says "never."
c) _____No, because the clock could change values between the execution of the `date` command on the fourth line and the `date` command on the twelfth line.
d) _____No, because of the Y2K problem.
e) _____Yes. I still say they will always be the same because it takes no time at all to execute the commands between the `date` command on the fourth line and the `date` command on the twelfth line.

3) How could `s1021` be modified so the "now" date always agrees with the next execution's "last" date?

a) _____No change needed, they will always agree without changing the script. (*Hint:* Look at the hint for the previous question.)
b) _____There is no way to make them always agree.
c) _____Put a `sleep -1` command between lines four and five of the script to move the clock back one second.

d) ____Capture the date in a variable before line four, then use the value of that variable in place of the command substitution on the fourth line and again in the *here document* on the twelfth line.
e) ____Put in a test to see whether they are different, and subtract one from the time if the second one is too big.

4) What will be the contents of `~/.s1022_current_report` after running the following two commands?

```
rm ~/.s1022_current_report
s1022 -report-
```

a) _____Nothing, because the first command removed the file.
b) _____Nothing, because you can't have a report named `-report-`.
c) _____The string, `-report-`.
d) _____The contents of the file named `-report-`.
e) _____An error message, because you can't start `-report-` until you complete work on the previous report.

5) Assume your computer's name is "Mozart." What would the following command print?

```
print This computer\'s name is $(hostname).
```

a) _____`This computer\'s name is $(hostname).`
b) _____`This computer\'s name is Mozart.`
c) _____`This computer's name is Mozart.`
d) _____`This computer's name is .`
e) _____`This computer's name is hostname.`

Quiz answers appear in Appendix A, Section 10.2.

LAB 10.3

PARAMETER EXPANSION

LAB OBJECTIVES

After this lab, you will be able to:

✓ Manage Defaults and Errors
✓ Distinguish Between Null and Unset Variables
✓ Work with Strings and Substrings

This lab deals with *parameter expansion,* which you have already seen in its basic form when you learned about variable references. The KornShell has extended the basic syntax of putting a variable name inside `${ ... }` to provide a rich set of operations you can do with the values of variables. Some of these operations give you efficient ways of dealing with common tests that would otherwise require double-bracket or `if` commands. Others give you ways of selecting parts of a variable's value in systematic ways.

There are some constructs that use the `${ ... }` syntax that are not covered here. They are all listed in Appendix B, "Built-In Command."

LAB 10.3 EXERCISES

10.3.1 MANAGE DEFAULTS AND ERRORS

Shell variables provide a convenient way for users to indicate their personal preferences when there is more than one way to do something. Such variables are typically initialized in the user's *ENV* file when the user logs in, but what if the user hasn't initialized one of these preference variables? The two most common ways to deal with this situation are to use a *default value* or to issue an *error message*. Parameter expansion lets you do either easily.

FOR EXAMPLE

Imagine a script that will run the user's web browser. There might be several browsers on the user's system, so the problem is to determine which one to use.

Run the following commands:

```
unset BROWSER
print Your browser is ${BROWSER:-lynx}.
```

You could run the browser by using `${BROWSER:-lynx}` *as a command name, but actually running a web browser in this exercise would be too distracting, so we'll just print out its name.*

a) What did the first command accomplish?

b) What prints when you run this command?

Now run the following commands:

```
BROWSER=netscape
print Your browser is ${BROWSER:-lynx}.
```

c) What prints this time?

This mechanism for providing a default value is very convenient, provided that you know that the default value will work. However, what if BROWSER isn't defined and lynx isn't installed on the user's system? In that case, using ${BROWSER:-lynx} as a command would fail, which is definitely uncool in a shell script! Run the following commands to see one way to manage this situation. (If you do have lynx installed on your computer, choose some other program name that you don't have.)

```
unset BROWSER
if    ! whence ${BROWSER:-lynx} >/dev/null
then  print -u2 no browser
fi
```

d) What printed when you ran these commands?

e) What does the > on the second line accomplish?

Another approach would be to *require* the user to set the BROWSER variable before running your script or function, using the KornShell's :? parameter expansion.

Create the following function definition:

```
function f1030 {
  print Your browser is ${BROWSER:?"must be defined"}.
  print Pretending to run $BROWSER.
  }
```

Now run the following commands:

```
unset BROWSER
f1030
```

f) What printed, and why?

____

____

Now run the following commands:

```
BROWSER=
f1030
```

g) What printed, and why?

____

____

Now run the following commands:

```
BROWSER=lynx
f1030
```

h) What printed, and why?

____

____

You can also use parameter expansion to combine variable assignment with default substitution.

Run the following commands:

```
unset BROWSER
print ${BROWSER:-lynx}
print $BROWSER
print ${BROWSER:=lynx}
print $BROWSER
```

i) What is the difference between `:-` and `:=`?

10.3.2 Distinguish Between Null and Unset Variables

Until now, we haven't paid much attention to the difference between a variable that isn't set and one that has the empty string as its value. If you print them, they both print the same thing (which is nothing, unless you have the shell's `nounset` option turned on). However, it can be important sometimes to differentiate between the two situations. If a variable is set to the empty string, it means that the user has done something to give that value to the variable. However if the variable is unset, it means the user has done nothing with the variable and perhaps doesn't even know about it.

Run the following commands:

```
unset BROWSER
BROKER=
[[ $BROWSER == $BROKER ]] && print They are the same
```

a) Does the message print?

b) Are the two variables really the same?

You will sometimes see the word null *used to mean "the empty string," which is fine for shell programs. However, languages like C, C++, and Java, distinguish very strongly between a variable that holds nothing and one that references the empty string.*

*All this talk about "*the empty string*" instead of "*an empty string*" is another bit of pedantry that has more meaning with other programming languages than with shell programming. You can use either phrase interchangeably when talking about shell programs. Just be aware that you may need to make the distinction when doing other kinds of programming.*

Each of the expansion operators in the previous exercise (`:-`, `:?`, and `:=`) can also be written without the colons, which make them work only if the variable is *unset*.

Run the following commands:

```
unset BROWSER
print ${BROWSER-lynx}
BROWSER=
print ${BROWSER-lynx}
BROWSER=netscape
print ${BROWSER-lynx}
```

c) Explain the outputs of the three `print` commands.

---

d) Which expansion operator would you use if you want to assign a default value to a variable only if it is unset?

10.3.3 WORK WITH STRINGS AND SUBSTRINGS

The shell provides a rich set of parameter expansions that you can use to work with the value part of string variables. The simplest tells you how many characters there are in a variable's value. To see this, run the following commands:

```
ThisVar="Hello, . . . hello?"
print "ThisVar has ${#ThisVar} characters."
```

a) What does the number sign (#) to the right of the opening brace ({) do?

FOR EXAMPLE

You can also extract part of a variable's value. For example, the following two commands will print the current time. (If you are not familiar with the `date` command's formatting options, you can probably figure out what you need to understand from the example. If not, consult your documentation for the UNIX `date` command.)

```
date +%T
NOW=$(date); print ${NOW:11:8}
```

b) What do the two numbers after the colons (:) tell the shell?

You can also substitute a string for a pattern that occurs in a variable's value. To see this, run the following command line:

```
NOW=$(date)
print ${NOW/[0-9][0-9]:[0-9][0-9]:[0-9][0-9]/"Very Late!"}
```


c) What is the code between the slashes?

d) Explain the output of the `print` command.

Here are four variations on this theme of substituting strings for patterns, starting with the one you just looked at:

1. **`${name/pattern/string}`** Substitute *string* for the *first* occurrence of *pattern*.
2. **`${name//pattern/string}`** Substitute *string* for *all* occurrences of *pattern*.
3. **`${name/#pattern/string}`** Substitute only if *pattern* is at the *start* of the value.
4. **`${name/%pattern/string}`** Substitute only if *pattern* is at the *end* of the value.

To see how these work, run the following commands:

```
SAMPLE=aaabbbccc
print ${SAMPLE/b/x}
```

```
print ${SAMPLE//b/x}
print ${SAMPLE/#b/x}
print ${SAMPLE/#a*b/x}
print ${SAMPLE/%c*c/x}
```

e) Explain the output of each of the `print` commands.

____

____

____

____

____

There are four manipulations that are very widely used because they can manipulate values that represent file pathnames. They can be used with any strings, of course, but pathnames are "naturals" for these operations. Here they are:

1.	**${**name**#**pattern**}**	Remove shortest left pattern.
2.	**${**name**##**pattern**}**	Remove longest left pattern.
3.	**${**name**%**pattern**}**	Remove shortest right pattern.
4.	**${**name**%%**pattern**}**	Remove shortest right pattern.

To see how these work, run the following commands:

```
SAMPLE=/usr/local/bin/fringle
print ${SAMPLE#*/}
print ${SAMPLE##*/}
print ${SAMPLE%/*}
print ${SAMPLE%%/*}
```

f) Explain the outputs of these four `print` commands.

Finally, there is also a set of parameter expansions that you can use to work with a subset of positional parameter lists (the special variables (`@`) and (`*`) that you covered in Exercise 5.1.3, "Use Special Parameter Variables (`#` `@` `*`)"), indexed arrays, and associative arrays, covered in Lab 6.2, "Arrays and Compound Variables." The syntax is analogous to the substring syntax you looked at in Question b of this exercise.

Enter the following commands:

```
integer i=( 99 88 77 66 55 )
typeset -A a
a[aa]=99 a[bb]=88 a[cc]=77 a[dd]=66 a[ee]=55
set 99 88 77 66 55
print $@       $'\n' ${@:1:2}
print ${a[@]} $'\n' ${a[@]:1:2}
print ${i[@]} $'\n' ${i[@]:1:2}
```

g) Explain the outputs of the three `print` commands.

Lab 10.3 Answers

This section gives you some suggested answers to the questions in Lab 10.3, with discussion related to those answers. Your answers may vary, but the most important thing is whether or not your answer works. Use this discussion to analyze differences between your answers and those presented here.

If you have alternative answers to the questions in this exercise, you are encouraged to post your answers and to discuss them at the companion web site for this book, located at:

`http://www.phptr.com/phptrinteractive/`

10.3.1 Answers

Run the following commands:

```
unset BROWSER
print Your browser is ${BROWSER:-lynx}.
```

a) What did the first command accomplish?

Answer: It made sure the variable `BROWSER` *does not have a value.*

It's possible that you had already assigned a value to a variable with this name, so we just made sure that it is undefined when you ran the second command.

b) What prints when you run this command?

Answer: Your interaction should look like the following:

```
[1035]: unset BROWSER
[1036]: print Your browser is ${BROWSER:-lynx}.
Your browser is lynx.
[1037]:
```

The *default parameter value* symbol (:-) tells the shell to substitute whatever follows the dash for the value of the variable named before the colon, if that variable is either undefined or has the empty string as its value. In the present case, `BROWSER` is undefined, so the value printed is lynx.

```
BROWSER=netscape
print Your browser is ${BROWSER:-lynx}.
```

c) What prints this time?

Answer: Your interaction should look like the following:

```
[1037]: BROWSER=netscape
[1038]: print Your browser is ${BROWSER:-lynx}.
Your browser is netscape.
[1039]:
```


This time, `BROWSER` does have a value, and that's what gets substituted for the `${ ... }`.

```
unset BROWSER
if    ! (whence ${BROWSER:-lynx} >/dev/null)
then  print -u2 no browser
fi
```

d) What printed when you ran these commands?

Answer: "no browser" prints.

If you recall, the shell's `whence` command tells you whether a command is a function or an external command, and if it is external, where it is located in the file system. In this code, we are using the fact that `whence` sets its exit code to *false* if the shell cannot find the command anywhere. The exclamation mark changes the logical value being tested into *true* if the value of the `${ ... }` is not the name of an executable file, and if this is the case, the `print` command gets executed.

e) What does the > on the second line accomplish?

Answer: It redirects the output of the whence *command.*

If the parameter passed to `whence` *is* the name of something executable, `whence` prints a message telling you about it, but we don't want to see that message, so we redirect it to `/dev/null`. We're interested only in the value of `whence`'s exit code in this `if` statement, so we get rid of the message.

```
unset BROWSER
f1030
```

f) What printed, and why?

Answer: Your interaction should look like the following:

```
[1039]: unset BROWSER
[1040]: f1030
ksh: f1030: line 1: BROWSER: must be defined
[1041]:
```


Because BROWSER was not set when you ran the function, the shell printed an error message telling you the function name, the line number in the function where the error occurred, the name of the variable that caused the problem and, finally, the string that you wrote after the :? in the first print command.

Note that neither print command executed. The shell does parameter expansion before it runs a command. (This makes sense, because it does parameter expansion to produce the value that will be passed to the command when it executes, so it has to do the expansion before the execution.) As soon as the shell found the unset variable, it printed its own error message and *stopped executing the function.* It's not just the first print command that doesn't execute, it's everything else in the function as well.

Whenever the shell finds an unset or empty variable using the :? expansion, it sets the script or function's exit code to 1 (indicating failure) and abandons the remainder of the script or function that contained the :? expansion.

```
BROWSER=
f1030
```

g) What printed, and why?

Answer: Your interaction should look like the following:

```
[1041]: BROWSER=
[1042]: f1030
ksh: f1030: line 1: BROWSER: must be defined
[1043]:
```

You got the same error message, even though BROWSER was defined this time because it was defined to have the empty string as its value. The :? considers both an unset variable and a variable set to the empty string to be errors.

```
BROWSER=lynx
f1030
```

h) What printed, and why?

Answer: Your interaction should look like the following:

```
[1043]: BROWSER=lynx
[1044]: f1030
Your browser is lynx.
Pretending to run lynx.
[1045]:
```

Now you have assigned a nonempty string to BROWSER, so the :? does not fail, and both print commands run.

Run the following commands:

```
unset BROWSER
print ${BROWSER:-lynx}
print $BROWSER
print ${BROWSER:=lynx}
print $BROWSER
```

i) What is the difference between :- and :=?

Answer: Your interaction should look like the following:

```
[1045]: unset BROWSER
[1046]: print ${BROWSER:-lynx}
lynx
[1047]: print $BROWSER

[1048]: print ${BROWSER:=lynx}
lynx
[1049]: print $BROWSER
lynx
[1050]:
```

Both :- and := cause the ${ ... } to expand to the value *lynx*, but in the first case the variable BROWSER keeps its original value (nothing, which is printed after line 1047), whereas the := assigns the default value to the variable so that it can be used later on, as when its value is printed on line 1049.

10.3.2 Answers

Run the following commands:

```
unset BROWSER
BROKER=
[[ $BROWSER == $BROKER ]] && print They are the same
```

a) Does the message print?

Answer: Yes.

`BROWSER` is not set, but `BROKER` is set to the empty string. If you print them, you will get nothing in both cases. They appear to be indistinguishable.

b) Are the two variables really the same?

Answer: No.

`BROWSER` has explicitly been unset, given no value. However, `BROKER` has been set, it's just that the value to the right of the equal sign is the empty string. The assignment to `BROKER` could also have been written as follows:

```
BROKER=""
```

Run the following commands:

```
unset BROWSER
print ${BROWSER-lynx}
BROWSER=
print ${BROWSER-lynx}
BROWSER=netscape
print ${BROWSER-lynx}
```

c) Explain the outputs of the three `print` commands.

Answer: Your interaction should look like the following:

```
[1050]: unset BROWSER
[1051]: print ${BROWSER-lynx}
lynx
```

```
[1052]: BROWSER=
[1053]: print ${BROWSER-lynx}

[1054]: BROWSER=netscape
[1055]: print ${BROWSER-lynx}
netscape
[1056]:
```

The command on line 1051 substitutes the default value because BROWSER is not set, but on line 1053 the substitution does not take place because BROWSER is defined, even though it is the empty string. If these two commands had used :- instead of just -, both commands would have printed the default value. Line 1055 shows that - works the same way as := if the variable is set to a nonempty string, also.

d) Which expansion operator would you use if you want to assign a default value to a variable only if it is unset?

Answer: Use = in this case.

Just as the dash operator works only if the variable is unset. The equal operator follows the same rule.

10.3.3 Answers

a) What does the number sign (#) to the right of the opening brace ({) do?

Answer: It tells the shell to use the number of characters in the variable's value as the value of the reference. Your interaction should have looked like the following:

```
[1056]: ThisVar="Hello, . . . hello?"
[1057]: print "ThisVar has ${#ThisVar} characters."
ThisVar has 19 characters.
[1058]:
```

All the characters in the value, including any embedded spaces, punctuation marks, and so forth, are included in the value returned by this expansion.

b) What do the two numbers after the colons (:) tell the shell?

Answer: Where in the string to start and how many additional characters to include in the value returned. Your interaction should look like the following:

```
[1058]: date +%T
18:36:34
[1059]: NOW=$(date); print ${NOW:11:8}
18:36:37
[1060]:
```


Line 1058 shows how you can print just the time using the system's `date` command. Line 1059 captures the output of a `date` command in the variable *NOW*, then prints eight characters, starting at position 11 from the value of *NOW*. Note that the leftmost position in the string is numbered 0, not 1.

If you leave out the length part of a substring specifier (the `:8` part of line 1059), the shell will return all the characters in the string, from the first one specified (position 11 in line 1059) to the end of the string.

c) What is the code between the slashes?

Answer: It is a pattern that specifies two digits, a colon, two digits, a colon, and two more digits.

This sort of pattern was covered in Exercise 10.1.3, "Use Square brackets (`[]`) to Match Character Sets."

d) Explain the output of the `print` command.

Answer: Your interaction should look like the following:

```
[1060]: NOW=$(date)
[1061]: print ${NOW/[0-9][0-9]:[0-9][0-9]:[0-9][0-9]/ \
"Very Late!"}
Wed Sep 30 Very Late! EDT 1998
[1062]:
```

The `print` command prints the output of the `date` command, but with the string `"Very Late!"` substituted for the pattern of characters that matches the `HH:MM:SS` part (that is, the part that matches the pattern described in Question c).

e) Explain the output of each of the `print` commands.

Answer: Your interaction should look like the following:

```
[1062]: SAMPLE=aaabbbccc
[1063]: print ${SAMPLE/b/x}
aaaxbbccc
[1064]: print ${SAMPLE//b/x}
aaaxxxccc
[1065]: print ${SAMPLE/#b/x}
aaabbbccc
[1066]: print ${SAMPLE/#a*b/x}
xccc
[1067]: print ${SAMPLE/%c*c/x}
aaabbbx
[1068]:
```


Line 1063 prints the value of *SAMPLE* with the first *b* changed to an x, whereas line 1064 changes all bs to xs. Line 1065 prints the original value of SAMPLE because the specified pattern, a character b, does not occur at the beginning of the string. However, line 1066 does make a substitution of x for the pattern #aaab, which tells the shell to look for "an a, followed by zero or more characters, followed by a b, starting at the beginning of the string." Line 1067 uses a pattern that tells the shell to look for "a c, followed by any number of characters, followed by a c, ending at the end of the string," which matches the three cs at the end of *SAMPLE*.

f) Explain the outputs of these four `print` commands.

Answer: Your interaction should look like the following:

```
[1068]: print ${SAMPLE#*/}
usr/local/bin/fringle
[1069]: print ${SAMPLE##*/}
fringle
[1070]: print ${SAMPLE%/*}
/usr/local/bin
[1071]: print ${SAMPLE%%/*}

[1072]:
```

The pattern in line 1068 is #*/, which tells the shell to "delete the shortest sequence of characters (#) that consists of any number of characters (*), followed by a slash (/), starting at the beginning of the string." In this case, the shortest such sequence is just the slash at the beginning of the value of *SAMPLE*. Remember, "any number of characters" can mean, as in this case, "none."

The pattern in line 1069 is `##*/` which is the same as the previous one, except that the shell is to match the longest matching sequence that it can find. So, in this case the asterisk (`*`) matches everything up to the last slash (`/`), leaving just the characters following that slash after the deletion.

The command `print ${SAMPLE##*/}` *behaves much like the UNIX command* `basename $SAMPLE`*, provided that the value of* SAMPLE *is a valid pathname.*

The pattern in line 1070 is `%/*` which tells the shell to "delete the shortest sequence of characters that consist of a slash, followed by any number of characters, ending at the end of the string." In this case, the shell deletes the last slash and everything to the right of it.

The command `print ${SAMPLE%/*}` *is much like the UNIX command* `dirname $SAMPLE` *provided that the value of* `SAMPLE` *is a valid pathname.*

The pattern in line 1071 is `%%/*`, which is the same as the previous one, except that the shell is to match the *longest* matching sequence that it can find. In this case, the slash is found at the beginning of the string and the asterisk matches everything else, resulting in everything being deleted, and a blank line prints.

g) Explain the outputs of the three `print` commands.

Answer: Your interaction should look like the following:

```
[1072]: integer i=( 99 88 77 66 55 )
[1073]: typeset -A a
[1074]: a[aa]=99 a[bb]=88 a[cc]=77 a[dd]=66 a[ee]=55
[1075]: set 99 88 77 66 55
[1076]: print $@       $'\n' ${@:1:2}
99 88 77 66 55
 99 88
[1077]: print ${a[@]} $'\n' ${a[@]:1:2}
77 55 88 66 99
 55 88
```

```
[1078]: print ${i[@]} $'\n' ${i[@]:1:2}
99 88 77 66 55
 88 77
[1079]:
```

Lines 1072–1075 establish variable `i` as an indexed array of integers, variable *a* as an associative array, and the special variable @ (the list of command line parameters, as discussed in Exercise 5.1.3, "Use Special Parameter Variables (`# @ *`)"); each of which has a similar set of values.

Line 1076 prints the value of @, and then uses colons to select two elements, starting with element 1. As the output shows, the two elements selected are the first two parameters given on the `set` command. You may recall that element number 0 of the @ variable is the name of the command, and is not affected by the `set` command.

Line 1077 prints the value of all the elements in the associative array *a*, then prints two elements, starting with element 1. You may recall from Exercise 6.2.2, "Declare and Use Associative Arrays," that the sequence of elements in an associative array is related neither to the values of the subscripts nor to the order in which the elements were added to the array, as the first output line from this command shows. The two elements selected for printing are the second and third elements of the array because the positions in the list generated by `${a[@] ... }` are numbered starting with 0.

Line 1078 prints all the elements of the indexed array *i*, then selects two elements, starting with subscript 1. The results agree with the notion that the first element of an indexed array has a subscript value of 0.

LAB 10.3 SELF-REVIEW QUESTIONS

To test your progress, you should be able to answer the following questions.

1) Which expansion operator would you use to assign a value to a variable if it is either null or unset?

   a) _____:
   b) _____:-
   c) _____-
   d) _____:=
   e) _____=

2) What value does the following variable reference represent?
`$(abc=abc}`

a) ______None, because you can't assign a variable to itself.
b) ______The value `abc` if the variable `abc` is not set; otherwise, whatever the value of the variable `abc` is.
c) ______The value of the variable `abc`.
d) ______The characters, `abc`.
e) ______The characters, `abc=abc`.

3) What does this command line print?
`x="12345678"; print -- ${#x} ${x:5}`

a) ______`12345678 8 55555555`
b) ______`678`
c) ______`-- ${#x} ${x:5}`
d) ______`8 5`
e) ______`#12345678 5678`

Quiz answers appear in Appendix A, Section 10.3.

CHAPTER 10

TEST YOUR THINKING

The projects in this section are meant to have you utilize all of the skills that you have acquired throughout this chapter. The answers to these projects can be found at the companion web site to this book, located at:

`http://www.phptr.com/phptrinteractive/`

Visit the Web site periodically to share and discuss your answers.

1) Modify `s1022` so that it uses the user's preferred editor, if the *EDITOR* variable is set. Otherwise, use `vi`.

Optional: Is there a better way to handle this issue? One idea would be to introduce another variable, for example, `REPORT_EDITOR`, to hold the user's preference for what editor to use. Modify the script to manage the use of this variable.

2) Modify `s1022` so that it checks that the file to be edited exists and that the user has read/write access to it. If it is a new file, make sure the user has write access to the directory that contains it.

Optional: The user might start a new report, in the sense that there is no `~/.s1022_current_report` file, but the file might already exist. Decide what would be a reasonable way to handle this situation, and implement it.

3) Continuing `s1022`, write another script or function named, `s1022_finish`, that (*i*) mails the current report to an email address specified on the command line (use the `mailx` command to do this). If there is no email address given, skip this step); (*ii*) moves the current report to an archive directory—the pathname of the archive directory may be specified by the setting of a shell variable or by the contents of a file in the user's home directory; you decide which is more reasonable and implement it; and (*iii*) provided that the current report is archived successfully, deletes `~/.s1022_current_report`, indicating that the current report is finished and the user may start a new one.

Optional: Write `s1022_initialize`, which sets up the archive directory based on a command line argument or through an interactive dialog with the user.

CHAPTER 11

I/O AND TRAP PROCESSING

Read'n, Rite'n, and Respond'n

The three Rs

CHAPTER OBJECTIVES

In this chapter, you will learn about:

The labs in this chapter cover features of the KornShell shell that take advantage of services provided by the operating system's kernel to achieve some powerful programming effects.

These services include I/O processing, process management, and signal processing. How the kernel implements these services are topics in "systems programming." In this chapter you will learn how the KornShell makes these services available to your shell programs.

THE `READ` AND `PRINTF` COMMANDS

LAB OBJECTIVES

After this lab, you will be able to:

- ✓ Use the `read` Command
- ✓ Format Output

In this lab, you will learn how to "get inside" a text file so that you can perform operations using its contents. Until now (except for the `select` statement), you have seen only how to get a file's contents sent to other programs, such as the filter programs you used in Lab 3.1.3, "Pipelines," for processing. However, your scripts and functions can read the contents of a text file just as well as any other program can by using the shell's built-in `read` command.

Also, the `print` command by itself does not make it very easy for you to format the output generated by your program—for example, to make columns of numbers line up neatly. This issue is not so important when the output consists of messages you want to display for the user to read, but it becomes significant when you need to generate a report that people will read "off line," where appearances matter more. The `printf` command and some options for the `typeset` command will give you the control over formatting your output that you will need for this sort of operation.

Lab 11.1 Exercises

11.1.1 Use the read Command

There are a couple of points to make before we start working with the `read` command. The first is that in this exercise we will use `read` to process information coming from *stdin* (`fd` number zero), but the command has an option, `-u`, that you can use to process a file using `fd`s other than number zero. You will learn to work with different `fd`s in the next lab. The principles covered in this exercise carry over directly to performing input from all `fd`s, not just *stdin*.

The second point has to do with the distinction between *text* and *binary* files. UNIX treats all files equivalently, as streams of bytes, but we can use the term *text file* to mean a file that contains only ASCII character codes, such as one you prepare using a text editor or generate using the output of `print` commands. Binary files, on the other hand, contain arbitrary bit patterns, such as the machine language code generated by a compiler when it processes a C/C++ or Java program. You can use the `read` command to process text files very nicely, but it won't work very well with binary files because `read` uses ASCII codes in the file to determine where lines begin and end and where words within a line begin and end, but having non-ASCII codes in a file makes the concepts of lines and words meaningless.

Here is the syntax of the `read` command:

```
read [-Aprs] [-U [n] ] [-d char] [-t sec] [name?prompt] [name ... ]
```

As you can see, the command has a lot of options and parameters you can use, but they are all shown in square brackets, which means that they are all optional. So we'll start with as simple a `read` command as possible, one with no parameters or arguments. When you run that command, the shell will wait for you to type a line of text, which it will read, then the shell will show a prompt for you to enter another command.

LAB 11.1

Type the following three lines to see this happen:

```
read
Hello, how are you?
print $REPLY
```

a) What was the value of *REPLY* after the `read` command completed?

____

____

Now type these three lines:

```
read answer
OK.  How are you now?
print $answer
```

b) What was the value of *answer* after the `read` command completed?

____

____

Now type the following lines:

```
read r1?"Type something: " r2 r3
This really is something.
print "r1 is \"$r1\", r2 is \"$r2\", and r3 is \"$r3\""
```

c) What is the string after the question mark (`?`) used for?

____

____

d) What are the values of the three variables, `r1`, `r2`, and `r3` after the `read` command completed?

To learn more about the `read` command, we'll work with a function that works sort of like the external `wc` command that you used in Chapter 2, "Command Syntax." The idea is to count the number of lines, words, and characters in a file.

Enter the following function definition into a file named `~/fun/mywc`:

```
# mywc Count the lines, words, and characters in a file
function mywc {

integer lines words chars
typeset IFS

  IFS=
  while read -r
  do
    IFS=$' \t\n'
    print -- $REPLY | read -rA inWords
    (( lines++ ))
    (( words += ${#inWords[@]} ))
    (( chars += ${#REPLY} ))
    IFS=
  done

  print -- "\t$lines \t$words \t$chars"

  }
```

We need a file with some test data in it, so enter the following text into a file named `wctest`:

```
This is a nice text file.
I hope you like it.
Good-bye.
```

There is a lot of material in here, so let's summarize the main features of the function before learning about how the individual parts work:

1. There is a `while` loop at the heart of this function that uses the value returned by a `read` command to decide whether to continue executing.
2. The value of a variable named *IFS* is saved when the function starts and restored to its original value before the function exits. The value of *IFS* is changed before entering the loop and in two different places inside the loop.
3. Inside the loop, the value of the input buffer from the first `read` is read again by piping the output of a `print` command to a second `read` command.

A `read` command has an exit status of false if it tries to read beyond the end of the input file and true otherwise, so "`while read; do...done`" is a common programming idiom for reading all the lines in a file.

Now run the following two command lines to compare the output of `mywc` and the version of `wc` that is available on your computer:

```
wc < wctest
mywc < wctest
```

e) How does the output of these two commands compare?

____

____

The shell uses the variable `IFS` as its Internal Field Separator, the character(s) it uses for doing token splitting. By default, it is the "whitespace" characters, space, tab, and new line, but you can change it if you wish. In particular, if you give `IFS` an empty string as its value, the shell will not do field splitting when executing `read` commands.

The shell also uses `IFS` when it does field splitting during command substitution, parameter expansion, and for the words after `in`, `for`, and `select`.

f) Does the shell do field splitting when the `read` at the top of the loop is executed?

---

g) What does the expression `(( chars += ${#REPLY} ))` compute?

---

h) Does the shell do field splitting when the `read` command inside the loop is executed?

---

i) What does the expression `(( words += ${#inWords[@]} ))` compute?

---

j) What is it in the code that makes the variable *inWords* an array?

---

k) What is the purpose of the statement `typeset IFS`?

There are two options for `read` that we haven't covered here: `-d` and `-u`. The `-d` option can be employed to use some character other than linefeed as the end-of-line delimiter, and the `-u` option will be covered when we look at the `exec` command in the next lab. As you might infer from the `-u` option of the `print` command, it is used to tell `read` to get its input from an `fd` other than zero (*stdin*).

11.1.2 Format Output

The KornShell provides three different ways to control the appearance of your programs' output. You have already seen the simplest form of control you have, which is to embed control codes such as tabs (`\t`) and new lines (`\n`) into the messages that you print. However, the shell provides two other ways to control output formatting, one of which is based on options to the `typeset` command, and the other of which is provided by the `printf` command, which is patterned on a statement of the same name in the C programming language.

You can use `typeset` to affect how a variable's value is kept internally, and this will (normally) determine how the variable looks when it is printed using the `print` command. If you use `printf`, you provide a *format string* as the first parameter of the command, and the format string describes how the remaining parameters are to be formatted for printing. If you use `typeset` to establish how a variable is stored internally by the shell, then print the variable using `printf`, the `printf` format string controls how the internal value will be printed but does not affect the internal value in any way.

Both `typeset` and `printf` provide more features than we will cover here. For further details, consult Appendix B, "Built-In Command Reference."

Normally, the values you print are *left-justified*, but you can use `typeset's -R` option to make a variable print *right-justified*. To see this, enter the following commands:

```
a1=a a2=aa a3=aaa a4=aaaa a5=aaaaa
for x in $a1 $a2 $a3 $a4 $a5 ; do print "$x"; done
typeset -R6 x
for x in $a1 $a2 $a3 $a4 $a5 ; do print "$x"; done
```

a) What variable is affected by the `typeset` command?

---

b) By examining the output of the second `for` statement, tell what the `R6` does in the `typeset` command.

Now run the following commands:

```
typeset -R3 x
for x in $a1 $a2 $a3 $a4 $a5 ; do print "$x"; done
typeset -R16 x
for x in $a1 $a2 $a3 $a4 $a5 ; do print "$x"; done
```

c) What happens if the width of `x` is too small to hold a value assigned to it?

---

d) What does the output of the second loop prove?

To see how `typeset`'s upper and lowercase options work, run the following commands:

```
typeset -u x
for x in $a1 $a2 $a3 $a4 $a5 ; do print "$x"; done
typeset -l x
typeset -u a3
for x in $a1 $a2 $a3 $a4 $a5 ; do print "$x"; done
```

```
typeset +l x
for x in $a1 $a2 $a3 $a4 $a5 ; do print "$x"; done
```

e) What does the `-u` do to the values assigned to `x` in the first `for` loop?

---

f) Explain the output of the second `for` loop.

---

g) Based on the output of the last `for` loop, what does the `+l` option do?

Other typeset formatting options you might want to investigate include `-E` (exponential number format), `-F` (floating-point number format), `-LZ` (left-justify and remove leading zeros), and `-Z` (right-justify and fill with leading zeros).

The `printf` command's format string can be a mixture of text to print and *conversion control strings*, which begin with a percent (`%`) symbol.

Run the following command to see the KornShell's equivalent of the classic "first program" shown to C-language programmers:

```
printf "Hello, World!\n"
```

h) Why is the parameter in quotes? (There are two answers to this.)

The conversion control strings consist of the percent symbol, up to four optional qualifiers and, finally, a required *conversion character.* Two commonly used conversion characters are `d`, for printing integer values, and `s`, for printing strings. Some other interesting conversions include `e`, `f`, and `g` for various floating-point formats, as well as `o`, `x`, and `X` for octal and hexadecimal values. To see some examples of how these conversions work, run the following commands:

```
integer i=12345
printf "%d\n %10d\n %-10d\n %o\n %x\n" i i i i i
h=hello
printf "%s\n %10s\n %-10s\n" $h $h $h
```

i) In the first `printf` command, how many conversion control strings are there in the format string, and how many times is the variable *i* given after the format string?

j) What does a number between the percent symbol and the conversion character do?

LAB 11.1

k) What does a minus sign in front of the number do?

Now run the following commands:

```
typeset -uL7 h
printf "\"%10s\"\n" "$h"
```

l) What did the `typeset` command do, and how did it affect the output of the `printf` command?

Run the following command to observe the difference between the `%s` conversion and another related one, `%b`:

```
printf "%s -- %b\n" "hello\there" "hello\there"
```

m) What is the difference between the `%s` and the `%b` conversion codes?

LAB 11.1 ANSWERS

This section gives you some suggested answers to the questions in Lab 11.1, with discussion related to those answers. Your answers may vary, but the most important thing is whether or not your answer works. Use this discussion to analyze differences between your answers and those presented here.

If you have alternative answers to the questions in this exercise, you are encouraged to post your answers and to discuss them at the companion web site for this book, located at:

`http://www.phptr.com/phptrinteractive/`

11.1.1 ANSWERS

a) What was the value of *REPLY* after the `read` command completed?

Answer: It contains the second line you typed in. Your interaction should look like the following:

```
[11000]: read
Hello, how are you?
[11001]: print $REPLY
Hello, how are you?
[11002]:
```

You could have typed anything you wanted to after line 11000, and whatever you typed would have been displayed as the value of the variable *REPLY*. You can think of the variable *REPLY* as the default *buffer* that receives the line of text input by a `read` command.

b) What was the value of *answer* after the `read` command completed?

Answer: It contains the second line you typed in. Your interaction should look like the following:

```
[11002]: read answer
OK.  How are you now?
[11003]: print $answer
OK. How are you now?
[11004]:
```

The shell uses *REPLY* as the variable to serve as the input buffer by default, but you can give another variable name to use for this purpose if you wish. In this case, we used *answer* as the input variable.

Did you notice the difference between what you typed in and what was printed as the value of *answer*? If you typed in exactly what was shown for the second line, you should have typed two spaces after the "`OK.`" in the second line, but the value of *answer* has only one space following the dot. This is a clue that the `read` command is doing *token splitting* on the input line, as you will see next.

c) What is the string after the question mark (`?`) used for?

Answer: It serves as a prompt string. Your interaction should have looked like the following:

```
[11004]: read r1?"Type something:  " r2 r3
Type something: This really is something.
[11005]:print "r1 is \"$r1\", r2 is \"$r2\", and r3 is \"$r3\""
r1 is "This", r2 is "really", and r3 is "is something."
[11006]:
```

You could use any string as the prompt that you want to. If it contains spaces, as this one does, you need to enclose it in quotes or to escape the spaces with backslashes (\ ).

d) What are the values of the three variables, `r1`, `r2`, and `r3` after the `read` command completed?

Answer: They are "This," "really," and "is something," *respectively.*

The `read` command lets you have multiple input buffers; simply list their names on the command line. The shell does token splitting on the command line, putting the first token in the first buffer, the second token in the second buffer, and so forth. If there are more tokens than there are buffers, any tokens remaining go in the last buffer you name, as in `r3` in this example. Whenever a single variable receives multiple tokens, they are separated from each other by a single space. We will look at token splitting more carefully shortly.

If you are supplying a prompt string and using multiple input buffers, as in the present example, the prompt string must follow the first input buffer name.

You can use the default input buffer, REPLY, *and also have a prompt string by naming* REPLY *explicitly, as in the following command:*

```
read REPLY?"Your input: "
```

e) How does the output of these two commands compare?

Answer: Your interaction should look like the following:

```
[11006]:  wc < wctest
3       12       56
[11007]:  mywc < wctest
3        12        53
[11008]:
```

Both commands print out three similar numbers, but they are not identical, and their spacing is different. The reasons for the differences can be attributed to the difference between how the shell's `read` command operates compared with the logic of the C language code that was used to generate the `wc` command. The matter of how the numbers are spaced is not important here, but the fact that the final numbers output by the two programs are different is significant: The new line characters (the ASCII "linefeed" code) at the end of each line are removed by the `read` command, but the system's `wc` command reads and counts them the same as any other characters in the file. If you used a non-UNIX editor to prepare your data file, there would be both an ASCII "carriage return" code, as well as a new line at the end of each line, and your results would differ accordingly. (The values would be 59 and 56, instead of 56 and 53.)

f) Does the shell do field splitting when the `read` at the top of the loop is executed?

Answer: No, because IFS *is the empty string whenever this* `read` *command is executed.*

The empty string is assigned to *IFS* before the `while` loop is entered the first time, then again as the last statement of the loop, before returning to the top to execute `read` again.

g) What does the expression `(( chars += ${#REPLY} ))` compute?

Answer: It adds the number of characters in each line to the variable `chars`.

Because there is no field splitting when the `read` command at the top of the loop is executed, *REPLY* contains *all* the characters in each line, including all spaces and tabs. (We'll deal with those new lines later.) We covered the use of `${# ... }` to find the number of characters in a string in Exercise 10.3.3, "Work with Strings and Substrings."

h) Does the shell do field splitting when the `read` command inside the loop is executed?

Answer: It uses the default value of `IFS` *to do field splitting "in the usual way."*

The idea here is that by manipulating the value of `IFS` you can get the first `read` to input each line as an image of what is in the input file (except for the new lines) and then to get the second `read` to split the line into words, where a *word* is defined as a sequence of non-whitespace characters.

When a `read` *command does field splitting, it normally treats a backslash (\ ) at the end of a line as a continuation marker and appends the "next" line of the file to the first one automatically. The* `-r` *option suppresses this behavior and is used in* `mywc` *so that whatever looks like a line in the file is counted as such.*

i) What does the expression, `(( words += ${#inWords[@]} ))` compute?

Answer: It adds the number of elements in the array `inWords` *to the integer variable* words.

You can infer from this line and from the output of the program that the second `read` command has split the input line into tokens and stored them as separate values in the array *inWords*. This is an extension of the idea of having multiple input buffers already discussed in the present exercise. By using `${#inWords[@]}`, which was covered in Exercise 10.3.3, "Work with Strings and Substrings," we get a count of how many elements there are in the array, which is the same as the number of tokens in the line.

j) What is it in the code that makes the variable *inWords* an array?

Answer: It's the `-A` *option on the second* `read` *command.*

This option is a very useful feature for this type of application. The variable you name is automatically made into an indexed array with the number of elements equal to the number of tokens obtained by splitting the input line.

Don't confuse the `-A` *option of the* `read` *command with the* `-A` *option of the* `typeset` *command. With* `read` *you get an indexed array, but with* `typeset` *you get an associative array.*

k) What is the purpose of the statement `typeset IFS`?

Answer: It guarantees that executing this function will not change the value of `IFS` *from whatever value it had beforehand.*

Imagine an unwitting user who has set *IFS* to a colon (:) in order to split the fields in, for example, the *PATH* variable, then runs `mywc`. The user would not automatically expect that running your function would affect his or her working environment. A change to *IFS* could be confusing. The `typeset` command makes *IFS* a local variable (Exercise 6.1.4, "Control the Scope of Variables"), so changing it inside the function will have no effect on the user's environment.

If you wrote `mywc` *as a script instead of as a function you wouldn't need to worry about saving and restoring the value of* IFS*. The shell gives* IFS *its default value at the beginning of every script it runs. Functions, however, normally share this variable (and all other variables) with the environment from which they are run.*

11.1.2 ANSWERS

a) What variable is affected by the `typeset` command?

Answer: Just the variable `x`.

Be sure you understand that the `for` statement assigns the values of *a1, a2,* and so forth to *x,* and it is those assignment operations that will be affected by the `typeset` command.

b) By examining the output of the second for statement, tell what the `R6` does in the `typeset` command.

Answer: Your interaction should look like the following:

```
[11008]: a1=a a2=aa a3=aaa a4=aaaa a5=aaaaa
[11009]: for x in $a1 $a2 $a3 $a4 $a5 ; do print "$x"; done
a
aa
aaa
aaaa
aaaaa
[11010]: typeset -R6 x
[11011]: for x in $a1 $a2 $a3 $a4 $a5 ; do print "$x"; done
     a
    aa
   aaa
  aaaa
 aaaaa
[11012]:
```

The second loop prints the values right-justified in fields that are six characters wide. The default behavior is to left-justify the values.

Note the quotes around `$x` in the `print` command. Without them, the spaces causing the output to be right-justified would be lost.

You can put a space between the `R` and the `6` in the `typeset` command, which might make your code easier to read.

c) What happens if the width of `x` is too small to hold a value assigned to it?

Answer: The answer is truncated, as the following interaction shows:

```
[11012]: typeset -R3 x
```

```
[11013]: for x in $a1 $a2 $a3 $a4 $a5 ; do print "$x";
  done
  a
 aa
aaa
aaa
aaa
[11014]: typeset -R16 x
[11015]: for x in $a1 $a2 $a3 $a4 $a5 ; do print "$x";
  done
               a
              aa
             aaa
            aaaa
           aaaaa
[11016]:
```

The values of a1, a2, and a3 are printed in their entireties, but only the rightmost three characters of a4 and a5 are printed. (See Self-Review Question 4 for a follow-up on this.)

d) What does the output of the second loop prove?

Answer: It shows that the values of a1, a2, *and so forth are not affected by assigning them to* x *with a field width of 3.*

Although some information is lost in the printing, the original variables are not affected.

e) What does the -u do to the values assigned to x in the first *for* loop?

Answer: It converts them to uppercase, as the following interactions show:

```
[11016]: typeset -u x
[11017]: for x in $a1 $a2 $a3 $a4 $a5 ; do print "$x"; done
A
AA
AAA
AAAA
AAAAA
[11018]: typeset -l x
[11019]: typeset -u a3
[11020]: for x in $a1 $a2 $a3 $a4 $a5 ; do print "$x"; done
```

```
a
aa
aaa
aaaa
aaaaa
[11021]: typeset +l x
[11022]: for x in $a1 $a2 $a3 $a4 $a5 ; do print "$x"; done
a
aa
AAA
aaaa
aaaaa
[11023]:
```

The first loop prints all uppercase letters because *x* has been made into an uppercase-only variable using the `-u` option.

f) Explain the output of the second `for` loop.

Answer: Now `x` *is a lowercase-only variable, and it always prints lowercase letters.*

This statement is true, even though the value of `a3` has been declared to be uppercase.

g) Based on the output of the last `for` loop, what does the `+l` option do?

Answer: It turns off the lowercase option for `x`.

In the last loop, `x` is neither uppercase-only nor lowercase-only, so its value is whatever is assigned to it. In this case, `a3` has been made into an uppercase variable, and the middle row of letters is all uppercase.

```
printf "Hello, World!\n"
```

h) Why is the parameter in quotes? (There are two answers to this.)

Answer: The first answer is that we want the entire parameter to be the format string, so the quotes prevent token splitting due to the embedded space. The second answer is that the `\n` *has to be inside quotes to be treated as a newline character.*

Without quotes, the format string would have been "Hello," so that is all that would have printed. Unless the format string contains conversion control strings (indicated by percent symbols), `printf` will not look for additional parameters to print. Because "Hello," has no percent symbols in it, that's all that prints.

If the `\n` wasn't inside quotes, the shell would treat it as an escaped *n* because of the special meaning of the backslash character, and just the character immediately after the slash (the *n*) would have been passed to `printf`. Putting the `\n` inside quotes removes the special meaning of backslash, and `printf` receives both the backslash and the *n* as part of the format string parameter.

In addition to `\n` for new line, the `printf` and `print` commands recognize the following *escape conventions*, which are based on the C language:

\a	Alert (bell character)
\b	Backspace
\c	Do not put a newline at the end of the line. Anything after this code will be skipped.
\f	Formfeed (for printers)
\n	Newline
\t	Horizontal Tab
\v	Vertical Tab
\\	Backslash itself
\E	Escape. Used to introduce ANSI escape sequences, such as `\E[2J` to clear the screen
\0n	The character with ASCII code `n`, given in octal, such as `\007` for the bell character.

Don't use the `\c` code with `printf` because that command never prints a new line unless you expressly put it in the format string or in one of the values to be printed. Likewise, you don't need to use `\n` with `print` (unless you want to print extra new lines) because that command always puts a new line an the end of what it prints (unless you use its `-n` option.)

"If we had some tea, we could have some tea and crumpets ...

... if we had some crumpets."

LAB 11.1

i) In the first `printf` command, how many conversion control strings are there in the format string, and how many times is the variable `i` given after the format string?

Answer: There were five conversion control strings, and five references to the variable `i`*, as the following interaction shows:*

```
[11023]: integer i=12345
[11024]: printf "%d\n %10d\n %-10d\n %o\n %x\n" i i i i i
12345
      12345
12345
30071
3039
[11025]: h=hello
[11026]: printf "%s\n %10s\n %-10s\n" $h $h $h
hello
      hello
 hello
[11027]:
```

In both lines 11024 and 11026, the number of conversion strings (the number of percent symbols) is equal to the number of variable references on the remainder of the command line. Note that you don't need dollar signs when referencing integer variables using the `%d` conversion string in `printf` commands, but you do need them when referencing string variables.

If the number of conversion strings doesn't match the number of variable references in the format string, `printf` *will reuse the entire format string from the beginning to print the remainder of the variables.*

j) What does a number between the percent symbol and the conversion character do?

Answer: It tells how many character positions to use for the value of the variable being printed.

If you don't use a number, the command will use just as many character positions as needed to represent the value. If the number you give is not large enough, the shell will use the minimum number of characters that it needs to show the value, just as if you didn't give any number at all.

k) What does a minus sign in front of the number do?

Answer: It causes the value to be left-justified in the field.

Normally, values are printed right-justified in their field.

```
typeset -uL7 h
printf "\"%10s\"\n" "$h"
```

l) What did the `typeset` command do, and how did it affect the output of the `printf` command?

Answer: Your interaction should look like the following:

```
[11027]: typeset -uL7 h
[11028]: printf "\"%10s\"\n" "$h"
"   HELLO  "
[11029]: cp2
[11030]:
```

The `typeset` command set the width of the variable *h* to seven characters, left-justified, and made the characters uppercase. By printing quotes just before and after the `%10s`, you can see that the five characters in "hello" are left-justified within the seven allocated to them, but that those seven characters are right-justified in the ten character field specified by the `printf` conversion string.

m) What is the difference between the `%s` and the `%b` conversion codes?

Answer: Your interaction should look like the following:

```
[11030]: printf "%s -- %b\n" "hello\there" "hello\there"
hello\there -- hello    here
[11031]:
```

The key is that `\t` in the middle of the two stings being printed. If you use `%s`, they are printed literally as the characters backslash-*t* (`/t`), but if you use the `%b` conversion code, they are interpreted as an ASCII `<tab>` code.

C escape conventions are always recognized in the format string of `printf` commands, but not in string values being printed unless you use the `%b` conversion code.

LAB 11.1 SELF-REVIEW QUESTIONS

To test your progress, you should be able to answer the following questions:

1) How do you specify a prompt string to use in a `read` command?

a) _____Enter it as the argument of the `-p` option.
b) _____Assign a value to the environment variable `PS4`.
c) _____Name a variable to use as an input buffer and put the prompt after a question mark following the variable's name.
d) _____You can't. The only way to accomplish this is with a `print -n` command before the `read` command.
e) _____You can't. The only way to accomplish this is with a `printf` command before the `read` command.

2) What variable is used as the input buffer of a `read` command if you don't specify on the command line?

a) _____`REPLY`
b) _____`RESPONSE`
c) _____`INPUT`
d) _____`PS4`
e) _____No variable. The input is discarded in this case.

3) Which of the following command lines would assign the value *hello* to `in[0]` and *there* to `in[1]` assuming the user types `hello:there` in response to the `read` command?

a) _____`read in[0]=hello in[1]=there`
b) _____`read in`
c) _____`read -A in`
d) _____`IFS=: read -A in`
e) _____`read -A in?"Type hello:there "`

4) How would you verify that it was the rightmost characters that were printed in Question 11.1.2c?

a) _____Change the value of `a5` to *abcde*
b) _____Change the value of `a4` to *abcd*
c) _____Change the value of `a5` to *12345*
d) _____Either *a)* or *b)*, but not *c)*.
e) _____Any of *a)*, *b)*, or *c)*.

5) What is the difference between `typeset -R5 x` and `printf %5s x`?

a) _____The `typeset` command affects how a variable is stored, but the `printf` command affects how it is displayed.
b) _____The `printf` command affects how a variable is stored, but the `typeset` command affects how it is displayed.
c) _____Nothing. Both add 5 to the variable's value.
d) _____The `typeset` command adds 5 to the variable's value, but the `printf` subtracts 5 from its value.
e) _____The `typeset` command prints a new line after showing the value of `x`, but the `printf` command does not.

Quiz answers appear in Appendix A, Section 11.1.

LAB 11.2

THE exec COMMAND

LAB OBJECTIVES

After this lab, you will be able to:

- ✓ Use exec to Execute Another Program
- ✓ Use exec to Open and Close Files
- ✓ Use exec to Read and Write "Interesting" Devices

The `exec` command has two distinct uses. One is to cause another program to execute in place of the one that is running when `exec` is executed, and the other, which might be used in combination with the first, is to open and close `fds`. In this lab, we'll look briefly at the first use, from which `exec` gets its name, but we will spend most of our time looking at the second, more common use for this versatile command.

LAB 11.2 EXERCISES

11.2.1 USE exec TO EXECUTE ANOTHER PROGRAM

Enter the following commands in a script named `tryexec`, and run it:

Be sure you make this a script rather than a function! If you run it as a function, it will log you off the system.

```
# tryexec -- Use exec to execute another program.

exec ls > ls.out
print "If you can read this . . . well, you can't."
```

a) Was the file `ls.out` created with the output of the `ls` command?

b) Was the `print` command executed?

c) What would have happened if you created a function with these commands and ran it, or had run the commands from the shell prompt, or dotted the script?

11.2.2 USE exec TO OPEN AND CLOSE FILES

So far, you have learned to work with the three standard I/O file descriptors, *stdin* (*fd* number 0), *stdout* (*fd* number 1), and *stderr* (*fd* number 2). You saw how to redirect and copy them in Lab 2.3, "Redirect Input and Output," and you have seen the `-u` option for the `print` command as another way of accomplishing output redirection. You also saw earlier in this chapter that the `read` command also accepts a `-u` option, but you haven't used it yet.

Now it's time to generalize your understanding of I/O processing a bit. The KornShell lets you work with up to 10 file descriptors, numbered 0–9 at a time, by writing I/O redirection operators on `exec` commands. Normally, you do the I/O redirection without specifying a command for `exec` to run.

FOR EXAMPLE

The usual sequence of events when processing a file is to *open* the file using `exec`, then to execute a sequence of `read` or `print` commands with the file, then to *close* the file using another `exec` command. For example, the following two sets of commands would copy `file1` to `file2`. The second version clearly is not an efficient way to accomplish this task, but it illustrates the use of `exec`.

The normal way to copy a file:

```
cp file1 file2
```

Doing the same thing using `exec`:

```
exec 3< file1
exec 4> file2
while read -ru3
do    print -u4 "$REPLY"
done
exec 3<&-
exec 4<&-
```

a) What do the first two `exec` commands do?

____

____

b) What do the last two `exec` commands do?

____

____

c) What does the `-ru3` on the `read` command accomplish?

d) What do the quotes around the reference to `REPLY` accomplish?

e) What is inefficient about the second version compared with the first version?

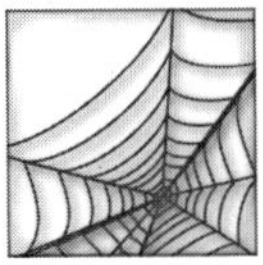

The following script, named `shuffle`, allows a user to perform a "perfect shuffle" on pairs of files. (A perfect shuffle means to shuffle a deck of cards so that cards from two halves of the deck alternate one by one with each other.) The following questions are based on that script, and "Test Your Thinking" question 1 gives you a chance to make some needed improvements to it.

You can download a copy of the script from:

http://www.phptr.com/phptrinteractive/

```
# shuffle -- Performs perfect shuffles of pairs of files.

while read -A inFiles?"Name two files that you want to shuffle: "

do [[ ${inFiles[0]} == "." || ${inFiles[0]} == "q" ]] && return
      [[ ${#inFiles[@]} != 2 ]] && {
        print -u2 \
       "Enter exactly two file names. Use quotes if necessary."
        continue
        }
```

```
    exec 3< "${inFiles[0]}"
    exec 4< "${inFiles[1]}"

    read outFile?"Where do you want the shuffled output? "
    exec 5> "$outFile"

IFS=
    while read  -ru3
    do    print -u5 "$REPLY"
          read  -ru4
          print -u5 "$REPLY"
    done
IFS=$' \t\n'

    exec 3<&-
    exec 4<&-
    exec 5<&-

done
print
```

f) What are four things the user could type to cause this script to stop executing?

____

____

____

____

g) What is the purpose of the `print` command at the end of the script?

____

____

h) What happens if the user enters the name of a nonexistent file for either of the two files to be shuffled?

____

____

i) What happens if the user enters the name of a file that already exists as the output file?

____

____

j) What happens if the user enters the name of one of the input files as the name of the output file? (*Hint:* Don't try this on a file that you care about keeping!)

____

____

11.2.3 USE `exec` TO READ AND WRITE "INTERESTING" DEVICES

There are several file names that you can use for I/O as if they were files, but that actually give you access to I/O devices or even to programs running on other computers. You can access these devices using either I/O redirection or the `exec` command, but we've put them off until now because one of them is almost always accessed using `exec`. However, the three we will look at are all similar, in that their names look like disk files, but they are actually not. Here are the three we will look at in this exercise:

- `/dev/null`
- `/dev/tty`
- `/dev/tcp`

The first one, `/dev/null` is normally used as a place to send unwanted output. A common use in scripts is when you want to test whether a command completed successfully or not, but when you don't care about its output. (A similar device, /dev/zero, contains an infinite supply of null bytes.)

Enter the following command lines:


```
if grep "^${USER}:" /etc/passwd > /dev/null
then print "You have a local account on this system."
else print "You have a network account for accessing this system."
fi
```

a) What does this `if` statement do, and why is the output of the `grep` command redirected to /dev/null?

____

____

The second one, /dev/tty, always represents the user's terminal, no matter what has happened to *stdout* and *stderr.*

Enter the following command in a script named `insist`:

```
print "Hey, pay attention to me!" > /dev/tty
```

Now invoke the script as follows:

```
insist > /dev/null 2>&1
```

b) What does the I/O redirection on the command line do?

____

____

c) Did the "pay attention" message print on the screen?

____

____

Finally, let's look at the last "interesting" item on the list, `/dev/tcp`. This one can be used on most systems (sorry, this example may not work on some systems, such as Solaris, and your computer does have to be connected to the Internet to complete this exercise) to make a TCP/IP socket connection to a program running on a computer running elsewhere on the net.

Try entering the following commands. If you get an error message when you enter the first one, you won't be able to run the remaining commands, and you will have to answer the questions by just studying the code.

```
exec 4< /dev/tcp/149.4.4.122/80
exec 3>&4
print -u3 GET /KornShell
while read -ru4
do print "$REPLY"
done
```

d) What do the two `exec` commands accomplish?

____

____

e) What are the numbers after `/dev/tcp` on the first line?

____

____

____

f) What sequence of `read` and `print` commands must the program at the other end of the TCP/IP connection do in order for these commands to work?

____

____

Lab 11.2 Answers

This section gives you some suggested answers to the questions in Lab 11.2, with discussion related to those answers. Your answers may vary, but the most important thing is whether or not your answer works. Use this discussion to analyze differences between your answers and those presented here.

If you have alternative answers to the questions in this exercise, you are encouraged to post your answers and to discuss them at the companion web site for this book, located at:

`http://www.phptr.com/phptrinteractive/`

11.2.1 Answers

a) Was the file `ls.out` created, containing the output of the `ls` command?

Answer: Yes, it was.

If you ran a command such as, `more ls.out`, you would see the output of the `ls` command, implying that the `ls` command that was passed as an argument to `exec` was indeed executed successfully, with its output redirected to the file.

b) Was the `print` command executed?

Answer: No, it wasn't.

The reason you didn't see the output of the `print` command was that it really wasn't executed. *The* `exec` *command replaces whatever command is running with the command given as its parameter list.* In this case, the `tryexec` script is *replaced* by the `ls > ls.out` command. It's the executing program in memory that's replaced, not the script file itself, of course. When the `ls` command completes, control returns to the command line, not to the `tryexec` script.

c) What would have happened if you had created a function with these commands and run it, or had run the commands from the shell prompt, or dotted the script?

Answer: You would have been logged out from your KornShell session!

In all three situations listed, the `exec` command would have caused your interactive shell process to be replaced by the `ls` command, and when it terminated, you would have been logged out. When it finishes generating its output, the `ls` command internally does the equivalent of the shell's `exit` command, thus logging you off the system.

Self-Review Question 1 shows a somewhat more realistic way that you might make use of the `exec` command in a script.

11.2.2 ANSWERS

```
exec 3< file1
exec 4> file2
while read -ru3
do    print -u4 "$REPLY"
done
exec 3<&-
exec 4<&-
```

a) What do the first two `exec` commands do?

Answer: They open `file1` *for reading and* `file2` *for writing.*

Although these look like commands to redirect I/O for the `exec` command, they do it for the program that runs `exec`. That is, if you run these commands from the command line (from an *interactive shell*), they open *fd*s 3 and 4 for the interactive shell you are running, but if you do them from inside a script, they take effect for the code inside the script. Dotting a script or running a function with these commands in them would have the same effect as entering `exec`s from the command line.

Inside a script the standard I/O fds (0, 1, and 2) will be copies of those in effect in your interactive shell, but all fds greater than number 2 will be closed. However, all the interactive shell's fds will still be open when control returns to it.

b) What do the last two lines do?

Answer: They close the two fds that were opened by the first two command lines.

Closing files when you are finished with them is a good thing to do, although failing to do so will generally not have much effect on your life. Doing so prevents your program from doing more `read`s or `print`s using the *fd* until it is opened again. You saw that `m>&n` is the syntax for connecting *fd m* to the same file or device as *fd n* in Lab 2.3, "Redirect Input and Output." Now you can see that using a dash (-) for *n* means that *fd m* gets closed and cannot be used for I/O.

c) What does the `-ru3` on the `read` command accomplish?

Answer: It makes the command read from the first input file.

The `-r` part says to treat backslashes (\ ) at the ends of lines as normal characters rather than as line-continuation characters. The `u3` part says to read from *fd* number 3. You could have typed this as `-r -u3`, if you prefer.

It's almost always a good idea to use `-r` when you read from a file; line continuation is really designed for interactive use.

d) What do the quotes around the reference to `REPLY` accomplish?

Answer: They preserve the spacing in the lines being printed.

The *IFS* variable was set to the empty string before entering the loop that does the shuffle so that no token splitting would be done by the two `read` commands inside the loop, and the `print` commands use quotes to prevent the spacing from being lost in the output. The value of *IFS* is restored to its default value after doing the copying, so that the `read` command asking for the next two file names will do token splitting as required.

Don't try to use these commands to copy anything but text files. Trying to `read` *and* `print` *non-ASCII character codes will almost always lead to unpredictable results.*

e) What is inefficient about the second version compared with the first version?

Answer: In the second version, two shell commands are executed for every line of the input file, whereas the `cp` *command executes no shell commands to do the copy.*

Shell commands, even built-in ones such as `read` and `print`, almost always take longer to execute than do the equivalent machine language instructions inside an external "binary" command.

The reason for using a shell program to read a file is so that you can do something special with its contents. If you can, use the external commands that came with your system, such as `cp`, `mv`, `grep`, `sort`, `uniq`, `head`, *and* `tail` *to do "standard" things with files.*

f) What are four things the user could type to cause this script to stop executing?

Answer: (.), q, Ctrl-D, or Ctrl-C.

The program checks whether the user types a dot or a `q` as the first token on the command line, and exits the outer `while` loop (by executing `return` in either case). Because the outer `while` loop continues for as long as the `read` command returns *true,* the user can press Ctrl-D (or Ctrl-Z on DOS/Windows systems, or whatever the user has set as his/her end-of-file character, to use the system's `stty eof` command) to indicate end of input. Finally, if the user types Ctrl-C (or whatever his/her interrupt character is to use the system's `stty intr` command), the program will terminate abruptly.

g) What is the purpose of the `print` command at the end of the script?

Answer: It positions the cursor properly in case the user presses Ctrl-D.

Because the cursor does not move to the start of a new line on the screen in this case, the script does a `print` command if execution gets past the end of the outer `while` loop.

h) What happens if the user enters the name of a nonexistent file for either of the two files to be shuffled?

Answer: The shell will print an error message, as in the following interaction:

```
[11031]: shuffle
Name two files that you want to shuffle: x y
/home/vickery/bin/shuffle[12]: x: cannot open [No \
such file or directory]
[11032]:
```

In this example, there was no file named `x` in my working directory, the error message was printed as soon as the `exec 3<` command was reached, and the script terminated immediately. The `exec 4<` command was not reached in this case (it would have failed too, because I didn't have a file named `y`, either), nor were any of the other commands in the script. So "the name of a nonexistent file" would have been a fifth thing you could have mentioned in your answer to Question f.

i) What happens if the user enters the name of a file that already exists as the output file?

Answer: It would have been overwritten.

Even if the user had set the interactive shell's `noclobber` option before running the script, the file would have been silently overwritten because the shell resets almost all of its options whenever it starts running a script. (The exceptions are the `emacs` and `vi` options, so the user can use his/her preferences for command line editing when responding to `read` commands, and the `trackall` option, which means the shell will remember where it finds external commands while running the script.)

Be aware of this feature of the shell when writing scripts. Users don't like to be surprised. The first Test Your Thinking question at the end of this chapter deals with this matter further.

j) What happens if the user enters the name of one of the input files as the name of the output file? (*Hint:* Don't try this on a file that you care about keeping!)

Answer: The file gets truncated to zero bytes.

Consider the following interaction:

```
[11032]: ls -l junk Months
-rw-r--r-- 1 Administrator None 86 Jul 28 13:04 Months
-rw-r--r-- 1 Administrator None  539 Oct  4 17:59 junk
[11033]: shuffle
Name two files that you want to shuffle: junk Months
Where do you want the shuffled output? junk
Name two files that you want to shuffle: q
[11034]: ls -l junk
-rw-r--r--  1 Administrator None   0 Oct  4 18:19 junk
[11035]:
```

The output from line 11032 shows that there are two nice files named `junk` and `Months` sitting in my working directory, with dozens of bytes of information in them. However, by specifying `junk` as both an input file and an output file, as line 11034 shows, I ended up with nothing left in `junk`. Fortunately, "junk" describes original contents of the file.

This pattern of destroying the contents of input files that are used for output is not unique to this script. Don't let it "bite" you when using normal UNIX commands. For example, the following command makes `in1` into an empty file before concatenating it with `in2`; you end up with just what was in `in2` in `in1`:

```
cat in1 in2 >| in1
```

As soon as the shell sees an output redirection operation, it immediately creates an empty new file to hold the expected output. If the file already exists and you have either set `noclobber` off or used `>|`, the shell truncates the length of the file, discarding its former contents.

11.2.3 ANSWERS

```
if grep "^${USER:?"Unable to determine user"}:" /etc/
  passwd > /dev/null
then print "You have a local account on this system."
else print "You have a network account for accessing \
this system."
fi
```

a) What does this `if` statement do, and why is the output of the `grep` command redirected to `/dev/null`?

Answer: It uses `grep` *to look for the user's name in the* `/etc/password` *file, discarding the output of the* `grep` *command, then prints one of two messages based on the value of the return code from the* `grep` *command.*

The basic idea here is that we want to use the `grep` command to see whether a file contains a string, but we are not interested in seeing the line that `grep` prints if it does find the string, so we throw that output line away by redirecting the output of the `grep` command to `/dev/null`. The `grep` command will have an exit code of *true* (0) if it does find the string, and *false* (1) if it does not, so the `if` statement prints the first message if the user's name is found in the local `/etc/passwd` file, and the second message if not.

```
print "Hey, pay attention to me!" > /dev/tty
insist > /dev/null 2>&1
```

b) What does the I/O redirection on the command line do?

Answer: It forces the standard output from the script, both `stdout` *and* `stderr`*, to be discarded.*

The `insist` command line redirects both *stdout* and *stderr* to `/dev/null`, which means that the user wants to discard all output that would normally be written to the screen.

c) Did the "pay attention" message print on the screen?

Answer: Yes, it did.

The script still manages to show its message because it writes to the device directly without using an *fd*.

Reading and writing `/dev/tty` *can be a useful capability, but don't use it because you think you know better than the user what the user "should" do. If the user redirects all output away from the screen, your program should normally honor that setting.*

Most often, this feature is used when you temporarily close one of the standard I/O *fds* inside a script, then want to restore the standard setting.

```
exec 4< /dev/tcp/149.4.4.122/80
exec 3>&4
```

d) What do the two `exec` commands accomplish?

Answer: They open fds 3 and 4 for writing and reading a tcp "socket" connection.

The shell does not let you `read` and `print` using the same *fd*, so the code opens the socket for reading, using *fd* 4, then copies that *fd* to *fd* 3.

e) What are the numbers after `/dev/tcp` on the first line?

Answer: They are the Internet address (149.4.4.122) and port number (80) that uniquely identify a program running on a computer that is ready to reply to messages that we send to it.

In this case, I've given you the Internet address and port number for the web server running on my computer.

If your version of `ksh` *is new enough, you may be able to use a "fully qualified domain name" (FQDN) instead of the "dotted-decimal" address format shown. In this example, the FQDN is "babbage.cs.qc.edu."*

f) What sequence of `read` and `print` commands must the program at the other end of the TCP/IP connection do in order for these commands to work?

Answer: Because this program first prints one line and then reads as many lines as it can get, we can infer that the other program first reads a line, then writes one or more lines back to us.

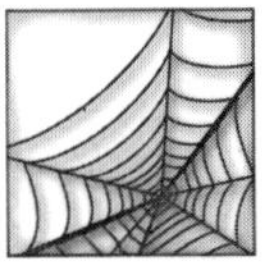

If you can't get this exercise to work on your computer, go to `www.phptr.com/phptrinteractive/` to see what the interaction should look like. We're not giving away the surprise here!

What we have described is a subset of the Hypertext Transfer Protocol (http). This program is acting as a *web browser,* which makes an http *protocol request* (`GET /KornShell`—be sure to capitalize it exactly as shown), then reads the server's reply, a series of text lines that the program prints on your screen. In this case, `KornShell` is the name of a text file in my server's web-page directory.

Using the KornShell to build a web browser may seem to be an odd thing to do, but it is actually an example of what shell programming is very good for: We were able to write a few lines of code to check out our connection to the server. Writing the equivalent "quick and dirty" program in C would have taken dozens of lines of code.

LAB 11.2 SELF-REVIEW QUESTIONS

To test your progress, you should be able to answer the following questions.

1) What would a script named `doit` containing the following commands do if you dot it from an interactive shell prompt?

```
[[ -n $DO1 ]] && exec do1
[[ -n $DO2 ]] && exec do2
print Did not do do1 and did not do do2.
```

a) _____If `DO1` is a non-zero-length string, execute command `do1`, then if `DO2` is a non-zero-length string, execute command `do2`, then print the message.
b) _____If `DO1` is a non-zero-length string, execute the command `do1` and log off the system. But if `DO1` is not a non-zero-length string, and `DO2` is a non-zero-length string, execute the command `do2`, and log off the system. If neither `DO1` nor `DO2` is a non-zero-length string, print the message and prompt for the next command line.
c) _____If `DO1` is a non-zero-length string, execute the command `do1` and log off the system. But if `DO1` is not a non-zero-length string, and `DO2` is a non-zero-length string, execute the command `do2`, and log off the system. If neither `DO1` nor `DO2` is a non-zero-length string, print the message, and log off the system.
d) _____It always prints "Do do do what you done done done before!"
e) _____It logs you off the system and sends e-mail to the administrator reporting your attempt to perform an illegal operation.

2) A script contains the following lines of code. What is going on here?

```
exec 0< commands
a_prog
exec 0< /dev/tty
```

a) _____a_prog will abort because stdin is closed.
b) _____Everything that is written to /dev/tty will be read by a_prog.
c) _____A trap has been set to prevent a_prog from executing.
d) _____Whatever a_prog reads from stdin will actually come from the file commands. But stdin will not be changed for the user of this script.
e) _____Whatever a_prog reads from stdin will actually come from /dev/tty. However, anything read from /dev/tty will actually be written to *fd* number 0.

3) What does this command line do?

```
3>&-
```

a) _____It redirects *fd* 3 to a file named -.
b) _____It opens *fd* 3 for writing.
c) _____It opens *fd* 3 for reading.
d) _____It closes *fd* 3.
e) _____It generates an error message because you can't do I/O redirection without a command to go with it.

Quiz answers appear in Appendix A, Section 11.2.

LAB 11.3

INTERCEPTING AND GENERATING TRAPS

LAB OBJECTIVES

After this lab, you will be able to:

- ✓ Intercept `INT` and `EXIT` Traps
- ✓ Use the `DEBUG` Trap

The KornShell's trap command is built on the UNIX *signal* mechanism. You use the `trap` command to set up a *trap handler* (a command) that you want to run whenever a *trap event* occurs. The trap event can be any of the UNIX signals (use the command `kill -l` to see a list of UNIX signal names) or any of several events specific to KornShell processing.

In this lab you will learn how to set up trap handlers for some of the more common trap events.

LAB 11.3 EXERCISES

11.3.1 INTERCEPT INT AND EXIT TRAPS

If you ever pressed Ctrl-C to stop a program, you've delivered a signal to a process. It's not as convenient, but you could accomplish the same thing using the system's `kill` command.

If you have changed your interrupt character to something other than Ctrl-C, either mentally change all references to "Ctrl-C" in this exercise to whatever character you are using, or run the following command before proceeding:

```
stty intr ^C
```

That's literally the characters caret (^) and (C) at the end of the line, not Ctrl-C.

For this exercise, we will use the following program to study trap processing. Put it in a script named `tt1` (for "first trap test"):

```
# trap-test 1

sleep 30
print -- "$0 Completed Normally"
```

If you run the program in the foreground and press Ctrl-C while it is running, it will terminate, and nothing will print. Not very interesting. However, run it in the background by ending the command line with an ampersand (&), as discussed in Exercise 3.1.2, "Parallel execution (&)," and observe the job and process numbers that are displayed. Assuming that the job number is `[1]`, enter the following command during the 30 seconds that `tt1` is sleeping:

```
kill -INT %1
```

Alternatively, you could use the process number in place of the `%1` at the end of that command.

a) What was displayed when you ran the `kill` command?

As mentioned at the beginning of this lab, you can use the following command to list all the signal names available on your system:


```
kill -l
```

Run the following sequence of commands. Be sure to wait a full 30 seconds after the last one:

```
tt1 &
kill -USR1 %1
tt1 &
kill -HUP %1
tt1 &
kill -CHLD %1
```

b) What does delivering these three types of signals do when they are delivered to a process?

Now run the following sequence of commands. Pause for about 10 seconds between entering the first `kill` command and the second one. Wait 30 seconds after entering the second one.

```
tt1 &
kill -STOP %1
kill -CONT %1
```

c) What did you observe?

The shell's `trap` command has the following syntax:

```
trap [ <handler> <condition> ]
```

Here, `<handler>` is a command that you want to have executed when the trap named by `<condition>` occurs. If you don't supply a `<handler>` and a `<condition>`, the command prints a list of all trap conditions and handlers that are in effect. In addition to the condition names you saw when you ran the `kill -l` command, the shell lets you set handlers using the following additional condition names:

EXIT	When a script or your interactive shell exits.
ERR	Whenever a command terminates with a nonzero exit code.
DEBUG	Every time a command executes.
KEYBD	Every time you press a key in an interactive session. Used so that arrow keys can be used to recall previous commands, for example.

In addition, the system's `CHLD` signal name can be used as a condition that will happen whenever a background job stops or exits.

d) What happens if you press Ctrl-C in response to the shell's command prompt?

Run the following command, and press Ctrl-C when the shell prompts for the next command.

```
trap "print INT occurred." INT
```

e) What happened when you pressed Ctrl-C?

Now run the following two commands:

```
tt1 &
kill -INT %1
```


f) Does the trap handler affect signal handling for the script?

You can clear the setup for a condition (or a list of conditions) by entering a `trap` command with a dash in the position where the handler goes, followed by the condition name(s) that you want to restore to default operation.

Enter the following sequence of commands:

```
trap
trap - INT
trap
```

g) What did the three `trap` commands do?

Now create a new version of our test program for this exercise, called `tt2`, that looks like the following:

```
#  test-trap 2
trap 'print "$0: Resetting" ; sleep 30' INT
trap 'print "$0: Exit Trap"'              EXIT
```

```
sleep 30
print "$0: Exiting Normally"
```

Run the program in the foreground and press Ctrl-C as it runs.

h) What happens each time you press Ctrl-C?

Now run the program in the background and enter the following sequence of commands:

```
tt2 &
kill -INT %1
kill -USR1 %1
```

i) What printed when the program terminated?

We won't work with `ERR` or `KEYBD` conditions here. You should be able to see how to use the `ERR` condition based on the examples you have done so far. The `KEYBD` condition is used to customize your interactive environment, but we are focusing our attention on programming the shell rather than using it interactively.

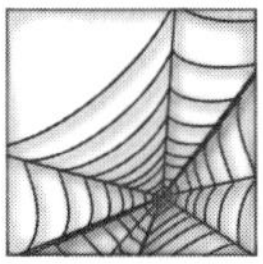

You can find tips for customizing your interactive environment, including an example of how to use the `KEYBD` trap, at the companion web site for this book, located at:

```
http://www.phptr.com/phptrinteractive/
```

11.3.2 USE THE DEBUG TRAP

We'll end this lab with an introduction to the shell's debugging features. For the small pieces of code we have been using to introduce the shell's features, you really don't need to use these features, but as you progress to larger and larger scripts and functions, you will find them invaluable.

Before we look at the DEBUG trap condition, we need to introduce the debug option that is always available to you. Enter the following commands in a script named tt3:


```
# trap-test 3
set -x
print This is the first command in this script
print This is the second command in this script
print This is the last command in this script > /dev/null
```

a) What happened when you executed tt3?

Now create another script named tt4 that looks like the following:

```
# test-trap 4

function showVars {
  print Variable values are:  X=$X Y=$Y Z=$Z
  }

trap showVars DEBUG

X=abc Y=cba Z=bac
X=hello
Y=greetings!
Z=Farewell
```

b) What happened when you executed tt4?

As you might guess, you can combine the shell's `xtrace` option with the `DEBUG` trap condition to see the commands being executed, as well as whatever debugging information you want to display with your trap handler.

LAB 11.3 ANSWERS

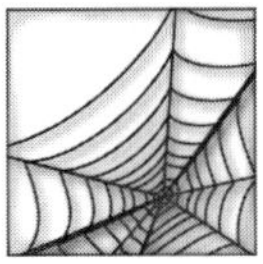

This section gives you some suggested answers to the questions in Lab 11.3, with discussion related to those answers. Your answers may vary, but the most important thing is whether or not your answer works. Use this discussion to analyze differences between your answers and those presented here.

If you have alternative answers to the questions in this exercise, you are encouraged to post your answers and to discuss them at the companion web site for this book, located at:

`http://www.phptr.com/phptrinteractive/`

11.3.1 ANSWERS

a) What was displayed when you ran the `kill` command?

Answer: Your interaction should look like the following:

```
[11035]: tt1 &
[1]     328
[11036]: kill -INT %1
[1] +                           tt1 &
[11037]:
```

Line 11035 starts the `tt1` command running in the background, then the `kill` command sends an `INT` signal to the job, causing it to terminate immediately, just as if it was running in the foreground and you pressed `Ctrl-C`. Note that the program does not print its "Normal Termination" message.

b) What does delivering these three types of signals do when they are delivered to a process?

Answer: Your interaction should look like the following:

```
[11037]: tt1 &
[1]      281
[11038]: kill -USR1 %1
[1] + User signal 1              tt1 &
[11039]: tt1 &
[1]      328
[11040]: kill -HUP %1
[1] + Hangup                     tt1 &
[11041]: tt1 &
[1]      349
[11042]: kill -CHLD %1
[11043]: /home/vickery/bin/tt1 Completed Normally
```

On line 11043, the prompt string was printed, then after 30 seconds, the "Completed Normally" message printed, leaving the cursor at the beginning of the line below. When I pressed the `Enter` *key, the last two lines below printed.*

```
[1] +  Done                      tt1 &
[11043]:
```

The `USR1` and `HUP` signals cause the program to terminate abruptly (without printing its "Normal Termination" message). In addition, the shell displays the "full name" of the signal that caused the job to terminate in its message, telling that the background job is finished. The `HUP` signal was originally designed to tell a program when a user's dial-in connection to a program has been lost (a "hangup") but now is often used to tell long-running programs that they should reinitialize themselves. The `USR1` and `USR2` signals are provided for any use you might wish to make of them. However, unless you create a trap handler for these or most other signal types, the default behavior is to terminate the process to which they are sent.

The `CHLD` signal is an example of a signal that, by default, does *not* cause the process receiving it to be terminated. As the interaction with `tt1` on line 11042 shows, sending this signal has no effect on the program, which continues to run and finally prints its "Normal Completion" message. This signal is automatically delivered to a process any time one of its child processes terminates. For example, if you run a program in the background, your interactive shell receives this signal when the background job finishes. Internally, that's how the shell knows when it is time to print its "Done" message for the job.

c) What did you observe?

Answer: Your interaction should look like the following:

```
[11043]: tt1 &
[1]     282
[11044]: kill -STOP %1
[1] + Stopped (SIGSTOP)        tt1 &
[11045]: kill -CONT %1
[11046]: /home/vickery/bin/tt1 Completed Normally
[1] +  Done                    tt1 &
[11046]:
```


The sequence of events here was basically the same as in the previous example. The difference is that the total time between lines 11043 and 11046 (the one above) was 30 seconds plus the time I waited between entering lines 11044 and 11045.

The range of features implemented using UNIX signals is broad. This example shows that the `STOP` and `CONT` (continue) signals, as their names imply, start and stop a process' execution. We'll concentrate on the ones that are most useful in constructing shell scripts here.

d) What happens if you press Ctrl-C in response to the shell's command prompt?

Answer: You get another prompt string.

The point of mentioning this is that according to normal UNIX signal processing rules, pressing Ctrl-C while the shell is executing its code to read a command line from you should cause the shell process to terminate. Clearly, there is some way to override the shell's default behavior, and that's where the shell's `trap` command comes in. (The shell accomplishes the equivalent of what we are about to look at for itself by making machine-language calls to the operating system to control how signals are handled.)

e) What happened when you pressed Ctrl-C?

Answer: Your interaction should look like the following:

```
[11046]: trap "print INT occurred." INT
[11047]: INT occurred.
[11048]: INT occurred.
```

```
[11048]: helloINT occurred.
[11048]:
```

Here we have used the trap command to establish a trap handler that prints "INT occurred" whenever the `INT` signal is delivered to out interactive shell process. Normally, you will do this sort of thing inside a script, as you will see below, but the trap command can be used at any level of your session.

On line 11048 I typed "hello" before pressing Ctrl-C, and that partially completed command line was discarded by the shell, and it reissued the prompt string for command 11048.

f) Does the trap handler affect signal handling for the script?

Answer: Your interaction should look the same as your interaction for Question a. Entering the `trap` command at the command prompt has no effect on signal processing for a command that runs as a subprocess.

If a process wants to manage signals it has to do it itself. The way in which signals are handled in one process does not affect the way they are handled by other processes. (If you are familiar with the UNIX systems' programming, note that this is different from the behavior of the `fork()` system call.)

g) What did the three `trap` commands do?

Answer: The first and last ones print a list of trap handlers that are set. The middle one clears the trap handler for `INT`.

Your interaction should look something like the following:

```
[11048]: trap
trap -- 'print INT occurred.' INT
trap -- 'eval "${Keytable[${.sh.edchar}]}"' KEYBD
[11049]: trap - INT
[11050]: trap
trap -- 'eval "${Keytable[${.sh.edchar}]}"' KEYBD
[11051]:
```

Line 11048 shows that I had two trap handlers set when I issued the `trap` command, the one for `INT` that we entered earlier in this exercise, plus one for `KEYBD` that was set when I logged into the system. Entering the command on line 11049 cleared the `INT` handler, and line 11050 shows that only the `KEYBD` trap remains set.

h) What happens each time you press Ctrl-C?

Answer: Your interaction should look something like the following:

```
[11051]: tt2
/home/vickery/bin/tt2: Resetting
/home/vickery/bin/tt2: Resetting
/home/vickery/bin/tt2: Exiting Normally
/home/vickery/bin/tt2: Exit Trap
[11052]:
```


This script illustrates setting two trap handlers for a script. Each time you press Ctrl-C, the `INT` handler prints the "Resetting" message and starts a new sleep command. Finally, when you don't press Ctrl-C for 30 seconds, the script prints its "Exiting Normally" message and finishes, then the `EXIT` handler runs and prints the "Exit Trap" message, and the shell issues a new prompt.

i) What printed when the program terminated?

Answer: Your interaction should look like the following:

```
[11052]: tt2 &
[1]     280
[11053]: kill -INT %1
/home/vickery/bin/tt2: Resetting
[11054]: kill -USR1 %1
/home/vickery/bin/tt2: Exit Trap
[1] + User signal 1             tt2 &
[11055]:
```

First, we see that an `INT` signal is caught by the script, and the "Resetting" message prints in the usual way. When we deliver a `USR1` signal, for which the script has not set a trap, the program terminates immediately, and the "Exiting Normally" message does not get printed. However, the `EXIT` trap still gets handled, even though the script did not reach the end.

The `EXIT` trap is great for "cleaning up," even when an unusual condition prevents a script from doing its full job.

11.3.2 Answers

a) What happened when you executed `tt3`?

Answer: Your interaction should look like the following:

```
[11055]: tt3
[3]+ print This is the first command in this script
This is the first command in this script
[4]+ print This is the second command in this script
This is the second command in this script
[5]+ print This is the last command in this script
[5]+ 1> /dev/null
[11056]:
```

The `set -x` command turns on the shell's `xtrace` facility. (You can turn it off with the `set +x` command.) As you can see, every command that the shell executes is printed before it is executed, along with its line number in the script. Note that the output redirection on the third print command is treated as a separate command by the shell. This is consistent with the fact that the shell allows you to use redirection without a command, for example, to create files.

You can change what the shell prints to the left of each command in `xtrace` *mode by giving a value to the variable* `PS4`*. The default value of* `PS4`*, as shown above, is "*`[$LINENO]+ ]`*."*

As you can see, this can be a valuable tool for finding out what your program is doing, although the output can get voluminous. (Don't try turning it on from the command line if you have a `KEYBD` trap set! You'll get a line of output for every character you type!)

b) What happened when you executed `tt4`?

Answer: Your interaction should look like the following:

```
[11056]: tt4
Variable values are: X= Y= Z=
Variable values are: X=abc Y=cba Z=bac
Variable values are: X=hello Y=cba Z=bac
Variable values are: X=hello Y=greetings! Z=bac
[11057]:
```

A `DEBUG` trap handler is executed just before each command is executed. Unlike the `xtrace` option, which just prints the command about to be executed, the trap handler can do anything you want it to. In this case, we defined a function that prints the values of some variables. Naturally, you can put any number of commands inside such a function.

Debugging is a skill that requires careful analysis of a program that isn't working right. If a program goes into an endless loop, you can locate the problem by turning the `xtrace` *option on and off at different places in the code. If a value is computed incorrectly, judicious use of* `DEBUG` *traps to print key values can help you locate the problem.*

You can save a lot of debugging time by writing and testing code incrementally. Write a little bit, and test everything carefully. Then write a little bit more, and test again. If a problem crops up during testing, it has to be because of that little bit of code that you just wrote, reducing the scope of the problem greatly.

LAB 11.3 SELF-REVIEW QUESTIONS

To test your progress, you should be able to answer the following questions:

1) What does the `trap` command do?

- **a)** _____It sends a signal to a process.
- **b)** _____It receives a signal from a process.
- **c)** _____It tells what code you want to execute when a signal occurs.
- **d)** _____It stops a script when it is executed.
- **e)** _____It prints the time of day.

2) What are two ways of sending an `INT` signal to a process?
   a) _____Press Ctrl-C or run a `kill` command.
   b) _____Run a `trap` or a `signal` command.
   c) _____Run a `trap` or a `kill` command.
   d) _____Press Ctrl-C or run a `signal` command.
   e) _____Run a `signal` or a `kill` command.

3) Signal handlers set at the command line are automatically passed on to scripts that you run from the command line.
   a) _____True
   b) _____False

4) What is the shell's `xtrace` option used for?
   a) _____It is used to execute X Window System applications.
   b) _____It is used to show the values of variables whenever the shell executes a command.
   c) _____It is used to set a trap for Ctrl-C.
   d) _____It is used to print each command before it is executed.
   e) _____It isn't used for anything.

5) What would this command do:

```
trap ' print ouch! ; trap - INT ' INT
```

   a) _____When the user presses Ctrl-C once, it prints "ouch," but not if the user presses Ctrl-C a second time.
   b) _____It prints "ouch!" and then causes an I/O interrupt.
   c) _____It prints "ouch" and then sends an `INT` signal to the shell.
   d) _____It causes "ouch" to print every time the user presses any key.
   e) _____Nothing, because you can't put a trap command inside a trap handler.

Quiz answers appear in Appendix A, Section 11.3.

CHAPTER 11

TEST YOUR THINKING

The projects in this section are meant to have you utilize all of the skills that you have acquired throughout this chapter. The answers to these projects can be found at the companion web site to this book, located at:

http://www.phptr.com/phptrinteractive/

Visit the Web site periodically to share and discuss your answers.

1) Modify the "shuffle" script from Exercise 11.2.2 to perform the following:

- If either of the input files does not exist or is not readable, print an error message, don't ask for an output file name, and prompt for another pair of input files.
- If the output file already exists, ask the user whether it is all right to overwrite it (and respond appropriately!).
- If the user presses `Ctrl-C`, be sure the cursor is positioned at the beginning of the next line before the script exits.
- As written, the program includes all the lines from both files only if the first one has more or an equal number of lines, compared with the second one. Modify it so that the output always contains all lines from both files.

2) Write the equivalent of the `du -k` command, which prints the name of each directory under the current one, preceded by the number of kilobytes in all the files in that directory and all its descendants. *Hint: You can redirect the output of an* `ls -l` *command to a temporary file, and read that file back in to get the file sizes.*

APPENDIX A

ANSWERS TO SELF-REVIEW QUESTIONS

CHAPTER 1

Lab 1.1 ■ Self-Review Answers

Question	Answers	Comments
1)	A	If you selected B ("something else") you aren't running a current version of the KornShell! You need to get set up properly before you proceed.

Lab 1.2 ■ Self-Review Answers

Question	Answers	Comments
1)	D	
2)	A	
3)	C	
4)	D	
5)	A-5, B-1, C-4, D-3, E-2, F-6	

Lab 1.3 ■ Self-Review Answers

Question	Answers	Comments
1)	E	
2)	B	
3)	B	
4)	B	
5)	A	

CHAPTER 2

Lab 2.1 ■ Self-Review Answers

Question	Answer	Comments
1)	D	You will sometimes see choice C's terminology, but D is "correct."
2)	C	
3)	B, D	The command name is wrong. All the other choices are valid.
4)	A, D	

Lab 2.2 ■ Self-Review Answers

Question	Answers	Comments
1)	A	
2)	B	The `whence` command will also tell you the location of an external command, but it will not tell you the location of an arbitrary file, so choice A is close, but not right. (To find any file, use the UNIX `find` command.)
3)	B	It's almost true, but as you saw in Chapter 1, functions run in the shell's context whereas scripts, unless they are dotted, run in their own context, which can lead to differences.
4)	C	Unless you have a command named `Functions` on your system, you will get an error message saying that there is no such file or directory. If you used `functions *` (first letter lowercase), nothing will print—unless there is a file or subdirectory in the current directory with the same name as one of the functions defined for the shell, in which case the definition of that function will not be printed. That's because the shell does pathname expansion and substitutes the names of all files in the current directory in place of the asterisk. Pathname expansion wil be covered in Chapter 10 ("Patterns, Expansions, and Substitutions"). If you selected choice D (all functions defined in your shell), note the presence of the asterisk in the command. To list all functions, there must be nothing after the command.
5)	C	

Lab 2.3 ■ Self-Review Answers

Question	Answer	Comments
1)	B	
2)	A	Unless you link `fds`.
3)	D	
4)	B	
5)	B, D, E	D is correct because `fd 1` is `stdout`.
6)	A	
7)	C	
8)	B	

CHAPTER 3

Lab 3.1 ■ Self-Review Answers

Question	Answer	Comments
1)	A	
2)	C	The `cat` command might run before the `print` command completes, at least in principle.
3)	D	
4)	C	
5)	B	
6)	A	

Lab 3.2 ■ Self-Review Answers

Question	Answer	Comments
1)	B	
2)	B	The closing brace is taken as an argument to the `print` command, so the shell prompts for another one to match the opening brace at the beginning. You could put a semicolon before the closing brace to mark the end of the `print` command if this behavior is not what you want.
3)	A	
4)	B	It goes to the first command in the group that actually reads from `stdin`.
5)	C	
6)	A	

CHAPTER 4

Lab 4.1 ■ Self-Review Answers

Question	Answer	Comments
1)	A	
2)	C	
3)	B	The dollar sign is used to reference variables; it is never part of a variable's name.
4)	E	Choices B–D all have spaces around the equal sign.

Lab 4.2 ■ Self-Review Answers

Question	Answer	Comments
1)	A	
2)	B	
3)	B	
4)	D	
5)	D	
6)	C	

Lab 4.3 ■ Self-Review Answers

Question	Answer	Comments
1)	E	
2)	D	
3)	E	

CHAPTER 5

Lab 5.1 ■ Self-Review Answers

Question	Answer	Comments
1)	C	
2)	D	
3)	E	
4)	A	You could write a function that underdefines itself each time (which can be a useful debugging trick), in which case the answer would be *False*.
5)	B	
6)	A	
7)	B	

Lab 5.2 ■ Self-Review Answers

Question	Answer	Comments
1)	B	
2)	C	
3)	A	
4)	A	
5)	E	

CHAPTER 6

Lab 6.1 ■ Self-Review Answers

Question	Answer	Comments
1)	D	
2)	C	
3)	B	
4)	B	In this case, the dollar sign is not needed to reference the value of *hello*
5)	E	
6)	C	The division is done first because it has higher precedence than addition.
7)	D	
8)	D	
9)	E	

Lab 6.2 ■ Self-Review Answers

Question	Answer	Comments
1)	B	
2)	C	
3)	C	
4)	C	
5)	C	

Chapter 7

Lab 7.1 ■ Self-Review Answers

Question	Answer	Comments
1)	A	
2)	B	
3)	B	There don't have to be any `else` commands.
4)	A	
5)	A	How would you get rid of the error message from the `ls` command if there is no junk?
6)	D	

Lab 7.2 ■ Self-Review Answers

Question	Answer	Comments
1)	B	
2)	B	
3)	B	
4)	C	`-eq` is used for comparing arithmetic expressions

Chapter 8

Lab 8.1 ■ Self-Review Answers

Question	Answer	Comments
1)	E	
2)	E	
3)	A	
4)	A	
5)	B	
6)	C	

Lab 8.2 ■ Self-Review Answers

Question	Answer	Comments
1)	B	But it might be if you omit the `in` part.
2)	E	
3)	B	
4)	A	
5)	C	

CHAPTER 9

Lab 9.1 ■ Self-Review Answers

Question	Answer	Comments
1)	E	
2)	D	
3)	E	
4)	E	
5)	B	
6)	A	
7)	C	
8)	C	

CHAPTER 10

Lab 10.1 ■ Self-Review Answers

Question	Answer	Comments
1)	A	
2)	D	
3)	D	
4)	E	
5)	E	
6)	C	
7)	B	
8)	F	

Lab 10.2 ■ Self-Review Answers

Question	Answer	Comments
1)	B	This puts it in the user's home directory, makes it hidden from normal directory listings, and makes it clear what program is responsible for it or depends on it.
2)	C	
3)	D	
4)	C	
5)	C	

Lab 10.3 ■ Self-Review Answers

Question	Answer	Comments
1)	D	
2)	B	
3)	B	

CHAPTER 11

Lab 11.1 ■ Self-Review Answers

Question	Answer	Comments
1)	C	
2)	A	
3)	D	
4)	E	
5)	A	

Lab 11.2 ■ Self-Review Answers

Question	Answer	Comments
1)	B	Note that if you run the script as a command instead of dotting it, control always returns to the console.
2)	D	This is an example of writing code so you don't surprise an unsuspecting user.
3)	D	

Lab 11.3 ■ Self-Review Answers

Question	Answer	Comments
1)	C	
2)	A	This assumes you haven't changed your interrupt character from `Ctrl-C` to something else.
3)	B	
4)	D	
5)	A	

APPENDIX B

BUILT-IN COMMAND REFERENCE

The material in this Appendix is excerpted from *The New KornShell Command and Programming Language* by Morris I. Bolsky and David G. Korn, Prentice-Hall, 1995. Reproduced by permission.

This Appendix uses a slightly different typographic convention from the remainder of this book. Names of comands, symbols and words that you must type exactly as shown are in **boldface**. Items for which you must substitute actual values are shown in *italics*. Throughout this Appendix, *name* typically refers to the name of a variable, and *compound-list* refers to one or more simple commands separated by Newlines or by the symbols covered in Chapter 3, "Compound Command Syntax". The remainder of the conventions used here were introduced in Chapter 2, "Command Syntax": Square brackets ([ ]) surround optional items and ellipses (...) follow items that may be repeated zero or more times. Be careful to differentiate the square brackets that indicate optional items ([ ]) from the ones that you must type explicitly (**[ ]**).

. Dot Command

. *name* [*arg* ...]

If *name* refers to a function defined with the **function** *name* syntax, **ksh** executes this function in the current environment. Otherwise, **ksh** reads the complete file (called a dot script) and executes commands from it in the current environment. **ksh** uses the search path specified by the *PATH* variable to find the file. Dotting a file that is not a script or function leads to unpredictable results. **For more inforamtion**: see Chapter 1 (Setting Up.)

to unpredictable results. **For more inforamtion**: see Chapter 1 (Setting Up.)

{ ... } Brace Grouping Operator

{ *compound-list* }

ksh runs *compound-list* in the current environment. The return value is the return value of the last command in *compound-list.* **For more information:** see Chapter 3 (Compound Command Syntax).

(...) Subshell Grouping Operator

(*compound-list*)

ksh runs *compound-list* in a subshell environment. For **more information:** see Chapter 3 (Compound Command Syntax).

(...) Array Initialization

varname= (*value* ...)
varname= ([*expression*]=*value* ...)
varname= (*assignment* ...)

The first form assigns values to the indexed array *varname,* starting with index position 0.

The second form assigns values to the associative array *varname* using *expression* as the array subscript.

The third form assigns values to a set of variables whose names are of the form *varname.name,* where *name* is the left-hand side of an *assignment.* **typeset** commands are allowed in *assignments* provided they are separated by semicolons or newlines. **For more information:** see Chapter 6 (Advanced Variable Usage).

((...)) Arithmetic Command

((*word* ...))

ksh does command substitution, parameter expansion, arithmetic expansion, and quote removal for each *word* to generate an arithmetic expression that is evaluated as follows:

ksh performs all calculations using the double precision floating point arithmetic type on your system. **ksh** does not check for overflow.

A floating point constant has the form [(]*number*[.*number*][*exponent*], where *number* is any non-negative decimal number, and *exponent* is **E** or **e** optionally followed by **+** or **-** and a non-negative decimal number.

An integer constant has the form [*base*#]*number*, where *base* is a decimal integer between 2 and 64 that defines the arithmetic base (default is 10), and *number* is any non-negative number.

A variable is denoted by a *varname*. If a variable in an arithmetic expression has the integer attribute, then **ksh** uses the value of the variable. Otherwise, **ksh** assumes that

the value of the variable is an arithmetic expression, and tries to evaluate it.

An arithmetic function is denoted by *function*(*expression*), where *function* is one of the following: **abs** (absolute value), **acos** (arc cosine of angle in radians), **asin** (arc sine), **atan** (arc tangent), **cos** (cosine), **cosh** (hyperbolic cosine), **exp** (exponential with base *e* (2.718281828459045), **int** (greatest integer less than or equal to value of *expression*, **log** (logarithm base *e*), **sin** (sine), **sinh** (hyperbolic sine), **sqrt** (square root), **tan** (tangent), **tanh** (hyperbolic tangent).

An expression is a constant, a variable, or is constructed with the following operators. The value of an expression with a comparison operator or a logical operator is **1** if non-zero (true) or **0** (false) otherwise. Operators are listed in order of precedence, with the highest ones first. Items of the same precedence are listed under the same bullet. **ksh** evaluates all items of the same precedence left-to-right, except for = and *op*= and other assignment operators, which it evaluates right-to-left.

• (*expression*)	Overrides precedence rules.
• *varname*++/++*varname*	Postfix/prefix increment.
varname--/--*vaname*	Postfix/prefix decrement.
+*expression*	Unary plus.
-*expression*	Unary minus.
!*expression*	Logical negation. The value is **0** for any espression whose value is **0**.

~expression — Bit-wise negation.

• *expression * expression* — Multiplication.

expression / expression — Division.

expression % expression — Remainder of 1st expression after dividing by the 2nd expression.

• *expression + expression* — Addition.

expression - expression — Subtractioin.

• *expression << expression* — Left shift first expression by the number of bits given by the second expression.

expression >> expression — Right shift expression by the number of bits given by the second expression.

• *expression <= expression* — Less than or equal to.

expression >= expression — Greater than or equal to.

expression < expression — Less than.

expression > expression — Greater than.

• *expression == expression* — Equal to.

expression != expression — Not equal to.

• *expression & expression* — Bit-wise OR. Both expressions are always evaluated.

• *expression ^ expression* — Bit-wise Exclusive OR.

• *expression | expression* — Bit-wise OR. Both expressions are always evaluated.

• *expression && expression* — Logical AND. If the first expression is non-zero, then the second expression is not evaluated.

• *expression || expression* — Logical OR. If the first expression is non-zero, then the second expression is not evaluated.

• *expression ? expression: expression* — Conditional operator. If the first expression is non-zero, then the second expression is evaluated. Otherwise the third expression is evaluated.

• *varname = expression*	Assignment.
• *varname* **op** = *expression*	Compound assignment. The is equivalent to *varname* = varname op expression. **op** must be * / % + - << >> & ^ or [
• *expression, expression*	Comma operator. Both expressions are evaluated. The resulting value is the value of the second expression.

For more information: see Chapter 6 (Advanced Variable Usage).

[...] Left Bracket Command

[[*expression*]]
test [*expression*]

The **[[...]]** compound command makes **test** and **[** obsolescent.

[[...]] Conditional Command

[[*test-expression* [Newline ...]]]

test-expression must be a conditional expression primitive or some combination of conditional primitives formed by combining one or more of them with one of the following, The following are listed in order of precedence, from highest to lowest:

• **(** *test-expression* **)**	Evaluates to value of test-expression. The ( ) are used to override normal precedence rules.
• **!** *test-expression*	Logical negation of of *test-expression.*
• *test-expression* **&&** *test_expression*	Evaluates to True if both test expressions are True. The second test expression is expanded and evaluated only if the first test expression is True.
• *test-expression* || *test-expression*	Evaluates to True if either of the test expressions is True. The second test expression is expanded and evaluated only if the first test expression is False.

Conditional expression primitives are unary and binary expressions that evaluate to True or False. Spaces or tabs are required to separate operators from operands.

-e *file*	True if *file* exists.
-a *file*	True if *file* exists. Do not use this primitive; use **-e** instead.
-r *file*	True if *file* exists and is readable.
-w *file*	True if *file* exists and is writable. *file* will not be writable on a readonly file system even if this test indicates True.
-x *file*	True if *file* exists and is executable. If *file* is a directory, True indicates that the directory can be searched.
-f *file*	True if *file* exists and is a regular file.
-d *file*	True if *file* exists and is a directory.
-c *file*	True if *file* exists and is a character special file.
-b *file*	True if *file* exists and is a block special file.
-p *file*	True if *file* exists and is a named pipe (fifo).
-u *file*	True if *file* exists and its set-user-id bit is set.
-g *file*	True if *file* exists and its set-group-id bit is set.
-k *file*	True if *file* exists and its sticky bit is set.
-s *file*	True if *file* exists and it has a size greater than zero.
-L *file*	True if *file* exists and is a symbolic link.
-h *file*	True if *file* exists and is a symbolic link.
-O *file*	True if *file* exists and its owner is the effective user id.
-G *file*	True if *file* exists and its group is the effective group id.
-S *file*	True if *file* exists and is a special file of type socket.
-t *fildes*	True if the file whose file descriptor number is *fildes* is open and is associated with a terminal device.
file1 **-nt** *file 2*	True if *file1*is newer than *file2* or if *file2* does not exist.
file1 **-ot** *file2*	True if *file1*is older than *file2* or if *file2* does not exist.

file1 **-et** *file2*	True if *file1*is another name for *file2*. This will be true if *file1* is a hard link or a symbolic link to *file2*.
-o *option*	True if *option* is on.
-z *string*	True if length of *string* is zero.
-n *string*	True if length of *string* is non-zero.
string	True if *string* is not Null
string == pattern	True if *string* matches *pattern*. Quote *pattern* to treat it as a string.
string **!=** *pattern*	True if *string* does not match *pattern*.
string1 < *string2*	True if *string1* comes before *string2* in the collation order defined by the current locale.
string1 > *string2*	True if *string1* comes after *string2* in the collation order defined by the current locale.
exp1 **-eq** *exp2*	True if arithmetic expression *exp1* is equal to arithmetic expression *exp2*.
exp1 **-ne** *exp2*	True if arithmetic expression *exp1* is not equal to arithmetic expression *exp2*.
exp1 **-gt** *exp2*	True if arithmetic expression *exp1* is greater than arithmetic expression *exp2*.
exp1 **-ge** *exp2*	True if arithmetic expression *exp1* is greater than or equal to arithmetic expression *exp2*.
exp1 **-lt** *exp2*	True if arithmetic expression *exp1* is less than arithmetic expression *exp2*.
exp1 **-le** *exp2*	True if arithmetic expression *exp1* is less than or equal to arithmetic expression *exp2*.

For more information: see Chapter 7 (Basic Tests).

: NULL COMMAND

Use **:** where you must have a command, as in the **then** condition of an **if** command, but you do not want the command to do anything. The arguments to **:** are expanded. Returns True.

ALIAS

alias [**-pt**] [*name*[=*value*] ...]

Do not specify any *name* arguments if you want to display aliases. **ksh** displays the list of aliases, one per line, on standard output, in the form *name=value*. The **-p** option causes the word **alias** to precede each one so that it is displayed in a re-enterable format. If you specify **-t**, then **ksh** displays only tracked aliases.

If you specify *name* only, then:

- Without **-t**, **ksh** displays the name and value of the alias *name*.
- With **-t**, **ksh** set the tracked attribute, and sets the value of the alias *name* to the pathname obtained by doing a path search.

value can contain any valid shell text. During alias substitution, if the last character of *value* is a space or tab, **ksh** also checks the word following the alias to see if it should do alias substitution. Use a trailing space or a tab when the next argument is supposed to be a command name.

Enclose *value* in single quotes if you want *value* expanded only when **ksh** executes a reference to the alias. Otherwise, **ksh** also expands *value* when it processes the **alias** command. **For more information:** see Chapter 2 (Command Syntax).

AUTOLOAD

autoload is a predefined alias for '**typeset -fu**'.

BG

bg [*job*]

Use **bg** to resume stopped jobs and run them in the background. Use **bg** without arguments to refer to the current job the job that you most recently stopped). Use **bg** *jobs* to refer to specific jobs. *job* may be a process id or one of the following:

%*number*	To refer to the job by number.
%*string*	The job whose name begins with *string*.
%?*string*	The job whose name contains *string*.
%+or %%	Current job.
%-	Previous job.

For more information: see Chapter 3 (Compound Command Syntax).

BREAK

break [*n*]

break exits from the smallest enclosing **for, while, until,** or **select** loop, or from the nth enclosing loop if you specify *n*. Execution continues with the command immediately following the loop(s). For **more information:** see Chapters 8 (Loops) and Chapter 9 (The *case* and *select* Statements).

BUILTIN

builtin [**-ds**] [**-f** *file*] [*pathname* ...]

If *pathname* is not specified, and no **-f** option is specified, the built-ins are displayed on standard output. The **-s** option displays only the special built-ins. The **-f** and *pathname* options are used for adding new built-ins to the shell. **For more information:** see Chapter 2 (Command Syntax) and the Web site for this book to see how to add built-ins to the shell.

CASE

```
case word in
[ [(] pattern [ | pattern] ... ) compound-list ;; ]
[ [(] pattern [ | pattern] ... ) compound-list ;& ]
...
esac
```

ksh runs the first *compound-list* for which *word* matches *pattern*. **For more information:** see Chapter 9 (The *case* and *select* Statements).

CD

cd [**-LP**] [*directory*]

cd [**-LP**] *oldstring newstring*

Use **cd** to change the working directory.

If *directory* is a dash (-) **ksh** changes the working directory to the previous directory. If *directory* is specified, does not begin with slash, (/), dot-slash (./), or dot-dot-slash (../), and *CDPATH* is set, **ksh** prepends, in turn, each directory in the *CDPATH* variable to *directory* to construct a directory name, and changes the working directory to the first constructed name, if any, that corresponds to a directory that you have permission to change to.

In the second form, **ksh** substitutes *newstring* for *oldstring* in the working directory name, *PWD*, and tries to change to this new directory.

If you specify **-L**, **ksh** displays the logical name, and does not resolve symbolic links. If you specify **-P**, **ksh** resolves all symbolic links and displays the resulting physical name.

COMMAND

command [**-pvV**] *command* [*arg*]

Executes *command* with the specified arguments, with functions eliminated from the search order. If you specify **-p**, then **ksh** performs the command search using the default value for *PATH*. **command -v** is equivalent to **whence**. **command -V** is equivalent to **whence -v**.

CONTINUE

continue [*n*]

Goes to the top of the smallest enclosing **for**, **while**, **until**, or **select** loop, or to the top of the nth enclosing loop if *n* is specified, and causes it to repeat execution. **For more information:** see Chapters 8 (Loops) and Chapter 9 (The *case* and *select* Statements).

DISOWN

disown [*job* ...]

Use **disown** to prevent **ksh** from sending a *HUP* signal to each of the given *job*s (or all active jobs if *jobs* is omitted) when it terminates a login session. See the **bg** command for how to specify *job*.

ECHO

Use the **print** command instead of **echo.**

EXEC

exec [**-c**] [**-a** *name*] [*command* [*arg* ...]]

Use **exec** to replace **ksh** with *command* without creating a new process. If you specify **-c**, **ksh** clears the environment of all variables before execution except variable assignments that are part of the current **exec** command. If you specify **-a**, **ksh** passes *name* as the zeroth argument of *command*.

If you do not specify any options, *command*, or *arg*, **exec** will open, close, and/or copy file descriptors as specified by I/O redirection.

exec [*n*]< *readfile*	Open *readfile* as file descriptor *n* for reading. *n* is 0 (*stdin*) if omitted.
exec [*n*]< *writefile*	Open *writefile* as file descriptor *n* for writing. *n* is 1 (*stdout*) if omitted.
exec *m*<&*n*	Make file unit *m* a copy of file descriptor *n*.
exec *n*<&-	Close file descriptor *n*.

For more information: see Chapters 2 (Command Syntax) and Chapter 11 (I/O and Trap Processing).

EXIT

exit [*n*]

Causes **ksh** to exit. If this is the login shell, **ksh** logs you out. Otherwise, **ksh** returns to the program that invoked **ksh**. If set, a trap on *EXIT* is executed before **ksh** terminates. If specified, *n* is the return value.

EXPORT

export [**-p**] [*name*[=*value*]] ...

name(s) are marked for automatic export to the environment of subsequently executed commands. If you don't supply any arguments, **ksh** displays a list of variables with the export attribute, and their values. If you specify **-p**, **ksh** displays the list of variables in re-enterable format.

FALSE

This command evaluates any arguments and then returns the value False.

FC

fc is a built-in alias for the **hist** command.

FG

fg [*job*]

Use **fg** to move background jobs into the foreground one at a time. See the **bg** command for options.

FLOAT

float is a predefined alias for **'typeset -E'**.

FOR

for *varname* [**in** *word* ...]

do *compound-list*

done

ksh does command substitution, parameter expansion, arithmetic expansion, field splitting, pathname expansion, and quote removal for each *word* to generate a list of items. If you do not specify **in** *word*, **ksh** uses the positional parameters starting at *1* as the list of items as if you had specified **in "$@"**. **ksh** sets *varame* to each item in turn, and runs *compound-list.* Execution ends when there are no more items.

for (([*init_expression*] **;** [*loop_condition*] **;** [*loop_expression*]))

do *compound-list*

done

init_expression, loop_condition, and *loop_expression* are arithmetic expressions. **ksh** evaluates *init_expression* before executing the **for** loop. **ksh** evaluates *loop_condition* before each iteration. If *loop_condition* is non-zero, then *compound-list* is executed again. *loop_expression* specifies an expression that is executed after each iteration. **For more information:** see Chapter 8 (Loops).

FUNCTION

function [*varname.*]*identifier* **{**

compound_list

}

Define a function which is referenced by *varname.identifier* or *identifier.* **ksh** executes the function in a separate function environment. **For more information:** see Chapters 1 (Setting Up) and Chapter 5 (Parameters).

FUNCTIONS

functions is a predefined alias for '**typeset -f**'.

GETCONF

getconf [*name* [*pathname*]]

Without arguments, **getconf** prints a list of POSIX configuration parameters and their values. The options can be used to see the values of particular parameters.

GETOPTS

getopts [**-a** *name*] *optstring varname* [*arg* ...]

getopts checks the argument list *arg* for legal options. If *arg* is omitted, **getopts** uses the positional parameters instead. See Lab 5.2 (Processing Option Parameters) for information on using this command.

HASH

hash is a predefined alias for '**alias -t** --'.

HIST

hist [**-e** *editor*} {**-nlr**] [*first* [*last*]]

hist provides access to your history file, which is a copy of previously-entered interactive command lines. Interactive command processing is not specifically covered in this book.

HISTORY

history is a predefined alias for '**hist -l**', which lists the last 16 commands entered.

IF

if *compound-list*

then *compound-list*

[**elif** *compound-list*

then *compound-list*

...

[**else** *compound-list*

fi

ksh runs the **if** *compound-list.* If the return value is True, **ksh** runs the **then** *compound-list.* If the return value is False, **ksh** runs each **elif** *compound-list*(s) (if any) in turn, until one has a return value of True. If there are no **elif** *compound-list*(s), or if none have a return value of True, **ksh** runs the **else** *compound-list,* if any. **For more information:** see Chapter 7 (Basic Tests).

INTEGER

integer is a predefined alias for **'typeset -i'**

JOBS

jobs [-lnp] [*job* ...]

Use **jobs** to display information about specified *job*s (or all active *job*s if *job* is omitted) that the current **ksh** started. See the **bg** command for information on specifying *job.*

KILL

kill [**-s** *signame*] *job* ...

kill [**-n** *signum*] *job* ...

kill [-*sig*] *job* ...

Use **kill** to send a signal to the specified jobs. *signum* is a signal number, *signame* is a signal name (see below), and *sig* is either a *signum* or a *signame* with no space after the dash.

kill -l [*sig*]

Use **kill -l** without arguments to display signal names. If *sig* is a name, **ksh** displays the respective signal number. If *sig* is a number, **ksh** displays the respective signal name.

LET

let *arg*

Use **let** to evaluate one or more arithmetic expressions. If you use **((...))** instead of **let** you do not have to quote spaces, tabs, or any other special characters in *arg*.

NAMEREF

nameref is a predefined alias for **'typeset -n'**.

NOHUP

Use the **nohup** command to cause a job to ignore any *HUP* signal that it receives so that it can continue running even after you log out. The standard output and standard error are redirected to the file named nohup.out in the working directory.

PRINT

print [**-Rnprs**] [**-f** *format*] [**-u** [*n*]] [**--**] [*arg* ...]

Use **print** to write output to standard output. If you specify **-u** output is written to file descriptor *n*, which must be 1, 2, or a file descriptor that you opened with **exec**. The **-u** option has the same effect as redirecting the standard output of **print** but does not cause the file to be opened and closed each time.

Unless you specify **-R** or **-r**, **print** formats output using the following escape conventions:

\a	Bell character
\b	Backspace
\c	Print line without adding a newline. Additional args are ignored.
\f	Formfeed

\n	Newline
\r	Return
\t	Tab
\v	Vertical tab
****	Backslash
\E	Escape
\0*x*	The 8-bit character whose ASCII code is the 1-, 2-, 3-digit octal number *x*.

The **-f** option causes arguments to be processed as described for the **printf** command (see below). The **-n** option causes **ksh** not to add a trailing Newline to the output. The **-p** option redirects output to the co-process. The **-s** option redirects output to the history file. **For more information:** see throughout the book.

PRINTF

format [*arg* ...]

Use **printf** to format and display output on standard output. **printf** displays all characters in *format* except for escape sequences, listed for the **print** command, and conversion control strings, which begin with the **%** character. The syntax of a conversion control string is

% [*flags*][*fieldwidth*][*precision*][*base*]*conversion*

conversion specifies how the corresponding *arg* is to be displayed. You must specify exactly one of the following conversion characters:

b	String with the **print** escape conventions followed.
c	Unsigned character.
d	Signed decimal.
e,E	Scientific notation.
f	Floating point.
g,G	Scientific notation with significant digits.
n	The number of bytes printed at this point is stored in a variable whose name is given by *arg*.
o	Unsigned octal.

P	Regular expression is printed as a shell pattern.
q	String with special characters quoted.
s	String
u	Unsigned decimal
x,X	Unsigned hexadecimal. Letters match case of conversion character.
%	**%** character

flags are - to left-justify *arg* within the field, **+** to prefix all numbers with +or -; space to prefix all numbers with Space or -; **#** to prefix octal numbers with **0**, hexadecimal numbers with **0x**; to display the radix point when used with **e, E, f, g,** or **G**, or to display trailing zeros when used with **g** or **G**; or **0** to pad field width with leading zeros when used with **d, e, E, f, g, G, x,** or **X.**

A *field-width* is the minimum number of character positions displayed. The * character may be used to cause the value of the next *arg* to specify *field-width*. *precision* may be **.***n* to specify a width of *n* characters, **.*** to specify a variable width specified by the next *arg*, or **.** to specify a width of zero. The exact meaning of *precision* depends on the conversion type.

format is reused as often as necessary to satisfy the *arg* list. **For more information:** see Chapter 11 (I/O and Trap Processing).

PWD

pwd [**-LP**]

Use **pwd** to display the working directory. See the **cd** command for description of the options.

R

r is a predefined alias for '**hist -s**'

READ

read [**-Aprs**] [**-u** [*n*]] [**-d** *char*] [**-t** *sec*] [*name***?***prompt*] [*name* ...]

Use **read** to read a line and split it into fields, using the characters in the *IFS* variable as delimiters. If you specify *name***?***prompt*, **ksh** displays *prompt* on standard error if it is interactive. The first field is assigned to the first *name*, the second field to the second, *name*, etc., with leftover fields assigned to the last *name*. The default *name* is *REPLY*.

The **-A** option causes **ksh** to store the fields in *name* as an indexed array starting at index 0. The **-p** option causes **ksh** to read the input line from the co-process. An end-of-file causes **ksh** to disconnect the co-process so that you can create another co-process. The **-r** option causes a \ at the end of a line not to signify line continuation. The **-s** option causes **ksh** to save a copy of the input line as a command in the history file. The **-u** option causes **ksh** to read from file descriptor *n*; default is 0. Before you specify **read** with a file descriptor other than 0 or 2, you must open a file on the descriptor, typically with **exec**. The **-d** option terminates the **read** at delimiter *char* rather than Newline. The **-t** option puts a limit of *sec* seconds on the user response time. **For more information:** see Chapter 11 (I/O and Trap Processing).

READONLY

readonly [**-p**] [*name*=*value*]] ...

*name*s are given the readonly attribute. You cannot change *name* by subsequent variable assignment in this **ksh**. For **more information:** see Chapter 4 (Simple Variables).

REDIRECT

redirect is a predefined alias for **'command exec'**

RETURN

return [*n*]

Causes a **ksh** function or dot script to return to the invoking shell script. **return** outside a function or dot script is equivalent to **exit**. If set, a trap on *EXIT* defined in a non-POSIX function is executed in the environment of the calling program after the function returns.

SELECT

select *varname* [**in** *word* ...]

do *compound-list*

done

ksh does command substitution, parameter expansion, arithmetic expansion, field splitting, pathname expansion, and quote removal for each *word* to generate a list of items, before it processes the **do** *compound-list* command. If you do not specify **in** *word,* **ksh** uses the positional parameters starting at *1* as the list of items as if you had specified **in** "**$@**".

ksh displays the items in one or more columns on standard error, each preceded by a number, and then displays the *PS3* prompt. **ksh** then reads a selection line from standard input. If the line is the number of one of the displayed items, **ksh** sets the value of *varname* to the item corresponding to this number. If the line is empty, **ksh** again displays the list of items and the *PS3* prompt; **ksh** does not run *compound-list.* Otherwise, **ksh** sets *varname* to Null. **ksh** saves the contents of the selection line read from standard input in the variable *REPLY.* **ksh** runs *compound-list* for each selection until **ksh** encounters a **break**, **return**, or **exit** command in *compound-list.* If the value of the *TMOUT* variable is greater than zero, **select** will time out after the number of seconds given by *TMOUT.*

SET

set [(**Cabefhkmnopstuvx-**] [(**o** *option*]... [(**A** *name*] [*arg*...]

Use **(A** to assign values *arg* to array *name* starting sequentially from zero. Use **-A** to cause **ksh** to unset *name* prior to the assignment.

The **-s** option is used to sort positional parameters or, in the case of **A**, the values assigned to *name.*

If you specify **-o** with no *option,* **ksh** displays options settings on standard output.

If you specify no options at all, **ksh** displays the names and values of all variables.

Use **-o** *option* to turn an option on, and **+o** *option* to turn it off, where *option* is one of the option names listed below. Alternatively, you may use *-letter* or *+letter* to accomplish the same thing, where *letter* is the letter listed in parentheses after the names in the following list.

allexport (a)	While **allexport** is set, **ksh** sets the export attribute for each variable whose name does not contain a . (dot) to which you assign a value.
bgnice	**ksh** runs all background jobs at a lower priority
emacs	Puts you in the **emacs** built-in editor. (Not covered in this book.)
errexit (e)	If a command has False return value, **ksh** executes the *ERR* trap if set, and immediately exits.
gmacs	Puts you in the **gmacs** built-in editor. (Not covered in this book.)
ignoreeof	When the **interactive** option is also set, **ksh** does not exit on end-of-file (default is when you type Control-D).
keyword (k)	Provided for only backward compatibility with the Bourne shell.
markdirs	**ksh** appends a trailing / to all directory names resulting from pathname expansion
markdirs (m)	**ksh** runs background jobs in a separate process group, and displays a line upon completion.
noclobber (C)	**ksh** will not overwrite an existing file with the > redirection operator. You must specify >| to overwrite an existing file.
noexec (n)	**ksh** reads commands but does not execute them. You can use this option to have **ksh** check your shell script for syntax errors.
noglob (f)	**ksh** disables pathname expansion.
nolog	**ksh** does not store function definitions in the history file.

notify (b)	**ksh** displays a completion message on standard error immediately after each background job completes.
nounset (u)	**ksh** displays an error message when it tries to expand a variable that is unset.
privileged (p)	Not covered in this book.
trackall (h)	**ksh** causes each command whose name has the suyntax of an alias name to become a tracked alias when it is first encountered.
verbose (v)	**ksh** displays its input on standard error as it is read.
vi	Puts you in the **vi** built-in editor. Not covered in this book
viraw	Specifies **vi** character-at-a-time input.
xtrace (x)	After expanding each simple command, **ksh** expands *PS4* and displays it on standard error followed by the command and its expanded arguments.

SHIFT

shift [*n*]

ksh shifts positional parameter(s) to the left by *n*. **ksh** discards the first *n* positional parameters. *n* is an arithmetic expression that must evaluate to zero, or a positive number less than or equal to the value of special parameter #. Default is 1.

STOP

stop is a predefined alias for **'kill -s STOP'.**

TEST

See the **[** (left bracket) command, above. Use[[...]] instead.

TIME

time [*pipeline*]

If *pipeline* is specified, **ksh** executes *pipeline,* and displays on standard error the elapsed time, user time, and system time. Otherwise, **ksh** displays the cumulative time for the shell and its children.

TIMES

times is a predefined alias for **'{ {time;}2>&1;}'** Provided for backward compatibility with old scripts.

TRAP

trap [*action condition...*]

trap -p [*condition*]

Specify the action for **ksh** to take when the *condition*(s) arise. If *action* is Null, when any specified *condition* arises, **ksh** ignores it. If *action* is a dash (-), **ksh** resets *condition*(s) to their original value(s). If *action* is *n,* then **ksh** performs the action described for dash, and *n* becomes the first *condition.* If *action* is a command, then **ksh** executes the command each time that any of the *condition*(s) arise.

Use **trap** with no *action* and no *condition* to list all your trap settings. Use the **-p** option to display *action*(s) corresponding to each *condition* in re-enterable form. **For more information:** see Chapter 11 (I/O and Trap Processing).

TRUE

Same as the **:** (Null) command.

TYPESET

typeset +f[**tu**] [*name...*]

Use this form of **typeset** to display function names and values, and to set and unset function attributes.

Use **t** to specify the **xtrace** option for the function(s) specified via *name.* Use **u** to specify that *name* refers to a function that has not yet been defined. Use **-f** to display function names and definitions; use **+f** to display function names only. Definitions are displayed only if they are in your history file.

typeset [(**AHlnprtux**] [(**ELFRZi**[*n*]] [*name*[=*value*]] ...

With no options, **typeset** displays all variable names and attributes. With just **-p**, all names, attributes, and values are displayed in re-enterable format.

The options letters stand for the attributes listed below. Use - to set an attribute, and use + to unset an attribute. If you don't give any *name*(s), variables with that attribute set (or unset for +) will be listed.

u	Uppercase
l	Lowercase
i	Integer. If given, *n* specifies the arithmetic base.
n	Name reference
A	Associative array
E	Exponential number. *n* specifies significant figures.
F	Floating point number. *n* specifies decimal places.
L	Left-justifies. *n* specifies field width.
LZ	Left-justifies and strips leading zeros. *n* specifies field width.
R	Right-justifies. *n* specifies field width.
RZ	Right-justifies. *n* specifies field width, and fills with leading zeros.
Z	Same as **RZ**
r	readonly
x	export
H	UNIX system-to-host operating system pathname mapping.
t	User-defined tag

For more information: see Chapter 6 (Advanced Variable Usage) and Chapter 11 (I/O and Trap Processing).

ULIMIT

ulimit [**-HSacdfmnstv**] [*n*]

Use **ulimit** to set or display system resource limits. If you specify *n,* **ksh** sets the specified resource limit to *n. n* can be any arithmetic expression or **unlimited.** If you do not specify *n,* **ksh** displays the specified limit. If you specify **-H** a hard limit is set or displayed. If you specify **-S** as soft limit is set or displayed if soft limits exist. If you specify neither **-H** nor **-S**, both hard and soft limits are set; soft limits are displayed.

a displays all current resource limits. **c** specifies the limit on the size of core dumps, in 512-byte blocks. **d** specifies the size of the data area, in kilobytes. **f** specifies the size of files written by child processes, in 512-byte blocks. **m** specifies the size of physical memory that this process or any of its children can use, in kilobytes. **n** specifies the maximum number of file descriptors per process. **s** specifies the size of the stack area, in kilobytes. **t** specifies the number of seconds to be used by each process. **v** specifies the size of virtual memory that this process or any of its children can use.

UMASK

The *KornShell* **umask** command is the same as the same as the UNIX external command with the same name, except that it allows you to use the same symbolic notation for permissions as the UNIX **chmod** command. Use the **-S** option to introduce a symbolic mask value.

UNALIAS

unalias [**-a**] *name*

unalias removes the *name*(s) from the alias list. If you specify **-a**, then all of the aliases are cleared from memory.

UNTIL

until *compound-list*

do *compound-list*

done

The **until** command repeatedly runs the **until** *compound-list*. Each time, if the return value of the *compound-list* is False, runs **do** *compound-list*. If True, loop terminates. A **break** command within the **do** *compound-list* causes the **until** command to terminate with a value of True. A **continue** command causes the **do** *compound-list* to terminate and the **until** *compound-list* to be run again. **For more information:** see Chapter 8 (Loops).

WAIT

wait [*job...*]

Use **wait** to have **ksh** wait for the specified *job*(s) to terminate. If you specify *job* as a number, **ksh** waits for the given process. Otherwise, **ksh** waits fo all child processes of the specified *job* to terminate. If you omit *job*, **ksh** waits for all currently active child processes to complete.

WHENCE

whence [**-afpv**] *name...*

Use **whence** without **-v** to find the absolute pathname, if any, corresponding to each *name*. You can also use **whence** to find out what type of item each *name* is: specify **-v**. For each *name* you specify, **ksh** displays a line that indicates if the *name* is a reserved word, an alias, a built-in, an undefined function, a function, a tracked alias, a program, or "not found." If you specify **-f, ksh** does not check to see if *name* is a function. If you specify **-p**, **ksh** does not check to see if *name* is a reserved word, a built-in, an alias, or a function. If you specify **-a**, **ksh** displays all uses for *name*.

WHILE

while *compound-list*

do *compound-list*

done

The **while** command repeatedly runs the **while** *compound-list*. Each time, if the return value of the *compound-list* is True, runs **do** *compound-list*. If False, loop terminates. A **break** command within the **do** *compound-list* causes the **while** command to terminate with a value of True. A **continue** command causes the **do** *compound-list* to terminate and the **while** *compound-list* to be run again. **For more information:** see Chapter 8 (Loops).

Parameter Expansions

${*parameter:-word*}	**Use Default Value**. If *parameter* is null or unset, **ksh** substitutes the expanded value of *word*. Otherwise, **ksh** substitutes the value of *parameter*.
${*parameter-word* }	**Use Default Value**. If *parameter* is unset, **k s h** substitutes the expanded value of *word*. Otherwise, **ksh** substitutes the value of *parameter*.
${*parameter: =word*}	**Assign Default Value**. If *parameter* is null or unset, **ksh** assigns the expanded value of *word* to *parameter*. **ksh** then substitutes the value of *parameter*.
${*parameter=word*}	**Assign Default Value**. If *parameter* is unset, **ksh** assigns the expanded value of *word* to *parameter*. **ksh** then substitutes the value of *parameter*.
${*parameter:?word*}	**Display Error**. If *parameter* is null or unset, **ksh** expands and displays *word* on standard error, and causes your shell script, if any, to terminate with a return value of False (1). Otherwise, **ksh** substitutes the value of *parameter*.
${*parameter?word*}	**Display Error**. If *parameter* is unset, **ksh** expands and displays *word* on standard error, and causes your shell script, if any, to terminate with a return value of False (1). Otherwise, **ksh** substitutes the value of *parameter*.
${*parameter:+word*}	**Use Alternate Value**. If *parameter* is null or unset, **ksh** substitutes null. But if *parameter* is not null or unset, **ksh** substitutes the expanded value of *word*.
${*parameter+word*}	**Use Alternate Value**. If *parameter* is unset, **ksh** substitutes null. But if *parameter* is not null or unset, **ksh** substitutes the expanded value of *word*.

${*parameter#word*}	**Remove Small Left Pattern**. The value of this expansion is the value of *parameter* with the smallest portion matched on the left by *pattern* deleted.
${*parameter##word*}	**Remove Large Left Pattern**. The value of this expansion is the value of *parameter* with the largest portion matched on the left by *pattern* deleted.
${*parameter%word*}	**Remove Small Right Pattern**. The value of this expansion is the value of *parameter* with the smallest portion matched on the right by *pattern* deleted.
${*parameter%%word*}	**Remove Large Right Pattern**. The value of this expansion is the value of *parameter* with the largest portion matched on the right by *pattern* deleted.
${*parameter:offset:length*}	**Substring**. The value of this expansion is a substring of *parameter* starting at the character position defined by the arithmetic expression *offset*, and terminating after *length* characters. If *:length* is omitted or is too long, then substring terminates with the last character in *parameter.*
${*parameter/pattern/string*}	**Substitute First**. The first occurrence of *pattern* in *parameter* is replaced by *string*.
${*parameter/#pattern/string*}	**Substitute at Beginning**. If *pattern* occurs at the beginning of *parameter,* it is replaced by *string*.
${*parameter/%pattern/string*}	**Substitute at End**. If *pattern* occurs at the end of *parameter,* it is replaced by *string*.
${*parameter//pattern/string*}	**Substitute All**. All occurrences of *pattern* in *parameter* are replaced by *string*.

${#*parameter*}	**String Length**. If *parameter* is * or @, **ksh** substitutes the number of positional parameters. Otherwise, **ksh** substitutes the length of the value of *parameter.*
${#*varname*[*]}	**Number of Array Elements**. Expands to the number of elements in the array *varname* that are set.
${#*varname*[@]}	**Number of Array Elements**. Expands to the number of elements in the array *varname* that are set.
${!*varname*[@]}	**Name of Variable**. Expands to the name of the variable that *varname* that is set to. Used with namerefs.
${!*prefix*@}	**Name of Variables**. Expands to a list of variable names that begin with *prefix* and are set.
${!*prefix**}	**Name of Variables**. Expands to a list of variable names that begin with *prefix* and are set.
${!*varname*[@]}	**Name of Subscripts**. Expands to a list of subscripts of the array *varname* that are set. For a variable that is not an array, the value is 0 if the variable is set, or null otherwise.
${!*varname*[*]}	**Name of Subscripts**. Expands to a list of subscripts of the array *varname* that are set. For a variable that is not an array, the value is 0 if the variable is set, or null otherwise.

${*varname*[@]:*offset*:*length*}	**Sub-array**. Expands to a sub-array of *varname* starting at the index defined by the arithmetic expression *offset* and continuing for *length* (also an arithmetic expression) positions or to the end of the array, whichever comes first. If :*length* is omitted, the sub-array continues to the end of the defined elements in *varname*. If *varname* is omitted, the positional parameters, considered as an array, are used in its place.
${*varname*[*]:*offset*:*length*}	**Sub-array**. Expands to a sub-array of *varname* starting at the index defined by the arithmetic expression *offset* and continuing for *length* (also an arithmetic expression) positions or to the end of the array, whichever comes first. If :*length* is omitted, the sub-array continues to the end of the defined elements in *varname*. If *varname* is omitted, the positional parameters, considered as an array, are used in its place.

Subpatterns

?(*pattern-list*)	Matches zero or one occurrences of *pattern-list.*
*(*pattern-list*)	Matches zero or more occurrences of *pattern-list.*
+(*pattern-list*)	Matches one or more occurrences of *pattern-list.*
@(*pattern-list*)	Matches exactly one occurrence of *pattern-list.*
!(*pattern-list*)	Matches all strings except those matched by *pattern-list.*

Character Classes

[:alnum:]	Digits, lowercase letters, and uppercase letters.
[:alpha:]	Lowercase and uppercase letters.
[:blank:]	Horizontal `<tab>` or `<space>`.
[:cntrl:]	Control characters.
[:digit:]	Decimal digits.
[:graph:]	Digits, letters, and punctuation.
[:lower:]	Lowercase letters.
[:print:]	Digits, letters, punctuation, and spaces.
[:punct:]	Punctuation.
[:space:]	Horizontal `<tab>` or `<space>`.
[:upper:]	Uppercase letters.
[:xdigit:]	Hexadecimal digits.

APPENDIX C

GLOSSARY

Just knowing what these terms mean won't make you into a shell programmer, but it sure will be hard to write shell programs if you don't know what they mean. Except maybe the last one. Chapter references, where given, indicate a good place to start looking for more information on the term, but many of these terms are used throughout the book.

argument
: Many commands recognize option parameters (the ones that start with - or +) and that some option parameters are followed by an "argument." Unfortunately, the same term is sometimes used for any parameter variable inside a script or function, or sometimes even for positional parameters in a command line. You have to figure out which meaning of the term is intended by the context it's used in. Chapter 2 [Command Line Syntax].

arithmetic expansion
: The shell substitutes the value of *expression* for $((*expression*)), where *expression* is an arithmetic expression.

assign
: You *assign* a value to a variable in order to make the association between the name and its value. There are commands for making the assignment explicitly, and the shell sometimes assigns values to variables as part of its normal housekeeping operations. Chapter 6 [Advanced Variable Usage].

associative array
: A variable that holds a set of values. Elements are accessed using arbitrary strings as subscript values. Chapter 6 [Advanced Variable Usage].

command substitution
: The shell substitutes whatever *command* writes to its standard output for $(*command*). Chapter 10 [Patterns, Expansions, and Substitutions].

co-process
: A command that runs concurrently with a script having the additional feature that the script can read from the co-process' standard output and write to its standard input. Chapter 3 [Compound Command Syntax].

discipline function	A function with a name in the form *varname.action*, where *varname* is the name of a variable, and action is one of set, get, or unset. The function is automatically run when the indicated action is applied to the named variable. Chapter 6 [Advanced Variable Usage].
dot (a script)	The dot (.) is a command that takes a script or function command as its argument. The script or function is run in the same environment as the shell that runs the dot command. Chapter 1 [Setting Up].
environment file	A file whose name is the value of the *ENV* variable. If such a file is defined, the shell executes the commands in it before issuing its first prompt in an interactive session. Normally, you put an assignment to *ENV* in your `~/.profile` to establish an environment file. Chapter 1 [Setting Up].
environment variable	Any variable that is defined in a script or function's environment.
environment	The environment of a script or function consists of a set of variables as well as a collection of parameter settings determined by the user's file access rights, current working directory, trap settings, and other information that can be tested or can control the behavior of the program.
evaluate	When the shell sees a reference to a variable in a command, it substitutes the value of the variable for the reference to it before executing the command. This substitution is called "evaluating a reference" or "evaluating a variable." Chapter 4 [Simple Variables].
field splitting	The operation of breaking a string into a sequence of tokens using the *IFS* variable to determine what characters serve as token delimiters. Chapter 11 [I/O and Trap Processing].
initialize	The first time you assign a value to a variable you are said to initialize it. Before that, the variable is "uninitialized." Chapter 4 [Simple Variables].
interactive shell	When you run the *KornShell* so that it reads its commands from your keyboard and writes its output to your screen. A non-interactive shell would be when you run a script or function in a separate invocation of the *KornShell*.
job	A process that executes a command entered from the keyboard. You can use the **fg** and **bg** commands, among others, to manage the execution of jobs. Chapter 3 [Compound Command Syntax].

lvalue	Short for "left-hand side value." The things that are valid to put on the left side of an equal sign, such as a variable name.
name	A variable name is any combination of letters, underscores, and digits, but must not start with a digit. Upper and lower-case letters are *not* the same. Chapter 4 [Simple Variables].
option argument	The value, such as a file name, that must follow certain option letters. Chapter 5 [Parameters].
option letter	Commands that process command line values in the standard way use option letters, indicated by a dash followed by the letter, to specify execution alternatives. Chapter 5 [Parameters].
option parameter	Command line values that are option letters or option arguments. Chapter 5 [Parameters].
parameter expansion	In its simplest form, the shell substitutes the value of a parameter for a reference to it in the form ${*parameter*}, where *parameter* is the name of a variable. There are several expansion operators, such as : :- := :? :+ # ## % %% that cause the shell to modify the value being substituted and/or the variable named by *parameter*. Chapter 10 [Patterns, Expansions, and Substitutions].
parameter	When you run a command, including a shell script or function, you can type parameters after the command name. The shell assigns these parameters as the values of *parameter variables,* which can be referenced by code inside the script or function. Chapter 2 [Command Line Syntax].
pathname expansion	If a command takes a list of files as arguments, the *KornShell* will generate a list of file names matching the files in the current directory using * to match any string of characters, ? to match any single character, [...] to match sets of characters, and any of several pattern matching rules (defined next) to generate the file names. Chapter 10 [Patterns, Expansions, and Substitutions].
pattern matching rule	Also called sub-patterns. Any of the symbols * ? @ + or ! followed by a pattern list enclosed in parentheses. Chapter 10 [Patterns, Expansions, and Substitutions].
positional parameter	The values entered on a command line are passed to the command as the values of a set of positional parameters, which are variables with small integers as their names. *0* is the name of the command, *1* is the first parameter following the command name, and so forth. Chapter 5 [Parameters].

precedence	When evaluating an expression, the shell calculates the result of higher precedence operators before doing the calculation for lower-precedence operators. Generally, operators of equal precedence are evaluated in left to right order; exceptions are the assignment operators such as = +=. For example, multiplication has a higher precedence than addition, so a+b*c would be evaluated as a+(b*c). Use parentheses to override precedence rules if necessary. Chapter 6 [Advanced Variable Usage].
process ID	Every process that is running on the computer at any time has a unique integer assigned to it by the kernel called its process id.
process	The operating system construct that executes programs. When it is created, a process has a thread of execution that is scheduled for CPU usage by the kernel and an address space, which includes its environment and the code that it executes. Chapter 1 [Setting Up].
program	Executable code.
quote removal	The last step the shell performs on a command line before executing a command, in which single and double quotation marks are removed, as well as escape characters (back slashes). Chapter 2 [Command Line Syntax].
reference	You reference a variable by putting a dollar sign ($) before its name in a command line. Sometimes the variable's name has to be enclosed in curly braces to make it clear where the name begins and ends. Chapter 4 [Simple Variables]
she-bang	She-bang notation gets its name from the first two characters that may appear in the first line of a script file: (#!). The first one is sometimes called sharp, and the second one is often called "bang" because that's easier to say than "exclamation mark." The rest of the line gets the pathname of the program that will process the commands in the file. Depending on where your copy of the KornShell is installed, it might look like /bin/ksh or something similar. Chapter 1 [Setting Up].
subscript	The expression inside square brackets that tells what element of an array you want to access or modify. Use a number for indexed arrays, or an arbitrary string for associative arrays. Chapter 6 [Advanced Variable Usage].

subshell — Not necessarily a separate process, a subshell refers to executing a command or command list in a separate environment from the shell that started the command, accomplished by putting the command inside single parentheses. Chapter 3 [Compound Command Syntax].

trap condition — The signal or other event (DEBUG, ERR, EXIT, KEYBD) to be intercepted by a `trap` command. Chapter 11 [I/O and Trap Processing].

trap handler — The code to be executed when a *trap condition* occurs. Chapter 11 [I/O and Trap Processing].

value — The value of a variable is normally a string of characters, but you can give a variable a numeric *type* so that it will be handled as either an *integer*, a *floating-point*, an *exponential* number, or a *reference* to another variable. Chapters 4 [Simple Variables] and 6 [Advanced Variable Usage].

variable — A variable is a *name* and an associated *value*. You or the shell can *assign* a value to a name, and the shell will *substitute* the value when you reference the name in your programs. Chapter 4 [Simple Variables].

xtrace — An option you can set (**set -x**) so that the shell prints each command just before it executes it. Very useful for debugging scripts and functions. Turn it off with **set +x**.

zythepsary — A brewery.

INDEX

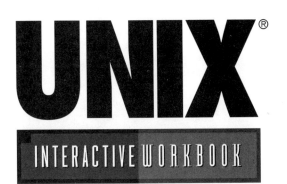

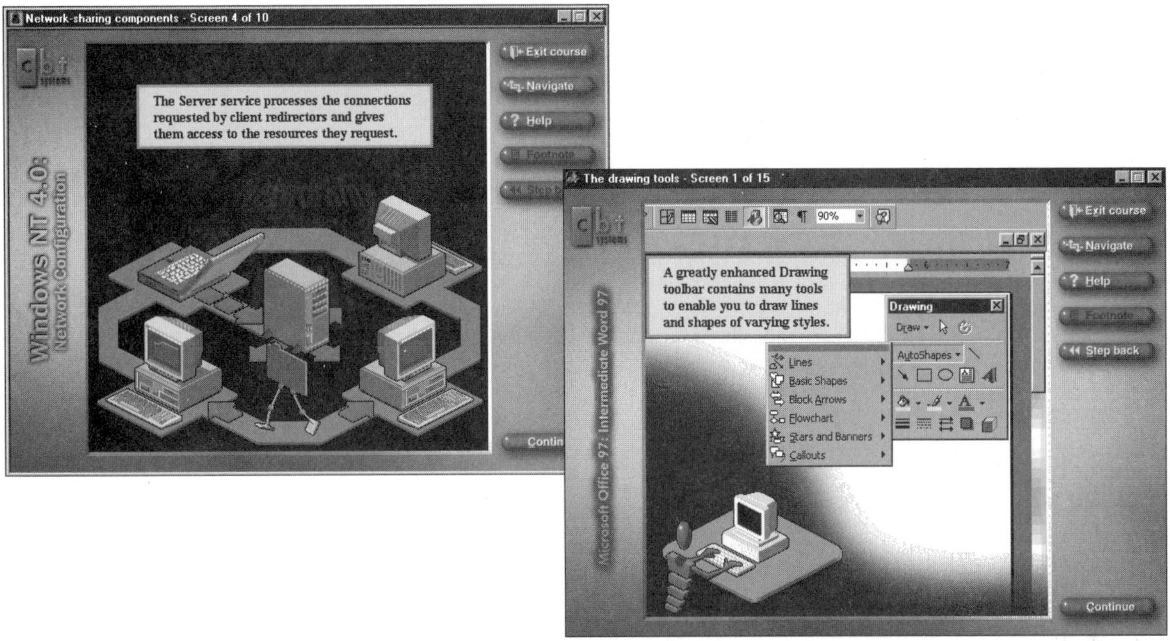

Other curricula available from CBT Systems:

- Cisco
- Informix
- Java
- Marimba
- Microsoft
- Netscape
- Novell
- Oracle
- SAP
- Sybase
- C/C++
- Centura
- Information Technology/ Core Concepts
- Internet and Intranet Skills
- Internetworking
- UNIX

cbt™ systems

To order additional CBT Systems courseware today call 800.789.8590 or visit www.clbooks.com/training/cbt.htm

CBT SOFTWARE LICENSE AGREEMENT

IF YOU DO NOT AGREE WITH THESE TERMS AND CONDITIONS, DO NOT INSTALL THE SOFTWARE.

This is a legal agreement you and CBT System Ltd. ("Licensor"). The licensor ("Licensor") from whom you have licensed the CBT Group PLC courseware (the "Software"). By installing, copying or otherwise using the Software, you agree to be bound by the terms of this Agreement License Agreement (the "License"). If you do not agree to the terms of this License, the Licensor is unwilling to license the Software to you. In such event, you may not use or copy the Software, and you should promptly contact the Licensor for instructions on the return of the unused Software.

1. **Use.** Licensor grants to you a non-exclusive, nontransferable license to use Licensor's software product (the "Software") the Software and accompanying documentation in accordance with the terms and conditions of this license agreement ("License") License and as specified in your agreement with Licensor (the "Governing Agreement"). In the event of any conflict between this License and the Governing Agreement, the Governing Agreement shall control.

You may:

a. (if specified as a "personal use" version) install the Software on a single stand-alone computer or a single network node from which node the Software cannot be accessed by another computer, provided that such Software shall be used by only one individual; <u>or</u>

b. (if specified as a "workstation" version) install the Software on a single stand-alone computer or a single network node from which node the Software cannot be accessed by another computer, provided that such Software shall be used by only one individual; <u>or</u>

c. (if specified as a "LAN" version) install the Software on a local area network server that provides access to multiple computers, up to the maximum number of computers or users specified in your Governing Agreement, provided that such Software shall be used only by employees of your organization; <u>or</u>

d. (if specified as an "enterprise" version) install the Software or copies of the Software on multiple local or wide area network servers, intranet servers, stand-alone computers and network nodes (and to make copies of the Software for such purpose) at one or more sites, which servers provide access to a multiple number of users, up to the maximum number of users specified in your Governing Agreement, provided that such Software shall be used only by employees of your organization.

<u>This License is not a sale. Title and copyrights to the Software, accompanying documentation and any copy made by you remain with Licensor or its suppliers or licensors.</u>

2. **Intellectual Property**. The Software is owned by Licensor or its licensors and is protected by United States and other jurisdictions' copyright laws and international treaty provisions. Therefore, you may not use, copy, or distribute the Software without the express written authorization of CBT Group PLC. This License authorizes you to use the Software for the internal training needs of your employees only, and to make one copy of the Software solely for backup or archival purposes. You may not print copies of any user documentation provided in "online" or electronic form. Licensor retains all rights not expressly granted.

3. **Restrictions**. You may not transfer, rent, lease, loan or time-share the Software or accompanying documentation. You may not reverse engineer, decompile, or disassemble the Software, except to the extent the foregoing restriction is expressly prohibited by applicable law. You may not modify, or create derivative works based upon the Software in whole or in part.

1. **Confidentiality**. The Software contains confidential trade secret information belonging to Licensor, and you may use the software only pursuant to the terms of your Governing Agreement, if any, and the license set forth herein. In addition, you may not disclose the Software to any third party.

2. **Limited Liability**. IN NO EVENT WILL THE Licensor's LIABILITY UNDER, ARISING OUT OF OR RELATING TO THIS AGREEMENT EXCEED THE AMOUNT PAID TO LICENSOR FOR THE SOFTWARE. LICENSOR SHALL NOT BE LIABLE FOR ANY SPECIAL, INCIDENTAL, INDIRECT OR CONSEQUENTIAL DAMAGES, HOWEVER CAUSED AND ON ANY THEORY OF LIABILITY., REGARDLESS OR WHETHER LICENSOR HAS BEEN ADVISED OF THE POSSIBILITY OF SUCH DAMAGES. WITHOUT LIMITING THE FOREGOING, LICENSOR WILL NOT BE LIABLE FOR LOST PROFITS, LOSS OF DATA, OR COSTS OF COVER.

3. **Limited Warranty**. LICENSOR WARRANTS THAT SOFTWARE WILL BE FREE FROM DEFECTS IN MATERIALS AND WORKMANSHIP UNDER NORMAL USE FOR A PERIOD OF THIRTY (30) DAYS FROM THE DATE OF RECEIPT. THIS LIMITED WARRANTY IS VOID IF FAILURE OF THE SOFTWARE HAS RESULTED FROM ABUSE OR MISAPPLICATION. ANY REPLACEMENT SOFTWARE WILL BE WARRANTED FOR A PERIOD OF THIRTY (30) DAYS FROM THE DATE OF RECEIPT OF SUCH REPLACEMENT SOFTWARE. THE SOFTWARE AND DOCUMENTATION ARE PROVIDED "AS IS". LICENSOR HEREBY DISCLAIMS ALL OTHER WARRANTIES, EXPRESS, IMPLIED, OR STATUTORY, INCLUDING WITHOUT LIMITATION, THE IMPLIED WARRANTIES OF MERCHANTABILITY AND FITNESS FOR A PARTICULAR PURPOSE.

4. **Exceptions**. SOME STATES DO NOT ALLOW THE LIMITATION OF INCIDENTAL DAMAGES OR LIMITATIONS ON HOW LONG AN IMPLIED WARRANTY LASTS, SO THE ABOVE LIMITATIONS OR EXCLUSIONS MAY NOT APPLY TO YOU. This agreement gives you specific legal rights, and you may also have other rights which vary from state to state.

5. **U.S. Government-Restricted Rights**. The Software and accompanying documentation are deemed to be "commercial computer Software" and "commercial computer Software documentation," respectively, pursuant to FAR Section 227.7202 and FAR Section 12.212, as applicable. Any use, modification, reproduction release, performance, display or disclosure of the Software and accompanying documentation by the U.S. Government shall be governed solely by the terms of this Agreement and shall be prohibited except to the extent expressly permitted by the terms of this Agreement.

6. **Export Restrictions**. You may not download, export, or re-export the Software (a) into, or to a national or resident of, Cuba, Iraq, Libya, Yugoslavia, North Korea, Iran, Syria or any other country to which the United States has embargoed goods, or (b) to anyone on the United States Treasury Department's list of Specially Designated Nations or the U.S. Commerce Department's Table of Deny Orders. By installing or using the Software, you are representing and warranting that you are not located in, under the control of, or a national resident of any such country or on any such list.

7. **General**. This License is governed by the laws of the United States and the State of California, without reference to conflict of laws principles. The parties agree that the United Nations Convention on Contracts for the International Sale of Goods shall not apply to this License. If any provision of this Agreement is held invalid, the remainder of this License shall continue in full force and effect.

8. **More Information**. Should you have any questions concerning this Agreement, or if you desire to contact Licensor for any reason, please contact: CBT Systems USA Ltd., 1005 Hamilton Court, Menlo Park, California 94025, Attn: Chief Legal Officer.

IF YOU DO NOT AGREE WITH THE ABOVE TERMS AND CONDITIONS, SO NOT INSTALL THE SOFTWARE AND RETURN IT TO THE LICENSOR.

About the CD-ROM

The CD-ROM that accompanies this book contains the source code for all of the illustrative programs, starting with the SQUARES example in Chapter 1 and continuing all the way to the explorations of compiler output in Chapter 13.

The CD-ROM has been manufactured to have partitions that present the files appropriately to either a Macintosh or a Windows desktop client system. On a Macintosh, the files can be viewed with BBEDIT (see Suggested Resources), SimpleText, or a word processor. On a Windows system, the files can be viewed with WordPad or a word processor, as well as with the TYPE command at the DOS prompt.

Files that are independent of operating system are at the top directory level. Those files include programs in various high level languages as well as miscellaneous test data files. Assembly language files specific to MACRO-64 are in an OpenVMS subdirectory (folder). Similarly, files specific to the UNIX assembler for the Alpha are in a UNIX subdirectory (folder).

Technical Support

Prentice Hall does not offer technical support for this software. However, if there is a problem with the media, you may obtain a replacement copy by emailing us with your problem at:

`discexchange@phptr.com`